COMPLETE BIBLE CURRICULUM: HOW TO EXAMINE PASTORS, VOL. 4

FUNDAMENTAL CONCEPTS FOR SUCCESSFUL CHRISTIAN LIFE

COVERING: 1 & 2 CORINTHIANS

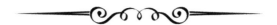

Rev. Prof. PETER PRYCE,

DSEF, BA, MA, B.SOC.SC POL SCI, IBA, PHD

PROFESSOR OF FRENCH, USA

===============================

COMPLETE BIBLE CURRICULUM: HOW TO EXAMINE PASTORS, VOL. 4

FUNDAMENTAL CONCEPTS FOR SUCCESSFUL CHRISTIAN LIFE

COVERING: 1 & 2 CORINTHIANS

United States Library of Congress Catalog in Publication Data – Rev. Prof. Peter Pryce: *Complete Bible Curriculum: How to Examine Pastors, Vol. 4 – Fundamental Concepts for Successful Christian Life: Covering 1 & 2 Corinthians.*

ISBN 978-1-77637-662-9 Paper Edition

Printed and Published in the USA

ACKNOWLEDGEMENT

I acknowledge the Holy Spirit and dedicate this book to the Holy Spirit for giving me the wisdom to understand the Holy Scriptures to write this book in order to help others to also come to the understanding of The Word of God.

Isaiah 28:26 (KJV) For his God doth instruct him to discretion, *and* doth teach him.

Jeremiah 30:2 (KJV) Thus speaketh the LORD God of Israel, saying, Write thee all the words that I have spoken unto thee in a book.

John 14:26 (KJV) But the Comforter, *which is* the Holy Ghost, whom the Father will send in my name, he shall teach you all things, and bring all things to your remembrance, whatsoever I have said unto you.

Ephesians 5:11 (KJV) And have no fellowship with the unfruitful works of darkness, but rather reprove *them*.

Rev. Prof. PETER PRYCE,
DSEF, BA, MA, B.Scs. Pol Sci, IBA, PhD
A Scribe of the Law of the God of Heaven
Prophet of the Word of God
Professor of French, USA
Silver Spring, MD, USA
WWW.THEBIBLEUNIVERSITY.ORG
Accreditation Number: 07-QCTO/SDP120723172836
SAQA QUAL ID: Identification # 101997
WWW.BOOKSTORESITE.ORG
WWW.THEBIBLEUNIVERSITYCHURCH.ORG

DEDICATION

𝕴 dedicate this book to the Ministers of Jesus Christ who are obeying this commission:

Matthew 28:18 (KJV) And Jesus came and spake unto them, saying, All power is given unto me in heaven and in earth.

Matthew 28:19 (KJV) Go ye therefore, and teach all nations, baptizing them in the name of the Father, and of the Son, and of the Holy Ghost:

Matthew 28:20 (KJV) Teaching them to observe all things whatsoever I have commanded you: and, lo, I am with you alway, *even* unto the end of the world. Amen.

Acts 1:7 (KJV) And he said unto them, It is not for you to know the times or the seasons, which the Father hath put in his own power.

Acts 1:8 (KJV) But ye shall receive power, after that the Holy Ghost is come upon you: and ye shall be witnesses unto me both in Jerusalem, and in all Judaea, and in Samaria, and unto the uttermost part of the earth.

Rev. Prof. PETER PRYCE,
DSEF, BA, MA, B.Scs. Pol Sci, IBA, PhD

ABOUT THE AUTHOR

Rev. Prof. Peter Pryce served for 10 years as a Public Servant French Teacher of the Maryland State Department of Education, USA, with competence in the IB Program, and is currently a Professor of Translation and Interpretation, a bilingual Scholar of Translation and Interpretation of the Holy Bible and the Qur'an, a French Language Scholar, a Theological Researcher and Scholar, a Christian Publisher, an Ordained Minister of the Gospel of Jesus Christ, an Anti-Racism Educator, a Bilingual Conference Interpreter, an Education Consultant, a Translator and Interpreter, and a Technical Writer. Rev. Prof. Peter Pryce holds a Ph.D. in Translation and Interpretation of French and English, with research interests in Translation Theory and Practice, and Sacred Text Analyses of the Bible and Qur'an.

I am a native-level English and French language expert. I hold the following School Administrator credentials for School Principal and Assistant Principal: Maryland Candidate ID # 03779397 ETS SCHOOL LEADERSHIP SERIES 02/02/2006 - ADMIN 1 & 2.

Rev. Prof. Peter Pryce taught Translation and Techniques of Expression in the Department of French, University of Education, Winneba, GHANA. He also taught Translation and Interpreting (French and English) in the Department of Modern Languages, University of Ghana, LEGON.

I am an Author of French and English textbooks for University Students. I have more than 35 textbook publications in the academic field of English and French Translation and Interpretation that are registered with the United States Library of Congress.

Rev. Prof. Peter Pryce often teaches on Radio and TV in the Bible and Qur'an Lecture Series drawing from his long experience as a Bible Commentary Writer, Corporate Language Instructor, Technical Writer with Nokia Corporation, French Embassy award-winning Poet, Conference Speaker, Book Editor, Presidential Speech Writer, and Author with intellectual properties registered with the United States Library of Congress Copyright Office in Washington, DC.

Four Presidents have encountered the writings of Rev. Prof. Peter Pryce namely: President Léopold Sédar Senghor of Senegal when Prof. Pryce was a student of French in the University of Dakar, Head of State Ibrahim Badamosi Babangida of Nigeria when Prof. Pryce was a student of French in the University of Dakar, President Jerry John Rawlings of Ghana when Prof. Pryce was a Ph.D. Lecturer of French in the University of Education, Winneba and was selected to write the President's speech.

In July 2020, Rev. Prof. Peter Pryce received a formal Letter of Appreciation from the United States White House; from President Donald Trump, in appreciation, after the US President received some free textbooks from Rev. Prof. Peter Pryce.

Rev. Prof. Peter Pryce is currently devoting his time and energy to the writing and publishing of Christian Theological Research Textbooks for The Bible University and to the following services:

1. Anti-Racism Awareness Training and Education
2. Anti-Racism Research, Racism Policy and Social Justice Initiatives
3. Post-Racism Traumatic Syndrome Alleviation Counseling
4. Mental and Spiritual Health Counseling Therapy for Post-Racism Rehabilitate and Traumatic Stress Alleviation
5. Inter-Ministerial Pastoral Training and Pastoral Accountability
6. Theological Research and Christian Publishing
7. Bilingual Conference Interpretation and Translation
8. Technical Writing

Rev. Prof. PETER PRYCE,
DSEF, BA, MA, B.Soc.Sc Pol Sci, IBA, PhD
A Scribe of the Law of the God of Heaven
Prophet of the Word of God
Professor of French, USA
Silver Spring, MD, USA
WWW.THEBIBLEUNIVERSITY.ORG
Accreditation Number: 07-QCTO/SDP120723172836
SAQA QUAL ID: Identification # 101997
WWW.BOOKSTORESITE.ORG
WWW.THEBIBLEUNIVERSITYCHURCH.ORG

SUMMARY OF FORMAL EDUCATION

1. L'Université de Dakar, Diplôme Supérieur d'Études de Français (3e degré Supérieur), 1987
2. University of Calabar, B.A. (HONS.) French/German, 1988
3. University of Lagos, M.A. French (Emphasis on Translation), 1992
4. University of Helsinki, Finland, B.Scs. in Political Science, 1st Class, 1999
5. University of Applied Sciences, Finland, IBA Degree: Int. Business Acumen, 2000
6. Catholic University of America, USA, Graduate Teacher Certification Program, 2003
7. McDaniel University, USA, School Leadership and Administration I, 2005
8. School Leaders Licensure Assessment, SLLA Administration II, USA, 2006
9. University of Helsinki, Finland, PhD in Translation and Interpretation, English and French, 2007

SKILLS SUMMARY

1. French-English Translation and Interpretation
2. French Language Immersion Teacher
3. Conference Translator and Interpreter
4. Competence in IB and AP Program Implementation
5. Native-level English and French Language Expert
6. Editor of Publication Articles
7. Author of Textbooks with 37 publications registered with the US Library of Congress
8. Ordained Minister of the Gospel of Jesus Christ
9. Qur'an Scholar
10. Scholar of the Institute of Theologians, USA
11. Holder of School Administrator credentials for School Principal and Assistant Principal: Maryland Candidate ID # 03779397 ETS SCHOOL.

PUBLICATIONS BY REV. PROF., PETER PRYCE, PH. D.

Monographs and Books:

1. Pryce, Peter. (2003, 2018, 2019). *Foreignising Finnish – Necessary and Unnecessary English Imports into Translations* is peer-reviewed, accepted, and has a journal publication in 2003 by the University of Natal in South Africa. However, September 2018 is the first time that it was published as an e-book online and subsequently appeared as a hard cover book in March 2019. ISBN: 978-9988-8799-4-5

2. Pryce, Peter. (2006). *Measuring Attitudes in Translation: A Study of Nokia Business Reports*. Helsinki: Helsinki University Translation Studies Monographs 2, Vol. 2 Peter Pryce: Helsinki University Printing House. 324 pages. ISSN 1459-3246. ISBN 952-10-3414-9 (Paperback). ISBN 952-10-3415-7 (PDF)

3. Pryce, Peter. (2012, 2018, 2019). *Change as a Distinct Property of Language – Aspects of Language Variation, Acquisition, and Use* is peer-reviewed, accepted, and has a journal publication in 2012 by the University of Cape Coast, in Ghana. However, September 2018 is the first time that it was published as an e-book online and subsequently appeared as a hard cover book in March 2019. ISBN 978-9988-8799-0-7

4. Pryce, Peter. (2012, 2018, 2019). *Attitudes to Translation – Linguistique et didactique de langue et de littérature: problématiques contemporaines et perspectives* is peer-reviewed, accepted, and has a journal publication by the University of Lagos in Nigeria in 2012. However, September 2018 is the first time that it was published as an e-book online and subsequently appeared as a hard cover book in March 2019. ISBN 978–9988–2–7248–7

5. Pryce, Peter. (2013, 2018, 2019). *Techniques of Expression – The Conference Rapporteur* is peer-reviewed, accepted, and has a journal publication in 2013 by the University of Education, Winneba, in Ghana. However, September 2018 is the first time that it was published as an e-book online and subsequently appeared as a hard cover book in March 2019. ISBN 978-9988-8799-5-2

6. Pryce, Peter. (2013, 2018, 2019). *Norms of Academic Writing* is peer-reviewed, accepted, and was presented at the 3rd Annual International Colloquium of Language,

Literature and Communication: Contexts, Practice and Pedagogy, Faculty of Languages Education, the University of Education, Winneba, in Ghana, from Wednesday 13th November - Thursday 14th November 2013. However, September 2018 was its first publication, as an e-book online and subsequently appeared for the first time in print as a hard cover book in March 2019. ISBN 978-9988-8799-3-8

7. Pryce, Peter. (2018). *Topics in Translation Review – Testing the Perfect Harmony Theory of Translation and Interpreting*. Legon: Ghana Universities Press. 953 pages. ISBN 978-9988-2-2741-8.

8. Pryce, Peter. (2018). *Salvation – Anointed Teachings*. INGRAM. One Ingram Blvd., La Vergne, Tennessee, 37086: 615-793-5000. 756 pages. ISBN 978-9988-8799-1-4

9. Pryce, Peter. (2019). *Thematic Dictionary of Matthew – Intralingual Translation of Spiritual Themes*. INGRAM. One Ingram Blvd., La Vergne, Tennessee, 37086: 615-793-5000. 617 pages. ISBN 978-9988-8800-2-6

10. Pryce, Peter. (2019). *Language Migration* was first peer-reviewed, and accepted for journal publication by *Translation Watch Quarterly*, official journal of the Translation Standards Institute in Australia. However, September 2018 was its first publication, as an e-book online and subsequently appeared for the first time in print as a hard cover book in March 2019. ISBN 978-9988-8799-2-1

11. Pryce, Peter. (2019). *Français aux Anglophones – French for English Speakers*. INGRAM. One Ingram Blvd., La Vergne, Tennessee, 37086: 615-793-5000. 600 pages. ISBN: 978-9988-8801-4-9 (paper edition). ISBN: 978-9988-8803-1-6 (e-Book edition)

12. Pryce, Peter. (2020). *The Counseling Manual - Case Studies*. INGRAM. One Ingram Blvd., La Vergne, Tennessee, 37086: 615-793-5000. 416 pages. ISBN 978-9988-8800-4-0 – paper edition. ISBN 978-9988-8800-9-5 – eBook edition.

13. Pryce, Peter. (2020). *Threatened…by the Truth*. INGRAM. One Ingram Blvd., La Vergne, Tennessee, 37086: 615-793-5000. 654 pages. ISBN 978-9988-8801-8-7– paper edition. ISBN 978-9988-8800-1-9 – eBook edition.

14. Pryce, Peter. (2020). *Marriage is a Blood Covenant*. INGRAM. One Ingram Blvd., La Vergne, Tennessee, 37086: 615-793-5000. 348 pages. ISBN: 978-9988-8801-5-6 (Paper Edition). ISBN: 978-9988-8799-7-6 (e-Book Edition)

15. Pryce, Peter. (2020). *Strategies for Church Growth*. INGRAM. One Ingram Blvd., La Vergne, Tennessee, 37086: 615-793-5000. 456 pages. ISBN: 978-9988-8802-1-7 (Paper Edition). ISBN:978-9988-8802-2-4 (e-Book Edition)

16. Pryce, Peter. (2020). *But Suppose God is Black – What God says about Racism*. INGRAM. One Ingram Blvd., La Vergne, Tennessee, 37086: 615-793-5000. 284

pages. ISBN: 978-9988-8803-0-9 (paper edition). ISBN: 978-9988-8803-1-6 (e-Book edition)

17. Pryce, Peter. (2020). ***Anti-Racism Program for Christians – Methodology for Racist Detoxification***. INGRAM. One Ingram Blvd., La Vergne, Tennessee, 37086: 615-793-5000. 434 pages. ISBN: 978-9988-8799-9-0(paper edition). ISBN: 978-9988-8803-2-3(e-Book edition)

18. Pryce, Peter. (2020). ***Key to unlock Romans – 1449 Spiritual Revelations***. INGRAM. One Ingram Blvd., La Vergne, Tennessee, 37086: 615-793-5000. 582 pages. ISBN: 978-9988-8801-9-4 (paper edition). ISBN: 978-9988-8802-0-0(e-Book edition)

19. Pryce, Peter. (2020). ***Praise and Worship***. INGRAM. One Ingram Blvd., La Vergne, Tennessee, 37086: 615-793-5000. 276 pages. ISBN: 978-9988-8802-7-9 (paper edition). ISBN: 978-9988-8802-8-6(e-Book edition)

20. Pryce, Peter. (2020). ***Tithing – A Comprehensive Study from Genesis to Revelation***. INGRAM. One Ingram Blvd., La Vergne, Tennessee, 37086: 615-793-5000. 276 pages. ISBN: 978-9988-8800-0-2 (paper edition). ISBN: 978-9988-8802-9-3 (e-Book edition)

21. Pryce, Peter. (2020). ***Sermon Preparation – A Training Program for Pastors***. INGRAM. One Ingram Blvd., La Vergne, Tennessee, 37086: 615-793-5000. 276 pages. ISBN: 978-9988-8803-3-0 (paper edition). ISBN: 978-9988-8803-4-7 (e-Book edition)

22. Pryce, Peter. (January 2021). ***Theory of Bible Errors and Contradictions – Ministers' Essential Reference***. INGRAM. One Ingram Blvd., La Vergne, Tennessee, 37086: 615-793-5000. 1186 pages. ISBN: **978-9988-8803-5-4** (paper edition). ISBN: **978-9988-8803-6-1** (e-Book edition)

23. Pryce Peter. (July 2021). ***Key tothe Bible – Complete Bible Curriculum***. A 2600-page Christian Theological Research Textbook of Holy Spirit inspired Bible Teachings from Genesis to Revelation with search engine, as a Mobile App, for Android and IOS devices. Available on Google Play Store. Mobile App User Experience Functionality:

     i. Search engine for any word or topic in the Bible
    ii. Search results total count
   iii. Subject teachings with Book of the Bible references
    iv. Reading or audio functionality
     v. Font size increase or decrease
    vi. Text-to-voice audio function
   vii. https://play.google.com/store/apps/details?id=com.majesty.keytothebible

24. Pryce, Peter. (January 2022) *Méthode d'Enseignement de Traduction – Translation Textbook for Students*. INGRAM. One Ingram Blvd., La Vergne, Tennessee, 37086: 615-793-5000. 1098 pages. ISBN – 978-9988-8803-8-5 (Hard Cover Edition). ISBN – 978-9988-8803-9-2 (e-Book edition).

25. Pryce, Peter. (February 2022) *Spirituals of Money – Principles of Church Accounting*. INGRAM. One Ingram Blvd., La Vergne, Tennessee, 37086: 615-793-5000. 1166 pages. ISBN: 9781776376650 (Hard Cover Edition). ISBN: 9781776376681 (e-Book edition).

26. Pryce, Peter. (March 2022) *Complete Bible Curriculum Vol. 1 – Genesis – Exodus*. INGRAM. One Ingram Blvd., La Vergne, Tennessee, 37086: 615-793-5000. 695 pages. ISBN: 978-1-77637-622-3 (Hard Cover Edition). ISBN: 978-1-77637-623-0 (e-Book edition).

27. Pryce, Peter. (April 2022) *Complete Bible Curriculum Vol. 2 – Leviticus, Numbers, Deuteronomy*. INGRAM. One Ingram Blvd., La Vergne, Tennessee, 37086: 615-793-5000. 584 pages. ISBN: 978-1-77637-624-7 (Hard Cover Edition). ISBN: 978-1-77637-625-4 (e-Book edition).

28. Pryce, Peter. (May 2022) *Complete Bible Curriculum Vol. 3 – Joshua, Judges, Ruth, 1 and 2 Samuel*. INGRAM. One Ingram Blvd., La Vergne, Tennessee, 37086: 615-793-5000. 606 pages. **ISBN 978-1776376261** (Hard Cover Edition). **ISBN 9781776376278** (e-Book edition).

29. Pryce, Peter. (June 2022) *Topics in Qur'an and Bible Translation*. Legon: Ghana Universities Press, 2018. INGRAM. One Ingram Blvd., La Vergne, Tennessee, 37086: 615-793-5000. 707 pages. ISBN: (Hard Cover Edition). ISBN: (e-Book edition)

30. Pryce, Peter. (July 2022) *Complete Bible Curriculum Vol. 4 – 1 and 2 Kings, 1 and 2 Chronicles*. INGRAM. One Ingram Blvd., La Vergne, Tennessee, 37086: 615-793-5000. 604 pages. **ISBN 978-1776376261** (Hard Cover Edition). **ISBN 9781776376278** (e-Book edition).

31. Pryce, Peter. (August 2022) *Complete Bible Curriculum Vol. 5 – Ezra, Nehemiah, Esther, Job*. INGRAM. One Ingram Blvd., La Vergne, Tennessee, 37086: 615-793-5000. 382 pages. **ISBN 978-1-77637-630-8** (Hard Cover Edition). **ISBN 978-1-77637-631-5** (e-Book edition).

32. Pryce, Peter. (September 2022) *The Law of Writing Scriptures – A Comprehensive Research from Genesis to Revelation*. **ISBN 978-1-77637-632-2 – paper edition. ISBN 978-1-77637-633-9 – e-Book edition.** 779 pages. AMAZON PUBLISHING SOL, 5201 Great America Pkwy Unit 320 Santa Clara, CA 95054 United States, info@amazonpublishingsol.com, +(855) 408-6467.

33. Pryce, Peter. (October 2022) *Complete Bible Curriculum Vol. 6 – The Book of Psalms*. **ISBN 978-1-77637-634-6 – paper edition. ISBN 978-1-77637-635-3 – e-**

Book edition. 523 pages. AMAZON PUBLISHING SOL, 5201 Great America Pkwy Unit 320 Santa Clara, CA 95054 United States, info@amazonpublishingsol.com, +(855) 408-6467.

34. Pryce, Peter. (November 2022) *Complete Bible Curriculum Vol. 7 – Hermeneutics and Exegesis of the Book of Proverbs*. ISBN 978-1-77637-637-7 – paper edition. ISBN 978-1-77637-636-0 – e-Book edition. 502 pages. AMAZON PUBLISHING SOL, 5201 Great America Pkwy Unit 320 Santa Clara, CA 95054 United States, info@amazonpublishingsol.com, +(855) 408-6467.

35. Pryce, Peter. (December 2022) *Complete Bible Curriculum Vol. 8 – Ecclesiastes, Song of Solomon*. ISBN 978-1-77637-638-4 – paper edition. ISBN 978-1-77637-639-1 – e-Book edition. 523 pages. AMAZON PUBLISHING SOL, 5201 Great America Pkwy Unit 320 Santa Clara, CA 95054 United States, info@amazonpublishingsol.com, +(855) 408-6467.

36. Pryce, Peter. (July 2023) *Complete Bible Curriculum Vol. 9 - THE BOOK OF ISAIAH*. ISBN – INGRAM. One Ingram Blvd., La Vergne, Tennessee, – Hard Cover paper edition, 650 pages. ISBN 978-1-77637-650-6. eBook edition ISBN 978-1-77637-651-3.

37. Pryce, Peter. (August 2023) *Her hair is given her for a Covering* –. ISBN 979 8859067831 – **Amazon Kindle Direct Publishing Paperback.** Sunday 27th August 2023. 233 pages.

38. Pryce, Peter. (September 2023) *Marriage Counseling Textbook for Ministers Vol. 1.* Print ISBN 978-1-77637-640-7. E-book ISBN 978-1-77637-641-4. INGRAM Publishing. 518 pages.

39. Pryce, Peter. (September 2023) THE LAW OF HOLY COMMUNION, VOL. 1: WHAT LAWS GOVERN HOLY COMMUNION? – ISBN 979 8861352727 – Amazon Kindle Direct Publishing Paperback. Thursday 14th September 2023. 123 pages.

40. Pryce, Peter. (October 2023) THE LAW OF HOLY COMMUNION, VOL. 2: WHO HAS THE RIGHT TO SUPPLY HOLY COMMUNION BREAD? –. ISBN 979-8868078910 – Amazon Kindle Direct Publishing Paperback. Monday 2nd October 2023. 114 pages.

41. Pryce, Peter. (October 2023) THE LAW OF HOLY COMMUNION, VOL. 3: THIS DO, IN REMEMBRANCE OF ME! –. ISBN 979-8863155616 – Amazon Kindle Direct Publishing Paperback. Monday 2nd October 2023. 266 pages.

42. Pryce, Peter. (October 2023) THE BIBLE UNIVERSITY PASTORAL CERTIFICATE TRAINING: MODULE 1 # 263601004-KM-01. – ISBN 9798863610375. Amazon Kindle Direct Publishing Paperback. Release date: October 6, 2023. 107 pages.

43. Pryce, Peter. (October 2023) THE BIBLE UNIVERSITY PASTORAL CERTIFICATE TRAINING: MODULE 2 # 263601004-KM-01. – **ISBN 979-8863800417. Amazon Kindle Direct Publishing Paperback.** Release date: October 8, 2023.136 pages.

44. Pryce, Peter. (October 2023) THE BIBLE UNIVERSITY PASTORAL CERTIFICATE TRAINING: MODULE 3 # 263601004-KM-01. – **ISBN 979-8863905266. Amazon Kindle Direct Publishing Paperback.** Release date: October 9, 2023.121 pages.

45. Pryce, Peter. (October 2023) THE BIBLE UNIVERSITY PASTORAL CERTIFICATE TRAINING MODULE 4: THEORY AND PRACTICE OF BIBLE TRANSLATION AND INTERPRETATION. – **ISBN 9798863978338. Amazon Kindle Direct Publishing Paperback.** Release date: October 10, 2023. 104 pages.

46. Pryce, Peter. (October 2023) THE BIBLE UNIVERSITY PASTORAL CERTIFICATE TRAINING MODULE 5: TEMPLATE FOR BIBLE TRANSLATION, TEACHING, AND INTERPRETATION. – **ISBN 979-8864084694. Amazon Kindle Direct Publishing Paperback.** Release date: October 11, 2023. 114 pages.

47. Pryce, Peter. (October 2023) THE BIBLE UNIVERSITY PASTORAL CERTIFICATE TRAINING MODULE 6: METHODOLOGY FOR BIBLE INTERPRETATION. – **ISBN 979-8864196045. Amazon Kindle Direct Publishing Paperback.** Release date: October 12, 2023. 102 pages.

48. Pryce, Peter. (October 2023) THE BIBLE UNIVERSITY PASTORAL CERTIFICATE TRAINING MODULE 7: METHODOLOGY OF SPIRITUAL INTERPRETATION. – **ISBN 979-8864307342. Amazon Kindle Direct Publishing Paperback.** Release date: October 13, 2023. 131 pages.

49. Pryce, Peter. (October 2023) THE BIBLE UNIVERSITY PASTORAL CERTIFICATE TRAINING MODULE 8: DO I NEED HEBREW, GREEK, ARAMAIC, OR ARABIC TO UNDERSTAND GOD? – **ISBN 979-8864408537. Amazon Kindle Direct Publishing Paperback.** Release date: October 13, 2023. 119 pages.

50. Pryce, Peter. (October 2023) THE BIBLE UNIVERSITY PASTORAL CERTIFICATE TRAINING MODULE 9: METHODOLOGY FOR CHRISTIAN APOLOGETICS. – **ISBN 979-8864600184. Amazon Kindle Direct Publishing Paperback.** Release date: October 17, 2023. 129 pages.

51. Pryce, Peter. (October 2023) THE BIBLE UNIVERSITY PASTORAL CERTIFICATE TRAINING MODULE 10: SONG MINISTRATION AS A METHODOLOGY FOR GOSPEL IMPARTATION. **ISBN-979-8864757185.**

Amazon Kindle Direct Publishing Paperback. Release date: October 18, 2023. 129 pages.

52. Pryce, Peter. (October 2023) THE BIBLE UNIVERSITY PASTORAL CERTIFICATE TRAINING MODULE 11: TEACHING BIBLICAL HERMENEUTICS AND EXEGESIS. **ISBN 979-8865077749. Amazon Kindle Direct Publishing Paperback.** Release date: October 21, 2023. 132 pages.

53. Pryce, Peter. (October 2023) **SPIRITUAL SUPERIORITY OF THE BLACK MAN**, INGRAM. One Ingram Blvd., La Vergne, Tennessee, **– Hard Cover Color Paper Edition, ISBN 978-1-77637-652-0. 150 pages.** Release Date 13-OCT-2023.

54. Pryce, Peter. (September 14, 2023). **THE LAW OF HOLY COMMUNION, VOL. 1: WHAT LAWS GOVERN HOLY COMMUNION? Amazon Kindle Direct Publishing Paperback. ISBN-13: 979-8861352727.** 123 pages.

55. Pryce, Peter. (October 2, 2023). **THE LAW OF HOLY COMMUNION, VOL. 2: WHO HAS THE RIGHT TO SUPPLY HOLY COMMUNION BREAD? Amazon Kindle Direct Publishing Paperback. ISBN-13: 979-8863155616.** 114 pages

56. Pryce, Peter. (October 2, 2023). **THE LAW OF HOLY COMMUNION, VOL. 3: THIS DO, IN REMEMBRANCE OF ME! Amazon Kindle Direct Publishing Paperback. ISBN-13: 979-8863155616.** 266 pages.

57. Pryce, Peter. (November 18, 2023) **THE DOCTRINE OF CHRISTMAS AND BIRTHDAYS, VOL. 1. Amazon Kindle Direct Publishing Paperback. ISBN-13: 979-8868075650.** 153 pages.

58. Pryce, Peter. (November 18, 2023) **THE DOCTRINE OF CHRISTMAS AND BIRTHDAYS, VOL. 2. Amazon Kindle Direct Publishing Paperback. ISBN-13: 979-8868078910.** 124 pages

59. Pryce, Peter. (November 18, 2023). **THE DOCTRINE OF CHRISTMAS AND BIRTHDAYS, VOL. 3. ISBN-13: 979-8868080302.** 132 pages.

60. Pryce, Peter. (December 8, 2023). **FEMALE ORDINATION – VOL. 1. Amazon Kindle Direct Publishing Paperback. ISBN-13:** 979-8871181256. 114 pages.

61. Pryce, Peter. (December 8, 2023). **FEMALE ORDINATION – VOL. 2. Amazon Kindle Direct Publishing Paperback. ISBN-13:** 979-8871184752. 115 pages.

62. Pryce, Peter. (December 8, 2023). **FEMALE ORDINATION – VOL. 3. Amazon Kindle Direct Publishing Paperback. ISBN-13:** 979-8871186282. 134 pages.

63. Pryce, Peter. (December 13, 2023). **FEMALE ORDINATION – VOL. 4. Amazon Kindle Direct Publishing Paperback. ISBN** 979-8871747872. 203 Pages.

64. Pryce, Peter. (1ˢᵗ January 2024) *Complete Bible Curriculum Vol. 10 - THE BOOK OF JEREMIAH.* INGRAM. One Ingram Blvd., La Vergne, Tennessee, **– Hard**

Cover paper edition ISBN 978-1-77637-655-1. eBook edition ISBN 978-1-77637-656-8. **332 pages.**

65. Pryce, Peter. (1st February 2024) *Complete Bible Curriculum: How to Examine Pastors, Vol. 1 – What is the Church and why does it Matter?* One Ingram Blvd., La Vergne, Tennessee, – **Hard Cover paper edition ISBN 978-1-77637-654-4. eBook edition ISBN. 332 pages.**

66. Pryce, Peter. (1st March 2024) **Complete Bible Curriculum:** *How to Examine Pastors, Vol. 2 – Fundamental Concepts for Successful Christian Life: Covering: Matthew, Mark, Luke, John.* One Ingram Blvd., La Vergne, Tennessee, – **Hard Cover. ISBN 978-1-77637-657-5 – paper edition.** 300 pages.

67. Pryce, Peter. (1st April 2024) **Complete Bible Curriculum:** *How to Examine Pastors, Vol. 3 – Fundamental Concepts for Successful Christian Life: Covering: Acts, Romans.* One Ingram Blvd., La Vergne, Tennessee, – **Hard Cover. ISBN – paper edition.** 372 pages.

68. Pryce, Peter (1st May 2024) *Can the Minister of God also function as a Minister of Government?* One Ingram Blvd., La Vergne, Tennessee, – **Hard Cover. ISBN 9781776376421 – paper edition.** 470 pages.

69. Pryce, Peter. (1st June 2024) **Complete Bible Curriculum:** *How to Examine Pastors, Vol. 4 – Fundamental Concepts for Successful Christian Life: Covering: 1 and 2 Corinthians.* One Ingram Blvd., La Vergne, Tennessee, – **Hard Cover. ISBN – paper edition.** 422 pages.

70. Pryce, Peter. (1st July 2024) **Complete Bible Curriculum:** *How to Examine Pastors, Vol. 5 – Fundamental Concepts for Successful Christian Life: Covering: Galatians, Ephesians, Philippians, Colossians.* One Ingram Blvd., La Vergne, Tennessee, – **Hard Cover. ISBN – paper edition.** ?? pages.

71. Pryce, Peter. (1st August 2024) **Complete Bible Curriculum:** *How to Examine Pastors, Vol. 6 – Fundamental Concepts for Successful Christian Life: Covering: Galatians, Ephesians, Philippians, Colossians.* One Ingram Blvd., La Vergne, Tennessee, – **Hard Cover. ISBN – paper edition.** ?? pages.

72. Pryce, Peter. (1st September 2024) **Complete Bible Curriculum:** *How to Examine Pastors, Vol. 7 – Fundamental Concepts for Successful Christian Life: Covering: Titus, Philemon, Hebrews.* One Ingram Blvd., La Vergne, Tennessee, – **Hard Cover. ISBN – paper edition.** ?? pages.

COMPLETED MANUSCRIPTS AND UP-COMING TEXTBOOKS

73. Pryce, Peter. (September 2023) *Water Baptism Vol. 1 - From Genesis to Revelation.*

74. Pryce, Peter. (November 2023) *Water Baptism Vol. 2 - From Genesis to Revelation*.
75. Pryce, Peter. (December 2023) *Water Baptism Vol. 3 - From Genesis to Revelation*.
76. Pryce, Peter. (January 2024) *Water Baptism Vol. 4 - From Genesis to Revelation*.
77. Pryce, Peter. (February 2024) *Water Baptism Vol. 5 - From Genesis to Revelation*.
78. Pryce, Peter. (2024) *Holy Communion - From Genesis to Revelation*.

REFEREED ARTICLES IN BLIND PEER-REVIEWED ACADEMIC JOURNALS:

1. Pryce, Peter. (2003). Foreignising Finnish: Necessary/Unnecessary English Imports into Translations. *Current Writing: Text and Reception in Southern Africa 14/2* (October, 2003), 203-12.
2. Pryce, Peter. (2011). Gemeinschaft Concept of Community in Schools: Case Study of Prince George's County Public Schools. *International Journal of Basic Education*, vol. 2(1), 1-9.
3. Pryce, Peter. (2012). Attitudes to Translation. *Linguistique et didactique de langue et de littérature : Problématiques contemporaines et perspectives (Linguistics and Language / Literature Didactics : Contemporary Challenges and Prospects)*, 343-377.
4. Pryce, Peter. (2012). Change as a Distinct Property of Language. In Bariki, I., Kuupole, D. D. and Kambou, M. K. (Eds.), *Aspects of Language Variation and Use*. Cape Coast: University of Cape Coast Press, 1-14.
5. Pryce, Peter. (2013). Techniques of Expression. *International Journal of Educational Research and Development*, vol. 2 (1), 1-9. 235-246.

EVIDENCE OF ACCEPTANCE FOR PUBLICATION IN A REFEREED JOURNAL:

6. Pryce, Peter. (2006). Nokia's Role as an Agent of Language Migration. *Translation Watch Quarterly*. Patterson Lakes, Victoria, Australia: Translation Standards Institute.

PUBLICATION OF CONFERENCE PROCEEDINGS:

7. Pryce, Peter. (2002). Translation as a Medium for Transmitting New Ideas: Finland as a Case Study. In H. Kucerova & B. Knowlden (Eds.), XVI Vancouver World Congress

of the International Federation of Translators: Translation: New Ideas for a New Century (151-155). Paris: Fédération internationale des traducteurs (FIT).

INTERNET PRESENCE

Professional Website: WWW.THEBIBLEUNIVERSITY.ORG
Author website: WWW.BOOKSTORESITE.ORG
Church Website: WWW.THEBIBLEUNIVERSITYCHURCH.ORG

SOCIAL MEDIA LINKS

Skype link: https://join.skype.com/invite/a7xNskRQG2Fj
https://www.facebook.com/BibleLecturesAndHumanServices
www.instagram.com/thebibleuniversity
www.twitter.com/TheBibleUniv
https://youtu.be/G2bMwBpt0jk
https://www.youtube.com/channel/UCa0RgmXpGm7bJhtY7j_-UHw
LinkedIn URL: https://www.linkedin.com/in/the-bible-university-by-rev-prof-peter-pryce-ph-d-38b021127/

Association of African Universities (AAU) TV Discussion Program with Rev. Prof. Peter Pryce:
Topic: How Religion Contributes to Peace and Security in Africa:
https://kzread.info/dash/aau-talks-how-religion-contributes-to-peace-and-security-in-africa/lHiu1NeJgrjKgaQ.html

https://thebibleuniversity.org/blog/

Author Website Bookstore: WWW.BOOKSTORESITE.ORG

United States Patent and Trademark Office (USPTO): TRADEMARK:
https://furm.com/trademarks/the-bible-university-by-rev-prof-peter-pryce-phd-97075519

Contact Info:
Phone: +1-301-793-7190
E-mail: Dr.Pryce@gmail.com

TRADEMARK INFORMATION

United States of America
United States Patent and Trademark Office

The Bible University by Rev. Prof. Peter Pryce, P.H.D.

Reg. No. 6,999,146

Registered Mar. 14, 2023

Int. Cl.: 41

Service Mark

Principal Register

Presentation Copy

THE BIBLE UNIVERSITY INC.
11779 Carriage House Drive
Silver Spring, MARYLAND 20904

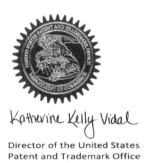

Katherine Kelly Vidal

Director of the United States
Patent and Trademark Office

TABLE OF CONTENTS

Table of Contents

FOREWORD

HOW CAN I KNOW THAT A PROPHECY IS TRUE AND CORRECT AND FROM GOD?

Question 2455

1. Here is the **#52 physical sacrifice and offering of God-worship**.
2. How can I know that a prophecy is true and correct and from God?
3. You can know when the prophecy is 100% from the Word of God as **Romans 12:6 (KJV)** reveals, because Faith is the Word of God, and because all prophecies come from Faith, and Faith is the Word of God!
    i. **Romans 12:6 (KJV)** Having then gifts differing according to the grace that is given to us, whether prophecy, *let us prophesy* according to the proportion of faith;
    ii. **Romans 10:8 (KJV)** But what saith it? The word is nigh thee, *even* in thy mouth, and in thy heart: that is, the word of faith, which we preach;
4. Normally, what you preach is the Word of God and that preaching Word is called Faith in **Romans 10:8 (KJV)**, therefore, Faith is the Word of God, and if all true prophecies MUST come from Faith as **Romans 12:6 (KJV)** says, then, all true prophecies MUST come 100% from the Word of God, and if any prophecy comes from any Prophet from outside the Word of God, then, that Prophet is a Prophet of Satan who uses the evil spirit of divination to prophesy!
    i. **Acts 16:16 (KJV)** And it came to pass, as we went to prayer, a certain damsel possessed with a spirit of divination met us, which brought her masters much gain by soothsaying:
    ii. **Acts 16:17 (KJV)** The same followed Paul and us, and cried, saying, These men are the servants of the most high God, which shew unto us the way of salvation.
    iii. **Acts 16:18 (KJV)** And this did she many days. But Paul, being grieved, turned and said to the spirit, I command thee in the name of Jesus Christ to come out of her. And he came out the same hour.
5. Here is another evidence of where true and correct prophecies come from: they come from the Gospel/Testimony of Christ!

      i. **Revelation 19:10 (KJV)** And I fell at his feet to worship him. And he said unto me, See *thou do it* not: I am thy fellowservant, and of thy brethren that have the testimony of Jesus: worship God: for the testimony of Jesus is the spirit of prophecy.

6. You have seen clearly from the Word of God that prophecy comes from Faith and Faith is what we preach and what we preach is the Word of God, therefore prophecy comes 100% from the Word of God!

      i. **Romans 12:6 (KJV)** Having then gifts differing according to the grace that is given to us, whether prophecy, *let us prophesy* according to the proportion of faith;

      ii. **Romans 10:8 (KJV)** But what saith it? The word is nigh thee, *even* in thy mouth, and in thy heart: that is, the word of faith, which we preach;

7. Now, when prophecy comes from outside the Word of God/Faith, see what the LORD God says it is: IT IS SIN!

      i. **Romans 14:23 (KJV)** And he that doubteth is damned if he eat, because *he eateth* not of faith: for whatsoever *is* not of faith is sin.

8. So, when your Prophet claims to have prophecies from Angels like J. Y. Adu in Ghana, from Heaven, from the air, directly from God, from spirits, from ancestors, or from anywhere that is outside the Word of God, then know immediately that they are Satan's Prophets working with the evil spirit of divination!

The LORD Jesus Christ be with your spirit. The LORD Jesus Christ give you understanding.

Rev. Prof. PETER PRYCE,
DSEF, BA, MA, B.Soc.Sc Pol Sci, IBA, PhD
A Scribe of the Law of the God of Heaven
Prophet of the Word of God
Professor of French, Silver Spring, MD, USA
Scholar of the Institute of Theologians, USA
WWW.THEBIBLEUNIVERSITY.ORG
Accreditation Number: 07-QCTO/SDP120723172836
SAQA QUAL ID: Identification # 101997
WWW.BOOKSTORESITE.ORG
WWW.THEBIBLEUNIVERSITYCHURCH.ORG

Monday 1st January 2024 @ 4:37 PM – 4:40 PM
While hearing and meditating on the Word of God.

PREFACE
THE NEW COMMAND REGARDING HOLY COMMUNION

Question 2463

1. The same way that the LORD God Almighty sacrificed the LORD Jesus Christ for our sins that HE took upon Himself, same way also you must purge that fornicator away from your midst!

    i. **1 Corinthians 5:7 (KJV)** Purge out therefore the old leaven, that ye may be a new lump, as ye are unleavened. For even Christ our passover is sacrificed for us:

    ii. **1 Corinthians 5:8 (KJV)** Therefore let us keep the feast, not with old leaven, neither with the leaven of malice and wickedness; but with the unleavened *bread* of sincerity and truth.

2. At the same time as the LORD God in **1 Corinthians 5:7-8 (KJV)** is commanding to purge the fornicator out of the church, same time the LORD is also revealing how to perform the spiritual Holy Communion, NOT with physical bread, wine, and wafers as it is corruptly done in all the churches today, but with the spiritual bread, wine, and wafers called: "the unleavened *bread* of sincerity and truth"!

3. So, in **1 Corinthians 5:8 (KJV)**, the new command regarding Holy Communion is this:

    i. "Therefore let us keep the feast with the unleavened *bread* of sincerity and truth"!

4. What that means in practise is that, since now "sincerity and truth" are the real Holy Communion bread, wine, and wafers, you as the Christian will set your daily target to accomplish your living in Truth and Righteousness in all things: in your thoughts, in your words, and in your deeds, and as you do that daily, then, it is counted for you as your righteousness in Heaven, just the same way as Abraham's believing in God and obeying God in Truth and Righteousness earned him his own righteousness in Heaven!

    i. **Genesis 15:6 (KJV)** And he believed in the LORD; and he counted it to him for righteousness.

ii. **Romans 4:3 (KJV)** For what saith the scripture? Abraham believed God, and it was counted unto him for righteousness.

iii. **Galatians 3:6 (KJV)** Even as Abraham believed God, and it was accounted to him for righteousness.

iv. **James 2:23 (KJV)** And the scripture was fulfilled which saith, Abraham believed God, and it was imputed unto him for righteousness: and he was called the Friend of God.

5. But, why is the LORD God including this Word on Holy Communion in a chapter on how to judge fornicators and other sinners in the congregation?

6. The reason is that the current Holy Communion as it is practiced in the present form in all the churches, is wrong and a sin, seeing that Pastors, Bishops, and Church Leaders are carnal, corrupt, and practising idolatry by reason of the physical oblations that they use in their filthy Holy Communion whereby, those physical items themselves are contrary to the commandment of the LORD Jesus Christ!

i. **John 4:23 (KJV)** But the hour cometh, and now is, when the true worshippers shall worship the Father in spirit and in truth: for the Father seeketh such to worship him.

ii. **John 4:24 (KJV)** God *is* a Spirit: and they that worship him must worship *him* in spirit and in truth.

iii. **Ephesians 5:9 (KJV)** (For the fruit of the Spirit *is* in all goodness and righteousness and truth;)

7. Furthermore, the LORD God included Holy Communion in the subject of how to judge fornicators because all the Pastors, Bishops, and Church Leaders who have this Holy Communion doctrine that is contrary to **John 4:23-24 (KJV)**, they are also fornicators, harlots, and whores and here is the evidence!

i. **Hosea 1:2 (KJV)** The beginning of the word of the LORD by Hosea. And the LORD said to Hosea, Go, take unto thee a wife of whoredoms and children of whoredoms: for the land hath committed great whoredom, *departing* from the LORD.

ii. **Hebrews 3:12 (KJV)** Take heed, brethren, lest there be in any of you an evil heart of unbelief, in departing from the living God.

The LORD Jesus Christ be with your spirit. The LORD Jesus Christ give you understanding.

Rev. Prof. PETER PRYCE,
DSEF, BA, MA, B.Soc.Sc Pol Sci, IBA, PhD
A Scribe of the Law of the God of Heaven
Prophet of the Word of God

Professor of French, Silver Spring, MD, USA
Scholar of the Institute of Theologians, USA
WWW.THEBIBLEUNIVERSITY.ORG
Accreditation Number: 07-QCTO/SDP120723172836
SAQA QUAL ID: Identification # 101997
WWW.BOOKSTORESITE.ORG
WWW.THEBIBLEUNIVERSITYCHURCH.ORG

Monday 8th January 2024 @ 10:21 AM – 11:44 AM
While hearing and meditating on the Word of God.

CHAPTER 1
INTRODUCTION TO BIBLICAL HERMENEUTICS AND BIBLICAL EXEGESIS

ADINKRAHENE
"Chief of Adinkra symbols"
Asante philosophical symbol of Greatness, Charisma, Leadership

Hermeneutics is the study and establishment of the principles by which you interpret the Word of God. Thus, any rules, theoretical or practical, that you follow in order to bring out the meaning of a Bible text, is called "Biblical Hermeneutics".

The theoretical part is called "Hermeneutics" and then the actual application and implementation of the rules of Bible translation and interpretation, in order to bring out the hidden meaning, that is called "Biblical Exegesis"!

This introduction contains the entire theory that is at the foundation of how I teach the Word of God the way that I teach it, in other words: the why behind the what.

ABSTRACT

The aim of this research was to discover a scientific method of intralingual Bible interpreting where scientific means that (1) the faithfulness and accuracy of the translation are verifiable and (2) replicability of meaning at the message level of the interpreting process is assured once the method is mastered. The method used for the research was simple: (1) explain the Perfect Harmony Method for Bible Translation and Interpreting and the aim of interpreting, (2) read the entire English Bible: King James Version, (3) discover how meaning was rendered in the Bible using only the Bible (KJV), (4) in the light of the Scriptures, examine the rendered meaning for perfect harmony at the lexical level, at the message level, and at the context level such that the accuracy of the rendering or the accuracy of the intralingual interpretation is assured by its perfect harmony with the rest of the entire Bible. We found two illustrations of the Perfect Harmony Method of Bible Translation and Interpreting in Mark 12 and Mark 15. Thus, by using the Bible as its own interpreter, we achieve faithfulness to the source text and accuracy of expression apart from the assurance that the interpretation is not contradicted by any other verse in the entire Bible.

To the extent that there are University Professors and academics who are still ignorant of the three levels of translation to wit: Intralingual Translation (One language translation), Intralingual Translation (two or more language translation), and Intersemiotic Translation (non-verbal, non-linguistic translation), it is important to state plainly and categorically that this textbook is a work of interpretation and translation. It is a work of both interpretation and translation because we interpret to translate and we translate to interpret!

Keywords: Method, Intralingual Translation, Bible Interpreting, Perfect Harmony.

INTRODUCTION TO THE PERFECT HARMONY THEORY

T ranslation is the process of rendering meaning from an initiator to a receptor in order to achieve understanding of communication. In this paper, both translation and interpretation are used interchangeably given that during the cognitive process of translation, there is an interpretation segment that intervenes prior to writing the translation whereas, on the other hand, the act of note taking during interpreting is a clear intervention of a major translation activity of writing (cf. Seleskovitch, Danica, et Lederer, Marianne 2001).

We identify three types of translation known as *interlingual translation, intralingual translation* and *intersemiotic translation*. First, it is possible to render meaning from one language into another…that is called *interlingual translation*. Secondly, it is possible to render meaning within the same language such as when you take a Bible verse and explain it or when you explain a proverb in the same language to another…that practice is called *intralingual translation*.

Therefore Bible teaching, paraphrasing, summarizing, rephrasing, deverbalization, rapporteuring, commentary, journalistic reporting, recasting just to name those few, are all examples of *intralingual translation*. Thirdly, it is possible to render meaning by means of signs and objects such as road signs and drawings…that is called *intersemiotic translation* (Jakobson, 1971: 266).

The type of Bible interpreting exemplified in this book is intralingual translation and the English Bible: King James Version was used throughout. It is well understood that in translation, you render meaning by means of entities called words or signs or symbols. Therefore, words are vehicles that carry meanings. Just as meaning cannot be independent of the context, so Bible translation, whether interlingual or intralingual, must respect the *perfect harmony of the Scriptures*. The P*erfect Harmony Method of Bible Translation and Interpreting* simply means that Bible teaching or interpreting must not in any way contradict any part of the Bible from Genesis to Revelation.

THE LAW OF BIBLE TRANSLATION AND INTERPRETATION

1. Here in **Proverbs 21:16 (KJV)** is the Law of Bible Translation and Interpretation, otherwise known as Hermeneutics (Theory) and Exegesis (Interpretation)!

2. What is Understanding? What is the Way of Understanding?

     i. **Proverbs 21:16 (KJV)** The man that wandereth out of the way of understanding shall remain in the congregation of the dead.

3. "Understanding" is another name for the Word of God!

     i. **Deuteronomy 4:5 (KJV)** Behold, I have taught you statutes and judgments, even as the LORD my God commanded me, that ye should do so in the land whither ye go to possess it.

     ii. **Deuteronomy 4:6 (KJV)** Keep therefore and do *them*; for this *is* your wisdom and your understanding in the sight of the nations, which shall hear all these statutes, and say, Surely this great nation *is* a wise and understanding people.

     iii. **Job 28:12 (KJV)** But where shall wisdom be found? and where *is* the place of understanding?

     iv. **Job 28:20 (KJV)** Whence then cometh wisdom? and where *is* the place of understanding?

     v. **Psalm 119:104 (KJV)** Through thy precepts I get understanding: therefore I hate every false way.

     vi. **Psalm 119:130 (KJV)** The entrance of thy words giveth light; it giveth understanding unto the simple.

     vii. **Psalm 119:169 (KJV)** TAU. Let my cry come near before thee, O LORD: give me understanding according to thy word.

     viii. **Proverbs 2:6 (KJV)** For the LORD giveth wisdom: out of his mouth *cometh* knowledge and understanding.

     ix. **Proverbs 4:5 (KJV)** Get wisdom, get understanding: forget *it* not; neither decline from the words of my mouth.

     x. **Proverbs 4:7 (KJV)** Wisdom *is* the principal thing; *therefore* get wisdom: and with all thy getting get understanding.

     xi. **Proverbs 8:14 (KJV)** Counsel *is* mine, and sound wisdom: I *am* understanding; I have strength.

       xii. **Proverbs 9:10 (KJV)** The fear of the LORD *is* the beginning of wisdom: and the knowledge of the holy *is* understanding.

      xiii. **Proverbs 16:22 (KJV)** Understanding *is* a wellspring of life unto him that hath it: but the instruction of fools *is* folly.

4. Therefore, the real message in **Proverbs 21:16 (KJV)** is that: The moment you stray outside the Word of God, you have entered the territory of Death!

      i. **Proverbs 21:16 (KJV)** The man that wandereth out of the way of understanding shall remain in the congregation of the dead.

5. Do you now understand why we say that in The Bible University, our ONLY textbook for the entire University is the Word of God, the Holy Bible the Gospel of the LORD Jesus Christ, from Genesis to Revelation?

6. So, then, as a true Man of God, you are forbidden to use any book aside the Word of God!

7. Are you a Pastor?

8. Do you have and do you consult other books that you keep in your Pulpit and in your Church Office, and you even use them to preach to the congregation?

9. Show me just one evidence where the LORD Jesus Christ used any other book aside the Word of God the Prophets!

      i. **Luke 24:27 (KJV)** And beginning at Moses and all the prophets, he expounded unto them in all the scriptures the things concerning himself.

      ii. **Luke 10:26 (KJV)** He said unto him, What is written in the law? how readest thou?

      iii. **Matthew 4:4 (KJV)** But he answered and said, It is written, Man shall not live by bread alone, but by every word that proceedeth out of the mouth of God.

      iv. **Matthew 4:7 (KJV)** Jesus said unto him, It is written again, Thou shalt not tempt the Lord thy God.

      v. **Matthew 4:10 (KJV)** Then saith Jesus unto him, Get thee hence, Satan: for it is written, Thou shalt worship the Lord thy God, and him only shalt thou serve.

10. Do you also now understand why the same Law in **Proverbs 21:16 (KJV)** forbids you to use any other book when you want to translate and interpret the Word of God!

11. The entire theory of Bible Translation and Interpretation rests in this one verse:

      i. **Proverbs 21:16 (KJV)** The man that wandereth out of the way of understanding shall remain in the congregation of the dead.

12. In other words, when you remove **Proverbs 21:16 (KJV)**, or when you despise and disregard **Proverbs 21:16 (KJV)**, then you have no Hermeneutics and Exegesis!

      i.   **Isaiah 8:20 (KJV)** To the law and to the testimony: if they speak not according to this word, *it is* because *there is* no light in them.

      ii.   **Proverbs 21:30 (KJV)** *There is* no wisdom nor understanding nor counsel against the LORD.

      iii.   **Galatians 1:8 (KJV)** But though we, or an angel from heaven, preach any other gospel unto you than that which we have preached unto you, let him be accursed.

      iv.   **Galatians 1:9 (KJV)** As we said before, so say I now again, If any *man* preach any other gospel unto you than that ye have received, let him be accursed.

13. Except when you are a fool and an ignorant person, that is when you will go outside of the Holy Bible to seek a theory, false theory, to use to teach, translate, examine, research, and interpret the Holy Bible, and then, in that case, your Hermeneutics and Exegesis will be from Satan!

14. Here in **Proverbs 21:30 (KJV)** is another Law of Bible Translation and Interpretation!

      i.   **Proverbs 21:30 (KJV)** *There is* no wisdom nor understanding nor counsel against the LORD.

15. Proper Hermeneutics and Exegesis come from **Proverbs 21:30 (KJV)** and stipulates that you cannot translate and interpret the Word of God against the Word of God!

16. Instead, by that Theory of Bible Translation and Interpretation that you see in **Proverbs 21:30 (KJV)**, you must teach the Word of God to agree with the Word of God, you must translate the Word of God to agree with the Word of God, you must interpret the Word of God to agree with the Word of God!

      i.   **Mark 9:39 (KJV)** But Jesus said, Forbid him not: for there is no man which shall do a miracle in my name, that can lightly speak evil of me.

      ii.   **John 3:34 (KJV)** For he whom God hath sent speaketh the words of God: for God giveth not the Spirit by measure *unto him.*

      iii.   **John 17:22 (KJV)** And the glory which thou gavest me I have given them; that they may be one, even as we are one:

      iv.   **John 17:23 (KJV)** I in them, and thou in me, that they may be made perfect in one; and that the world may know that thou hast sent me, and hast loved them, as thou hast loved me.

17. That is the ONLY way, that is the only Theory, that is the only Hermeneutics available by which you can correctly teach, examine, research, expound, and interpret (Exegesis) the Word of God!

BIBLICAL EXEGESIS

Hermeneutics is the study and establishment of the principles by which you interpret the Word of God. Thus, any rules, theoretical or practical, that you follow in order to bring out the meaning of a Bible text, is called "Biblical Hermeneutics".

The theoretical part is called "Hermeneutics" and then the actual application and implementation of the rules of Bible translation and interpretation, in order to bring out the hidden meaning: that is called "Biblical Exegesis"! In the following paragraphs, we shall see an illustration of Biblical Exegesis.

SUMMARY OF THE THEORY OF BIBLICAL HERMENEUTICS

1. The Lord Jesus Christ used Psalm 110:1 (KJV) to teach Deductive Reasoning as a Methodology for Gospel Impartation!

    i. **Psalm 110:1 (KJV)** A Psalm of David. The LORD said unto my Lord, Sit thou at my right hand, until I make thine enemies thy footstool.

    ii. **Matthew 22:41 (KJV)** While the Pharisees were gathered together, Jesus asked them,

    iii. **Matthew 22:42 (KJV)** Saying, What think ye of Christ? whose son is he? They say unto him, *The Son* of David.

    iv. **Matthew 22:43 (KJV)** He saith unto them, How then doth David in spirit call him Lord, saying,

    v. **Matthew 22:44 (KJV)** The LORD said unto my Lord, Sit thou on my right hand, till I make thine enemies thy footstool?

    vi. **Matthew 22:45 (KJV)** If David then call him Lord, how is he his son?

    vii. **Matthew 22:46 (KJV)** And no man was able to answer him a word, neither durst any *man* from that day forth ask him any more *questions*.

2. First of all, the LORD Jesus Christ confirms in Matthew 22:41-46 (KJV) that David was saved in the Old Testament because David knew the LORD Jesus Christ in the Old Testament hence, he was writing about HIM!

3. Secondly, the LORD Jesus Christ is laying down "Deduction Reasoning" as an essential aspect of the Methodology for Gospel Impartation, saying that:

    i. If what you are teaching, affirming, explaining, translating, preaching, interpreting, evangelizing, and writing, does not make sense, then you are wrong in your Gospel Doctrine and in the Word of God!

    ii. If what you are teaching, affirming, explaining, translating, preaching, interpreting, evangelizing, and writing, violates any part of the entire Word of God from Genesis to Revelation, then you are wrong in your Gospel Doctrine and in the Word of God!

    iii. If what you are teaching, affirming, explaining, translating, preaching, interpreting, evangelizing, and writing, contradicts any part of the entire Word of God from Genesis to Revelation, then you are wrong in your Gospel Doctrine and in the Word of God!

    iv. If what you are teaching, affirming, explaining, translating, preaching, interpreting, evangelizing, and writing, does not perfectly harmonize and agree with the entire remainder of the Word of God from Genesis to Revelation, then you are wrong in your Gospel Doctrine and in the Word of God!

     v.   In other words, you cannot teach the Word of God against the Word of God!

    vi.   In other words, you must teach the Word of God to agree with the Word of God!

4.   Here are the evidences for the Perfect Harmony Theory for Bible Translation and Interpreting that the LORD Jesus Christ was teaching the erudite Pharisees, Sadducees, Synagogue Rulers, High Priests, Pastors, and Church Leaders!

5.   In **Isaiah 8:20 (KJV)**, the LORD God Almighty declares that if you fail to teach the Word of God to agree with the Word of God, then it means that you are not even saved or born again!

     i.   **Isaiah 8:20 (KJV)** To the law and to the testimony: if they speak not according to this word, *it is* because *there is* no light in them.

6.   In **Luke 10:25-28 (KJV)**, the LORD Jesus Christ is pointing out that, if you fail to seek, read, and study Salvation according to all that is written in the Law of God, then you will NOT be saved and you will NOT enter Heaven, effectively meaning that Salvation is actually a School Curriculum that you must read and study!

     i.   **Luke 10:25 (KJV)** And, behold, a certain lawyer stood up, and tempted him, saying, Master, what shall I do to inherit eternal life?

    ii.   **Luke 10:26 (KJV)** He said unto him, What is written in the law? how readest thou?

    iii.   **Luke 10:27 (KJV)** And he answering said, Thou shalt love the Lord thy God with all thy heart, and with all thy soul, and with all thy strength, and with all thy mind; and thy neighbour as thyself.

    iv.   **Luke 10:28 (KJV)** And he said unto him, Thou hast answered right: this do, and thou shalt live.

     v.   **2 Timothy 2:15 (KJV)** Study to shew thyself approved unto God, a workman that needeth not to be ashamed, rightly dividing the word of truth.

7.   In **Acts 17:10-12 (KJV)**, the LORD God Almighty is revealing that Salvation is a Taught School Activity where the Salvation is attained when the Doctrine of Salvation is taught to Bible Students and where the Student of Salvation in turn reads and researches the Holy Bible to verify that what he/she has been taught conforms to the rest of the Word of God, before he/she proceeds to believe what he/she has been taught, and then he/she will now attain unto Salvation!

      i. **Acts 17:10 (KJV)** And the brethren immediately sent away Paul and Silas by night unto Berea: who coming *thither* went into the synagogue of the Jews.

     ii. **Acts 17:11 (KJV)** These were more noble than those in Thessalonica, in that they received the word with all readiness of mind, and searched the scriptures daily, whether those things were so.

   iii. **Acts 17:12 (KJV)** Therefore many of them believed; also of honourable women which were Greeks, and of men, not a few.

8. In **Galatians 1:8-9 (KJV)**, the LORD God reveals that even if Angels from Heaven come and engage in teaching, affirming, explaining, translating, preaching, interpreting, evangelizing, and writing the Gospel of the LORD Jesus Christ, and then what the Angels teach do not perfectly harmonize and agree with the entire remainder of the Word of God from Genesis to Revelation, then those Angels are wrong in their Gospel Doctrine and in the Word of God, and for that matter, you the Man of God are even authorized to curse all such Angels!

      i. **Galatians 1:8 (KJV)** But though we, or an angel from heaven, preach any other gospel unto you than that which we have preached unto you, let him be accursed.

     ii. **Galatians 1:9 (KJV)** As we said before, so say I now again, If any *man* preach any other gospel unto you than that ye have received, let him be accursed.

9. In **1 Thessalonians 5:21 (KJV)** and in **1 John 4:1 (KJV)**, the LORD God Almighty reveals to us that if you fail to prove the Word of God by the Word of God, and if you fail to test, examine, and reason out the Word of God by the Word of God, then you are a false Christian and a false Prophet!

      i. **1 Thessalonians 5:21 (KJV)** Prove all things; hold fast that which is good.

     ii. **1 John 4:1 (KJV)** Beloved, believe not every spirit, but try the spirits whether they are of God: because many false prophets are gone out into the world.

10. All the above is the Perfect Harmony Theory for Bible Translation and Interpreting (Pryce, 2011) that I have been teaching in The Bible University and which the LORD Jesus Christ was first teaching the erudite Pharisees, Sadducees, Synagogue Rulers, High Priests, Pastors, and Church Leaders!

      i. **Matthew 22:41 (KJV)** While the Pharisees were gathered together, Jesus asked them,

     ii. **Matthew 22:42 (KJV)** Saying, What think ye of Christ? whose son is he? They say unto him, *The Son* of David.

  iii. **Matthew 22:43 (KJV)** He saith unto them, How then doth David in spirit call him Lord, saying,

  iv. **Matthew 22:44 (KJV)** The LORD said unto my Lord, Sit thou on my right hand, till I make thine enemies thy footstool?

  v. **Matthew 22:45 (KJV)** If David then call him Lord, how is he his son?

  vi. **Matthew 22:46 (KJV)** And no man was able to answer him a word, neither durst any *man* from that day forth ask him any more *questions.*

11. Specifically, the LORD Jesus Christ told them that there is contradiction (**Matthew 22:43 (KJV), Matthew 22:45 (KJV)**) in your reasoning and teaching of the Word of God, therefore, you are wrong!

12. Your ability as a Man of God to eliminate every contradiction in your teaching of the Word of God is your evidence that you have attained unto the Perfect Harmony of the Scriptures and unto the required Deductive Reasoning as the correct Methodology for Gospel Impartation!

THE BIBLE TRANSLATOR'S METHODOLOGY

THE BIBLE TRANSLATOR'S METHODOLOGY/THEORY (BIBLICAL HERMENEUTICS) TO EXPLAIN/TEACH/INTERPRET (BIBLICAL EXEGESIS) THE HOLY BIBLE

1. Here in **Isaiah 55:8-9 (KJV** is one of the major reasons why it is sheer folly and despicable beastly ignorance to try to explain the Word of God with human intellect and man-made methodologies!

    i. **Isaiah 55:8 (KJV)** For my thoughts *are* not your thoughts, neither *are* your ways my ways, saith the LORD.

    ii. **Isaiah 55:9 (KJV)** For *as* the heavens are higher than the earth, so are my ways higher than your ways, and my thoughts than your thoughts.

2. How can foolishness explain wisdom for it to be right?

    i. **1 Corinthians 2:14 (KJV)** But the natural man receiveth not the things of the Spirit of God: for they are foolishness unto him: neither can he know *them*, because they are spiritually discerned.

    ii. **Micah 7:3 (KJV)** That they may do evil with both hands earnestly, the prince asketh, and the judge *asketh* for a reward; and the great *man*, he uttereth his mischievous desire: so they wrap it up.

    iii. **1 Corinthians 1:20 (KJV)** Where *is* the wise? where *is* the scribe? where *is* the disputer of this world? hath not God made foolish the wisdom of this world?

    iv. **1 Corinthians 2:6 (KJV)** Howbeit we speak wisdom among them that are perfect: yet not the wisdom of this world, nor of the princes of this world, that come to nought:

    v. **1 Corinthians 3:19 (KJV)** For the wisdom of this world is foolishness with God. For it is written, He taketh the wise in their own craftiness.

3. How can corrupt thoughts produce an explanation or a methodology to assess and examine thoughts that are incorrupt and pure even as **Isaiah 55:8 (KJV)** reveals?

    i. **Proverbs 21:30 (KJV)** *There is* no wisdom nor understanding nor counsel against the LORD.

    ii. **Psalm 119:140 (KJV)** Thy word *is* very pure: therefore thy servant loveth it.

      iii. **Proverbs 30:5 (KJV)** Every word of God *is* pure: he *is* a shield unto them that put their trust in him.

4. How can continual liars (all men and all women) purport to examine, assess, evaluate, and offer a methodology/theory (Biblical Hermeneutics) to explain/teach (Biblical Exegesis) the words of He who never lied? Is that possible?

      i. **Genesis 6:5 (KJV)** And GOD saw that the wickedness of man *was* great in the earth, and *that* every imagination of the thoughts of his heart *was* only evil continually.

      ii. **Numbers 23:19 (KJV)** God *is* not a man, that he should lie; neither the son of man, that he should repent: hath he said, and shall he not do *it*? or hath he spoken, and shall he not make it good?

      iii. **1 Samuel 15:29 (KJV)** And also the Strength of Israel will not lie nor repent: for he *is* not a man, that he should repent.

      iv. **Proverbs 8:8 (KJV)** All the words of my mouth *are* in righteousness; *there is* nothing froward or perverse in them.

      v. **James 1:17 (KJV)** Every good gift and every perfect gift is from above, and cometh down from the Father of lights, with whom is no variableness, neither shadow of turning.

      vi. **1 Peter 2:21 (KJV)** For even hereunto were ye called: because Christ also suffered for us, leaving us an example, that ye should follow his steps:

      vii. **1 Peter 2:22 (KJV)** Who did no sin, neither was guile found in his mouth:

      viii. **John 14:6 (KJV)** Jesus saith unto him, I am the way, the truth, and the life: no man cometh unto the Father, but by me.

5. Ever since the world was created, was it ever possible for Darkness to dispel/explain Light? Was it ever possible for Darkness to examine, assess, evaluate, and offer a methodology/theory (Biblical Hermeneutics) to explain/teach (Biblical Exegesis) the words of He who is The Light?

      i. **John 8:12 (KJV)** Then spake Jesus again unto them, saying, I am the light of the world: he that followeth me shall not walk in darkness, but shall have the light of life.

      ii. **John 9:5 (KJV)** As long as I am in the world, I am the light of the world.

6. Shall He that brought Light (enlightenment) be examined by he that sat in darkness (the ignorant and the fools)?

      i. **Genesis 1:1 (KJV)** In the beginning God created the heaven and the earth.

ii. **Genesis 1:2 (KJV)** And the earth was without form, and void; and darkness *was* upon the face of the deep. And the Spirit of God moved upon the face of the waters.

iii. **Genesis 1:3 (KJV)** And God said, Let there be light: and there was light.

iv. **Genesis 1:4 (KJV)** And God saw the light, that *it was* good: and God divided the light from the darkness.

7. Shall one use the earthly to teach and to explain the Heavenly and not risk being called a fool?

i. **Luke 24:13 (KJV)** And, behold, two of them went that same day to a village called Emmaus, which was from Jerusalem *about* threescore furlongs.

ii. **Luke 24:14 (KJV)** And they talked together of all these things which had happened.

iii. **Luke 24:15 (KJV)** And it came to pass, that, while they communed *together* and reasoned, Jesus himself drew near, and went with them.

iv. **Luke 24:16 (KJV)** But their eyes were holden that they should not know him.

v. **Luke 24:17 (KJV)** And he said unto them, What manner of communications *are* these that ye have one to another, as ye walk, and are sad?

vi. **Luke 24:18 (KJV)** And the one of them, whose name was Cleopas, answering said unto him, Art thou only a stranger in Jerusalem, and hast not known the things which are come to pass there in these days?

vii. **Luke 24:19 (KJV)** And he said unto them, What things? And they said unto him, Concerning Jesus of Nazareth, which was a prophet mighty in deed and word before God and all the people:

viii. **Luke 24:20 (KJV)** And how the chief priests and our rulers delivered him to be condemned to death, and have crucified him.

ix. **Luke 24:21 (KJV)** But we trusted that it had been he which should have redeemed Israel: and beside all this, to day is the third day since these things were done.

x. **Luke 24:22 (KJV)** Yea, and certain women also of our company made us astonished, which were early at the sepulchre;

xi. **Luke 24:23 (KJV)** And when they found not his body, they came, saying, that they had also seen a vision of angels, which said that he was alive.

     xii. **Luke 24:24 (KJV)** And certain of them which were with us went to the sepulchre, and found *it* even so as the women had said: but him they saw not.

     xiii. **Luke 24:25 (KJV)** Then he said unto them, O fools, and slow of heart to believe all that the prophets have spoken:

     xiv. **Luke 24:26 (KJV)** Ought not Christ to have suffered these things, and to enter into his glory?

     xv. **Luke 24:27 (KJV)** And beginning at Moses and all the prophets, he expounded unto them in all the scriptures the things concerning himself.

8. Or, shall the profane and the physical be adequate to teach and to explain the holy and the spiritual without incurring the condemnation of fools?

     i. **John 3:1 (KJV)** There was a man of the Pharisees, named Nicodemus, a ruler of the Jews:

     ii. **John 3:2 (KJV)** The same came to Jesus by night, and said unto him, Rabbi, we know that thou art a teacher come from God: for no man can do these miracles that thou doest, except God be with him.

     iii. **John 3:3 (KJV)** Jesus answered and said unto him, Verily, verily, I say unto thee, Except a man be born again, he cannot see the kingdom of God.

     iv. **John 3:4 (KJV)** Nicodemus saith unto him, How can a man be born when he is old? can he enter the second time into his mother's womb, and be born?

     v. **John 3:5 (KJV)** Jesus answered, Verily, verily, I say unto thee, Except a man be born of water and *of* the Spirit, he cannot enter into the kingdom of God.

     vi. **John 3:6 (KJV)** That which is born of the flesh is flesh; and that which is born of the Spirit is spirit.

     vii. **John 3:7 (KJV)** Marvel not that I said unto thee, Ye must be born again.

     viii. **John 3:8 (KJV)** The wind bloweth where it listeth, and thou hearest the sound thereof, but canst not tell whence it cometh, and whither it goeth: so is every one that is born of the Spirit.

     ix. **John 3:9 (KJV)** Nicodemus answered and said unto him, How can these things be?

     x. **John 3:10 (KJV)** Jesus answered and said unto him, Art thou a master of Israel, and knowest not these things?

      xi.   **John 3:11 (KJV)** Verily, verily, I say unto thee, We speak that we do know, and testify that we have seen; and ye receive not our witness.

      xii.   **John 3:12 (KJV)** If I have told you earthly things, and ye believe not, how shall ye believe, if I tell you *of* heavenly things?

9.   When he that dwelt in the Darkness attempted to translate, interpret, explain, teach, examine, assess, evaluate, and offer a methodology/theory (Biblical Hermeneutics) to explain/teach (Biblical Exegesis) the words of He who dwells in The Bright Light, the result was a perpetual disaster of evil, wrath, condemnation, curses, and death!

      i.   **1 Timothy 6:14 (KJV)** That thou keep *this* commandment without spot, unrebukeable, until the appearing of our Lord Jesus Christ:

      ii.   **1 Timothy 6:15 (KJV)** Which in his times he shall shew, *who is* the blessed and only Potentate, the King of kings, and Lord of lords;

      iii.   **1 Timothy 6:16 (KJV)** Who only hath immortality, dwelling in the light which no man can approach unto; whom no man hath seen, nor can see: to whom *be* honour and power everlasting. Amen.

      iv.   **Romans 5:12 (KJV)** Wherefore, as by one man sin entered into the world, and death by sin; and so death passed upon all men, for that all have sinned:

      v.   **1 Corinthians 15:22 (KJV)** For as in Adam all die, even so in Christ shall all be made alive.

10.   Here is Professor Satan bringing his methodology/theory (Biblical Hermeneutics) to explain/teach (Biblical Exegesis) the words of He who dwells in The Bright Light!

      i.   **Genesis 3:1 (KJV)** Now the serpent was more subtil than any beast of the field which the LORD God had made. And he said unto the woman, Yea, hath God said, Ye shall not eat of every tree of the garden?

11.   Here is the ignorant and foolish Student of Professor Satan interacting with him in class when she had not prior read and assimilated her notes!

      i.   **Genesis 3:2 (KJV)** And the woman said unto the serpent, We may eat of the fruit of the trees of the garden:

      ii.   **Genesis 3:3 (KJV)** But of the fruit of the tree which *is* in the midst of the garden, God hath said, Ye shall not eat of it, neither shall ye touch it, lest ye die.

12.   Here is Professor Satan who immediately recognized that his Student was a lazy Student who had refused to read and assimilate her notes before coming to class, and so, he proceeded to impart unto her: false doctrines and an evil methodology/theory (Biblical Hermeneutics) on how best to understand the Word of God!

     i. **Genesis 3:4 (KJV)** And the serpent said unto the woman, Ye shall not surely die:

     ii. **Genesis 3:5 (KJV)** For God doth know that in the day ye eat thereof, then your eyes shall be opened, and ye shall be as gods, knowing good and evil.

13. Professor Satan's Student, Eve, has received the evil methodology/theory (Biblical Hermeneutics) on how best to understand the Word of God, and now, she is on her way to teach it and to implement it with her equally foolish and ignorant husband called Adam

     i. **Genesis 3:6 (KJV)** And when the woman saw that the tree *was* good for food, and that it *was* pleasant to the eyes, and a tree to be desired to make *one* wise, she took of the fruit thereof, and did eat, and gave also unto her husband with her; and he did eat.

14. Then, suddenly, they both died!

     i. **Genesis 3:7 (KJV)** And the eyes of them both were opened, and they knew that they *were* naked; and they sewed fig leaves together, and made themselves aprons.

     ii. **Genesis 2:16 (KJV)** And the LORD God commanded the man, saying, Of every tree of the garden thou mayest freely eat:

     iii. **Genesis 2:17 (KJV)** But of the tree of the knowledge of good and evil, thou shalt not eat of it: for in the day that thou eatest thereof thou shalt surely die.

     iv. **Hosea 13:1 (KJV)** When Ephraim spake trembling, he exalted himself in Israel; but when he offended in Baal, he died.

     v. **Romans 5:12 (KJV)** Wherefore, as by one man sin entered into the world, and death by sin; and so death passed upon all men, for that all have sinned:

15. What then shall we do, how shall we approach the Word of God, and with what methodology/theory (Biblical Hermeneutics) shall we approach and understand the Word of God?

16. Since every man and woman is corrupt and the Word of God is incorrupt, the only choice left is to use the methodology/theory (Biblical Hermeneutics) that the LORD God Himself has provided, and to learn from the ONLY Professor who is qualified to teach and to reveal the Word of God who is: The Holy Spirit!

17. Here is God's methodology to understand, to explain, and to teach the Word of God!

     i. **Proverbs 21:30 (KJV)** *There is* no wisdom nor understanding nor counsel against the LORD.

ii. **Isaiah 8:20 (KJV)** To the law and to the testimony: if they speak not according to this word, *it is* because *there is* no light in them.

iii. **1 Corinthians 2:6 (KJV)** Howbeit we speak wisdom among them that are perfect: yet not the wisdom of this world, nor of the princes of this world, that come to nought:

iv. **1 Corinthians 2:7 (KJV)** But we speak the wisdom of God in a mystery, *even* the hidden *wisdom*, which God ordained before the world unto our glory:

v. **1 Corinthians 2:8 (KJV)** Which none of the princes of this world knew: for had they known *it*, they would not have crucified the Lord of glory.

vi. **1 Corinthians 2:9 (KJV)** But as it is written, Eye hath not seen, nor ear heard, neither have entered into the heart of man, the things which God hath prepared for them that love him.

vii. **1 Corinthians 2:10 (KJV)** But God hath revealed *them* unto us by his Spirit: for the Spirit searcheth all things, yea, the deep things of God.

viii. **1 Corinthians 2:11 (KJV)** For what man knoweth the things of a man, save the spirit of man which is in him? even so the things of God knoweth no man, but the Spirit of God.

ix. **1 Corinthians 2:12 (KJV)** Now we have received, not the spirit of the world, but the spirit which is of God; that we might know the things that are freely given to us of God.

x. **1 Corinthians 2:13 (KJV)** Which things also we speak, not in the words which man's wisdom teacheth, but which the Holy Ghost teacheth; comparing spiritual things with spiritual.

18. The words: "comparing spiritual things with spiritual" means that you must compare each understanding of the Word of God that you get with all the remainder of the Scriptures from Genesis to Revelation, before you can claim to have understood anything!

19. The reason for the arduous, diligent, and painstaking comparison from Genesis to Revelation is that: There should be no confusion, violation, or contradiction between your understand and the rest of the Word of God, no, not even one contradiction, else, you do not have Truth but a false doctrine, if you fail to do the comparison!

20. Here is the LORD Yeshua the Christ teaching the same correct God's methodology that I have just shown you, and He is condemning their Bible Teaching, because it has a contradiction, and therefore, it is a lie and not acceptable!

i. **Matthew 22:41 (KJV)** While the Pharisees were gathered together, Jesus asked them,

    ii.   **Matthew 22:42 (KJV)** Saying, What think ye of Christ? whose son is he? They say unto him, *The Son* of David.

    iii.   **Matthew 22:43 (KJV)** He saith unto them, How then doth David in spirit call him Lord, saying,

    iv.   **Matthew 22:44 (KJV)** The LORD said unto my Lord, Sit thou on my right hand, till I make thine enemies thy footstool?

    v.   **Matthew 22:45 (KJV)** If David then call him Lord, how is he his son?

    vi.   **Matthew 22:46 (KJV)** And no man was able to answer him a word, neither durst any *man* from that day forth ask him any more *questions*.

21. Consequently, since a fool cannot teach a wise person wisdom, in other words, since humans cannot teach Holy Spirit the Word of God, then, the only correct methodology left for translating, interpreting, and teaching the Word of God is to teach the Word of God to agree with the Word of God! Any other methodology is false and a lie!

    i.   **1 Corinthians 2:6 (KJV)** Howbeit we speak wisdom among them that are perfect: yet not the wisdom of this world, nor of the princes of this world, that come to nought:

    ii.   **1 Corinthians 2:7 (KJV)** But we speak the wisdom of God in a mystery, *even* the hidden *wisdom*, which God ordained before the world unto our glory:

    iii.   **1 Corinthians 2:10 (KJV)** But God hath revealed *them* unto us by his Spirit: for the Spirit searcheth all things, yea, the deep things of God.

    iv.   **1 Corinthians 2:11 (KJV)** For what man knoweth the things of a man, save the spirit of man which is in him? even so the things of God knoweth no man, but the Spirit of God.

    v.   **1 Corinthians 2:12 (KJV)** Now we have received, not the spirit of the world, but the spirit which is of God; that we might know the things that are freely given to us of God.

    vi.   **1 Corinthians 2:13 (KJV)** Which things also we speak, not in the words which man's wisdom teacheth, but which the Holy Ghost teacheth; comparing spiritual things with spiritual.

22. The LORD Jesus Christ be with your spirit. The LORD Jesus Christ give you understanding.

Rev. Prof. PETER PRYCE,
DSEF, BA, MA, B.Soc.Sc Pol Sci, IBA, PhD
A Scribe of the Law of the God of Heaven

Prophet of the Word of God
Professor of French, Silver Spring, MD, USA
Scholar of the Institute of Theologians, USA
WWW.THEBIBLEUNIVERSITY.ORG
Accreditation Number: 07-QCTO/SDP120723172836
SAQA QUAL ID: Identification # 101997
WWW.BOOKSTORESITE.ORG
WWW.THEBIBLEUNIVERSITYCHURCH.ORG

Saturday 27th May 2023 @ 12:40 PM – 2:30 PM

GOD'S THEORY FOR BIBLE TRANSLATION AND INTERPRETATION

Question 2366

Answer:

1. God Almighty reveals a Theory for Bible Translation and Interpretation in **Jeremiah 10:14 (KJV)**!
2. Because every man is brutish, a fool, and ignorant of the knowledge of God, this is the reason why it is impossible, yea, beyond the capacity of man, to devise a methodology for Bible Translation and Interpretation!
3. That leaves us with only one choice!
4. When you exclude all humans, then, you are left with ONLY God Almighty!
5. Hence, only God has the correct methodology for Bible Translation and Interpretation!
6. It is NOT possible for the Superior God to give HIS Superior Word to an inferior man to figure out and to develop a methodology on how to Translate and Interpret that superior Word of God!
7. That is why you cannot find any correct methodology for Bible Translation and Interpretation outside of the Holy Bible!
8. The correct way, methodology, technique, approach, and theory to understand, translate, teach, explain, and interpret the Word of God, is in the Word of God and by the Word of God ONLY!
   i. **Jeremiah 10:14 (KJV)** Every man is brutish in *his* knowledge: every founder is confounded by the graven image: for his molten image *is* falsehood, and *there is* no breath in them.
   ii. **Job 32:8 (KJV)** But *there is* a spirit in man: and the inspiration of the Almighty giveth them understanding.
   iii. **John 14:26 (KJV)** But the Comforter, *which is* the Holy Ghost, whom the Father will send in my name, he shall teach you all things, and bring all things to your remembrance, whatsoever I have said unto you.
   iv. **John 15:26 (KJV)** But when the Comforter is come, whom I will send unto you from the Father, *even* the Spirit of truth, which proceedeth from the Father, he shall testify of me:
   v. **John 16:13 (KJV)** Howbeit when he, the Spirit of truth, is come, he will guide you into all truth: for he shall not speak of himself; but

whatsoever he shall hear, *that* shall he speak: and he will shew you things to come.

    vi. **Acts 2:4 (KJV)** And they were all filled with the Holy Ghost, and began to speak with other tongues, as the Spirit gave them utterance.

    vii. **2 Timothy 3:16 (KJV)** All scripture *is* given by inspiration of God, and *is* profitable for doctrine, for reproof, for correction, for instruction in righteousness:

    viii. **2 Timothy 3:17 (KJV)** That the man of God may be perfect, throughly furnished unto all good works.

9. Here is the theory in **Jeremiah 10:14 (KJV)**!

10. This declaration by God Almighty: "Every man is brutish in *his* knowledge" disqualifies every man from putting forth a theory to examine the Word of God since that theory will constitute "his knowledge"!

11. The LORD God Almighty is saying in **Jeremiah 10:14 (KJV** that, if you want to see the evidence of a man's foolishness, his brute capacity, his ignorance, his treachery, his stupid thoughts, his evil proclivity, then, examine his words/his knowledge!

    i. **Matthew 12:34 (KJV)** O generation of vipers, how can ye, being evil, speak good things? for out of the abundance of the heart the mouth speaketh.

    ii. **Luke 6:45 (KJV)** A good man out of the good treasure of his heart bringeth forth that which is good; and an evil man out of the evil treasure of his heart bringeth forth that which is evil: for of the abundance of the heart his mouth speaketh.

12. As you can see in **Jeremiah 10:14 (KJV**, there is no exception to the falsehood that is in man, because "Every man is brutish in *his* knowledge"!

    i. **Genesis 6:5 (KJV)** And GOD saw that the wickedness of man *was* great in the earth, and *that* every imagination of the thoughts of his heart *was* only evil continually.

    ii. **Jeremiah 17:9 (KJV)** The heart *is* deceitful above all *things*, and desperately wicked: who can know it?

13. Every theory or methodology devised by men for Bible Translation and Interpretation that does not come 100% from the Word of God, is a work of error!

    i. **Jeremiah 10:15 (KJV)** They *are* vanity, *and* the work of errors: in the time of their visitation they shall perish.

14. Furthermore, there are other injunctions in the Word of God that sets the Approach to Bible Translation! Here is one of them:

    i. **Proverbs 19:27 (KJV)** Cease, my son, to hear the instruction *that causeth* to err from the words of knowledge.

15. Now, here is the meaning of **Proverbs 19:27 (KJV)**!

16. The ONLY "words of knowledge" that we know is the Word of God the Holy Scriptures from Genesis to Revelation!

17. Now, God says in **Proverbs 19:27 (KJV)** that ANYTHING, ANY WORD, ANY INSTRUCTION, ANY THEORY, ANY METHODOLOGY, ANY APPROACH, ANY TEACHING, ANY PREACHING, ANY EXPLANATION, ANYTHING AND EVERYTHING that departs from, deviates from, separates from, decouples from, and diverges from "the words of knowledge", which is the Word of God the Holy Scriptures from Genesis to Revelation: "CEASE, MY SON, TO HEAR IT"!

18. That injunction means that:

    i. "The moment you as a Translator, Interpreter, Preacher, Pastor, Apostle, Bishop, or anyone, the moment you step outside the boundaries (Genesis to Revelation) of the Word of God, for any assistance, to bring that outside thing into the Word of God, you are in error"!

19. Here is a confirmation of the same injunction above, showing that anything and everything and everyone that is outside the realm of the Word of God: IS FOOLISHNESS AND IS A FOOL!

    i. **Proverbs 14:7 (KJV)** Go from the presence of a foolish man, when thou perceivest not *in him* the lips of knowledge.

20. Here is another confirmation of the same injunction above, this time from the LORD Jesus Christ, showing that "Garbage in, Garbage out", or, "when you leave aside the Word of God to go and take foolishness to examine the Word of God, you will surely get foolishness as your result"! Jesus also means that "If you are in the Word of God and you take heed to exclude everything that is outside the perimeter of the Word of God, then more revelation in the Word of God will be given to you"!

    i. **Mark 4:24 (KJV)** And he said unto them, Take heed what ye hear: with what measure ye mete, it shall be measured to you: and unto you that hear shall more be given.

21. Here is another confirmation of the same injunction above, this time from Apostle Paul, showing that the ONLY way you can successfully execute any Theory of Bible Translation is by excluding/separating that theory away from unbelievers, away from unrighteousness, away from darkness, away from Belial, away from infidels, and away from idols, since anything and everything that are outside the realm of the Word of God are certainly what I have just listed! Succinctly, therefore, your Theory for Bible Translation and Interpretation CANNOT come from outside the Word of God because anything and everything that are outside the Word of God are "unbelievers, unrighteousness, darkness, Belial, infidels, and idols"!

    i. **2 Corinthians 6:14 (KJV)** Be ye not unequally yoked together with unbelievers: for what fellowship hath righteousness with unrighteousness? and what communion hath light with darkness?

    ii. **2 Corinthians 6:15 (KJV)** And what concord hath Christ with Belial? or what part hath he that believeth with an infidel?

    iii. **2 Corinthians 6:16 (KJV)** And what agreement hath the temple of God with idols? for ye are the temple of the living God; as God hath said, I will dwell in them, and walk in *them*; and I will be their God, and they shall be my people.

    iv. **2 Corinthians 6:17 (KJV)** Wherefore come out from among them, and be ye separate, saith the Lord, and touch not the unclean *thing*; and I will receive you,

    v. **2 Corinthians 6:18 (KJV)** And will be a Father unto you, and ye shall be my sons and daughters, saith the Lord Almighty.

22. Here is another confirmation of the same injunction above, this time from King Solomon, showing that:

    i. "the moment your Bible Translation, Interpretation, Teaching, Explanation, Theory, Hermeneutics, Exegesis, Methodology, or Counsel goes against the LORD/Word of God, then, that is the same moment that you entered into error and falsehood"!

    ii. **Proverbs 21:30 (KJV)** *There is* no wisdom nor understanding nor counsel against the LORD.

23. Consequently, since anything that proceeds from the realm and imagination of all humans is "only evil continually, deceit above all things, and desperately wicked", therefore, the ONLY parameter within which you can find the true and correct theory for translating and interpreting the Word of God is the Word of God itself!

24. Having now understood the requirements of the theory, the next step now is to locate within the limits of the Holy Bible, from Genesis to Revelation, models of the translation and interpretation theory that the LORD God Almighty and the LORD Jesus Christ themselves have already successfully used and applied for our instruction!

The LORD Jesus Christ be with your spirit. The LORD Jesus Christ give you understanding.

Rev. Prof. Peter Pryce, Ph.D.
A Scribe of the Law of the God of Heaven
Prophet of the Word of God
Friday 3rd November 2023 @ 10:37 AM – 11:03 AM
While hearing and meditating on the Word of God in my bedroom

WWW.THEBIBLEUNIVERSITY.ORG
WWW.BOOKSTORESITE.ORG
WWW.THEBIBLEUNIVERSITYCHURCH.ORG

GOD'S METHODOLOGY FOR BIBLE TRANSLATION AND INTERPRETATION

Question 2388

1. In order to solve and answer spiritual controversies, the LORD God Almighty already gave us a 5-Step Approach and Methodology to handle Spiritual Controversies and Bible Questions!

    a. **STEP 1**: Identify the controversy, the Bible Question, or the misunderstanding!

    b. **Deuteronomy 17:8 (KJV)** If there arise a matter too hard for thee in judgment, between blood and blood, between plea and plea, and between stroke and stroke, *being* matters of controversy within thy gates: then shalt thou arise, and get thee up into the place which the LORD thy God shall choose;

    c. **STEP 2**: Go to the Priest, who is the God-appointed Judge of the Word of God, the Scribe of the Law of the God of Heaven, the Man of God, and bring the specific Bible Question to him, so that he can shew thee the sentence of judgment!

    d. **Deuteronomy 17:9 (KJV)** And thou shalt come unto the priests the Levites, and unto the judge that shall be in those days, and inquire; and they shall shew thee the sentence of judgment:

2. **STEP 3**: The contract for coming to the Man of God to shew thee the sentence of judgment of God is that, thou shalt observe to do according to all that they, the Men of God, inform thee!

    a. **Deuteronomy 17:10 (KJV)** And thou shalt do according to the sentence, which they of that place which the LORD shall choose shall shew thee; and thou shalt observe to do according to all that they inform thee:

    b. **STEP 4**: The Man of God shall teach and explain the controversy or Bible Question ONLY from within the Law of God and according to the sentence of the Law of God!

3. Once the Man of God has finished his work to teach you, to explain to you, and to show you the good understanding of the Bible Question or controversy, thou shalt not decline from the sentence which they shall shew thee, *to* the right hand, nor *to* the left! The moment you hear the Word of God from the mouth of a true Man of God, you are bound by that Word whether you like it or not!

a. **Deuteronomy 17:11 (KJV)** According to the sentence of the law which they shall teach thee, and according to the judgment which they shall tell thee, thou shalt do: thou shalt not decline from the sentence which they shall shew thee, *to* the right hand, nor *to* the left.

b. **STEP 5**: Now, here is the curse of death that comes with going to the Man of God to teach you the Word of God, especially if that man is a true Man of God living in Truth and Righteousness daily!

4. After you have heard the Word of God from the true Man of God, and you reject it, despise it, decline it, argue against it, cast it aside, despise the Man of God, lie to him, not take his advice, leave his teaching aside to carry on with your life…well, in that case, the LORD God Almighty says that only death is good for you then, because it is such a great evil for the Word of God to come to you and you refuse to obey it!

a. **Deuteronomy 17:12 (KJV)** And the man that will do presumptuously, and will not hearken unto the priest that standeth to minister there before the LORD thy God, or unto the judge, even that man shall die: and thou shalt put away the evil from Israel.

b. **Deuteronomy 17:13 (KJV)** And all the people shall hear, and fear, and do no more presumptuously.

5. We shall, therefore, use this **5-Step Approach and Methodology to handle Spiritual Controversies and Bible Questions** that I have just presented to you; to answer this question on Female Ordination in the Churches!

The LORD Jesus Christ be with your spirit. The LORD Jesus Christ give you understanding.

Rev. Prof. PETER PRYCE,
DSEF, BA, MA, B.Soc.Sc Pol Sci, IBA, PhD
A Scribe of the Law of the God of Heaven
Prophet of the Word of God
Professor of French, Silver Spring, MD, USA
Scholar of the Institute of Theologians, USA
WWW.THEBIBLEUNIVERSITY.ORG
Accreditation Number: 07-QCTO/SDP120723172836
SAQA QUAL ID: Identification # 101997
WWW.BOOKSTORESITE.ORG
WWW.THEBIBLEUNIVERSITYCHURCH.ORG

Tuesday 19th December 2023 @ 2:40 PM – 4:01 PM
While writing another Book.

THEORETICAL APPROACH TO BIBLE INTERPRETATION AND TRANSLATION

Question 2458

If you want to accomplish a successful Bible Interpretation and Translation, then follow this theoretical approach:

1. A correct translation of the Holy Bible begins with a correct understanding of the text (Hermeneutics) of the Holy Bible!
2. A correct understanding of the Holy Bible precedes a correct interpretation (Exegesis) of the text of the Holy Bible!
3. A correct interpretation of the Holy Bible requires achieving perfect harmony/coherence and zero conflict of thought and doctrine between your understanding of the Bible text in question and the entire remainder of the Holy Bible!
4. A correct translation of the Holy Bible is the final step and a rendering in writing of the above intellectual process!
5. The Holy Scriptures is The Book that prescribes its own Approach and Methodology of Interpretation and it is contained in the Book of 1 Corinthians chapter 1!
6. There is a restricted audience that is identified for the interpretation and translation of the Holy Scriptures!
    i. **1 Corinthians 1:1 (KJV)** Paul, called *to be* an apostle of Jesus Christ through the will of God, and Sosthenes *our* brother,
    ii. **1 Corinthians 1:2 (KJV)** Unto the church of God which is at Corinth, to them that are sanctified in Christ Jesus, called *to be* saints, with all that in every place call upon the name of Jesus Christ our Lord, both theirs and ours:
7. In other words, the Holy Scriptures is NOT for everyone, but ONLY for:
    i. Those who are called to its tenets and doctrines.
    ii. Those who are identified as the Church of Christ and profess themselves so to be.
    iii. Them that are sanctified/cleansed/washed in Christ Jesus.
    iv. To be sanctified/cleansed/washed means to be washed from all thoughts that are contrary to the mind of Christ and to take on in its place, or to be imbued, impregnated, inspired, filled with, permeated, infused, poured into, soaked, or endued with: the mind of Christ!

v. **Luke 24:49 (KJV)** And, behold, I send the promise of my Father upon you: but tarry ye in the city of Jerusalem, until ye be endued with power from on high.

vi. **Acts 1:5 (KJV)** For John truly baptized with water; but ye shall be baptized with the Holy Ghost not many days hence.

vii. **Acts 1:8 (KJV)** But ye shall receive power, after that the Holy Ghost is come upon you: and ye shall be witnesses unto me both in Jerusalem, and in all Judaea, and in Samaria, and unto the uttermost part of the earth.

viii. Them that in every place call upon the name of Jesus Christ as the LORD and Source of that knowledge that is derived from the Holy Scriptures!

8. Now, therefore, if you are NOT identified in the above portrait or profile of people who should access the text of the Holy Scriptures, then what are you doing with it?

i. **Psalm 50:16 (KJV)** But unto the wicked God saith, What hast thou to do to declare my statutes, or *that* thou shouldest take my covenant in thy mouth?

ii. **Psalm 50:17 (KJV)** Seeing thou hatest instruction, and castest my words behind thee.

9. The next cardinal step in the theoretical approach to Bible Interpretation and Translation is called: the reciprocal confirmation of the knowledge of Christ!

i. **1 Corinthians 1:5 (KJV)** That in every thing ye are enriched by him, in all utterance, and *in* all knowledge;

ii. **1 Corinthians 1:6 (KJV)** Even as the testimony of Christ was confirmed in you:

iii. **1 Corinthians 1:7 (KJV)** So that ye come behind in no gift; waiting for the coming of our Lord Jesus Christ:

iv. **1 Corinthians 1:8 (KJV)** Who shall also confirm you unto the end, *that ye may be* blameless in the day of our Lord Jesus Christ.

10. In other words, in **1 Corinthians 1:5-8 (KJV)**, we learn that the knowledge and understanding of the text of the Word of God that you have, must be reciprocated and confirmed in both what you understand, interpret, say, and write on the one hand, and then on the other hand, in what is written in the Holy Scriptures itself!

i. **Luke 20:9 (KJV)** Then began he to speak to the people this parable; A certain man planted a vineyard, and let it forth to husbandmen, and went into a far country for a long time.

ii. **Luke 20:10 (KJV)** And at the season he sent a servant to the husbandmen, that they should give him of the fruit of the vineyard: but the husbandmen beat him, and sent *him* away empty.

iii. **Luke 20:11 (KJV)** And again he sent another servant: and they beat him also, and entreated *him* shamefully, and sent *him* away empty.

iv. **Luke 20:12 (KJV)** And again he sent a third: and they wounded him also, and cast *him* out.

v. **Luke 20:13 (KJV)** Then said the lord of the vineyard, What shall I do? I will send my beloved son: it may be they will reverence *him* when they see him.

vi. **Luke 20:14 (KJV)** But when the husbandmen saw him, they reasoned among themselves, saying, This is the heir: come, let us kill him, that the inheritance may be ours.

vii. **Luke 20:15 (KJV)** So they cast him out of the vineyard, and killed *him*. What therefore shall the lord of the vineyard do unto them?

viii. **Luke 20:16 (KJV)** He shall come and destroy these husbandmen, and shall give the vineyard to others. And when they heard *it*, they said, God forbid.

ix. **Luke 20:17 (KJV)** And he beheld them, and said, What is this then that is written, The stone which the builders rejected, the same is become the head of the corner?

x. **Luke 20:18 (KJV)** Whosoever shall fall upon that stone shall be broken; but on whomsoever it shall fall, it will grind him to powder.

11. Quite simply, the singleness of thought must be evident in your Bible Interpretation as well as in the text of the Holy Bible itself, to the extent that discord, contrariness, and divergence of thought are outlawed!

12. In **Luke 20:9-15 (KJV)**, we see the LORD Jesus Christ engaged in a Bible Interpretation and Translation!

13. In **Luke 20:16 (KJV)**, the LORD Jesus Christ renders an interpretation that is in perfect harmony, in one accord, is consistent with the contents in **Luke 20:9-15 (KJV)**!

14. At the end of **Luke 20:16 (KJV)**, the other Bible Interpreters come to a different, divergent, inconsistent, contrary interpretation, rejecting the interpretation of the LORD Jesus Christ with their words: "God forbid"!

15. In **Luke 20:17 (KJV)**, the LORD Jesus Christ shows them the evidence of their error in Bible Interpretation by pointing out the actual text that refutes and contradicts their interpretation, thereby establishing that Perfect Harmony is the required standard in Bible Interpretation and Translation!

16. Finally, in **Luke 20:18 (KJV)**, the LORD Jesus Christ uses metaphoric language to illustrate that, either way, both from the perspective of the bad Bible Interpreter and the bad Bible interpretation itself, there will be brokenness and a shattering of harmony and coherence!

17. The next cardinal step in the theoretical approach to Bible Interpretation and Translation is called: Faithfulness in Interpretation and Translation!

    i. **1 Corinthians 1:9 (KJV)** God *is* faithful, by whom ye were called unto the fellowship of his Son Jesus Christ our Lord.

18. This is where you seek to replicate the faith attribute of the owner of the text, which translation requirement is also mentioned elsewhere in the Holy Bible!

    i. **2 Chronicles 19:9 (KJV)** And he charged them, saying, Thus shall ye do in the fear of the LORD, faithfully, and with a perfect heart.

    ii. **Jeremiah 23:28 (KJV)** The prophet that hath a dream, let him tell a dream; and he that hath my word, let him speak my word faithfully. What *is* the chaff to the wheat? saith the LORD.

19. It is a reiteration of the requirement for zero conflict of thought and doctrine between your understanding of the Bible text in question and the entire remainder of the Holy Bible!

20. The next cardinal step in the theoretical approach to Bible Interpretation and Translation is captured in:

    i. **1 Corinthians 1:10 (KJV)** Now I beseech you, brethren, by the name of our Lord Jesus Christ, that ye all speak the same thing, and *that* there be no divisions among you; but *that* ye be perfectly joined together in the same mind and in the same judgment.

21. Now, the correct interpretation of the command in **1 Corinthians 1:10 (KJV)** is this:

    i. Speak the same thing as the original Bible text is saying!

    ii. Ensure that there be no divisions at all between your translation and the Bible text!

    iii. An examination of your translation and the original Bible text must reveal your translation to be perfectly joined together in the same mind and in the same judgment as the original Bible text!

22. The reason to (1) speak and write the same thing, (2) that there be no divisions at all, and (3) that your translation be perfect in mind and in judgment, is that, as I wrote above, the Holy Scriptures is the only Book that prescribes its own Approach and Methodology of Interpretation and Translation whereby, there is nothing that you can understand, interpret, or write which is contrary to what is already contained in the Holy Bible itself that will stand! The Holy Bible itself, as a text, outlaws contrary opinion and interpretation!

      i. **Proverbs 21:30 (KJV)** *There is* no wisdom nor understanding nor counsel against the LORD.

23. Failure to heed to the command in **1 Corinthians 1:10 (KJV)** and in **Proverbs 21:30 (KJV)** draws the following condemnation!

      i. **Isaiah 8:20 (KJV)** To the law and to the testimony: if they speak not according to this word, *it is* because *there is* no light in them.

24. It is very important to understand that the Holy Bible does NOT lend itself to contentious interpretations neither in the persons of the many theorists of translation and interpretation nor in the doctrines, subjects, themes, and topics that they present!

25. The Holy Bible lends itself to only one interpretation and translation that come from within itself to create a perfect harmony, as I have shown above:

      i. **1 Corinthians 1:11 (KJV)** For it hath been declared unto me of you, my brethren, by them *which are of the house* of Chloe, that there are contentions among you.

      ii. **1 Corinthians 1:12 (KJV)** Now this I say, that every one of you saith, I am of Paul; and I of Apollos; and I of Cephas; and I of Christ.

      iii. **1 Corinthians 1:13 (KJV)** Is Christ divided? was Paul crucified for you? or were ye baptized in the name of Paul?

      iv. **1 Corinthians 1:14 (KJV)** I thank God that I baptized none of you, but Crispus and Gaius;

      v. **1 Corinthians 1:15 (KJV)** Lest any should say that I had baptized in mine own name.

      vi. **1 Corinthians 1:16 (KJV)** And I baptized also the household of Stephanas: besides, I know not whether I baptized any other.

26. Hence, it does not matter at all whether the Bible Scholar is called Paul, or Apollos; or Cephas, or Christ, and it also does not matter at all whether the doctrine, subject, theme, or topic is Crucifixion or Baptism or whatever!

27. What matters in Bible Interpretation and Translation is the exclusion of man's wisdom in the exposition of the Doctrine of Christ!

      i. **1 Corinthians 1:17 (KJV)** For Christ sent me not to baptize, but to preach the gospel: not with wisdom of words, lest the cross of Christ should be made of none effect.

      ii. **1 Corinthians 1:18 (KJV)** For the preaching of the cross is to them that perish foolishness; but unto us which are saved it is the power of God.

      iii. **1 Corinthians 1:19 (KJV)** For it is written, I will destroy the wisdom of the wise, and will bring to nothing the understanding of the prudent.

      iv. **1 Corinthians 1:20 (KJV)** Where *is* the wise? where *is* the scribe? where *is* the disputer of this world? hath not God made foolish the wisdom of this world?

28. Not only is the exclusion of man's wisdom in Bible Interpretation and Translation one of the cardinal requirements, but also the exclusion of man's theories, man's methodologies, man's approaches, and man's techniques in Bible Interpretation and Translation, because the Holy Bible has concluded all human wisdom as vile, corrupted, and as foolishness!

      i. **Isaiah 55:8 (KJV)** For my thoughts *are* not your thoughts, neither *are* your ways my ways, saith the LORD.

      ii. **Isaiah 55:9 (KJV)** For *as* the heavens are higher than the earth, so are my ways higher than your ways, and my thoughts than your thoughts.

      iii. **Micah 7:1 (KJV)** Woe is me! for I am as when they have gathered the summer fruits, as the grapegleanings of the vintage: *there is* no cluster to eat: my soul desired the firstripe fruit.

      iv. **Micah 7:2 (KJV)** The good *man* is perished out of the earth: and *there is* none upright among men: they all lie in wait for blood; they hunt every man his brother with a net.

      v. **Micah 7:3 (KJV)** That they may do evil with both hands earnestly, the prince asketh, and the judge *asketh* for a reward; and the great *man*, he uttereth his mischievous desire: so they wrap it up.

      vi. **Micah 7:4 (KJV)** The best of them *is* as a brier: the most upright *is sharper* than a thorn hedge: the day of thy watchmen *and* thy visitation cometh; now shall be their perplexity.

      vii. **1 Corinthians 2:14 (KJV)** But the natural man receiveth not the things of the Spirit of God: for they are foolishness unto him: neither can he know *them*, because they are spiritually discerned.

29. In other words, how can foolishness interpret and translate wisdom? Therefore, you must rely on the Holy Bible to interpret and translate itself! You CANNOT teach the Bible against the Bible! You MUST ALWAYS teach the Bible to agree with the Bible!

30. Your reliance on the Holy Bible to interpret and translate itself should bring you to believe the text/word and the self-interpretation and the self-translation that it says it is able to accomplish!

      i. **1 Corinthians 1:21 (KJV)** For after that in the wisdom of God the world by wisdom knew not God, it pleased God by the foolishness of preaching to save them that believe.

31. This act of believing in the text/word of the Holy Scriptures to self-interpret and to self-translate does NOT rise to the level of unverifiable faith/belief or impregnable

esoterism, but is the same act of using your pre-research data to believe in your scientific theory and research findings before you start the actual experiment!

    i. **1 Corinthians 1:22 (KJV)** For the Jews require a sign, and the Greeks seek after wisdom:

32. In fact, as you can see in **1 Corinthians 1:22 (KJV)**, this theoretical approach to Bible Interpretation excludes not only signs, miracles, and wonders as justification for believing in the efficacy of the theory, but also, this same theoretical approach excludes all human wisdom!

33. And so, yes, just as a scientific experiment would seem foolish in the beginning but later turn out to be viable, so also will a Bible Translation that uses this Bible-prescribed theoretical approach to Bible Interpretation seem foolish in the beginning, but as record has it, it has never been proved inadequate or wrong whereas all the theories of Bible Translation and Interpretation that men devised have all fallen short of complete reliability!

    i. **1 Corinthians 1:23 (KJV)** But we preach Christ crucified, unto the Jews a stumblingblock, and unto the Greeks foolishness;

34. What is certain is that all those who fall outside the above portrait or profile of people who should access the text of the Holy Scriptures, they will surely, like did the Jews in **1 Corinthians 1:23 (KJV)**, find this theoretical approach to Bible Interpretation a stumblingblock, and like did the Greeks, they will find it to be foolishness!

35. On the other hand, all those who are called or those who have received inspiration to understand the Word of God, shall attain unto much wisdom in the Gospel of Christ, NOT outside of it, because everything that is outside of the Gospel of Christ is foolishness!

    i. **1 Corinthians 1:24 (KJV)** But unto them which are called, both Jews and Greeks, Christ the power of God, and the wisdom of God.

    ii. **1 Corinthians 1:25 (KJV)** Because the foolishness of God is wiser than men; and the weakness of God is stronger than men.

36. They shall attain unto much wisdom in the Gospel of Christ and they shall also attain unto the Power of Christ that is in the text/word of the Holy Scriptures, which Power of Christ in the Text/Word of God is identifiable in its ability to transform the mind of the inquirer to the renewal of itself unto the reproduction of itself (Text/Word of God) by the thirties, by the sixties, and by the hundreds!

    i. **Matthew 13:3 (KJV)** And he spake many things unto them in parables, saying, Behold, a sower went forth to sow;

    ii. **Matthew 13:4 (KJV)** And when he sowed, some *seeds* fell by the way side, and the fowls came and devoured them up:

    iii. **Matthew 13:5 (KJV)** Some fell upon stony places, where they had not much earth: and forthwith they sprung up, because they had no deepness of earth:

    iv. **Matthew 13:6 (KJV)** And when the sun was up, they were scorched; and because they had no root, they withered away.

    v. **Matthew 13:7 (KJV)** And some fell among thorns; and the thorns sprung up, and choked them:

    vi. **Matthew 13:8 (KJV)** But other fell into good ground, and brought forth fruit, some an hundredfold, some sixtyfold, some thirtyfold.

    vii. **Matthew 13:9 (KJV)** Who hath ears to hear, let him hear.

37. In other words, a good Student of the Theoretical Approach to Bible Interpretation and Translation that I am showing you here, should, in the end, be able to replicate in his own words, the same Thoughts and Doctrines of Christ as contained in the Holy Bible, by the thirties, by the sixties, and by the hundreds:

    i. **Philippians 2:5 (KJV)** Let this mind be in you, which was also in Christ Jesus:

38. Again, the LORD God Almighty reiterates that the Theoretical Approach to Bible Interpretation and Translation requires the exclusion of all human wisdom in order to attain unto the wisdom which is in the Word of God!

    i. **1 Corinthians 1:26 (KJV)** For ye see your calling, brethren, how that not many wise men after the flesh, not many mighty, not many noble, *are called*:

39. Wherefore, even though the interpretation and translation of the Bible by the Bible may seem incongruous and foolish on the face of it, yet still must thou persist in its own foolishness, even though it is NOT foolishness but it seems and sounds foolish because of the very foolishness and corruption that are in all humans, therefore, do some see a mirror image of their own foolishness and corruption in the Holy Bible!

    i. **1 Corinthians 1:27 (KJV)** But God hath chosen the foolish things of the world to confound the wise; and God hath chosen the weak things of the world to confound the things which are mighty;

    ii. **1 Corinthians 1:28 (KJV)** And base things of the world, and things which are despised, hath God chosen, *yea*, and things which are not, to bring to nought things that are:

    iii. **1 Corinthians 1:29 (KJV)** That no flesh should glory in his presence.

40. But thou must persist in the Bible's own foolishness because the Holy Bible being a mirror of the human face and character that it is, the foolishness and the contradictions that you see in the Holy Bible are a reflection of your own foolishness and contradictions, and they do hide a multitude of wise counsel ONLY when you exclude

yourself, as **1 Corinthians 1:28-29 (KJV)** reveals, and allow the Word of God to speak, to translate itself, and to interpret itself!

    i. **Numbers 27:21 (KJV)** And he shall stand before Eleazar the priest, who shall ask *counsel* for him after the judgment of Urim before the LORD: at his word shall they go out, and at his word they shall come in, *both* he, and all the children of Israel with him, even all the congregation.

    ii. **Deuteronomy 32:28 (KJV)** For they *are* a nation void of counsel, neither *is there any* understanding in them.

    iii. **Judges 20:18 (KJV)** And the children of Israel arose, and went up to the house of God, and asked counsel of God, and said, Which of us shall go up first to the battle against the children of Benjamin? And the LORD said, Judah *shall go up* first.

    iv. **Psalm 33:11 (KJV)** The counsel of the LORD standeth for ever, the thoughts of his heart to all generations.

    v. **Proverbs 27:19 (KJV)** As in water face *answereth* to face, so the heart of man to man.

    vi. **Isaiah 58:13 (KJV)** If thou turn away thy foot from the sabbath, *from* doing thy pleasure on my holy day; and call the sabbath a delight, the holy of the LORD, honourable; and shalt honour him, not doing thine own ways, nor finding thine own pleasure, nor speaking *thine own* words:

    vii. **Ezekiel 3:4 (KJV)** And he said unto me, Son of man, go, get thee unto the house of Israel, and speak with my words unto them.

    viii. **Hebrews 4:12 (KJV)** For the word of God *is* quick, and powerful, and sharper than any twoedged sword, piercing even to the dividing asunder of soul and spirit, and of the joints and marrow, and *is* a discerner of the thoughts and intents of the heart.

41. In the end, the LORD God is showing you that the efficacy of your exercise of the Theoretical Approach to Bible Interpretation and Translation will be made evident in your true and faithful reflection of the meaning of the Word of God devoid of any form of contrariness when compared against the Word of God!

    i. **1 Corinthians 1:30 (KJV)** But of him are ye in Christ Jesus, who of God is made unto us wisdom, and righteousness, and sanctification, and redemption:

    ii. **1 Corinthians 1:31 (KJV)** That, according as it is written, He that glorieth, let him glory in the Lord.

42. In other words, by means of comparison, your interpretation and translation of the Word of God must be one with the Word of God!

The LORD Jesus Christ be with your spirit. The LORD Jesus Christ give you understanding.

Rev. Prof. PETER PRYCE,
DSEF, BA, MA, B.Soc.Sc Pol Sci, IBA, PhD
A Scribe of the Law of the God of Heaven
Prophet of the Word of God
Professor of French, Silver Spring, MD, USA
Scholar of the Institute of Theologians, USA
WWW.THEBIBLEUNIVERSITY.ORG
Accreditation Number: 07-QCTO/SDP120723172836
SAQA QUAL ID: Identification # 101997
WWW.BOOKSTORESITE.ORG
WWW.THEBIBLEUNIVERSITYCHURCH.ORG

Thursday 4th January 2024 @ 7:10 AM – 4:44 PM
While hearing and meditating on the Word of God.

APPROACHES TO BIBLE INTERPRETATION AND BIBLE TRANSLATION – 1

Question 2461

1. The Testimony of God, or, the Holy Scriptures, or, the Holy Bible, has only one theme, namely, Jesus Christ and Him crucified!

     i.   **1 Corinthians 2:1 (KJV)** And I, brethren, when I came to you, came not with excellency of speech or of wisdom, declaring unto you the testimony of God.

     ii. **1 Corinthians 2:2 (KJV)** For I determined not to know any thing among you, save Jesus Christ, and him crucified.

2. It means that all the Books and writings in the entire Holy Bible are about the LORD Jesus Christ!

     i.   **John 5:46 (KJV)** For had ye believed Moses, ye would have believed me: for he wrote of me.

     ii. **John 14:6 (KJV)** Jesus saith unto him, I am the way, the truth, and the life: no man cometh unto the Father, but by me.

     iii. **Acts 10:43 (KJV)** To him give all the prophets witness, that through his name whosoever believeth in him shall receive remission of sins.

3. Therefore, a successful Bible Interpretation or Translation is the one that also has as its theme: Jesus Christ and Him crucified.

4. It also means that a Bible Interpretation or Translation that deviates from the LORD Jesus Christ and the Doctrines of the LORD Jesus Christ, is incorrect and false, just the same way as you cannot argue against the Constitution of a Country and be successful, because normally, the correct and accepted norm is that Judges and Lawyers speak and write from the strength, from the point of view, from the spirit, and from the prescriptions of the Law whereby, a Judge or a Lawyer is NOT a Judge or a Lawyer anymore when he speaks and writes against and contrary to the Constitution of the Land, and the same is with the Holy Bible the Word of God and the Law Book of God!

5. The speech, the preaching, or the writings of a true Man of God must be presented in a way to enhance and demonstrate the Spirit and Power of God!

     i.   **1 Corinthians 2:4 (KJV)** And my speech and my preaching *was* not with enticing words of man's wisdom, but in demonstration of the Spirit and of power:

      ii. **1 Corinthians 2:5 (KJV)** That your faith should not stand in the wisdom of men, but in the power of God.

6. What do the Spirit and Power of God do?
7. Here is the answer:

      i. The Power of God produces Salvation in every person who believes the report and witness of the LORD Jesus Christ!

8. How does this production of Salvation happen? By what means?
9. By means of speaking, preaching, writing, and teaching the Gospel of Christ to people, to the effectual renewing of their mind toward God Almighty!

      i. **Romans 1:15 (KJV)** So, as much as in me is, I am ready to preach the gospel to you that are at Rome also.

      ii. **Romans 1:16 (KJV)** For I am not ashamed of the gospel of Christ: for it is the power of God unto salvation to every one that believeth; to the Jew first, and also to the Greek.

      iii. **Romans 1:17 (KJV)** For therein is the righteousness of God revealed from faith to faith: as it is written, The just shall live by faith.

10. The revelation in **Romans 1:15-17 (KJV)** is that, when a Man of God claims to have power from God in Ministry, then, you should be able to measure or identify the source of that power through the following two steps:

      i. ONE – Are the words of the Man of God 100% derived from the Gospel of Christ, from the Word of God, form the Holy Scriptures?

      ii. TWO – When that Man of God speaks, preaches, teaches, or writes his words, do people hear or read it and become convinced of its contents and believe the contents of the speech or writing such that they turn away from the thoughts that they previously held to now embrace the new thoughts of Christ that are contained in the speech or writings of the Man of God?

11. The moment that the above two steps are successfully accomplished through the speech or writings of a Man of God, then, that is the same moment that he has demonstrated the Power of God unto Salvation, because, Salvation is first measured in the mind before it appears in the deeds of the flesh!

      i. **Colossians 1:21 (KJV)** And you, that were sometime alienated and enemies in *your* mind by wicked works, yet now hath he reconciled

      ii. **Romans 12:2 (KJV)** And be not conformed to this world: but be ye transformed by the renewing of your mind, that ye may prove what *is* that good, and acceptable, and perfect, will of God.

iii. **Titus 3:5 (KJV)** Not by works of righteousness which we have done, but according to his mercy he saved us, by the washing of regeneration, and renewing of the Holy Ghost;

12. Since **Romans 1:16 (KJV)** tells us that the Gospel of Christ is the Power of God unto Salvation, your belief/faith should be anchored in this Power of God, meaning, in the Gospel of Christ!

   i. **Romans 1:16 (KJV)** For I am not ashamed of the gospel of Christ: for it is the power of God unto salvation to every one that believeth; to the Jew first, and also to the Greek.

   ii. **1 Corinthians 2:5 (KJV)** That your faith should not stand in the wisdom of men, but in the power of God.

13. This same Gospel of Christ, though it might sound foolish to some, yet it is the ultimate wisdom that can be accessed ONLY through the revelation and inspiration from the Holy Spirit of God!

   i. **1 Corinthians 2:6 (KJV)** Howbeit we speak wisdom among them that are perfect: yet not the wisdom of this world, nor of the princes of this world, that come to nought:

14. What are revelation and inspiration?

15. Revelation and inspiration are simply different shades of thought that come to your mind as a result of reading the text of the Gospel of Christ!

16. It is the same as what Academics, Judges, and Lawyers call "the spirit of the text", meaning that there is an unseen thought, imagery, picture, understanding, poetry that accompanies a text while still remaining invisible and untouchable!

17. When this unseen thought, imagery, picture, understanding, poetry accompanies an ordinary text, it is called "the spirit of the text"!

18. When this same unseen thought, imagery, picture, understanding, poetry accompanies the text of the Holy Scriptures, it is called "the Holy Spirit"!

   i. **Job 32:8 (KJV)** But *there is* a spirit in man: and the inspiration of the Almighty giveth them understanding.

   ii. **2 Timothy 3:16 (KJV)** All scripture *is* given by inspiration of God, and *is* profitable for doctrine, for reproof, for correction, for instruction in righteousness:

19. Therefore, according to **1 Corinthians 2:6 (KJV)**, when a man operates according to, or under "the spirit of the text", meaning that his life is predicated on all sorts of texts that are outside the realm of the Gospel of Christ such as all academic and intellectual and scientific texts and pursuits of study, then, such a man has wisdom but his wisdom is worldly wisdom and is vain wisdom!

    i. **1 Corinthians 2:6 (KJV)** Howbeit we speak wisdom among them that are perfect: yet not the wisdom of this world, nor of the princes of this world, that come to nought:

20. Such a worldly wisdom vain man is NOT yet one with the Holy Bible and its only one theme of Jesus Christ and Him crucified as **1 Corinthians 2:2 (KJV)** reveals!

    i. **1 Corinthians 2:1 (KJV)** And I, brethren, when I came to you, came not with excellency of speech or of wisdom, declaring unto you the testimony of God.

    ii. **1 Corinthians 2:2 (KJV)** For I determined not to know any thing among you, save Jesus Christ, and him crucified.

21. On the other hand, when the man is completely one with the Holy Bible and its singular theme of Jesus Christ and Him crucified as **1 Corinthians 2:2 (KJV)** reveals, then, his spirit and the Spirit of the Word of God have become one Spirit!

    i. **Philippians 1:27 (KJV)** Only let your conversation be as it becometh the gospel of Christ: that whether I come and see you, or else be absent, I may hear of your affairs, that ye stand fast in one spirit, with one mind striving together for the faith of the gospel;

    ii. **1 Corinthians 6:17 (KJV)** But he that is joined unto the Lord is one spirit.

22. On the other hand, according to the same **1 Corinthians 2:6 (KJV)**, when a man operates according to, or under "the Holy Spirit", meaning that his life is mainly predicated on the text of the Holy Scriptures and he believes in and lives by its contents, then, such a man has perfect wisdom, has the ultimate wisdom, and has wisdom that becomes his Key of entry into another realm of spirit existence called Heaven!

23. Now, this wisdom that has the ability to transform my thinking here on Earth as well as guarantee my entry into the next Realm of Heaven, how accessible is this wisdom?

    i. **1 Corinthians 2:7 (KJV)** But we speak the wisdom of God in a mystery, *even* the hidden *wisdom*, which God ordained before the world unto our glory:

24. The wisdom of God is either accessible or hidden "to every man according to his several ability"!

    i. **Matthew 25:15 (KJV)** And unto one he gave five talents, to another two, and to another one; to every man according to his several ability; and straightway took his journey.

    ii. **Romans 14:5 (KJV)** One man esteemeth one day above another: another esteemeth every day *alike*. Let every man be fully persuaded in his own mind.

25. The wisdom of God does NOT become more accessible because of one's social standing, money, rank, education, or intellectual ability!

    i. **1 Corinthians 2:8 (KJV)** Which none of the princes of this world knew: for had they known *it*, they would not have crucified the Lord of glory.

    ii. **1 Corinthians 2:10 (KJV)** But God hath revealed *them* unto us by his Spirit: for the Spirit searcheth all things, yea, the deep things of God.

26. Concerning **1 Corinthians 2:10 (KJV)**, the meaning is that, just as the understanding of literature or legal text is hard to some yet easy to others who are endowed with certain inexplicable abilities, so also is the understanding of the Word of God easy to those who are filled with the Word of God the Gospel of Christ!

    i. **Deuteronomy 17:14 (KJV)** When thou art come unto the land which the LORD thy God giveth thee, and shalt possess it, and shalt dwell therein, and shalt say, I will set a king over me, like as all the nations that *are* about me;

    ii. **Deuteronomy 17:15 (KJV)** Thou shalt in any wise set *him* king over thee, whom the LORD thy God shall choose: *one* from among thy brethren shalt thou set king over thee: thou mayest not set a stranger over thee, which *is* not thy brother.

    iii. **Deuteronomy 17:18 (KJV)** And it shall be, when he sitteth upon the throne of his kingdom, that he shall write him a copy of this law in a book out of *that which is* before the priests the Levites:

    iv. **Deuteronomy 17:19 (KJV)** And it shall be with him, and he shall read therein all the days of his life: that he may learn to fear the LORD his God, to keep all the words of this law and these statutes, to do them:

    v. **Deuteronomy 17:20 (KJV)** That his heart be not lifted up above his brethren, and that he turn not aside from the commandment, *to* the right hand, or *to* the left: to the end that he may prolong *his* days in his kingdom, he, and his children, in the midst of Israel.

    vi. **Joshua 1:8 (KJV)** This book of the law shall not depart out of thy mouth; but thou shalt meditate therein day and night, that thou mayest observe to do according to all that is written therein: for then thou shalt make thy way prosperous, and then thou shalt have good success.

    vii. **Proverbs 14:6 (KJV)** A scorner seeketh wisdom, and *findeth it* not: but knowledge *is* easy unto him that understandeth.

    viii. **Colossians 1:9 (KJV)** For this cause we also, since the day we heard *it*, do not cease to pray for you, and to desire that ye might be filled with the knowledge of his will in all wisdom and spiritual understanding;

27. Just as it requires interrogating a man in order to know the unseen intent and the thoughts of his deed, so also does it require interrogating the Word of God in the Word of God so that the unseen Spirit in the Text of the Word can yield inspiration and understanding of the Word unto you!

    i. **1 Corinthians 2:11 (KJV)** For what man knoweth the things of a man, save the spirit of man which is in him? even so the things of God knoweth no man, but the Spirit of God.

    ii. **Job 32:8 (KJV)** But *there is* a spirit in man: and the inspiration of the Almighty giveth them understanding.

    iii. **2 Timothy 3:16 (KJV)** All scripture *is* given by inspiration of God, and *is* profitable for doctrine, for reproof, for correction, for instruction in righteousness:

28. That is why it is impossible to access the Word of God from outside the Word of God, just as it is impossible to access the true meanings of the Constitution of a country from outside a prior legal training in its jurisprudence!

29. Therefore, the Spirit of God mentioned in **1 Corinthians 2:11 (KJV)**: that is the catalyst and the means to access and understand the Word of God the Holy Scriptures, and it is the equivalent of the legal training that you need in order to correctly access and understand the contents of a legal text!

    i. **1 Corinthians 2:12 (KJV)** Now we have received, not the spirit of the world, but the spirit which is of God; that we might know the things that are freely given to us of God.

30. Now, the means or the methodology through which to access and understand the Word of God the Holy Scriptures, by the teaching or inspiration of the Holy Spirit, is called: Comparing Spiritual Things with Spiritual!

    i. **1 Corinthians 2:13 (KJV)** Which things also we speak, not in the words which man's wisdom teacheth, but which the Holy Ghost teacheth; comparing spiritual things with spiritual.

31. Just as "the spirit of the text", as they say, is not seen but works in the mind as you read, to the effectual understanding of a literature text or a legal text, so also the Spirit of God is not seen but works in the mind to the effectual understanding of the Word of God as you read it, and when the understanding thereof is hidden, then, it is hidden, NOT because of some esoteric unverifiable non-faith clairvoyance or the lack thereof, because of the inherent incapacity and mental inadequacy of the person himself who lacks the intellectual capacity to grasp deep and difficult concepts!

      i. **1 Corinthians 2:14 (KJV)** But the natural man receiveth not the things of the Spirit of God: for they are foolishness unto him: neither can he know *them*, because they are spiritually discerned.

     ii. **2 Corinthians 4:3 (KJV)** But if our gospel be hid, it is hid to them that are lost:

32. What does it mean: Comparing Spiritual Things with Spiritual?

33. Based on **1 Corinthians 2:11-13 (KJV)**, we understand that "comparing spiritual things with spiritual" is the methodology to access and to understand the deep thoughts, the concepts, and the doctrines that are hidden in the Word of God!

34. In order to correctly understand the phrase "comparing spiritual things with spiritual", we first need to understand what "spiritual" is!

35. What does "spiritual" mean?

36. Here is the answer!

      i. **John 1:1 (KJV)** In the beginning was the Word, and the Word was with God, and the Word was God.

     ii. **John 1:2 (KJV)** The same was in the beginning with God.

    iii. **John 1:14 (KJV)** And the Word was made flesh, and dwelt among us, (and we beheld his glory, the glory as of the only begotten of the Father,) full of grace and truth.

    iv. **Romans 7:14 (KJV)** For we know that the law is spiritual: but I am carnal, sold under sin.

     v. **1 Corinthians 6:17 (KJV)** But he that is joined unto the Lord is one spirit.

    vi. **2 Corinthians 3:17 (KJV)** Now the Lord is that Spirit: and where the Spirit of the Lord *is*, there *is* liberty.

37. As you can see from the above body of evidence, we do not need to travel outside the Holy Scriptures the Word of God into some unknown esoteric great beyond, in order to pluck off the meaning of the word "spiritual"!

38. As you can see, you need a prior rich understanding of figures of speech in order to correctly understand the personification, the metaphor, the irony, the hyperbole, the paradox, the poetry, the geography, and every sort of human intellectual sphere that is contained in the Holy Scriptures the Word of God!

39. Hence, the Word of God the Holy Scriptures, is God!

40. Then, the same Word of God the Holy Scriptures is a Man with flesh called Yeshua Christ!

41. Then, the same Word of God the Holy Scriptures, is "spiritual"!

42. Then, the same Word of God the Holy Scriptures turns a person into a spirit once that person fully believes the same Word of God the Holy Scriptures!

43. Then, the same Word of God the Holy Scriptures is the Holy Spirit who gives you that inspiration and understanding to understand the same Word of God the Holy Scriptures!

     i. **Haggai 2:5 (KJV)** *According to* the word that I covenanted with you when ye came out of Egypt, so my spirit remaineth among you: fear ye not.

44. Now that we have understood the word "spiritual", we shall return to the question that says: What does it mean: Comparing Spiritual Things with Spiritual?

45. From our prior understanding of "the spiritual", it becomes easy to define the phrase: "Comparing Spiritual Things with Spiritual", and it means: "comparing the Word of God the Holy Scriptures with the Word of God the Holy Scriptures"!

     i. **1 Corinthians 2:13 (KJV)** Which things also we speak, not in the words which man's wisdom teacheth, but which the Holy Ghost teacheth; comparing spiritual things with spiritual.

46. Therefore, as a good Bible Interpreter and Translator, your success in rendering a good and correct Bible Interpretation and Translation lies in your ability to successfully compare your understanding and interpretation of the text of the Holy Bible to each and every verse in the entire Holy Bible, with the express aim of eliminating all contradiction to attain zero contradiction, zero variableness, and with the express aim of achieving "Perfect Harmony" between your translation and the entire remainder of the Holy Bible!

47. Can a Bible Interpreter or Translator set aside these approaches and still attain a good Bible Translation? NO!

     i. **1 Corinthians 2:14 (KJV)** But the natural man receiveth not the things of the Spirit of God: for they are foolishness unto him: neither can he know *them*, because they are spiritually discerned.

48. Your ability to come to the correct understanding of the Word of God the Holy Scriptures derives 100% from your 100% immersion into the Word of God the Holy Scriptures!

     i. **1 Corinthians 2:15 (KJV)** But he that is spiritual judgeth all things, yet he himself is judged of no man.

     ii. **1 Corinthians 2:16 (KJV)** For who hath known the mind of the Lord, that he may instruct him? But we have the mind of Christ.

The LORD Jesus Christ be with your spirit. The LORD Jesus Christ give you understanding.

Rev. Prof. PETER PRYCE,
DSEF, BA, MA, B.Soc.Sc Pol Sci, IBA, PhD

A Scribe of the Law of the God of Heaven
Prophet of the Word of God
Professor of French, Silver Spring, MD, USA
Scholar of the Institute of Theologians, USA
WWW.THEBIBLEUNIVERSITY.ORG
Accreditation Number: 07-QCTO/SDP120723172836
SAQA QUAL ID: Identification # 101997
WWW.BOOKSTORESITE.ORG
WWW.THEBIBLEUNIVERSITYCHURCH.ORG

Saturday 6th January 2024 @ 7:02 AM – 3:33 PM
While hearing and meditating on the Word of God.

APPROACHES TO BIBLE INTERPRETATION AND BIBLE TRANSLATION – 2

Question 2462

1. In Approaches to Bible Interpretation and Bible Translation – 1, I identified two men or two Translators:

2. The Worldly Wisdom Vain Man who is NOT yet one with the Holy Bible and its only one theme of Jesus Christ and Him crucified as required in **1 Corinthians 2:2 (KJV)**!

    i. **1 Corinthians 2:1 (KJV)** And I, brethren, when I came to you, came not with excellency of speech or of wisdom, declaring unto you the testimony of God.

    ii. **1 Corinthians 2:2 (KJV)** For I determined not to know any thing among you, save Jesus Christ, and him crucified.

3. Then, you have The Spiritual Man who has become completely one with the Holy Bible and its singular theme of Jesus Christ and Him crucified as **1 Corinthians 2:2 (KJV)** reveals, and, because of that oneness, his spirit and the Spirit of the Word of God have become one Spirit!

    i. **Philippians 1:27 (KJV)** Only let your conversation be as it becometh the gospel of Christ: that whether I come and see you, or else be absent, I may hear of your affairs, that ye stand fast in one spirit, with one mind striving together for the faith of the gospel;

    ii. **1 Corinthians 6:17 (KJV)** But he that is joined unto the Lord is one spirit.

4. Now, in this chapter, we are going to find out how to identify The Worldly Wisdom Vain Man whose other names are The Carnal Man and The Babe in Christ!

    i. **1 Corinthians 3:1 (KJV)** And I, brethren, could not speak unto you as unto spiritual, but as unto carnal, *even* as unto babes in Christ.

5. The Worldly Wisdom Vain Man, The Carnal Man, or, The Babe in Christ can be identified by reason of the milk that he drinks!

    i. **1 Corinthians 3:2 (KJV)** I have fed you with milk, and not with meat: for hitherto ye were not able *to bear it*, neither yet now are ye able.

6. To be a Babe in Christ who drinks milk is to be unable or to lack the mental and intellectual and spiritual capacity to grasp deep difficult spiritual concepts in the Holy Bible the Word of God!

    i. **John 16:12 (KJV)** I have yet many things to say unto you, but ye cannot bear them now.

ii. **John 16:13 (KJV)** Howbeit when he, the Spirit of truth, is come, he will guide you into all truth: for he shall not speak of himself; but whatsoever he shall hear, *that* shall he speak: and he will shew you things to come.

iii. **John 16:14 (KJV)** He shall glorify me: for he shall receive of mine, and shall shew *it* unto you.

iv. **2 Peter 3:14 (KJV)** Wherefore, beloved, seeing that ye look for such things, be diligent that ye may be found of him in peace, without spot, and blameless.

v. **2 Peter 3:15 (KJV)** And account *that* the longsuffering of our Lord *is* salvation; even as our beloved brother Paul also according to the wisdom given unto him hath written unto you;

vi. **2 Peter 3:16 (KJV)** As also in all *his* epistles, speaking in them of these things; in which are some things hard to be understood, which they that are unlearned and unstable wrest, as *they do* also the other scriptures, unto their own destruction.

7. Another way to identify The Worldly Wisdom Vain Man, The Carnal Man, or, The Babe in Christ is his penchant, because of his weakness in Christ Doctrine, and because he is destitute of the Truth of the Gospel of Christ, to go outside of the Holy Bible into the world to use theories, lessons, examples, thoughts, ideas, jokes, references, books, personalities, personal testimonies, and non-Biblical stories, to preach and to teach a sermon! That is wrong and promptly reveals the speaker as The Carnal Man!

i. **Proverbs 26:18 (KJV)** As a mad *man* who casteth firebrands, arrows, and death,

ii. **Proverbs 26:19 (KJV)** So *is* the man *that* deceiveth his neighbour, and saith, Am not I in sport?

iii. **Ephesians 5:4 (KJV)** Neither filthiness, nor foolish talking, nor jesting, which are not convenient: but rather giving of thanks.

iv. **1 Timothy 1:1 (KJV)** Paul, an apostle of Jesus Christ by the commandment of God our Saviour, and Lord Jesus Christ, *which is* our hope;

v. **1 Timothy 1:2 (KJV)** Unto Timothy, *my* own son in the faith: Grace, mercy, *and* peace, from God our Father and Jesus Christ our Lord.

vi. **1 Timothy 1:3 (KJV)** As I besought thee to abide still at Ephesus, when I went into Macedonia, that thou mightest charge some that they teach no other doctrine,

vii. **1 Timothy 1:4 (KJV)** Neither give heed to fables and endless genealogies, which minister questions, rather than godly edifying which is in faith: *so do.*

viii. **1 Timothy 4:6 (KJV)** If thou put the brethren in remembrance of these things, thou shalt be a good minister of Jesus Christ, nourished up in the words of faith and of good doctrine, whereunto thou hast attained.

ix. **1 Timothy 4:7 (KJV)** But refuse profane and old wives' fables, and exercise thyself *rather* unto godliness.

x. **2 Timothy 4:1 (KJV)** I charge *thee* therefore before God, and the Lord Jesus Christ, who shall judge the quick and the dead at his appearing and his kingdom;

xi. **2 Timothy 4:2 (KJV)** Preach the word; be instant in season, out of season; reprove, rebuke, exhort with all longsuffering and doctrine.

xii. **2 Timothy 4:3 (KJV)** For the time will come when they will not endure sound doctrine; but after their own lusts shall they heap to themselves teachers, having itching ears;

xiii. **2 Timothy 4:4 (KJV)** And they shall turn away *their* ears from the truth, and shall be turned unto fables.

xiv. **Titus 1:14 (KJV)** Not giving heed to Jewish fables, and commandments of men, that turn from the truth.

xv. **Titus 1:15 (KJV)** Unto the pure all things *are* pure: but unto them that are defiled and unbelieving *is* nothing pure; but even their mind and conscience is defiled.

xvi. **Titus 1:16 (KJV)** They profess that they know God; but in works they deny *him*, being abominable, and disobedient, and unto every good work reprobate.

xvii. **2 Peter 1:16 (KJV)** For we have not followed cunningly devised fables, when we made known unto you the power and coming of our Lord Jesus Christ, but were eyewitnesses of his majesty.

8. Another way to identify The Worldly Wisdom Vain Man, The Carnal Man, or, The Babe in Christ is the division, the deviation, the contradiction, the discord, the contrariness, the divergence, or the disharmony that his Bible Interpretation and Bible Translation reveal when compared to and examined in the entire Holy Bible!

i. **1 Corinthians 3:3 (KJV)** For ye are yet carnal: for whereas *there is* among you envying, and strife, and divisions, are ye not carnal, and walk as men?

9. In other words, his Bible Interpretation and Bible Translation do NOT reflect oneness or one accord with the entire Holy Bible hence that Bible Interpretation or Bible Translation has to be rejected! Here is the LORD Jesus Christ rejecting a Bible Interpretation that goes against another verse in the Holy Bible in another part of the Bible!

   i. **Luke 20:9 (KJV)** Then began he to speak to the people this parable; A certain man planted a vineyard, and let it forth to husbandmen, and went into a far country for a long time.

   ii. **Luke 20:10 (KJV)** And at the season he sent a servant to the husbandmen, that they should give him of the fruit of the vineyard: but the husbandmen beat him, and sent *him* away empty.

   iii. **Luke 20:11 (KJV)** And again he sent another servant: and they beat him also, and entreated *him* shamefully, and sent *him* away empty.

   iv. **Luke 20:12 (KJV)** And again he sent a third: and they wounded him also, and cast *him* out.

   v. **Luke 20:13 (KJV)** Then said the lord of the vineyard, What shall I do? I will send my beloved son: it may be they will reverence *him* when they see him.

   vi. **Luke 20:14 (KJV)** But when the husbandmen saw him, they reasoned among themselves, saying, This is the heir: come, let us kill him, that the inheritance may be ours.

   vii. **Luke 20:15 (KJV)** So they cast him out of the vineyard, and killed *him*. What therefore shall the lord of the vineyard do unto them?

   viii. **Luke 20:16 (KJV)** He shall come and destroy these husbandmen, and shall give the vineyard to others. And when they heard *it*, they said, God forbid.

   ix. **Luke 20:17 (KJV)** And he beheld them, and said, What is this then that is written, The stone which the builders rejected, the same is become the head of the corner?

10. Here, again, is the LORD Jesus Christ rejecting a Bible Interpretation that goes against another verse in the Holy Bible in another part of the Bible!

    i. **Matthew 22:41 (KJV)** While the Pharisees were gathered together, Jesus asked them,

    ii. **Matthew 22:42 (KJV)** Saying, What think ye of Christ? whose son is he? They say unto him, *The Son* of David.

    iii. **Matthew 22:43 (KJV)** He saith unto them, How then doth David in spirit call him Lord, saying,

    iv. **Matthew 22:44 (KJV)** The LORD said unto my Lord, Sit thou on my right hand, till I make thine enemies thy footstool?

    v. **Matthew 22:45 (KJV)** If David then call him Lord, how is he his son?

    vi. **Matthew 22:46 (KJV)** And no man was able to answer him a word, neither durst any *man* from that day forth ask him any more *questions*.

11. Another way to identify The Worldly Wisdom Vain Man, The Carnal Man, or, The Babe in Christ is that he uses men's theories to do his Bible Interpretation, Translation, and Sermon Preparation instead of using God's Theory for Bible Interpretation and Translation, as I have already identified in my writings!

    i. **1 Corinthians 3:4 (KJV)** For while one saith, I am of Paul; and another, I *am* of Apollos; are ye not carnal?

    ii. **1 Corinthians 3:5 (KJV)** Who then is Paul, and who *is* Apollos, but ministers by whom ye believed, even as the Lord gave to every man?

    iii. **1 Corinthians 3:6 (KJV)** I have planted, Apollos watered; but God gave the increase.

    iv. **1 Corinthians 3:7 (KJV)** So then neither is he that planteth any thing, neither he that watereth; but God that giveth the increase.

12. For the very reason that there is no wisdom of man that is qualified to examine the wisdom of God since all of man's wisdom is classified as foolishness, therefore being foolishness, it cannot be used to examine wisdom!

    i. **1 Corinthians 1:20 (KJV)** Where *is* the wise? where *is* the scribe? where *is* the disputer of this world? hath not God made foolish the wisdom of this world?

    ii. **1 Corinthians 2:6 (KJV)** Howbeit we speak wisdom among them that are perfect: yet not the wisdom of this world, nor of the princes of this world, that come to nought:

    iii. **1 Corinthians 3:19 (KJV)** For the wisdom of this world is foolishness with God. For it is written, He taketh the wise in their own craftiness.

13. So, then, Bible Interpretation and Bible Translation have to be Bible-centered and God-centered in order to correctly accomplish the task of transmitting the correct information, message, and meaning, for it is impossible for the Created to examine the Creator!

    i. **1 Corinthians 3:9 (KJV)** For we are labourers together with God: ye are God's husbandry, *ye are* God's building.

    ii. **1 Corinthians 3:10 (KJV)** According to the grace of God which is given unto me, as a wise masterbuilder, I have laid the foundation, and another buildeth thereon. But let every man take heed how he buildeth thereupon.

14. Now, even though the theory is one for all Bible Interpreters and Translators as **1 Corinthians 3:11 (KJV)** reveals, the final work will be different for all Bible Interpreters and Translators by reason of each other's training, several ability, and mental capacity!

    i. **1 Corinthians 3:8 (KJV)** Now he that planteth and he that watereth are one: and every man shall receive his own reward according to his own labour.

    ii. **1 Corinthians 3:11 (KJV)** For other foundation can no man lay than that is laid, which is Jesus Christ.

    iii. **Matthew 25:15 (KJV)** And unto one he gave five talents, to another two, and to another one; to every man according to his several ability; and straightway took his journey.

15. Another way to identify The Worldly Wisdom Vain Man, The Carnal Man, or, The Babe in Christ is through the testing of his Bible Interpretation, Bible Translation, and Sermon Preparation in the Holy Scriptures to see whether there is 100% harmony!

    i. **1 Corinthians 3:12 (KJV)** Now if any man build upon this foundation gold, silver, precious stones, wood, hay, stubble;

    ii. **1 Corinthians 3:13 (KJV)** Every man's work shall be made manifest: for the day shall declare it, because it shall be revealed by fire; and the fire shall try every man's work of what sort it is.

    iii. **1 Corinthians 3:14 (KJV)** If any man's work abide which he hath built thereupon, he shall receive a reward.

    iv. **1 Corinthians 3:15 (KJV)** If any man's work shall be burned, he shall suffer loss: but he himself shall be saved; yet so as by fire.

16. The testing of Bible Interpretation, Bible Translation, and Sermon Preparation in the Holy Scriptures is what is rendered in metaphorical language in **1 Corinthians 3:12-15 (KJV)** as: "it shall be revealed by fire; and the fire shall try every man's work of what sort it is", because of the very reason that the Word of God the Holy Scriptures itself is Fire, again, a metaphor!

    i. **Deuteronomy 4:24 (KJV)** For the LORD thy God *is* a consuming fire, *even* a jealous God.

    ii. **Deuteronomy 9:3 (KJV)** Understand therefore this day, that the LORD thy God *is* he which goeth over before thee; *as* a consuming fire he shall destroy them, and he shall bring them down before thy face: so shalt thou drive them out, and destroy them quickly, as the LORD hath said unto thee.

    iii. **John 1:1 (KJV)** In the beginning was the Word, and the Word was with God, and the Word was God.

     iv. **Hebrews 12:29 (KJV)** For our God *is* a consuming fire.

17. A Bible Interpreter and a Bible Translator who has become one with the Spirit of the Text of the Word of God, as I have already explained heretofore, is also called: The Temple of God!

     i. **1 Corinthians 3:16 (KJV)** Know ye not that ye are the temple of God, and *that* the Spirit of God dwelleth in you?

18. To become a Temple of God and fall back from the requirements of remaining a Temple of God through the total adherence to the Word of God the Holy Scriptures, is to make a shipwreck of your life!

     i. **1 Corinthians 3:17 (KJV)** If any man defile the temple of God, him shall God destroy; for the temple of God is holy, which *temple* ye are.

     ii. **1 Timothy 1:18 (KJV)** This charge I commit unto thee, son Timothy, according to the prophecies which went before on thee, that thou by them mightest war a good warfare;

     iii. **1 Timothy 1:19 (KJV)** Holding faith, and a good conscience; which some having put away concerning faith have made shipwreck:

     iv. **1 Timothy 1:20 (KJV)** Of whom is Hymenaeus and Alexander; whom I have delivered unto Satan, that they may learn not to blaspheme.

19. Again, as I mentioned before, you cannot hold the wisdom, concepts, and theories of this world and access the knowledge in the Word of God at the same time, no, you have to drop the one in order to take up the other, and since the Word of God the Holy Bible comes entirely in metaphors, in proverbs, in parables and in dark sayings, very often, the first impression from people on the Word of God is that it is foolishness and it does not make sense, and yes, it was deliberately made so, seemingly senseless, in order to weed out the misfits and the undesirables away from the Word of God!

     i. **1 Corinthians 3:18 (KJV)** Let no man deceive himself. If any man among you seemeth to be wise in this world, let him become a fool, that he may be wise.

     ii. **1 Corinthians 3:19 (KJV)** For the wisdom of this world is foolishness with God. For it is written, He taketh the wise in their own craftiness.

     iii. **1 Corinthians 3:20 (KJV)** And again, The Lord knoweth the thoughts of the wise, that they are vain.

20. Hence, you have to drop your worldly wisdom to become a fool in the Word of God in order to appreciate the foolishness of the Word of God!

     i. **Ecclesiastes 7:25 (KJV)** I applied mine heart to know, and to search, and to seek out wisdom, and the reason *of things*, and to know the wickedness of folly, even of foolishness *and* madness:

ii. **1 Corinthians 1:18 (KJV)** For the preaching of the cross is to them that perish foolishness; but unto us which are saved it is the power of God.

iii. **1 Corinthians 1:21 (KJV)** For after that in the wisdom of God the world by wisdom knew not God, it pleased God by the foolishness of preaching to save them that believe.

iv. **2 Corinthians 4:3 (KJV)** But if our gospel be hid, it is hid to them that are lost:

v. **Psalm 78:2 (KJV)** I will open my mouth in a parable: I will utter dark sayings of old:

vi. **Proverbs 1:6 (KJV)** To understand a proverb, and the interpretation; the words of the wise, and their dark sayings.

vii. **Matthew 13:34 (KJV)** All these things spake Jesus unto the multitude in parables; and without a parable spake he not unto them:

viii. **Mark 4:34 (KJV)** But without a parable spake he not unto them: and when they were alone, he expounded all things to his disciples.

21. As guided by the verses in the Holy Scriptures which often uses repetition for emphasis, we conclude this chapter with a repetition of what I wrote earlier regarding **1 Corinthians 3:4-7 (KJV)** saying: Another way to identify The Worldly Wisdom Vain Man, The Carnal Man, or, The Babe in Christ is that he uses men's theories to do his Bible Interpretation, Translation, and Sermon Preparation instead of using God's Theory for Bible Interpretation and Translation, and here, in this conclusion, the correct approach is: DO NOT USE MEN'S THEORIES TO DO BIBLE INTERPRETATION, BIBLE TRANSLATION, AND SERMON PREPARATION!

    i. **1 Corinthians 3:21 (KJV)** Therefore let no man glory in men. For all things are yours;

    ii. **1 Corinthians 3:22 (KJV)** Whether Paul, or Apollos, or Cephas, or the world, or life, or death, or things present, or things to come; all are yours;

    iii. **1 Corinthians 3:23 (KJV)** And ye are Christ's; and Christ *is* God's.

The LORD Jesus Christ be with your spirit. The LORD Jesus Christ give you understanding.

Rev. Prof. PETER PRYCE,
DSEF, BA, MA, B.Soc.Sc Pol Sci, IBA, PhD
A Scribe of the Law of the God of Heaven
Prophet of the Word of God

Professor of French, Silver Spring, MD, USA
Scholar of the Institute of Theologians, USA
WWW.THEBIBLEUNIVERSITY.ORG
Accreditation Number: 07-QCTO/SDP120723172836
SAQA QUAL ID: Identification # 101997
WWW.BOOKSTORESITE.ORG
WWW.THEBIBLEUNIVERSITYCHURCH.ORG

Sunday 7th January 2024 @ 6:11 AM – 8:21 AM
While hearing and meditating on the Word of God.

SEVEN STEPS ON HOW TO CORRECTLY TEACH THE WORD OF GOD

Question 2483

1. It is inconceivable that the LORD God should give us such an imeasurably powerful instrument of Salvation, which is the Gospel of Christ, and not also give us any methodology to administer it!

    i. **Romans 1:16 (KJV)** For I am not ashamed of the gospel of Christ: for it is the power of God unto salvation to every one that believeth; to the Jew first, and also to the Greek.

    ii. **2 Corinthians 4:7 (KJV)** But we have this treasure in earthen vessels, that the excellency of the power may be of God, and not of us.

2. Therefore, thinking along the lines of the error of a lack of a Bible Interpretation Methodology in the Holy Scriptures, many humans have come up with several theories for Bible Translation and Interpretation without reasoning whether it makes any sense that God would call all human wisdom *foolishness* and then, the same God would return and hand over the translation and interpretation of what God calls *wisdom* to the same humans whom God has already condemned as foolish!

    i. **1 Corinthians 1:21 (KJV)** For after that in the wisdom of God the world by wisdom knew not God, it pleased God by the foolishness of preaching to save them that believe.

    ii. **1 Corinthians 3:19 (KJV)** For the wisdom of this world is foolishness with God. For it is written, He taketh the wise in their own craftiness.

3. How can foolish human beings exercise the power of correct understanding and interpretation over that which is NOT foolish but pure wisdom? It takes a superior Judge to supervise and correct a lower ranking Judge, just as it takes a more experienced medical doctor to supervise and correct a freshman doctor out of University medical school! If that is so even with filthy foolish humans, then, how come humans are evaluating, assessing, and examining a far superior Word of God which Word of God is God Himself? Shall a fool who is devoid of wisdom be be asked to examine wisdom and supply a methodology for wisdom?

    i. **Deuteronomy 4:5 (KJV)** Behold, I have taught you statutes and judgments, even as the LORD my God commanded me, that ye should do so in the land whither ye go to possess it.

    ii. **Deuteronomy 4:6 (KJV)** Keep therefore and do *them*; for this *is* your wisdom and your understanding in the sight of the nations, which shall hear all these statutes, and say, Surely this great nation *is* a wise and understanding people.

iii. **Job 4:17 (KJV)** Shall mortal man be more just than God? shall a man be more pure than his maker?

iv. **Job 28:20 (KJV)** Whence then cometh wisdom? and where *is* the place of understanding?

v. **Job 28:21 (KJV)** Seeing it is hid from the eyes of all living, and kept close from the fowls of the air.

vi. **Psalm 119:140 (KJV)** Thy word *is* very pure: therefore thy servant loveth it.

vii. **Proverbs 30:5 (KJV)** Every word of God *is* pure: he *is* a shield unto them that put their trust in him.

viii. **Jeremiah 4:22 (KJV)** For my people *is* foolish, they have not known me; they *are* sottish children, and they have none understanding: they *are* wise to do evil, but to do good they have no knowledge.

ix. **Haggai 2:14 (KJV)** Then answered Haggai, and said, So *is* this people, and so *is* this nation before me, saith the LORD; and so *is* every work of their hands; and that which they offer there *is* unclean.

4. If sinful men, and NOT God, shall decide on the correct meaning of the instrument (Word of God) that takes men to Heaven, then where is the need for the LORD God to write the Word of God Himself and not rather leave it to men to do so?

i. **Exodus 34:28 (KJV)** And he was there with the LORD forty days and forty nights; he did neither eat bread, nor drink water. And he wrote upon the tables the words of the covenant, the ten commandments.

ii. **Exodus 31:18 (KJV)** And he gave unto Moses, when he had made an end of communing with him upon mount Sinai, two tables of testimony, tables of stone, written with the finger of God.

iii. **Deuteronomy 9:10 (KJV)** And the LORD delivered unto me two tables of stone written with the finger of God; and on them *was written* according to all the words, which the LORD spake with you in the mount out of the midst of the fire in the day of the assembly.

iv. **Exodus 34:1 (KJV)** And the LORD said unto Moses, Hew thee two tables of stone like unto the first: and I will write upon *these* tables the words that were in the first tables, which thou brakest.

v. **Deuteronomy 10:2 (KJV)** And I will write on the tables the words that were in the first tables which thou brakest, and thou shalt put them in the ark.

vi. **Jeremiah 31:33 (KJV)** But this *shall be* the covenant that I will make with the house of Israel; After those days, saith the LORD, I will put my law in their inward parts, and write it in their hearts; and will be their God, and they shall be my people.

vii. **Hebrews 8:10 (KJV)** For this *is* the covenant that I will make with the house of Israel after those days, saith the Lord; I will put my laws into their mind, and write them in their hearts: and I will be to them a God, and they shall be to me a people:

viii. **Hebrews 10:16 (KJV)** This *is* the covenant that I will make with them after those days, saith the Lord, I will put my laws into their hearts, and in their minds will I write them;

ix. **Revelation 3:12 (KJV)** Him that overcometh will I make a pillar in the temple of my God, and he shall go no more out: and I will write upon him the name of my God, and the name of the city of my God, *which is* new Jerusalem, which cometh down out of heaven from my God: and *I will write upon him* my new name.

5. That is why every Theory for Bible Translation and Interpretation, and every Methodology for Bible Translation and Interpretation, and every Approach to Bible Translation and Interpretation, that was devised by humans, is condemned as foolishness even before it sees the light of day, because man is the sum product of all his error thoughts, of all his error words, and of all his error deeds, which triple levels of error are also transferred into every Theory for Bible Translation and Interpretation that he devises!

i. **Matthew 12:37 (KJV)** For by thy words thou shalt be justified, and by thy words thou shalt be condemned.

ii. **John 3:18 (KJV)** He that believeth on him is not condemned: but he that believeth not is condemned already, because he hath not believed in the name of the only begotten Son of God.

iii. **Hebrews 11:7 (KJV)** By faith Noah, being warned of God of things not seen as yet, moved with fear, prepared an ark to the saving of his house; by the which he condemned the world, and became heir of the righteousness which is by faith.

iv. **Romans 11:32 (KJV)** For God hath concluded them all in unbelief, that he might have mercy upon all.

v. **Galatians 3:22 (KJV)** But the scripture hath concluded all under sin, that the promise by faith of Jesus Christ might be given to them that believe.

vi. **Romans 7:18 (KJV)** For I know that in me (that is, in my flesh,) dwelleth no good thing: for to will is present with me; but *how* to perform that which is good I find not.

vii. **2 Corinthians 2:17 (KJV)** For we are not as many, which corrupt the word of God: but as of sincerity, but as of God, in the sight of God speak we in Christ.

6. STEP #1:

7. In order to correctly teach or preach the Word of God, the first step is to learn how to "speak in Christ" as **2 Corinthians 2:17 (KJV)** reveals!

8. What does it mean to "speak in Christ"?

9. It simply means to speak ONLY what the Gospel of Christ speaks, permits, directs, and allows!

    i. **Numbers 22:20 (KJV)** And God came unto Balaam at night, and said unto him, If the men come to call thee, rise up, *and* go with them; but yet the word which I shall say unto thee, that shalt thou do.

    ii. **Ezekiel 3:4 (KJV)** And he said unto me, Son of man, go, get thee unto the house of Israel, and speak with my words unto them.

    iii. **John 3:34 (KJV)** For he whom God hath sent speaketh the words of God: for God giveth not the Spirit by measure *unto him.*

    iv. **Numbers 22:35 (KJV)** And the angel of the LORD said unto Balaam, Go with the men: but only the word that I shall speak unto thee, that thou shalt speak. So Balaam went with the princes of Balak.

    v. **Numbers 22:36 (KJV)** And when Balak heard that Balaam was come, he went out to meet him unto a city of Moab, which *is* in the border of Arnon, which *is* in the utmost coast.

    vi. **Numbers 22:37 (KJV)** And Balak said unto Balaam, Did I not earnestly send unto thee to call thee? wherefore camest thou not unto me? am I not able indeed to promote thee to honour?

    vii. **Numbers 22:38 (KJV)** And Balaam said unto Balak, Lo, I am come unto thee: have I now any power at all to say any thing? the word that God putteth in my mouth, that shall I speak.

    viii. **Revelation 19:10 (KJV)** And I fell at his feet to worship him. And he said unto me, See *thou do it* not: I am thy fellowservant, and of thy brethren that have the testimony of Jesus: worship God: for the testimony of Jesus is the spirit of prophecy.

10. In other words, if the power to speak is given to you by God according to **John 12:49 (KJV)**, and if the words that you are speaking are NOT yours but were given to you

by God according to **John 17:8 (KJV)**, then you have zero entitlement to profess any meanings to those same words that do NOT belong to you in the first place!

    i. **Jeremiah 23:30 (KJV)** Therefore, behold, I *am* against the prophets, saith the LORD, that steal my words every one from his neighbour.

    ii. **John 14:10 (KJV)** Believest thou not that I am in the Father, and the Father in me? the words that I speak unto you I speak not of myself: but the Father that dwelleth in me, he doeth the works.

    iii. **John 12:49 (KJV)** For I have not spoken of myself; but the Father which sent me, he gave me a commandment, what I should say, and what I should speak.

    iv. **John 17:8 (KJV)** For I have given unto them the words which thou gavest me; and they have received *them*, and have known surely that I came out from thee, and they have believed that thou didst send me.

11. The real Owner of the words, being God Almighty, retains the right to define what HIS Words mean hence, all human Theories for Bible Translation and Interpretation are nonsense, void, and excluded!

12. STEP #2:

13. The second step to correctly teach or preach the Word of God is to measure the efficacy of the teaching, NOT in terms of pastoral commendation and approval one of the other, but in terms of actual men and women who have received the teachings of Christ from you, and, being led of the Holy Spirit, are actually walking in Truth and Righteousness daily!

    i. **2 Corinthians 3:1 (KJV)** Do we begin again to commend ourselves? or need we, as some *others*, epistles of commendation to you, or *letters* of commendation from you?

    ii. **2 Corinthians 3:2 (KJV)** Ye are our epistle written in our hearts, known and read of all men:

    iii. **2 Corinthians 3:3 (KJV)** *Forasmuch as ye are* manifestly declared to be the epistle of Christ ministered by us, written not with ink, but with the Spirit of the living God; not in tables of stone, but in fleshy tables of the heart.

    iv. **2 Corinthians 10:12 (KJV)** For we dare not make ourselves of the number, or compare ourselves with some that commend themselves: but they measuring themselves by themselves, and comparing themselves among themselves, are not wise.

14. STEP #3:

15. The third step to correctly teach or preach the Word of God is to acknowledge our own insufficiency and yield our insufficiency to the sufficiency of God who owns the words that we are preaching and teaching!

    i. **2 Corinthians 3:4 (KJV)** And such trust have we through Christ to God-ward:

    ii. **2 Corinthians 3:5 (KJV)** Not that we are sufficient of ourselves to think any thing as of ourselves; but our sufficiency *is* of God;

16. STEP #4:

17. The fourth step to correctly teach or preach the Word of God is to identify and to recognize the two-prong meanings in the Word of God, which are "the letter of the text" (the physical meaning) and "the spirit of the text" (the spiritual meaning), and, then, in your preaching or teaching, to emphasize and focus on "the spirit of the text", because God is Spirit and never physical!

    i. **2 Corinthians 3:6 (KJV)** Who also hath made us able ministers of the new testament; not of the letter, but of the spirit: for the letter killeth, but the spirit giveth life.

    ii. **John 4:23 (KJV)** But the hour cometh, and now is, when the true worshippers shall worship the Father in spirit and in truth: for the Father seeketh such to worship him.

    iii. **John 4:24 (KJV)** God *is* a Spirit: and they that worship him must worship *him* in spirit and in truth.

    iv. **Acts 7:48 (KJV)** Howbeit the most High dwelleth not in temples made with hands; as saith the prophet,

    v. **Acts 17:24 (KJV)** God that made the world and all things therein, seeing that he is Lord of heaven and earth, dwelleth not in temples made with hands;

    vi. **Acts 17:25 (KJV)** Neither is worshipped with men's hands, as though he needed any thing, seeing he giveth to all life, and breath, and all things;

18. STEP #5:

19. The fifth step to correctly teach or preach the Word of God is to recognize the consequence of dwelling on the physical in God-worship, which consequence is death! That form of preaching and teaching the Word of God that considers the physical meaning of the Word of God as essential is called "the ministration of death"! In other words, all the Old Testament physical forms of God-worship were NOT unto life but into death!

    i. **2 Corinthians 3:7 (KJV)** But if the ministration of death, written *and* engraven in stones, was glorious, so that the children of Israel could not stedfastly behold the face of Moses for the glory of his countenance; which *glory* was to be done away:

    ii. **Romans 3:20 (KJV)** Therefore by the deeds of the law there shall no flesh be justified in his sight: for by the law *is* the knowledge of sin.

    iii. **Romans 8:13 (KJV)** For if ye live after the flesh, ye shall die: but if ye through the Spirit do mortify the deeds of the body, ye shall live.

    iv. **Romans 3:20 (KJV)** Therefore by the deeds of the law there shall no flesh be justified in his sight: for by the law *is* the knowledge of sin.

    v. **Galatians 2:16 (KJV)** Knowing that a man is not justified by the works of the law, but by the faith of Jesus Christ, even we have believed in Jesus Christ, that we might be justified by the faith of Christ, and not by the works of the law: for by the works of the law shall no flesh be justified.

20. Hence, for example, it is called "the ministration of death", or, it is understood that you the Pastor or Bishop, you are administering death to the congregation when you read **Luke 22:19-20 (KJV)** and then you proceed to think and to preach that the LORD Jesus Christ wants you to eat and drink physical bread, wafers, and wine!

    i. **Luke 22:19 (KJV)** And he took bread, and gave thanks, and brake *it*, and gave unto them, saying, This is my body which is given for you: this do in remembrance of me.

    ii. **Luke 22:20 (KJV)** Likewise also the cup after supper, saying, This cup *is* the new testament in my blood, which is shed for you.

21. The moment that you choose to stay with the physical meaning of **Luke 22:19-20 (KJV)**, that is the same moment that you fell into the condemnation of **2 Corinthians 3:6 (KJV)**, and also, are in violation of the same!

22. The same doctrine of "the ministration of death" is applicable in all instances of the Word of God where you choose to present/minister the physical instead of the spiriual side of the same, why? Because the physical is already done away with! When was that? The physical was abolished in **John 4:23-24 (KJV)**!

    i. **2 Corinthians 3:8 (KJV)** How shall not the ministration of the spirit be rather glorious?

    ii. **2 Corinthians 3:9 (KJV)** For if the ministration of condemnation *be* glory, much more doth the ministration of righteousness exceed in glory.

    iii. **2 Corinthians 3:10 (KJV)** For even that which was made glorious had no glory in this respect, by reason of the glory that excelleth.

    iv. **2 Corinthians 3:11 (KJV)** For if that which is done away *was* glorious, much more that which remaineth *is* glorious.

v. **John 4:23 (KJV)** But the hour cometh, and now is, when the true worshippers shall worship the Father in spirit and in truth: for the Father seeketh such to worship him.

vi. **John 4:24 (KJV)** God *is* a Spirit: and they that worship him must worship *him* in spirit and in truth.

23. STEP #6:

24. The sixth step to correctly teach or preach the Word of God is to be fully convinced that the greatness of dropping the physical aspects of God-worship and placing all hope in the "ministration of the Spirit", or, in the act of "speaking in Christ", lies in the fact that you assume zero responsibility for all things spiritual, because it is then the Holy Spirit who is in control and responsible for the words of the LORD God Almighty, and not you!

   i. **2 Corinthians 3:12 (KJV)** Seeing then that we have such hope, we use great plainness of speech:

   ii. **2 Corinthians 3:13 (KJV)** And not as Moses, *which* put a vail over his face, that the children of Israel could not stedfastly look to the end of that which is abolished:

25. STEP #7:

26. The seventh step to correctly teach or preach the Word of God is to learn that all the physical blindness that the LORD Jesus Christ healed were nothing in themselves since all of the healed people were going to die again anyway!

27. The reason being that the most precious healing of their blindness was NOT in their ability to physically see the world and the things in the world, but, rather, that the blindness of their minds hindering their ability to correctly understand the Word of God was taken away by Jesus Christ, and this is the same spiritual healing of the blind that you the Pastor and the Bishop should be practising and ministring in your preaching and teaching of the Word of God!

   i. **2 Corinthians 3:14 (KJV)** But their minds were blinded: for until this day remaineth the same vail untaken away in the reading of the old testament; which *vail* is done away in Christ.

28. Therefore, I testify to you by the Holy Ghost, that blindness is in the mind and in the head, and this is the real blindness that you are commanded to heal, given the fact that the eyes of man are in his head and NOT on his face!

   i. **Ecclesiastes 2:14 (KJV)** The wise man's eyes *are* in his head; but the fool walketh in darkness: and I myself perceived also that one event happeneth to them all.

   ii. **Matthew 10:8 (KJV)** Heal the sick, cleanse the lepers, raise the dead, cast out devils: freely ye have received, freely give.

iii. **Isaiah 42:6 (KJV)** I the LORD have called thee in righteousness, and will hold thine hand, and will keep thee, and give thee for a covenant of the people, for a light of the Gentiles;

iv. **Isaiah 42:7 (KJV)** To open the blind eyes, to bring out the prisoners from the prison, *and* them that sit in darkness out of the prison house.

v. **Acts 26:17 (KJV)** Delivering thee from the people, and *from* the Gentiles, unto whom now I send thee,

vi. **Acts 26:18 (KJV)** To open their eyes, *and* to turn *them* from darkness to light, and *from* the power of Satan unto God, that they may receive forgiveness of sins, and inheritance among them which are sanctified by faith that is in me.

vii. **Isaiah 61:1 (KJV)** The Spirit of the Lord GOD *is* upon me; because the LORD hath anointed me to preach good tidings unto the meek; he hath sent me to bind up the brokenhearted, to proclaim liberty to the captives, and the opening of the prison to *them that are* bound;

viii. **Luke 4:18 (KJV)** The Spirit of the Lord *is* upon me, because he hath anointed me to preach the gospel to the poor; he hath sent me to heal the brokenhearted, to preach deliverance to the captives, and recovering of sight to the blind, to set at liberty them that are bruised,

29. How very stupid are you as a Man of God teaching the physical meaning of the Word of God, when you claim that it was the LORD Jesus Christ who called you into Ministry, and yet you are blind in the spiritual meaning of the Word of God, not knowing what the Word of God means, NOT having the Holy Spirit who is The Teacher of Truth, and therefore, you go about teaching the Word of God in error and in corruption, alas, to the utter destruction of your own soul in Hell

    i. **2 Corinthians 3:15 (KJV)** But even unto this day, when Moses is read, the vail is upon their heart.

    ii. **2 Corinthians 3:16 (KJV)** Nevertheless when it shall turn to the Lord, the vail shall be taken away.

    iii. **2 Corinthians 2:17 (KJV)** For we are not as many, which corrupt the word of God: but as of sincerity, but as of God, in the sight of God speak we in Christ.

    iv. **Acts 13:10 (KJV)** And said, O full of all subtilty and all mischief, *thou* child of the devil, *thou* enemy of all righteousness, wilt thou not cease to pervert the right ways of the Lord?

    v. **Galatians 1:7 (KJV)** Which is not another; but there be some that trouble you, and would pervert the gospel of Christ.

30. In conclusion, the Man of God who focuses on the spiritual side of the Word of God is demonstrating liberty in Chirst! Liberty from what? Liberty or breaking away from the physical and affinity with the Spirit of the Lord!

    i. **2 Corinthians 3:17 (KJV)** Now the Lord is that Spirit: and where the Spirit of the Lord *is*, there *is* liberty.

    ii. **2 Corinthians 3:18 (KJV)** But we all, with open face beholding as in a glass the glory of the Lord, are changed into the same image from glory to glory, *even* as by the Spirit of the Lord.

The LORD Jesus Christ be with your spirit. The LORD Jesus Christ give you understanding.

Rev. Prof. PETER PRYCE,
DSEF, BA, MA, B.Soc.Sc Pol Sci, IBA, PhD
A Scribe of the Law of the God of Heaven
Prophet of the Word of God
Professor of French, Silver Spring, MD, USA
Scholar of the Institute of Theologians, USA
WWW.THEBIBLEUNIVERSITY.ORG
Accreditation Number: 07-QCTO/SDP120723172836
SAQA QUAL ID: Identification # 101997
WWW.BOOKSTORESITE.ORG
WWW.THEBIBLEUNIVERSITYCHURCH.ORG

Saturday 20th January 2024 @ 11:01 AM – 3:37 PM
While hearing and meditating on the Word of God at home.

CONCLUSION

In this research, we set out to discover a scientific method for intralingual Bible translation/interpretation whose scientific edge derives from the ability to verify the rendered interpretation across the entire Bible from Genesis to Revelation and replicate the understanding contained in the interpretation without any contradiction whatsoever from any part of the Bible.

We noted in the introduction that translation and interpreting overlap and are therefore one and same thing depending on what emphasis one applies to both terms.

We also explained three types of translation known as *interlingual translation*, *intralingual translation* and *intersemiotic translation* and subsequently noted that the type of Bible interpreting exemplified in this paper is intralingual translation.

We then explained the *Perfect Harmony Theory for Bible Translation and Interpreting* and provided Biblical justifications for its use. In the section titled "Ten Roadmaps to Understanding Perfect Harmony", we supplied the chronological development of thoughts that help to anchor the importance and efficacy of this Bible interpreting method while reiterating that to master the *Perfect Harmony Method for Bible Translation and Interpreting* is to successfully blend the communicative objective of translation and interpreting with thorough Bible scholarship enriched by research and study of the Word from Genesis to Revelation.

In order to see how this Bible interpreting method works, we illustrated it with the Book of Daniel and with Mark Chapter 12. We then we tested the illustration with an interpretation assessment or verification exercise, which equally provided ten lessons on how to replicate it.

With pertinent references and explanatory commentaries following Mark Chapter 12, and in order not to have it seem as a one-off attempt to explain the *Perfect Harmony Method for Bible Translation and Interpreting*, we presented a second exposé of the method with a view to increasing its threshold of credibility by examining Mark chapter 15 with its own interpretation assessment and verification exercise. In fact, we conducted four interpretation assessment or verification exercises just to prove that, indeed, the theory works!

We believe that by removing self and allowing the Bible to interpret itself, we achieve faithfulness to the source text and we ensure accuracy of Bible interpreting apart from the assurance that the interpretation is not contradicted by any other verse in the entire Bible:

> **Jeremiah 23:28 (KJV)** The prophet that hath a dream, let him tell a dream; and he that hath my word, let him speak my word faithfully. What *is* the chaff to the wheat? Saith the LORD.

One way forward would be an extended project where the *Perfect Harmony Theory for Bible Translation and Interpreting* is used to anchor a complete Commentary of the Bible. In that case, the objective would be to answer the perennial question: what does the verse mean?

REFERENCES

1. Bible, The. (1611). King James Version (Authorized Version) (Public domain).
2. Jakobson, Roman (1971[1959]). "On Linguistic Aspects of Translation." In R. Jakobson, Roman O. (1959). *Selected Writings, II*. The Hague, Mouton, pp. 260-266.
3. Jakobson, Roman O. (1959). On Linguistic Aspects of Translation. In L. Venuti (ed), (2004), *The Translation Studies Reader*. London, New York and Canada: Routledge, pp. 113-118.
4. Pryce, Peter. (2011). Méthode de Traduction intralinguale de thèmes bibliques, paper presented to 8th Inter-University Conference on the Co-Existence of Languages in West Africa, Department of French Education, University of Education, Winneba, Ghana, Monday June 13, 2011 – Saturday June 18, 2011.
5. Pryce, Peter. (2018). *Thematic Dictionary of Matthew*. Ingram, USA.
6. Seleskovitch, Danica. (1977). « Take care of the sense and the sounds will take care of themselves or Why interpreting is not tantamount to Translating Languages. » *The Incorporated Linguist*, 16, pp. 27-33.
7. Seleskovitch, Danica. & Lederer, Marianne. (1993). *Traduire pour interpréter*. Publication de la Sorbonne, Didier Erudition, Coll. « Traductologie 1 ».
8. Seleskovitch, Danica, et Marianne Lederer. (2001). *Interpréter pour traduire*, *Quatrième édition*. Paris, Didier Erudition.
9. Vinay, Jean-Paul, and Jean Darbelnet. (1958). *Stylistique Comparée du Français et de l'anglais : Méthode de Traduction*, Paris : Didier, 69-70, 103, 107-108, 110, 124.
10. Vinay, Jean-Paul, and Jean Darbelnet. (1995 [1958]). *Comparative Stylistics of French and English: a Methodology for Translation.* (Ed. And translators) Juan C. Sager and M.-J. Hamel, Amsterdam: John Benjamin.

The LORD Jesus Christ be with your spirit. The LORD Jesus Christ give you understanding.

Rev. Prof. PETER PRYCE,
DSEF, BA, MA, B.Soc.Sc Pol Sci, IBA, PhD
A Scribe of the Law of the God of Heaven
Prophet of the Word of God

Professor of French, Silver Spring, MD, USA
Scholar of the Institute of Theologians, USA
WWW.THEBIBLEUNIVERSITY.ORG
Accreditation Number: 07-QCTO/SDP120723172836
SAQA QUAL ID: Identification # 101997
WWW.BOOKSTORESITE.ORG
WWW.THEBIBLEUNIVERSITYCHURCH.ORG

Wednesday 8th July 2020 @ 6:37 AM
While hearing, and meditating on the Word of God

CHAPTER 2
THE BOOK OF 1 CORINTHIANS

AKOBEN
"War horn"
Asante philosophical symbol of Vigilance, Wariness

CHAPTER 1: THEORETICAL APPROACH TO BIBLE INTERPRETATION AND TRANSLATION

If you want to accomplish a successful Bible Interpretation and Translation, then follow this theoretical approach:

1. A correct translation of the Holy Bible begins with a correct understanding of the text (Hermeneutics) of the Holy Bible!
2. A correct understanding of the Holy Bible precedes a correct interpretation (Exegesis) of the text of the Holy Bible!
3. A correct interpretation of the Holy Bible requires achieving perfect harmony/coherence and zero conflict of thought and doctrine between your understanding of the Bible text in question and the entire remainder of the Holy Bible!
4. A correct translation of the Holy Bible is the final step and a rendering in writing of the above intellectual process!
5. The Holy Scriptures is The Book that prescribes its own Approach and Methodology of Interpretation and it is contained in the Book of 1 Corinthians chapter 1!
6. There is a restricted audience that is identified for the interpretation and translation of the Holy Scriptures!
   - i. **1 Corinthians 1:1 (KJV)** Paul, called *to be* an apostle of Jesus Christ through the will of God, and Sosthenes *our* brother,
   - ii. **1 Corinthians 1:2 (KJV)** Unto the church of God which is at Corinth, to them that are sanctified in Christ Jesus, called *to be* saints, with all that in every place call upon the name of Jesus Christ our Lord, both theirs and ours:
7. In other words, the Holy Scriptures is NOT for everyone, but ONLY for:
   - i. Those who are called to its tenets and doctrines.
   - ii. Those who are identified as the Church of Christ and profess themselves so to be.
   - iii. Them that are sanctified/cleansed/washed in Christ Jesus.
   - iv. To be sanctified/cleansed/washed means to be washed from all thoughts that are contrary to the mind of Christ and to take on in its place, or to be imbued, impregnated, inspired, filled with, permeated, infused, poured into, soaked, or endued with: the mind of Christ!
   - v. **Luke 24:49 (KJV)** And, behold, I send the promise of my Father upon you: but tarry ye in the city of Jerusalem, until ye be endued with power from on high.

vi.   **Acts 1:5 (KJV)** For John truly baptized with water; but ye shall be baptized with the Holy Ghost not many days hence.

vii. **Acts 1:8 (KJV)** But ye shall receive power, after that the Holy Ghost is come upon you: and ye shall be witnesses unto me both in Jerusalem, and in all Judaea, and in Samaria, and unto the uttermost part of the earth.

viii. Them that in every place call upon the name of Jesus Christ as the LORD and Source of that knowledge that is derived from the Holy Scriptures!

8. Now, therefore, if you are NOT identified in the above portrait or profile of people who should access the text of the Holy Scriptures, then what are you doing with it?

i.   **Psalm 50:16 (KJV)** But unto the wicked God saith, What hast thou to do to declare my statutes, or *that* thou shouldest take my covenant in thy mouth?

ii. **Psalm 50:17 (KJV)** Seeing thou hatest instruction, and castest my words behind thee.

9. The next cardinal step in the theoretical approach to Bible Interpretation and Translation is called: the reciprocal confirmation of the knowledge of Christ!

i.   **1 Corinthians 1:5 (KJV)** That in every thing ye are enriched by him, in all utterance, and *in* all knowledge;

ii.   **1 Corinthians 1:6 (KJV)** Even as the testimony of Christ was confirmed in you:

iii. **1 Corinthians 1:7 (KJV)** So that ye come behind in no gift; waiting for the coming of our Lord Jesus Christ:

iv.   **1 Corinthians 1:8 (KJV)** Who shall also confirm you unto the end, *that ye may be* blameless in the day of our Lord Jesus Christ.

10. In other words, in **1 Corinthians 1:5-8 (KJV)**, we learn that the knowledge and understanding of the text of the Word of God that you have, must be reciprocated and confirmed in both what you understand, interpret, say, and write on the one hand, and then on the other hand, in what is written in the Holy Scriptures itself!

i.   **Luke 20:9 (KJV)** Then began he to speak to the people this parable; A certain man planted a vineyard, and let it forth to husbandmen, and went into a far country for a long time.

ii.   **Luke 20:10 (KJV)** And at the season he sent a servant to the husbandmen, that they should give him of the fruit of the vineyard: but the husbandmen beat him, and sent *him* away empty.

iii. **Luke 20:11 (KJV)** And again he sent another servant: and they beat him also, and entreated *him* shamefully, and sent *him* away empty.

    iv. **Luke 20:12 (KJV)** And again he sent a third: and they wounded him also, and cast *him* out.

    v. **Luke 20:13 (KJV)** Then said the lord of the vineyard, What shall I do? I will send my beloved son: it may be they will reverence *him* when they see him.

    vi. **Luke 20:14 (KJV)** But when the husbandmen saw him, they reasoned among themselves, saying, This is the heir: come, let us kill him, that the inheritance may be ours.

    vii. **Luke 20:15 (KJV)** So they cast him out of the vineyard, and killed *him*. What therefore shall the lord of the vineyard do unto them?

    viii. **Luke 20:16 (KJV)** He shall come and destroy these husbandmen, and shall give the vineyard to others. And when they heard *it*, they said, God forbid.

    ix. **Luke 20:17 (KJV)** And he beheld them, and said, What is this then that is written, The stone which the builders rejected, the same is become the head of the corner?

    x. **Luke 20:18 (KJV)** Whosoever shall fall upon that stone shall be broken; but on whomsoever it shall fall, it will grind him to powder.

11. Quite simply, the singleness of thought must be evident in your Bible Interpretation as well as in the text of the Holy Bible itself, to the extent that discord, contrariness, and divergence of thought are outlawed!

12. In **Luke 20:9-15 (KJV)**, we see the LORD Jesus Christ engaged in a Bible Interpretation and Translation!

13. In **Luke 20:16 (KJV)**, the LORD Jesus Christ renders an interpretation that is in perfect harmony, in one accord, is consistent with the contents in **Luke 20:9-15 (KJV)**!

14. At the end of **Luke 20:16 (KJV)**, the other Bible Interpreters come to a different, divergent, inconsistent, contrary interpretation, rejecting the interpretation of the LORD Jesus Christ with their words: "God forbid"!

15. In **Luke 20:17 (KJV)**, the LORD Jesus Christ shows them the evidence of their error in Bible Interpretation by pointing out the actual text that refutes and contradicts their interpretation, thereby establishing that Perfect Harmony is the required standard in Bible Interpretation and Translation!

16. Finally, in **Luke 20:18 (KJV)**, the LORD Jesus Christ uses metaphoric language to illustrate that, either way, both from the perspective of the bad Bible Interpreter and the bad Bible interpretation itself, there will be brokenness and a shattering of harmony and coherence!

17. The next cardinal step in the theoretical approach to Bible Interpretation and Translation is called: Faithfulness in Interpretation and Translation!

       i. **1 Corinthians 1:9 (KJV)** God *is* faithful, by whom ye were called unto the fellowship of his Son Jesus Christ our Lord.

18. This is where you seek to replicate the faith attribute of the owner of the text, which translation requirement is also mentioned elsewhere in the Holy Bible!

       i. **2 Chronicles 19:9 (KJV)** And he charged them, saying, Thus shall ye do in the fear of the LORD, faithfully, and with a perfect heart.

       ii. **Jeremiah 23:28 (KJV)** The prophet that hath a dream, let him tell a dream; and he that hath my word, let him speak my word faithfully. What *is* the chaff to the wheat? saith the LORD.

19. It is a reiteration of the requirement for zero conflict of thought and doctrine between your understanding of the Bible text in question and the entire remainder of the Holy Bible!

20. The next cardinal step in the theoretical approach to Bible Interpretation and Translation is captured in:

       i. **1 Corinthians 1:10 (KJV)** Now I beseech you, brethren, by the name of our Lord Jesus Christ, that ye all speak the same thing, and *that* there be no divisions among you; but *that* ye be perfectly joined together in the same mind and in the same judgment.

21. Now, the correct interpretation of the command in **1 Corinthians 1:10 (KJV)** is this:

       i. Speak the same thing as the original Bible text is saying!

       ii. Ensure that there be no divisions at all between your translation and the Bible text!

       iii. An examination of your translation and the original Bible text must reveal your translation to be perfectly joined together in the same mind and in the same judgment as the original Bible text!

22. The reason to (1) speak and write the same thing, (2) that there be no divisions at all, and (3) that your translation be perfect in mind and in judgment, is that, as I wrote above, the Holy Scriptures is the only Book that prescribes its own Approach and Methodology of Interpretation and Translation whereby, there is nothing that you can understand, interpret, or write which is contrary to what is already contained in the Holy Bible itself that will stand! The Holy Bible itself, as a text, outlaws contrary opinion and interpretation!

       i. **Proverbs 21:30 (KJV)** *There is* no wisdom nor understanding nor counsel against the LORD.

23. Failure to heed to the command in **1 Corinthians 1:10 (KJV)** and in **Proverbs 21:30 (KJV)** draws the following condemnation!

       i. **Isaiah 8:20 (KJV)** To the law and to the testimony: if they speak not according to this word, *it is* because *there is* no light in them.

24. It is very important to understand that the Holy Bible does NOT lend itself to contentious interpretations neither in the persons of the many theorists of translation and interpretation nor in the doctrines, subjects, themes, and topics that they present!

25. The Holy Bible lends itself to only one interpretation and translation that come from within itself to create a perfect harmony, as I have shown above:

     i. **1 Corinthians 1:11 (KJV)** For it hath been declared unto me of you, my brethren, by them *which are of the house* of Chloe, that there are contentions among you.

     ii. **1 Corinthians 1:12 (KJV)** Now this I say, that every one of you saith, I am of Paul; and I of Apollos; and I of Cephas; and I of Christ.

     iii. **1 Corinthians 1:13 (KJV)** Is Christ divided? was Paul crucified for you? or were ye baptized in the name of Paul?

     iv. **1 Corinthians 1:14 (KJV)** I thank God that I baptized none of you, but Crispus and Gaius;

     v. **1 Corinthians 1:15 (KJV)** Lest any should say that I had baptized in mine own name.

     vi. **1 Corinthians 1:16 (KJV)** And I baptized also the household of Stephanas: besides, I know not whether I baptized any other.

26. Hence, it does not matter at all whether the Bible Scholar is called Paul, or Apollos; or Cephas, or Christ, and it also does not matter at all whether the doctrine, subject, theme, or topic is Crucifixion or Baptism or whatever!

27. What matters in Bible Interpretation and Translation is the exclusion of man's wisdom in the exposition of the Doctrine of Christ!

     i. **1 Corinthians 1:17 (KJV)** For Christ sent me not to baptize, but to preach the gospel: not with wisdom of words, lest the cross of Christ should be made of none effect.

     ii. **1 Corinthians 1:18 (KJV)** For the preaching of the cross is to them that perish foolishness; but unto us which are saved it is the power of God.

     iii. **1 Corinthians 1:19 (KJV)** For it is written, I will destroy the wisdom of the wise, and will bring to nothing the understanding of the prudent.

     iv. **1 Corinthians 1:20 (KJV)** Where *is* the wise? where *is* the scribe? where *is* the disputer of this world? hath not God made foolish the wisdom of this world?

28. Not only is the exclusion of man's wisdom in Bible Interpretation and Translation one of the cardinal requirements, but also the exclusion of man's theories, man's methodologies, man's approaches, and man's techniques in Bible Interpretation and

Translation, because the Holy Bible has concluded all human wisdom as vile, corrupted, and as foolishness!

    i.   **Isaiah 55:8 (KJV)** For my thoughts *are* not your thoughts, neither *are* your ways my ways, saith the LORD.

    ii.   **Isaiah 55:9 (KJV)** For *as* the heavens are higher than the earth, so are my ways higher than your ways, and my thoughts than your thoughts.

    iii.   **Micah 7:1 (KJV)** Woe is me! for I am as when they have gathered the summer fruits, as the grapegleanings of the vintage: *there is* no cluster to eat: my soul desired the firstripe fruit.

    iv.   **Micah 7:2 (KJV)** The good *man* is perished out of the earth: and *there is* none upright among men: they all lie in wait for blood; they hunt every man his brother with a net.

    v.   **Micah 7:3 (KJV)** That they may do evil with both hands earnestly, the prince asketh, and the judge *asketh* for a reward; and the great *man*, he uttereth his mischievous desire: so they wrap it up.

    vi.   **Micah 7:4 (KJV)** The best of them *is* as a brier: the most upright *is sharper* than a thorn hedge: the day of thy watchmen *and* thy visitation cometh; now shall be their perplexity.

    vii.   **1 Corinthians 2:14 (KJV)** But the natural man receiveth not the things of the Spirit of God: for they are foolishness unto him: neither can he know *them*, because they are spiritually discerned.

29. In other words, how can foolishness interpret and translate wisdom? Therefore, you must rely on the Holy Bible to interpret and translate itself! You CANNOT teach the Bible against the Bible! You MUST ALWAYS teach the Bible to agree with the Bible!

30. Your reliance on the Holy Bible to interpret and translate itself should bring you to believe the text/word and the self-interpretation and the self-translation that it says it is able to accomplish!

    i.   **1 Corinthians 1:21 (KJV)** For after that in the wisdom of God the world by wisdom knew not God, it pleased God by the foolishness of preaching to save them that believe.

31. This act of believing in the text/word of the Holy Scriptures to self-interpret and to self-translate does NOT rise to the level of unverifiable faith/belief or impregnable esoterism, but is the same act of using your pre-research data to believe in your scientific theory and research findings before you start the actual experiment!

    i.   **1 Corinthians 1:22 (KJV)** For the Jews require a sign, and the Greeks seek after wisdom:

32. In fact, as you can see in **1 Corinthians 1:22 (KJV)**, this theoretical approach to Bible Interpretation excludes not only signs, miracles, and wonders as justification for

believing in the efficacy of the theory, but also, this same theoretical approach excludes all human wisdom!

33. And so, yes, just as a scientific experiment would seem foolish in the beginning but later turn out to be viable, so also will a Bible Translation that uses this Bible-prescribed theoretical approach to Bible Interpretation seem foolish in the beginning, but as record has it, it has never been proved inadequate or wrong whereas all the theories of Bible Translation and Interpretation that men devised have all fallen short of complete reliability!

    i. **1 Corinthians 1:23 (KJV)** But we preach Christ crucified, unto the Jews a stumblingblock, and unto the Greeks foolishness;

34. What is certain is that all those who fall outside the above portrait or profile of people who should access the text of the Holy Scriptures, they will surely, like did the Jews in **1 Corinthians 1:23 (KJV)**, find this theoretical approach to Bible Interpretation a stumblingblock, and like did the Greeks, they will find it to be foolishness!

35. On the other hand, all those who are called or those who have received inspiration to understand the Word of God, shall attain unto much wisdom in the Gospel of Christ, NOT outside of it, because everything that is outside of the Gospel of Christ is foolishness!

    i. **1 Corinthians 1:24 (KJV)** But unto them which are called, both Jews and Greeks, Christ the power of God, and the wisdom of God.

    ii. **1 Corinthians 1:25 (KJV)** Because the foolishness of God is wiser than men; and the weakness of God is stronger than men.

36. They shall attain unto much wisdom in the Gospel of Christ and they shall also attain unto the Power of Christ that is in the text/word of the Holy Scriptures, which Power of Christ in the Text/Word of God is identifiable in its ability to transform the mind of the inquirer to the renewal of itself unto the reproduction of itself (Text/Word of God) by the thirties, by the sixties, and by the hundreds!

    i. **Matthew 13:3 (KJV)** And he spake many things unto them in parables, saying, Behold, a sower went forth to sow;

    ii. **Matthew 13:4 (KJV)** And when he sowed, some *seeds* fell by the way side, and the fowls came and devoured them up:

    iii. **Matthew 13:5 (KJV)** Some fell upon stony places, where they had not much earth: and forthwith they sprung up, because they had no deepness of earth:

    iv. **Matthew 13:6 (KJV)** And when the sun was up, they were scorched; and because they had no root, they withered away.

    v. **Matthew 13:7 (KJV)** And some fell among thorns; and the thorns sprung up, and choked them:

vi. **Matthew 13:8 (KJV)** But other fell into good ground, and brought forth fruit, some an hundredfold, some sixtyfold, some thirtyfold.

vii. **Matthew 13:9 (KJV)** Who hath ears to hear, let him hear.

37. In other words, a good Student of the Theoretical Approach to Bible Interpretation and Translation that I am showing you here, should, in the end, be able to replicate in his own words, the same Thoughts and Doctrines of Christ as contained in the Holy Bible, by the thirties, by the sixties, and by the hundreds:

    i. **Philippians 2:5 (KJV)** Let this mind be in you, which was also in Christ Jesus:

38. Again, the LORD God Almighty reiterates that the Theoretical Approach to Bible Interpretation and Translation requires the exclusion of all human wisdom in order to attain unto the wisdom which is in the Word of God!

    i. **1 Corinthians 1:26 (KJV)** For ye see your calling, brethren, how that not many wise men after the flesh, not many mighty, not many noble, *are called*:

39. Wherefore, even though the interpretation and translation of the Bible by the Bible may seem incongruous and foolish on the face of it, yet still must thou persist in its own foolishness, even though it is NOT foolishness but it seems and sounds foolish because of the very foolishness and corruption that are in all humans, therefore, do some see a mirror image of their own foolishness and corruption in the Holy Bible!

    i. **1 Corinthians 1:27 (KJV)** But God hath chosen the foolish things of the world to confound the wise; and God hath chosen the weak things of the world to confound the things which are mighty;

    ii. **1 Corinthians 1:28 (KJV)** And base things of the world, and things which are despised, hath God chosen, *yea*, and things which are not, to bring to nought things that are:

    iii. **1 Corinthians 1:29 (KJV)** That no flesh should glory in his presence.

40. But thou must persist in the Bible's own foolishness because the Holy Bible being a mirror of the human face and character that it is, the foolishness and the contradictions that you see in the Holy Bible are a reflection of your own foolishness and contradictions, and they do hide a multitude of wise counsel ONLY when you exclude yourself, as **1 Corinthians 1:28-29 (KJV)** reveals, and allow the Word of God to speak, to translate itself, and to interpret itself!

    i. **Numbers 27:21 (KJV)** And he shall stand before Eleazar the priest, who shall ask *counsel* for him after the judgment of Urim before the LORD: at his word shall they go out, and at his word they shall come in, *both* he, and all the children of Israel with him, even all the congregation.

ii. **Deuteronomy 32:28 (KJV)** For they *are* a nation void of counsel, neither *is there any* understanding in them.

iii. **Judges 20:18 (KJV)** And the children of Israel arose, and went up to the house of God, and asked counsel of God, and said, Which of us shall go up first to the battle against the children of Benjamin? And the LORD said, Judah *shall go up* first.

iv. **Psalm 33:11 (KJV)** The counsel of the LORD standeth for ever, the thoughts of his heart to all generations.

v. **Proverbs 27:19 (KJV)** As in water face *answereth* to face, so the heart of man to man.

vi. **Isaiah 58:13 (KJV)** If thou turn away thy foot from the sabbath, *from* doing thy pleasure on my holy day; and call the sabbath a delight, the holy of the LORD, honourable; and shalt honour him, not doing thine own ways, nor finding thine own pleasure, nor speaking *thine own* words:

vii. **Ezekiel 3:4 (KJV)** And he said unto me, Son of man, go, get thee unto the house of Israel, and speak with my words unto them.

viii. **Hebrews 4:12 (KJV)** For the word of God *is* quick, and powerful, and sharper than any twoedged sword, piercing even to the dividing asunder of soul and spirit, and of the joints and marrow, and *is* a discerner of the thoughts and intents of the heart.

41. In the end, the LORD God is showing you that the efficacy of your exercise of the Theoretical Approach to Bible Interpretation and Translation will be made evident in your true and faithful reflection of the meaning of the Word of God devoid of any form of contrariness when compared against the Word of God!

    i. **1 Corinthians 1:30 (KJV)** But of him are ye in Christ Jesus, who of God is made unto us wisdom, and righteousness, and sanctification, and redemption:

    ii. **1 Corinthians 1:31 (KJV)** That, according as it is written, He that glorieth, let him glory in the Lord.

42. In other words, by means of comparison, your interpretation and translation of the Word of God must be one with the Word of God!

CHAPTER 2: APPROACHES TO BIBLE INTERPRETATION AND BIBLE TRANSLATION – 1

43. The Testimony of God, or, the Holy Scriptures, or, the Holy Bible, has only one theme, namely, Jesus Christ and Him crucified!

    i. **1 Corinthians 2:1 (KJV)** And I, brethren, when I came to you, came not with excellency of speech or of wisdom, declaring unto you the testimony of God.

    ii. **1 Corinthians 2:2 (KJV)** For I determined not to know any thing among you, save Jesus Christ, and him crucified.

44. It means that all the Books and writings in the entire Holy Bible is about the LORD Jesus Christ!

    i. **John 5:46 (KJV)** For had ye believed Moses, ye would have believed me: for he wrote of me.

    ii. **John 14:6 (KJV)** Jesus saith unto him, I am the way, the truth, and the life: no man cometh unto the Father, but by me.

    iii. **Acts 10:43 (KJV)** To him give all the prophets witness, that through his name whosoever believeth in him shall receive remission of sins.

45. Therefore, a successful Bible Interpretation or Translation is the one that also has as its theme: Jesus Christ and Him crucified.

46. It also means that a Bible Interpretation or Translation that deviates from the LORD Jesus Christ and the Doctrines of the LORD Jesus Christ, is incorrect and false, just the same way as you cannot argue against the Constitution of a Country and be successful, because normally, the correct and accepted norm is that Judges and Lawyers speak and write from the strength, from the point of view, from the spirit, and from the prescriptions of the Law whereby, a Judge or a Lawyer is NOT a Judge or a Lawyer anymore when he speaks and writes against and contrary to the Constitution of the Land, and the same is with the Holy Bible the Word of God and the Law Book of God!

47. The speech, the preaching, or the writings of a true Man of God must be presented in a way to enhance and demonstrate the Spirit and Power of God!

    i. **1 Corinthians 2:4 (KJV)** And my speech and my preaching *was* not with enticing words of man's wisdom, but in demonstration of the Spirit and of power:

    ii. **1 Corinthians 2:5 (KJV)** That your faith should not stand in the wisdom of men, but in the power of God.

48. What do the Spirit and Power of God do?

49. Here is the answer:

i. The Power of God produces Salvation in every person who believes the report and witness of the LORD Jesus Christ!

50. How does this production of Salvation happen? By what means?

51. By means of speaking, preaching, writing, and teaching the Gospel of Christ to people, to the effectual renewing of their mind toward God Almighty!

i. **Romans 1:15 (KJV)** So, as much as in me is, I am ready to preach the gospel to you that are at Rome also.

ii. **Romans 1:16 (KJV)** For I am not ashamed of the gospel of Christ: for it is the power of God unto salvation to every one that believeth; to the Jew first, and also to the Greek.

iii. **Romans 1:17 (KJV)** For therein is the righteousness of God revealed from faith to faith: as it is written, The just shall live by faith.

52. The revelation in **Romans 1:15-17 (KJV)** is that, when a Man of God claims to have power from God in Ministry, then, you should be able to measure or identify the source of that power through the following two steps:

i. ONE – Are the words of the Man of God 100% derived from the Gospel of Christ, from the Word of God, form the Holy Scriptures?

ii. TWO – When that Man of God speaks, preaches, teaches, or writes his words, do people hear or read it and become convinced of its contents and believe the contents of the speech or writing such that they turn away from the thoughts that they previously held to now embrace the new thoughts of Christ that are contained in the speech or writings of the Man of God?

53. The moment that the above two steps are successfully accomplished through the speech or writings of a Man of God, then, that is the same moment that he has demonstrated the Power of God unto Salvation, because, Salvation is first measured in the mind before it appears in the deeds of the flesh!

i. **Colossians 1:21 (KJV)** And you, that were sometime alienated and enemies in *your* mind by wicked works, yet now hath he reconciled

ii. **Romans 12:2 (KJV)** And be not conformed to this world: but be ye transformed by the renewing of your mind, that ye may prove what *is* that good, and acceptable, and perfect, will of God.

iii. **Titus 3:5 (KJV)** Not by works of righteousness which we have done, but according to his mercy he saved us, by the washing of regeneration, and renewing of the Holy Ghost;

54. Since **Romans 1:16 (KJV)** tells us that the Gospel of Christ is the Power of God unto Salvation, your belief/faith should be anchored in this Power of God, meaning, in the Gospel of Christ!

      i. **Romans 1:16 (KJV)** For I am not ashamed of the gospel of Christ: for it is the power of God unto salvation to every one that believeth; to the Jew first, and also to the Greek.

      ii. **1 Corinthians 2:5 (KJV)** That your faith should not stand in the wisdom of men, but in the power of God.

55. This same Gospel of Christ, though it might sound foolish to some, yet it is the ultimate wisdom that can be accessed ONLY through the revelation and inspiration from the Holy Spirit of God!

      i. **1 Corinthians 2:6 (KJV)** Howbeit we speak wisdom among them that are perfect: yet not the wisdom of this world, nor of the princes of this world, that come to nought:

56. What are revelation and inspiration?

57. Revelation and inspiration are simply different shades of thought that come to your mind as a result of reading the text of the Gospel of Christ!

58. It is the same as what Academics, Judges, and Lawyers call "the spirit of the text", meaning that there is an unseen thought, imagery, picture, understanding, poetry that accompanies a text while still remaining invisible and untouchable!

59. When this unseen thought, imagery, picture, understanding, poetry accompanies an ordinary text, it is called "the spirit of the text"!

60. When this same unseen thought, imagery, picture, understanding, poetry accompanies the text of the Holy Scriptures, it is called "the Holy Spirit"!

      i. **Job 32:8 (KJV)** But *there is* a spirit in man: and the inspiration of the Almighty giveth them understanding.

      ii. **2 Timothy 3:16 (KJV)** All scripture *is* given by inspiration of God, and *is* profitable for doctrine, for reproof, for correction, for instruction in righteousness:

61. Therefore, according to **1 Corinthians 2:6 (KJV)**, when a man operates according to, or under "the spirit of the text", meaning that his life is predicated on all sorts of texts that are outside the realm of the Gospel of Christ such as all academic and intellectual and scientific texts and pursuits of study, then, such a man has wisdom but his wisdom is worldly wisdom and is vain wisdom!

      i. **1 Corinthians 2:6 (KJV)** Howbeit we speak wisdom among them that are perfect: yet not the wisdom of this world, nor of the princes of this world, that come to nought:

62. Such a worldly wisdom vain man is NOT yet one with the Holy Bible and its only one theme of Jesus Christ and Him crucified as **1 Corinthians 2:2 (KJV)** reveals!

      i. **1 Corinthians 2:1 (KJV)** And I, brethren, when I came to you, came not with excellency of speech or of wisdom, declaring unto you the testimony of God.

      ii. **1 Corinthians 2:2 (KJV)** For I determined not to know any thing among you, save Jesus Christ, and him crucified.

63. On the other hand, when the man is completely one with the Holy Bible and its singular theme of Jesus Christ and Him crucified as **1 Corinthians 2:2 (KJV)** reveals, then, his spirit and the Spirit of the Word of God have become one Spirit!

      i. **Philippians 1:27 (KJV)** Only let your conversation be as it becometh the gospel of Christ: that whether I come and see you, or else be absent, I may hear of your affairs, that ye stand fast in one spirit, with one mind striving together for the faith of the gospel;

      ii. **1 Corinthians 6:17 (KJV)** But he that is joined unto the Lord is one spirit.

64. On the other hand, according to the same **1 Corinthians 2:6 (KJV)**, when a man operates according to, or under "the Holy Spirit", meaning that his life is mainly predicated on the text of the Holy Scriptures and he believes in and lives by its contents, then, such a man has perfect wisdom, has the ultimate wisdom, and has wisdom that becomes his Key of entry into another realm of spirit existence called Heaven!

65. Now, this wisdom that has the ability to transform my thinking here on Earth as well as guarantee my entry into the next Realm of Heaven, how accessible is this wisdom?

      i. **1 Corinthians 2:7 (KJV)** But we speak the wisdom of God in a mystery, *even* the hidden *wisdom*, which God ordained before the world unto our glory:

66. The wisdom of God is either accessible or hidden "to every man according to his several ability"!

      i. **Matthew 25:15 (KJV)** And unto one he gave five talents, to another two, and to another one; to every man according to his several ability; and straightway took his journey.

      ii. **Romans 14:5 (KJV)** One man esteemeth one day above another: another esteemeth every day *alike*. Let every man be fully persuaded in his own mind.

67. The wisdom of God does NOT become more accessible because of one's social standing, money, rank, education, or intellectual ability!

      i. **1 Corinthians 2:8 (KJV)** Which none of the princes of this world knew: for had they known *it*, they would not have crucified the Lord of glory.

    ii. **1 Corinthians 2:10 (KJV)** But God hath revealed *them* unto us by his Spirit: for the Spirit searcheth all things, yea, the deep things of God.

68. Concerning **1 Corinthians 2:10 (KJV)**, the meaning is that, just as the understanding of literature or legal text is hard to some yet easy to others who are endowed with certain inexplicable abilities, so also is the understanding of the Word of God easy to those who are filled with the Word of God the Gospel of Christ!

    i. **Deuteronomy 17:14 (KJV)** When thou art come unto the land which the LORD thy God giveth thee, and shalt possess it, and shalt dwell therein, and shalt say, I will set a king over me, like as all the nations that *are* about me;

    ii. **Deuteronomy 17:15 (KJV)** Thou shalt in any wise set *him* king over thee, whom the LORD thy God shall choose: *one* from among thy brethren shalt thou set king over thee: thou mayest not set a stranger over thee, which *is* not thy brother.

    iii. **Deuteronomy 17:18 (KJV)** And it shall be, when he sitteth upon the throne of his kingdom, that he shall write him a copy of this law in a book out of *that which is* before the priests the Levites:

    iv. **Deuteronomy 17:19 (KJV)** And it shall be with him, and he shall read therein all the days of his life: that he may learn to fear the LORD his God, to keep all the words of this law and these statutes, to do them:

    v. **Deuteronomy 17:20 (KJV)** That his heart be not lifted up above his brethren, and that he turn not aside from the commandment, *to* the right hand, or *to* the left: to the end that he may prolong *his* days in his kingdom, he, and his children, in the midst of Israel.

    vi. **Joshua 1:8 (KJV)** This book of the law shall not depart out of thy mouth; but thou shalt meditate therein day and night, that thou mayest observe to do according to all that is written therein: for then thou shalt make thy way prosperous, and then thou shalt have good success.

    vii. **Proverbs 14:6 (KJV)** A scorner seeketh wisdom, and *findeth it* not: but knowledge *is* easy unto him that understandeth.

    viii. **Colossians 1:9 (KJV)** For this cause we also, since the day we heard *it*, do not cease to pray for you, and to desire that ye might be filled with the knowledge of his will in all wisdom and spiritual understanding;

69. Just as it requires interrogating a man in order to know the unseen intent and the thoughts of his deed, so also does it require interrogating the Word of God in the Word of God so that the unseen Spirit in the Text of the Word can yield inspiration and understanding of the Word unto you!

  i. **1 Corinthians 2:11 (KJV)** For what man knoweth the things of a man, save the spirit of man which is in him? even so the things of God knoweth no man, but the Spirit of God.

  ii. **Job 32:8 (KJV)** But *there is* a spirit in man: and the inspiration of the Almighty giveth them understanding.

  iii. **2 Timothy 3:16 (KJV)** All scripture *is* given by inspiration of God, and *is* profitable for doctrine, for reproof, for correction, for instruction in righteousness:

70. That is why it is impossible to access the Word of God from outside the Word of God, just as it is impossible to access the true meanings of the Constitution of a country from outside a prior legal training in its jurisprudence!

71. Therefore, the Spirit of God mentioned in **1 Corinthians 2:11 (KJV)**: that is the catalyst and the means to access and understand the Word of God the Holy Scriptures, and it is the equivalent of the legal training that you need in order to correctly access and understand the contents of a legal text!

  i. **1 Corinthians 2:12 (KJV)** Now we have received, not the spirit of the world, but the spirit which is of God; that we might know the things that are freely given to us of God.

72. Now, the means or the methodology through which to access and understand the Word of God the Holy Scriptures, by the teaching or inspiration of the Holy Spirit, is called: Comparing Spiritual Things with Spiritual!

  i. **1 Corinthians 2:13 (KJV)** Which things also we speak, not in the words which man's wisdom teacheth, but which the Holy Ghost teacheth; comparing spiritual things with spiritual.

73. Just as "the spirit of the text", as they say, is not seen but works in the mind as you read, to the effectual understanding of a literature text or a legal text, so also the Spirit of God is not seen but works in the mind to the effectual understanding of the Word of God as you read it, and when the understanding thereof is hidden, then, it is hidden, NOT because of some esoteric unverifiable non-faith clairvoyance or the lack thereof, because of the inherent incapacity and mental inadequacy of the person himself who lacks the intellectual capacity to grasp deep and difficult concepts!

  i. **1 Corinthians 2:14 (KJV)** But the natural man receiveth not the things of the Spirit of God: for they are foolishness unto him: neither can he know *them*, because they are spiritually discerned.

  ii. **2 Corinthians 4:3 (KJV)** But if our gospel be hid, it is hid to them that are lost:

74. What does it mean: Comparing Spiritual Things with Spiritual?

75. Based on **1 Corinthians 2:11-13 (KJV)**, we understand that "comparing spiritual things with spiritual" is the methodology to access and to understand the deep thoughts, the concepts, and the doctrines that are hidden in the Word of God!

76. In order to correctly understand the phrase "comparing spiritual things with spiritual", we first need to understand what "spiritual" is!

77. What does "spiritual" mean?

78. Here is the answer!

    i. **John 1:1 (KJV)** In the beginning was the Word, and the Word was with God, and the Word was God.

    ii. **John 1:2 (KJV)** The same was in the beginning with God.

    iii. **John 1:14 (KJV)** And the Word was made flesh, and dwelt among us, (and we beheld his glory, the glory as of the only begotten of the Father,) full of grace and truth.

    iv. **Romans 7:14 (KJV)** For we know that the law is spiritual: but I am carnal, sold under sin.

    v. **1 Corinthians 6:17 (KJV)** But he that is joined unto the Lord is one spirit.

    vi. **2 Corinthians 3:17 (KJV)** Now the Lord is that Spirit: and where the Spirit of the Lord *is*, there *is* liberty.

79. As you can see from the above body of evidence, we do not need to travel outside the Holy Scriptures the Word of God into some unknown esoteric great beyond, in order to pluck off the meaning of the word "spiritual"!

80. As you can see, you need a prior rich understanding of figures of speech in order to correctly understand the personification, the metaphor, the irony, the hyperbole, the paradox, the poetry, the geography, and every sort of human intellectual sphere that is contained in the Holy Scriptures the Word of God!

81. Hence, the Word of God the Holy Scriptures, is God!

82. Then, the same Word of God the Holy Scriptures is a Man with flesh called Yeshua Christ!

83. Then, the same Word of God the Holy Scriptures, is "spiritual"!

84. Then, the same Word of God the Holy Scriptures turns a person into a spirit once that person fully believes the same Word of God the Holy Scriptures!

85. Then, the same Word of God the Holy Scriptures is the Holy Spirit who gives you that inspiration and understanding to understand the same Word of God the Holy Scriptures!

    i. **Haggai 2:5 (KJV)** *According to* the word that I covenanted with you when ye came out of Egypt, so my spirit remaineth among you: fear ye not.

86. Now that we have understood the word "spiritual", we shall return to the question that says: What does it mean: Comparing Spiritual Things with Spiritual?

87. From our prior understanding of "the spiritual", it becomes easy to define the phrase: "Comparing Spiritual Things with Spiritual", and it means: "comparing the Word of God the Holy Scriptures with the Word of God the Holy Scriptures"!

      i. **1 Corinthians 2:13 (KJV)** Which things also we speak, not in the words which man's wisdom teacheth, but which the Holy Ghost teacheth; comparing spiritual things with spiritual.

88. Therefore, as a good Bible Interpreter and Translator, your success in rendering a good and correct Bible Interpretation and Translation lies in your ability to successfully compare your understanding and interpretation of the text of the Holy Bible to each and every verse in the entire Holy Bible, with the express aim of eliminating all contradiction to attain zero contradiction, zero variableness, and with the express aim of achieving "Perfect Harmony" between your translation and the entire remainder of the Holy Bible!

89. Can a Bible Interpreter or Translator set aside these approaches and still attain a good Bible Translation? NO!

      i. **1 Corinthians 2:14 (KJV)** But the natural man receiveth not the things of the Spirit of God: for they are foolishness unto him: neither can he know *them*, because they are spiritually discerned.

90. Your ability to come to the correct understanding of the Word of God the Holy Scriptures derives 100% from your 100% immersion into the Word of God the Holy Scriptures!

      i. **1 Corinthians 2:15 (KJV)** But he that is spiritual judgeth all things, yet he himself is judged of no man.

      ii. **1 Corinthians 2:16 (KJV)** For who hath known the mind of the Lord, that he may instruct him? But we have the mind of Christ.

CHAPTER 3: APPROACHES TO BIBLE INTERPRETATION AND BIBLE TRANSLATION – 2

91. In Approaches to Bible Interpretation and Bible Translation – 1, I identified two men or two Translators:

92. The Worldly Wisdom Vain Man who is NOT yet one with the Holy Bible and its only one theme of Jesus Christ and Him crucified as required in **1 Corinthians 2:2 (KJV)**!

    i. **1 Corinthians 2:1 (KJV)** And I, brethren, when I came to you, came not with excellency of speech or of wisdom, declaring unto you the testimony of God.

    ii. **1 Corinthians 2:2 (KJV)** For I determined not to know any thing among you, save Jesus Christ, and him crucified.

93. Then, you have the Spiritual Man who has become completely one with the Holy Bible and its singular theme of Jesus Christ and Him crucified as **1 Corinthians 2:2 (KJV)** reveals, and, because of that oneness, his spirit and the Spirit of the Word of God have become one Spirit!

    i. **Philippians 1:27 (KJV)** Only let your conversation be as it becometh the gospel of Christ: that whether I come and see you, or else be absent, I may hear of your affairs, that ye stand fast in one spirit, with one mind striving together for the faith of the gospel;

    ii. **1 Corinthians 6:17 (KJV)** But he that is joined unto the Lord is one spirit.

94. Now, in this chapter, we are going to find out how to identify The Worldly Wisdom Vain Man whose other names are The Carnal Man and The Babe in Christ!

    i. **1 Corinthians 3:1 (KJV)** And I, brethren, could not speak unto you as unto spiritual, but as unto carnal, *even* as unto babes in Christ.

95. The Worldly Wisdom Vain Man, The Carnal Man, or, The Babe in Christ can be identified by reason of the milk that he drinks!

    i. **1 Corinthians 3:2 (KJV)** I have fed you with milk, and not with meat: for hitherto ye were not able *to bear it*, neither yet now are ye able.

96. To be a Babe in Christ who drinks milk is to be unable or to lack the mental and intellectual and spiritual capacity to grasp deep difficult spiritual concepts in the Holy Bible the Word of God!

    i. **John 16:12 (KJV)** I have yet many things to say unto you, but ye cannot bear them now.

    ii. **John 16:13 (KJV)** Howbeit when he, the Spirit of truth, is come, he will guide you into all truth: for he shall not speak of himself; but

whatsoever he shall hear, *that* shall he speak: and he will shew you things to come.

iii. **John 16:14 (KJV)** He shall glorify me: for he shall receive of mine, and shall shew *it* unto you.

iv. **2 Peter 3:14 (KJV)** Wherefore, beloved, seeing that ye look for such things, be diligent that ye may be found of him in peace, without spot, and blameless.

v. **2 Peter 3:15 (KJV)** And account *that* the longsuffering of our Lord *is* salvation; even as our beloved brother Paul also according to the wisdom given unto him hath written unto you;

vi. **2 Peter 3:16 (KJV)** As also in all *his* epistles, speaking in them of these things; in which are some things hard to be understood, which they that are unlearned and unstable wrest, as *they do* also the other scriptures, unto their own destruction.

97. Another way to identify The Worldly Wisdom Vain Man, The Carnal Man, or, The Babe in Christ is his penchant, because of his weakness in Christ Doctrine, and because he is destitute of the Truth of the Gospel of Christ, to go outside of the Holy Bible into the world to use theories, lessons, examples, thoughts, ideas, jokes, references, books, personalities, personal testimonies, and non-Biblical stories, to preach and to teach a sermon! That is wrong and promptly reveals the speaker as The Carnal Man!

i. **Proverbs 26:18 (KJV)** As a mad *man* who casteth firebrands, arrows, and death,

ii. **Proverbs 26:19 (KJV)** So *is* the man *that* deceiveth his neighbour, and saith, Am not I in sport?

iii. **Ephesians 5:4 (KJV)** Neither filthiness, nor foolish talking, nor jesting, which are not convenient: but rather giving of thanks.

iv. **1 Timothy 1:1 (KJV)** Paul, an apostle of Jesus Christ by the commandment of God our Saviour, and Lord Jesus Christ, *which is* our hope;

v. **1 Timothy 1:2 (KJV)** Unto Timothy, *my* own son in the faith: Grace, mercy, *and* peace, from God our Father and Jesus Christ our Lord.

vi. **1 Timothy 1:3 (KJV)** As I besought thee to abide still at Ephesus, when I went into Macedonia, that thou mightest charge some that they teach no other doctrine,

vii. **1 Timothy 1:4 (KJV)** Neither give heed to fables and endless genealogies, which minister questions, rather than godly edifying which is in faith: *so do*.

viii. **1 Timothy 4:6 (KJV)** If thou put the brethren in remembrance of these things, thou shalt be a good minister of Jesus Christ, nourished up in the words of faith and of good doctrine, whereunto thou hast attained.

ix. **1 Timothy 4:7 (KJV)** But refuse profane and old wives' fables, and exercise thyself *rather* unto godliness.

x. **2 Timothy 4:1 (KJV)** I charge *thee* therefore before God, and the Lord Jesus Christ, who shall judge the quick and the dead at his appearing and his kingdom;

xi. **2 Timothy 4:2 (KJV)** Preach the word; be instant in season, out of season; reprove, rebuke, exhort with all longsuffering and doctrine.

xii. **2 Timothy 4:3 (KJV)** For the time will come when they will not endure sound doctrine; but after their own lusts shall they heap to themselves teachers, having itching ears;

xiii. **2 Timothy 4:4 (KJV)** And they shall turn away *their* ears from the truth, and shall be turned unto fables.

xiv. **Titus 1:14 (KJV)** Not giving heed to Jewish fables, and commandments of men, that turn from the truth.

xv. **Titus 1:15 (KJV)** Unto the pure all things *are* pure: but unto them that are defiled and unbelieving *is* nothing pure; but even their mind and conscience is defiled.

xvi. **Titus 1:16 (KJV)** They profess that they know God; but in works they deny *him*, being abominable, and disobedient, and unto every good work reprobate.

xvii. **2 Peter 1:16 (KJV)** For we have not followed cunningly devised fables, when we made known unto you the power and coming of our Lord Jesus Christ, but were eyewitnesses of his majesty.

98. Another way to identify The Worldly Wisdom Vain Man, The Carnal Man, or, The Babe in Christ is the division, the deviation, the contradiction, the discord, the contrariness, the divergence, or the disharmony that his Bible Interpretation and Bible Translation reveal when compared to and examined in the entire Holy Bible!

i. **1 Corinthians 3:3 (KJV)** For ye are yet carnal: for whereas *there is* among you envying, and strife, and divisions, are ye not carnal, and walk as men?

99. In other words, his Bible Interpretation and Bible Translation do NOT reflect oneness or one accord with the entire Holy Bible hence that Bible Interpretation or Bible Translation has to be rejected! Here is the LORD Jesus Christ rejecting a Bible

Interpretation that goes against another verse in the Holy Bible in another part of the Bible!

    i. **Luke 20:9 (KJV)** Then began he to speak to the people this parable; A certain man planted a vineyard, and let it forth to husbandmen, and went into a far country for a long time.

    ii. **Luke 20:10 (KJV)** And at the season he sent a servant to the husbandmen, that they should give him of the fruit of the vineyard: but the husbandmen beat him, and sent *him* away empty.

    iii. **Luke 20:11 (KJV)** And again he sent another servant: and they beat him also, and entreated *him* shamefully, and sent *him* away empty.

    iv. **Luke 20:12 (KJV)** And again he sent a third: and they wounded him also, and cast *him* out.

    v. **Luke 20:13 (KJV)** Then said the lord of the vineyard, What shall I do? I will send my beloved son: it may be they will reverence *him* when they see him.

    vi. **Luke 20:14 (KJV)** But when the husbandmen saw him, they reasoned among themselves, saying, This is the heir: come, let us kill him, that the inheritance may be ours.

    vii. **Luke 20:15 (KJV)** So they cast him out of the vineyard, and killed *him*. What therefore shall the lord of the vineyard do unto them?

    viii. **Luke 20:16 (KJV)** He shall come and destroy these husbandmen, and shall give the vineyard to others. **And when they heard** *it*, **they said, God forbid.**

    ix. **Luke 20:17 (KJV)** And he beheld them, and said, What is this then that is written, The stone which the builders rejected, the same is become the head of the corner?

100.   Here, again, is the LORD Jesus Christ rejecting a Bible Interpretation that goes against another verse in the Holy Bible in another part of the Bible!

    i. **Matthew 22:41 (KJV)** While the Pharisees were gathered together, Jesus asked them,

    ii. **Matthew 22:42 (KJV)** Saying, What think ye of Christ? whose son is he? They say unto him, *The Son* of David.

    iii. **Matthew 22:43 (KJV)** He saith unto them, How then doth David in spirit call him Lord, saying,

    iv. **Matthew 22:44 (KJV)** The LORD said unto my Lord, Sit thou on my right hand, till I make thine enemies thy footstool?

    v. **Matthew 22:45 (KJV)** If David then call him Lord, how is he his son?

vi. **Matthew 22:46 (KJV)** And no man was able to answer him a word, neither durst any *man* from that day forth ask him any more *questions.*

101.   Another way to identify The Worldly Wisdom Vain Man, The Carnal Man, or, The Babe in Christ is that he uses men's theories to do his Bible Interpretation, Translation, and Sermon Preparation instead of using God's Theory for Bible Interpretation and Translation, as I have already identified in my writings!

    i. **1 Corinthians 3:4 (KJV)** For while one saith, I am of Paul; and another, I *am* of Apollos; are ye not carnal?

    ii. **1 Corinthians 3:5 (KJV)** Who then is Paul, and who *is* Apollos, but ministers by whom ye believed, even as the Lord gave to every man?

    iii. **1 Corinthians 3:6 (KJV)** I have planted, Apollos watered; but God gave the increase.

    iv. **1 Corinthians 3:7 (KJV)** So then neither is he that planteth any thing, neither he that watereth; but God that giveth the increase.

102.   For the very reason that there is no wisdom of man that is qualified to examine the wisdom of God since all of man's wisdom is classified as foolishness, therefore being foolishness, it cannot be used to examine wisdom!

    i. **1 Corinthians 1:20 (KJV)** Where *is* the wise? where *is* the scribe? where *is* the disputer of this world? hath not God made foolish the wisdom of this world?

    ii. **1 Corinthians 2:6 (KJV)** Howbeit we speak wisdom among them that are perfect: yet not the wisdom of this world, nor of the princes of this world, that come to nought:

    iii. **1 Corinthians 3:19 (KJV)** For the wisdom of this world is foolishness with God. For it is written, He taketh the wise in their own craftiness.

103.   So, then, Bible Interpretation and Bible Translation have to be Bible-centered and God-centered in order to correctly accomplish the task of transmitting the correct information, message, and meaning, for it is impossible for the Created to examine the Creator!

    i. **1 Corinthians 3:9 (KJV)** For we are labourers together with God: ye are God's husbandry, *ye are* God's building.

    ii. **1 Corinthians 3:10 (KJV)** According to the grace of God which is given unto me, as a wise masterbuilder, I have laid the foundation, and another buildeth thereon. But let every man take heed how he buildeth thereupon.

104.   Now, even though the theory is one for all Bible Interpreters and Translators as **1 Corinthians 3:11 (KJV)** reveals, the final work will be different for all Bible

Interpreters and Translators by reason of each other's training, several ability, and mental capacity!

    i. **1 Corinthians 3:8 (KJV)** Now he that planteth and he that watereth are one: and every man shall receive his own reward according to his own labour.

    ii. **1 Corinthians 3:11 (KJV)** For other foundation can no man lay than that is laid, which is Jesus Christ.

    iii. **Matthew 25:15 (KJV)** And unto one he gave five talents, to another two, and to another one; to every man according to his several ability; and straightway took his journey.

105.   Another way to identify The Worldly Wisdom Vain Man, The Carnal Man, or, The Babe in Christ is through the testing of his Bible Interpretation, Bible Translation, and Sermon Preparation in the Holy Scriptures to see whether there is 100% harmony!

    i. **1 Corinthians 3:12 (KJV)** Now if any man build upon this foundation gold, silver, precious stones, wood, hay, stubble;

    ii. **1 Corinthians 3:13 (KJV)** Every man's work shall be made manifest: for the day shall declare it, because it shall be revealed by fire; and the fire shall try every man's work of what sort it is.

    iii. **1 Corinthians 3:14 (KJV)** If any man's work abide which he hath built thereupon, he shall receive a reward.

    iv. **1 Corinthians 3:15 (KJV)** If any man's work shall be burned, he shall suffer loss: but he himself shall be saved; yet so as by fire.

106.   The testing of Bible Interpretation, Bible Translation, and Sermon Preparation in the Holy Scriptures is what is rendered in metaphorical language in **1 Corinthians 3:12-15 (KJV)** as: "it shall be revealed by fire; and the fire shall try every man's work of what sort it is", because of the very reason that the Word of God the Holy Scriptures itself is Fire, again, a metaphor!

    i. **Deuteronomy 4:24 (KJV)** For the LORD thy God *is* a consuming fire, *even* a jealous God.

    ii. **Deuteronomy 9:3 (KJV)** Understand therefore this day, that the LORD thy God *is* he which goeth over before thee; *as* a consuming fire he shall destroy them, and he shall bring them down before thy face: so shalt thou drive them out, and destroy them quickly, as the LORD hath said unto thee.

    iii. **John 1:1 (KJV)** In the beginning was the Word, and the Word was with God, and the Word was God.

    iv. **Hebrews 12:29 (KJV)** For our God *is* a consuming fire.

107.   A Bible Interpreter and a Bible Translator who has become one with the Spirit of the Text of the Word of God, as I have already explained heretofore, is also called: The Temple of God!

    i.   **1 Corinthians 3:16 (KJV)** Know ye not that ye are the temple of God, and *that* the Spirit of God dwelleth in you?

108.   To become a Temple of God and fall back from the requirements of remaining a Temple of God through the total adherence to the Word of God the Holy Scriptures, is to make a shipwreck of your life!

    i.   **1 Corinthians 3:17 (KJV)** If any man defile the temple of God, him shall God destroy; for the temple of God is holy, which *temple* ye are.

    ii. **1 Timothy 1:18 (KJV)** This charge I commit unto thee, son Timothy, according to the prophecies which went before on thee, that thou by them mightest war a good warfare;

    iii. **1 Timothy 1:19 (KJV)** Holding faith, and a good conscience; which some having put away concerning faith have made shipwreck:

    iv. **1 Timothy 1:20 (KJV)** Of whom is Hymenaeus and Alexander; whom I have delivered unto Satan, that they may learn not to blaspheme.

109.   Again, as I mentioned before, you cannot hold the wisdom, concepts, and theories of this world and access the knowledge in the Word of God at the same time, no, you have to drop the one in order to take up the other, and since the Word of God the Holy Bible comes entirely in metaphors, in proverbs, in parables and in dark sayings, very often, the first impression from people on the Word of God is that it is foolishness and it does not make sense, and yes, it was deliberately made so, seemingly senseless, in order to weed out the misfits and the undesirables away from the Word of God!

    i.   **1 Corinthians 3:18 (KJV)** Let no man deceive himself. If any man among you seemeth to be wise in this world, let him become a fool, that he may be wise.

    ii. **1 Corinthians 3:19 (KJV)** For the wisdom of this world is foolishness with God. For it is written, He taketh the wise in their own craftiness.

    iii. **1 Corinthians 3:20 (KJV)** And again, The Lord knoweth the thoughts of the wise, that they are vain.

110.   Hence, you have to drop your worldly wisdom to become a fool in the Word of God in order to appreciate the foolishness of the Word of God!

    i.   **Ecclesiastes 7:25 (KJV)** I applied mine heart to know, and to search, and to seek out wisdom, and the reason *of things*, and to know the wickedness of folly, even of foolishness *and* madness:

    ii. **1 Corinthians 1:18 (KJV)** For the preaching of the cross is to them that perish foolishness; but unto us which are saved it is the power of God.

    iii. **1 Corinthians 1:21 (KJV)** For after that in the wisdom of God the world by wisdom knew not God, it pleased God by the foolishness of preaching to save them that believe.

    iv. **2 Corinthians 4:3 (KJV)** But if our gospel be hid, it is hid to them that are lost:

    v. **Psalm 78:2 (KJV)** I will open my mouth in a parable: I will utter dark sayings of old:

    vi. **Proverbs 1:6 (KJV)** To understand a proverb, and the interpretation; the words of the wise, and their dark sayings.

    vii. **Matthew 13:34 (KJV)** All these things spake Jesus unto the multitude in parables; and without a parable spake he not unto them:

    viii. **Mark 4:34 (KJV)** But without a parable spake he not unto them: and when they were alone, he expounded all things to his disciples.

111.   As guided by the verses in the Holy Scriptures which often uses repetition for emphasis, we conclude this chapter with a repetition of what I wrote earlier regarding **1 Corinthians 3:4-7 (KJV)** saying: Another way to identify The Worldly Wisdom Vain Man, The Carnal Man, or, The Babe in Christ is that he uses men's theories to do his Bible Interpretation, Translation, and Sermon Preparation instead of using God's Theory for Bible Interpretation and Translation, and here, in this conclusion, the correct approach is: DO NOT USE MEN'S THEORIES TO DO BIBLE INTERPRETATION, BIBLE TRANSLATION, AND SERMON PREPARATION!

    i. **1 Corinthians 3:21 (KJV)** Therefore let no man glory in men. For all things are yours;

    ii. **1 Corinthians 3:22 (KJV)** Whether Paul, or Apollos, or Cephas, or the world, or life, or death, or things present, or things to come; all are yours;

    iii. **1 Corinthians 3:23 (KJV)** And ye are Christ's; and Christ *is* God's.

CHAPTER 4: THE JOB DESCRIPTION OF A TRUE MINISTER OF CHRIST

112.   This chapter 4 in the Book of 1 Corinthians is the Job Description of a true Minister of Christ. In other words, the Portrait of a true Man of God! Or, when you give an account of a true Man of God, what elements or points should you consider?

     i. **1 Corinthians 4:1 (KJV)** Let a man so account of us, as of the ministers of Christ, and stewards of the mysteries of God.

113.   The Very **First Point in the Portrait of a True Minister of Christ** is that, he is "A Steward of the Mysteries of God"!

114.   Why does the LORD God Almighty call the Word of God the Holy Bible "The Mysteries of God"?

115.   Here is the reason!

     i. **1 Kings 4:32 (KJV)** And he spake three thousand proverbs: and his songs were a thousand and five.

     ii. **Psalm 49:4 (KJV)** I will incline mine ear to a parable: I will open my dark saying upon the harp.

     iii. **Ezekiel 20:49 (KJV)** Then said I, Ah Lord GOD! they say of me, Doth he not speak parables?

     iv. **Matthew 13:3 (KJV)** And he spake many things unto them in parables, saying, Behold, a sower went forth to sow;

     v. **Matthew 13:10 (KJV)** And the disciples came, and said unto him, Why speakest thou unto them in parables?

     vi. **Matthew 13:13 (KJV)** Therefore speak I to them in parables: because they seeing see not; and hearing they hear not, neither do they understand.

     vii. **Matthew 13:34 (KJV)** All these things spake Jesus unto the multitude in parables; and without a parable spake he not unto them:

     viii. **Matthew 13:35 (KJV)** That it might be fulfilled which was spoken by the prophet, saying, I will open my mouth in parables; I will utter things which have been kept secret from the foundation of the world.

     ix. **Matthew 13:53 (KJV)** And it came to pass, *that* when Jesus had finished these parables, he departed thence.

     x. **Matthew 21:45 (KJV)** And when the chief priests and Pharisees had heard his parables, they perceived that he spake of them.

     xi. **Matthew 22:1 (KJV)** And Jesus answered and spake unto them again by parables, and said,

xii. **Mark 3:23 (KJV)** And he called them *unto him*, and said unto them in parables, How can Satan cast out Satan?

xiii. **Mark 4:2 (KJV)** And he taught them many things by parables, and said unto them in his doctrine,

xiv. **Mark 4:11 (KJV)** And he said unto them, Unto you it is given to know the mystery of the kingdom of God: but unto them that are without, all *these* things are done in parables:

xv. **Mark 4:13 (KJV)** And he said unto them, Know ye not this parable? and how then will ye know all parables?

xvi. **Mark 4:33 (KJV)** And with many such parables spake he the word unto them, as they were able to hear *it*.

xvii. **Mark 12:1 (KJV)** And he began to speak unto them by parables. A *certain* man planted a vineyard, and set an hedge about *it*, and digged *a place for* the winefat, and built a tower, and let it out to husbandmen, and went into a far country.

xviii. **Luke 8:10 (KJV)** And he said, Unto you it is given to know the mysteries of the kingdom of God: but to others in parables; that seeing they might not see, and hearing they might not understand.

xix. **John 16:25 (KJV)** These things have I spoken unto you in proverbs: but the time cometh, when I shall no more speak unto you in proverbs, but I shall shew you plainly of the Father.

xx. **Romans 11:25 (KJV)** For I would not, brethren, that ye should be ignorant of this mystery, lest ye should be wise in your own conceits; that blindness in part is happened to Israel, until the fulness of the Gentiles be come in.

xxi. **Romans 16:25 (KJV)** Now to him that is of power to stablish you according to my gospel, and the preaching of Jesus Christ, according to the revelation of the mystery, which was kept secret since the world began,

xxii. **1 Corinthians 2:7 (KJV)** But we speak the wisdom of God in a mystery, *even* the hidden *wisdom*, which God ordained before the world unto our glory:

xxiii. **1 Corinthians 15:51 (KJV)** Behold, I shew you a mystery; We shall not all sleep, but we shall all be changed,

xxiv. **Ephesians 1:9 (KJV)** Having made known unto us the mystery of his will, according to his good pleasure which he hath purposed in himself:

xxv. **Ephesians 3:3 (KJV)** How that by revelation he made known unto me the mystery; (as I wrote afore in few words,

xxvi. **Ephesians 3:4 (KJV)** Whereby, when ye read, ye may understand my knowledge in the mystery of Christ)

xxvii. **Ephesians 3:9 (KJV)** And to make all *men* see what *is* the fellowship of the mystery, which from the beginning of the world hath been hid in God, who created all things by Jesus Christ:

xxviii. **Ephesians 5:32 (KJV)** This is a great mystery: but I speak concerning Christ and the church.

xxix. **Ephesians 6:19 (KJV)** And for me, that utterance may be given unto me, that I may open my mouth boldly, to make known the mystery of the gospel,

xxx. **Colossians 1:26 (KJV)** *Even* the mystery which hath been hid from ages and from generations, but now is made manifest to his saints:

xxxi. **Colossians 1:27 (KJV)** To whom God would make known what *is* the riches of the glory of this mystery among the Gentiles; which is Christ in you, the hope of glory:

xxxii. **Colossians 2:2 (KJV)** That their hearts might be comforted, being knit together in love, and unto all riches of the full assurance of understanding, to the acknowledgement of the mystery of God, and of the Father, and of Christ;

xxxiii. **Colossians 4:3 (KJV)** Withal praying also for us, that God would open unto us a door of utterance, to speak the mystery of Christ, for which I am also in bonds:

xxxiv. **2 Thessalonians 2:7 (KJV)** For the mystery of iniquity doth already work: only he who now letteth *will let*, until he be taken out of the way.

xxxv. **1 Timothy 3:9 (KJV)** Holding the mystery of the faith in a pure conscience.

xxxvi. **1 Timothy 3:16 (KJV)** And without controversy great is the mystery of godliness: God was manifest in the flesh, justified in the Spirit, seen of angels, preached unto the Gentiles, believed on in the world, received up into glory.

xxxvii. **Revelation 1:20 (KJV)** The mystery of the seven stars which thou sawest in my right hand, and the seven golden candlesticks. The seven stars are the angels of the seven churches: and the seven candlesticks which thou sawest are the seven churches.

xxxviii. **Revelation 10:7 (KJV)** But in the days of the voice of the seventh angel, when he shall begin to sound, the mystery of God should be finished, as he hath declared to his servants the prophets.

xxxix. **Revelation 17:5 (KJV)** And upon her forehead *was* a name written, MYSTERY, BABYLON THE GREAT, THE MOTHER OF HARLOTS AND ABOMINATIONS OF THE EARTH.

xl. **Revelation 17:7 (KJV)** And the angel said unto me, Wherefore didst thou marvel? I will tell thee the mystery of the woman, and of the beast that carrieth her, which hath the seven heads and ten horns.

116.   With the above 40 evidences showing that the Word of God is indeed a mystery, it means, therefore, that the Word of God the Holy Bible, just as medical books and law books are NOT mean for the non-initiated, so also the Word of God the Holy Bible is NOT meant for everyone, and by extension, Salvation is also NOT meant for everyone, and that is why those who do not possess the mental, intellectual, and spiritual capacity to understand the Word of God the Holy Bible, they often condemn it as foolishness!

i. **2 Corinthians 4:3 (KJV)** But if our gospel be hid, it is hid to them that are lost:

ii. **1 Corinthians 2:9 (KJV)** But as it is written, Eye hath not seen, nor ear heard, neither have entered into the heart of man, the things which God hath prepared for them that love him.

iii. **1 Corinthians 2:10 (KJV)** But God hath revealed *them* unto us by his Spirit: for the Spirit searcheth all things, yea, the deep things of God.

iv. **1 Corinthians 2:11 (KJV)** For what man knoweth the things of a man, save the spirit of man which is in him? even so the things of God knoweth no man, but the Spirit of God.

v. **1 Corinthians 2:12 (KJV)** Now we have received, not the spirit of the world, but the spirit which is of God; that we might know the things that are freely given to us of God.

vi. **1 Corinthians 2:13 (KJV)** Which things also we speak, not in the words which man's wisdom teacheth, but which the Holy Ghost teacheth; comparing spiritual things with spiritual.

vii. **1 Corinthians 2:14 (KJV)** But the natural man receiveth not the things of the Spirit of God: for they are foolishness unto him: neither can he know *them*, because they are spiritually discerned.

117.   Consequently, those who possess the insight to access and understand the Word of God the Holy Bible, they are called: "Stewards of the Mysteries of God"!

    i.   **1 Corinthians 4:1 (KJV)** Let a man so account of us, as of the ministers of Christ, and stewards of the mysteries of God.

118.   These "Stewards of the Mysteries of God", what do they do? What is their work specifically?

119.   Here is the answer!

    i.   **Proverbs 5:1 (KJV)** My son, attend unto my wisdom, *and* bow thine ear to my understanding:

    ii. **Proverbs 5:2 (KJV)** That thou mayest regard discretion, and *that* thy lips may keep knowledge.

    iii. **Jeremiah 3:15 (KJV)** And I will give you pastors according to mine heart, which shall feed you with knowledge and understanding.

    iv. **Malachi 2:5 (KJV)** My covenant was with him of life and peace; and I gave them to him *for* the fear wherewith he feared me, and was afraid before my name.

    v.   **Malachi 2:6 (KJV)** The law of truth was in his mouth, and iniquity was not found in his lips: he walked with me in peace and equity, and did turn many away from iniquity.

    vi. **Malachi 2:7 (KJV)** For the priest's lips should keep knowledge, and they should seek the law at his mouth: for he *is* the messenger of the LORD of hosts.

120.   The "Stewards of the Mysteries of God" are also called: "The Stewards of the Law of Truth" as you can see in **Malachi 2:6-7 (KJV)**, and they are also called: "The Scholar of the Law of the God of Heaven", or "The Scribe of the Law of the God of Heaven", because they read, research, and study the Word of God the Law of Truth day and night, comparing spiritual things with spiritual!

    i.   **1 Corinthians 2:13 (KJV)** Which things also we speak, not in the words which man's wisdom teacheth, but which the Holy Ghost teacheth; comparing spiritual things with spiritual.

    ii. **Joshua 1:7 (KJV)** Only be thou strong and very courageous, that thou mayest observe to do according to all the law, which Moses my servant commanded thee: turn not from it *to* the right hand or *to* the left, that thou mayest prosper whithersoever thou goest.

    iii. **Joshua 1:8 (KJV)** This book of the law shall not depart out of thy mouth; but thou shalt meditate therein day and night, that thou mayest observe to do according to all that is written therein: for then thou shalt make thy way prosperous, and then thou shalt have good success.

iv. **1 Chronicles 25:8 (KJV)** And they cast lots, ward against *ward*, as well the small as the great, the teacher as the scholar.

v. **Malachi 2:12 (KJV)** The LORD will cut off the man that doeth this, the master and the scholar, out of the tabernacles of Jacob, and him that offereth an offering unto the LORD of hosts.

vi. **Ezra 7:12 (KJV)** Artaxerxes, king of kings, unto Ezra the priest, a scribe of the law of the God of heaven, perfect *peace*, and at such a time.

vii. **Ezra 7:21 (KJV)** And I, *even* I Artaxerxes the king, do make a decree to all the treasurers which *are* beyond the river, that whatsoever Ezra the priest, the scribe of the law of the God of heaven, shall require of you, it be done speedily,

viii. **Luke 10:26 (KJV)** He said unto him, What is written in the law? how readest thou?

ix. **John 5:39 (KJV)** Search the scriptures; for in them ye think ye have eternal life: and they are they which testify of me.

x. **1 Timothy 4:13 (KJV)** Till I come, give attendance to reading, to exhortation, to doctrine.

xi. **2 Timothy 2:15 (KJV)** Study to shew thyself approved unto God, a workman that needeth not to be ashamed, rightly dividing the word of truth.

121.   Now that you know what the true work of the true Man of God, it means now that you are armed because knowledge is power, and, therefore, when you meet anyone who calls himself a Man of God, then, this ONLY is what you should expect from him, and if he proceeds to do or speak anything more than these, then, know immediately that you are dealing with a fraud, a charlatan, a thief, a robber, a quack, a false prophet, a criminal, a murderer, and an adulterer!

i. **Jeremiah 3:15 (KJV)** And I will give you pastors according to mine heart, which shall feed you with knowledge and understanding.

ii. **Malachi 2:7 (KJV)** For the priest's lips should keep knowledge, and they should seek the law at his mouth: for he *is* the messenger of the LORD of hosts.

122.   A true Man of God "shall feed you with knowledge and understanding from the Law of Truth the Holy Bible"!

123.   The **Second Point in the Portrait of a True Minister of Christ** is that, he must be "Faithful to the Law of Truth the Holy Bible"! This requirement of "faithfulness on the part of the Man of God to reflect the truth in the Word of God" as seen in **Jeremiah 23:28 (KJV)** is also a cardinal requirement in all non-sacred text translations, and this cardinal requirement in the Holy Bible preceded the same requirement in the public space, thereby, showing clearly that the wisdom in the Word of God was the source of and the great influence to all modern secular education, training, and knowledge!

i.   **2 Kings 12:15 (KJV)** Moreover they reckoned not with the men, into whose hand they delivered the money to be bestowed on workmen: for they dealt faithfully.

ii.   **2 Kings 22:7 (KJV)** Howbeit there was no reckoning made with them of the money that was delivered into their hand, because they dealt faithfully.

iii.   **2 Chronicles 19:9 (KJV)** And he charged them, saying, Thus shall ye do in the fear of the LORD, faithfully, and with a perfect heart.

iv.   **Proverbs 29:14 (KJV)** The king that faithfully judgeth the poor, his throne shall be established for ever.

v.   **Jeremiah 23:28 (KJV)** The prophet that hath a dream, let him tell a dream; and he that hath my word, let him speak my word faithfully. What *is* the chaff to the wheat? saith the LORD.

vi.   **1 Corinthians 4:2 (KJV)** Moreover it is required in stewards, that a man be found faithful.

vii.   **2 Timothy 2:2 (KJV)** And the things that thou hast heard of me among many witnesses, the same commit thou to faithful men, who shall be able to teach others also.

viii.   **Titus 3:8 (KJV)** *This is* a faithful saying, and these things I will that thou affirm constantly, that they which have believed in God might be careful to maintain good works. These things are good and profitable unto men.

ix.   **Revelation 2:10 (KJV)** Fear none of those things which thou shalt suffer: behold, the devil shall cast *some* of you into prison, that ye may be tried; and ye shall have tribulation ten days: be thou faithful unto death, and I will give thee a crown of life.

124.   The **Third Point in the Portrait of a True Minister of Christ** is that, he must be subject always to examination, scrutiny, judgment, and questioning!

Therefore, a Man of God who hates examination, scrutiny, judgment, and questioning of his stewardship in Ministry, is NOT a Man of God but a Man of Satan!

  i. **Luke 16:1 (KJV)** And he said also unto his disciples, There was a certain rich man, which had a steward; and the same was accused unto him that he had wasted his goods.

  ii. **Luke 16:2 (KJV)** And he called him, and said unto him, How is it that I hear this of thee? give an account of thy stewardship; for thou mayest be no longer steward.

  iii. **1 Corinthians 4:3 (KJV)** But with me it is a very small thing that I should be judged of you, or of man's judgment: yea, I judge not mine own self.

  iv. **1 Corinthians 4:4 (KJV)** For I know nothing by myself; yet am I not hereby justified: but he that judgeth me is the Lord.

  v. **1 Corinthians 4:5 (KJV)** Therefore judge nothing before the time, until the Lord come, who both will bring to light the hidden things of darkness, and will make manifest the counsels of the hearts: and then shall every man have praise of God.

  vi. **1 Corinthians 4:6 (KJV)** And these things, brethren, I have in a figure transferred to myself and *to* Apollos for your sakes; that ye might learn in us not to think *of men* above that which is written, that no one of you be puffed up for one against another.

125. The Fourth Point in the Portrait of a True Minister of Christ is that, he must demonstrate humility and he must be always thankful!

  i. **1 Corinthians 4:7 (KJV)** For who maketh thee to differ *from another*? and what hast thou that thou didst not receive? now if thou didst receive *it*, why dost thou glory, as if thou hadst not received *it*?

  ii. **Colossians 3:15 (KJV)** And let the peace of God rule in your hearts, to the which also ye are called in one body; and be ye thankful.

126. The Fifth Point in the Portrait of a True Minister of Christ is that, he must always first seek the prosperity of his congregation and not his own advantage! Today's Pastors and church leaders do NOT do this thing, and that is a curse on them!

  i. **1 Corinthians 4:8 (KJV)** Now ye are full, now ye are rich, ye have reigned as kings without us: and I would to God ye did reign, that we also might reign with you.

127. The Sixth Point in the Portrait of a True Minister of Christ is that, he must always be the last to be served! Contrary to **1 Corinthians 4:9 (KJV)**, in all the

churches, the Pastors and General Overseers are NOT the last, but the first to serve themselves of church money!

> i. **1 Corinthians 4:9 (KJV)** For I think that God hath set forth us the apostles last, as it were appointed to death: for we are made a spectacle unto the world, and to angels, and to men.

128.   The **Seventh Point in the Portrait of a True Minister of Christ** is that, he must become a fool in order to become wise! Today, we cannot find even one church Pastor or Bishop who agrees with this portrait of the true Man of God as revealed in **1 Corinthians 4:10 (KJV)**! In all the congregations in the world, the church members are rather the fools, the church members are rather the weak ones, the church members are rather the despised of the lot, when it should the other way round!

> i. **1 Corinthians 4:10 (KJV)** We *are* fools for Christ's sake, but ye *are* wise in Christ; we *are* weak, but ye *are* strong; ye *are* honourable, but we *are* despised.
>
> ii. **1 Corinthians 3:18 (KJV)** Let no man deceive himself. If any man among you seemeth to be wise in this world, let him become a fool, that he may be wise.

129.   The **Eighth Point in the Portrait of a True Minister of Christ** is that, he must be the first in his congregation to be hungry, and thirsty, and naked, and buffeted, and have no certain dwelling place! Whereas the Word of God calls for the Church Leaders to be those who are hungry, and thirsty, and naked, and buffeted, and have no certain dwelling place, it is rather the congregations whom the Church Leaders exploit who are in that sorry situation!

> i. **1 Corinthians 4:11 (KJV)** Even unto this present hour we both hunger, and thirst, and are naked, and are buffeted, and have no certain dwellingplace;

130.   The **Ninth Point in the Portrait of a True Minister of Christ** is that, he must labor and work with his own hands and NOT force the church to be chargeable for the entire expenses of himself and his family members! Here is the Word of God in **1 Corinthians 4:12 (KJV)** commanding Pastors and Church Leaders to labor and work with their own hands, and yet, we have evil Pastors and Church Leaders who preach against God and say loudly, that it is a sin and a shame for Pastors and Church Leaders to labor and work with their own hands! They have changed the Word of God to deceive and enslave the congregations to work for them and bring them their money as tithes and first fruits! They are robbers! Woe unto them!

> i. **1 Corinthians 4:12 (KJV)** And labour, working with our own hands: being reviled, we bless; being persecuted, we suffer it:

131.   The Tenth Point in the Portrait of a True Minister of Christ is that, they must be ready to be defamed as part of their Job Description! The Word of God calls for Church Leaders to be ready to be defamed as part of their Job Description and yet, you have Pastors, Bishops, Prophets, and Church Leaders such as Frank Dwomoh Sarpong of Restoration Chapel International in Capitol Heights in Prince George's County in Maryland, USA, who sued Rev. Prof. Peter Pryce in Court for exposing their lies, thefts, immigration fraud, and their Biblical ignorance in collaboration with another thief and fraudster from Ghana called Prophet Emmanuel Amoah and the other and fraudster called Prophet Frank Osei!

   i.   **1 Corinthians 4:13 (KJV)** Being defamed, we intreat: we are made as the filth of the world, *and are* the offscouring of all things unto this day.

   ii. **1 Corinthians 4:14 (KJV)** I write not these things to shame you, but as my beloved sons I warn *you*.

132.   The Eleventh Point in the Portrait of a True Minister of Christ is that, they must produce children through the Gospel of Christ! **1 Corinthians 4:15 (KJV)** is one evidence that we have showing that, in the spiritual procreation of children, you do not use the male sperm in a biological copulation with a woman, but instead, you use the Word of God to beget children in the LORD!

   i.   **1 Corinthians 4:15 (KJV)** For though ye have ten thousand instructors in Christ, yet *have ye* not many fathers: for in Christ Jesus I have begotten you through the gospel.

   ii. **1 Corinthians 4:16 (KJV)** Wherefore I beseech you, be ye followers of me.

133.   How does it work in practise, this spiritual procreation of children?

134.   The Two-Step Salvation process that I showed you in Chapter 2 above, that is the way it works to produce children in the Spirit realm! Here is what I said over there in Chapter 2 above:

135.   How does this production of Salvation happen? By what means?

136.   By means of speaking, preaching, writing, and teaching the Gospel of Christ to people, to the effectual renewing of their mind toward God Almighty!

   i.   **Romans 1:15 (KJV)** So, as much as in me is, I am ready to preach the gospel to you that are at Rome also.

   ii. **Romans 1:16 (KJV)** For I am not ashamed of the gospel of Christ: for it is the power of God unto salvation to every one that believeth; to the Jew first, and also to the Greek.

    iii. **Romans 1:17 (KJV)** For therein is the righteousness of God revealed from faith to faith: as it is written, The just shall live by faith.

137.   The revelation in **Romans 1:15-17 (KJV)** is that, when a Man of God claims to have power from God in Ministry, then, you should be able to measure or identify the source of that power through the following two steps:

    i. ONE – Are the words of the Man of God 100% derived from the Gospel of Christ, from the Word of God, form the Holy Scriptures?

    ii. TWO – When that Man of God speaks, preaches, teaches, or writes his words, do people hear or read it and become convinced of its contents and believe the contents of the speech or writing such that they turn away from the thoughts that they previously held to now embrace the new thoughts of Christ that are contained in the speech or writings of the Man of God?

138.   The moment that the above two steps are successfully accomplished through the speech or writings of a Man of God, then, that is the same moment that he has demonstrated the Power of God unto Salvation, because, Salvation is first measured in the mind before it appears in the deeds of the flesh!

    i. **Colossians 1:21 (KJV)** And you, that were sometime alienated and enemies in *your* mind by wicked works, yet now hath he reconciled

    ii. **Romans 12:2 (KJV)** And be not conformed to this world: but be ye transformed by the renewing of your mind, that ye may prove what *is* that good, and acceptable, and perfect, will of God.

    iii. **Titus 3:5 (KJV)** Not by works of righteousness which we have done, but according to his mercy he saved us, by the washing of regeneration, and renewing of the Holy Ghost;

139.   The **Twelfth Point in the Portrait of a True Minister of Christ** is that, they must be transparent and open to examination and scrutiny of all their works, especially, their finances! A Church Leader who will NOT agree to the examination of his finances and doctrines is already a thief, a robber, a deceiver, and a fraud! The very moment that a Pastor prefers his activities to be conducted in the dark and NOT in the open for everyone to see and judge him, that is the same moment that you should know that he is a thief, a robber, a deceiver, and a fraud!

    i. **1 Corinthians 4:17 (KJV)** For this cause have I sent unto you Timotheus, who is my beloved son, and faithful in the Lord, who shall bring you into remembrance of my ways which be in Christ, as I teach every where in every church.

140.   The Thirteenth Point in the Portrait of a True Minister of Christ is that, arrogancy/pride must NOT be found with him, because God hates proud people who resist correction in the Word!

    i. **1 Corinthians 4:18 (KJV)** Now some are puffed up, as though I would not come to you.

    ii. **1 Corinthians 4:19 (KJV)** But I will come to you shortly, if the Lord will, and will know, not the speech of them which are puffed up, but the power.

    iii. **Psalm 138:6 (KJV)** Though the LORD *be* high, yet hath he respect unto the lowly: but the proud he knoweth afar off.

    iv. **James 4:6 (KJV)** But he giveth more grace. Wherefore he saith, God resisteth the proud, but giveth grace unto the humble.

    v. **1 Peter 5:5 (KJV)** Likewise, ye younger, submit yourselves unto the elder. Yea, all *of you* be subject one to another, and be clothed with humility: for God resisteth the proud, and giveth grace to the humble.

141.   The Fourteenth Point in the Portrait of a True Minister of Christ is that, as **1 Corinthians 4:19-20 (KJV)** is saying, he must be able to demonstrate the Power of God in the Word of God by means of his ability to speak, preach, or write sermons that people will hear or read, become convinced, believe in the LORD Jesus Christ, turn away from their sins, and then begin to live daily in Truth and Righteousness! That is how to demonstrate the Power of God in Ministry!

    i. **1 Corinthians 4:20 (KJV)** For the kingdom of God *is* not in word, but in power.

142.   The words: "the kingdom of God *is* not in word, but in power" in **1 Corinthians 4:20 (KJV)** should NOT take your corrupt mind to begin to image esoteric voodoo practices of healing, signs, miracles, and wonders as some depraved children of Devils do!

    i. **Matthew 12:38 (KJV)** Then certain of the scribes and of the Pharisees answered, saying, Master, we would see a sign from thee.

    ii. **Matthew 12:39 (KJV)** But he answered and said unto them, An evil and adulterous generation seeketh after a sign; and there shall no sign be given to it, but the sign of the prophet Jonas:

    iii. **Matthew 16:4 (KJV)** A wicked and adulterous generation seeketh after a sign; and there shall no sign be given unto it, but the sign of the prophet Jonas. And he left them, and departed.

iv. **2 Thessalonians 2:7 (KJV)** For the mystery of iniquity doth already work: only he who now letteth *will let*, until he be taken out of the way.

v. **2 Thessalonians 2:8 (KJV)** And then shall that Wicked be revealed, whom the Lord shall consume with the spirit of his mouth, and shall destroy with the brightness of his coming:

vi. **2 Thessalonians 2:9 (KJV)** *Even him*, whose coming is after the working of Satan with all power and signs and lying wonders,

vii. **2 Thessalonians 2:10 (KJV)** And with all deceivableness of unrighteousness in them that perish; because they received not the love of the truth, that they might be saved.

viii. **2 Thessalonians 2:11 (KJV)** And for this cause God shall send them strong delusion, that they should believe a lie:

ix. **2 Thessalonians 2:12 (KJV)** That they all might be damned who believed not the truth, but had pleasure in unrighteousness.

143. On the contrary, the words: "the kingdom of God *is* not in word, but in power" in **1 Corinthians 4:20 (KJV)** mean the Two-Step Salvation process and its power to transform the sinner away from sin and toward God Almighty that I have already showed to you here above!

144. The **Fifteenth Point in the Portrait of a True Minister of Christ** is found in **1 Corinthians 4:21 (KJV)**, and it points to the oversight role of the true Man of God over all his Assistant Pastors and over any other person as well who also calls himself a Pastor!

i. **1 Corinthians 4:21 (KJV)** What will ye? shall I come unto you with a rod, or in love, and *in* the spirit of meekness?

ii. **John 7:24 (KJV)** Judge not according to the appearance, but judge righteous judgment.

iii. **Philippians 2:4 (KJV)** Look not every man on his own things, but every man also on the things of others.

iv. **1 Corinthians 14:29 (KJV)** Let the prophets speak two or three, and let the other judge.

145. In conclusion, here is the present exploitative situation of almost all the Pastors and Bishops in all the churches in the world today, no exception! They are all evil corrupt beasts who feed themselves fat on the money of the congregation, building massive lifeless church buildings, allocating salaries to the Head Pastor and his family, creating a life of luxury for the General Overseer at the same time as the entire

congregation is not able to afford and pay for the luxuries that the Pastors receive free of charge!

i. **Ezekiel 34:1 (KJV)** And the word of the LORD came unto me, saying,

ii. **Ezekiel 34:2 (KJV)** Son of man, prophesy against the shepherds of Israel, prophesy, and say unto them, Thus saith the Lord GOD unto the shepherds; Woe *be* to the shepherds of Israel that do feed themselves! should not the shepherds feed the flocks?

iii. **Ezekiel 34:3 (KJV)** Ye eat the fat, and ye clothe you with the wool, ye kill them that are fed: *but* ye feed not the flock.

iv. **Ezekiel 34:4 (KJV)** The diseased have ye not strengthened, neither have ye healed that which was sick, neither have ye bound up *that which was* broken, neither have ye brought again that which was driven away, neither have ye sought that which was lost; but with force and with cruelty have ye ruled them.

v. **Ezekiel 34:5 (KJV)** And they were scattered, because *there is* no shepherd: and they became meat to all the beasts of the field, when they were scattered.

vi. **Ezekiel 34:6 (KJV)** My sheep wandered through all the mountains, and upon every high hill: yea, my flock was scattered upon all the face of the earth, and none did search or seek *after them*.

146.   In the beginning of this this chapter 4 in the Book of 1 Corinthians, we set out to discover the Job Description of a true Minister of Christ. In other words, the Portrait of a true Man of God! I have just taught you **Fifteen Points in the Portrait of a True Minister of Christ** that you can use to examine all Pastors and Church Leaders in order to know if they are doing the right thing, if they were called into the Ministry by the LORD Jesus Christ, or, if they were called into the Ministry by Satan!

CHAPTER 5: HOW TO JUDGE FORNICATORS AND OTHER SINNERS IN THE CONGREGATION

147.   For the first time in his Ministry, Black Man Apostle Paul is coming into contact with a depravity among the while people Gentiles that he had never heard before whereby, both father and son are sleeping with the same woman!

    i.   **1 Corinthians 5:1 (KJV)** It is reported commonly *that there is* fornication among you, and such fornication as is not so much as named among the Gentiles, that one should have his father's wife.

    ii.   **Amos 2:6 (KJV)** Thus saith the LORD; For three transgressions of Israel, and for four, I will not turn away *the punishment* thereof; because they sold the righteous for silver, and the poor for a pair of shoes;

    iii.   **Amos 2:7 (KJV)** That pant after the dust of the earth on the head of the poor, and turn aside the way of the meek: and a man and his father will go in unto the *same* maid, to profane my holy name:

148.   Worse of all, they are proud of what they are doing and calling it their culture, just the same way as depraved culturally bankrupt hedonistic Europe in Holland will license prostitutes to sit and stand completely naked in glass cubicles in plain public to sell sex for money, publicly!

    i.   **1 Corinthians 5:2 (KJV)** And ye are puffed up, and have not rather mourned, that he that hath done this deed might be taken away from among you.

    ii.   **1 Corinthians 5:3 (KJV)** For I verily, as absent in body, but present in spirit, have judged already, as though I were present, *concerning* him that hath so done this deed,

149.   As a true Man of God, how do you judge such fornicators in the congregation?

150.   Put that sinner out of the church forthwith and immediately so that he/she does not corrupt the rest of the congregation! Treat his/her lifestyle as poison that can kill the entire congregation!

    i.   **1 Corinthians 5:4 (KJV)** In the name of our Lord Jesus Christ, when ye are gathered together, and my spirit, with the power of our Lord Jesus Christ,

    ii.   **1 Corinthians 5:5 (KJV)** To deliver such an one unto Satan for the destruction of the flesh, that the spirit may be saved in the day of the Lord Jesus.

    iii.   **1 Corinthians 5:6 (KJV)** Your glorying *is* not good. Know ye not that a little leaven leaveneth the whole lump?

151.   The same way that the LORD God Almighty sacrificed the LORD Jesus Christ for our sins that HE took upon Himself, same way also you must purge that fornicator away from your midst!

    i.   **1 Corinthians 5:7 (KJV)** Purge out therefore the old leaven, that ye may be a new lump, as ye are unleavened. For even Christ our passover is sacrificed for us:

    ii.   **1 Corinthians 5:8 (KJV)** Therefore let us keep the feast, not with old leaven, neither with the leaven of malice and wickedness; but with the unleavened *bread* of sincerity and truth.

152.   At the same time as the LORD God in **1 Corinthians 5:7-8 (KJV)** is commanding to purge the fornicator out of the church, same time the LORD is also revealing how to perform the spiritual Holy Communion, NOT with physical bread, wine, and wafers as it is corruptly done in all the churches today, but with the spiritual bread, wine, and wafers called: "the unleavened *bread* of sincerity and truth"!

153.   So, in **1 Corinthians 5:8 (KJV)**, the new command regarding Holy Communion is this:

    i.   "Therefore let us keep the feast with the unleavened *bread* of sincerity and truth"!

154.   What that means in practise is that, since now "sincerity and truth" are the real Holy Communion bread, wine, and wafers, you as the Christian will set your daily target to accomplish your living in Truth and Righteousness in all things: in your thoughts, in your words, and in your deeds, and as you do that daily, then, it is counted for you as your righteousness in Heaven, just the same way as Abraham's believing in God and obeying God in Truth and Righteousness earned him his own righteousness in Heaven!

    i.   **Genesis 15:6 (KJV)** And he believed in the LORD; and he counted it to him for righteousness.

    ii.   **Romans 4:3 (KJV)** For what saith the scripture? Abraham believed God, and it was counted unto him for righteousness.

    iii.   **Galatians 3:6 (KJV)** Even as Abraham believed God, and it was accounted to him for righteousness.

    iv.   **James 2:23 (KJV)** And the scripture was fulfilled which saith, Abraham believed God, and it was imputed unto him for righteousness: and he was called the Friend of God.

155.   But, why is the LORD God including this Word on Holy Communion in a chapter on how to judge fornicators and other sinners in the congregation?

156.   The reason is that the current Holy Communion as it is practiced in the present form in all the churches, is wrong and a sin, seeing that Pastors, Bishops, and Church

Leaders are carnal, corrupt, and practising idolatry by reason of the physical oblations that they use in their filthy Holy Communion whereby, those physical items themselves are contrary to the commandment of the LORD Jesus Christ!

    i. **John 4:23 (KJV)** But the hour cometh, and now is, when the true worshippers shall worship the Father in spirit and in truth: for the Father seeketh such to worship him.

    ii. **John 4:24 (KJV)** God *is* a Spirit: and they that worship him must worship *him* in spirit and in truth.

    iii. **Ephesians 5:9 (KJV)** (For the fruit of the Spirit *is* in all goodness and righteousness and truth;)

157.   Furthermore, the LORD God included Holy Communion in the subject of how to judge fornicators because all the Pastors, Bishops, and Church Leaders who have this Holy Communion doctrine that is contrary to **John 4:23-24 (KJV)**, they are also fornicators, harlots, and whores and here is the evidence!

    i. **Hosea 1:2 (KJV)** The beginning of the word of the LORD by Hosea. And the LORD said to Hosea, Go, take unto thee a wife of whoredoms and children of whoredoms: for the land hath committed great whoredom, *departing* from the LORD.

    ii. **Hebrews 3:12 (KJV)** Take heed, brethren, lest there be in any of you an evil heart of unbelief, in departing from the living God.

158.   The LORD God repeats the same command to purge the fornicator out of the church forthwith and immediately so that he/she does not corrupt the rest of the congregation!

    i. **1 Corinthians 5:9 (KJV)** I wrote unto you in an epistle not to company with fornicators:

    ii. **1 Corinthians 5:10 (KJV)** Yet not altogether with the fornicators of this world, or with the covetous, or extortioners, or with idolaters; for then must ye needs go out of the world.

    iii. **1 Corinthians 5:11 (KJV)** But now I have written unto you not to keep company, if any man that is called a brother be a fornicator, or covetous, or an idolater, or a railer, or a drunkard, or an extortioner; with such an one no not to eat.

159.   With this type of language: "with such an one no not to eat", it means that there should such a distinct separation between you the Christian and sinners to the extent that you should NOT be seen in their company reveling with them, celebrating feasts with them, observing days with them, festivals, anniversaries, Christmas, Easter, and birthdays with them! Neither should al such days of festivities and celebrations be brought into the church by the Pastor to be observed

160.   Well, what about a person who says that he/she is saved, born again, and a Christian but he/she is also a covetous/greedy person, or an idolater, or a railer/faultfinder/nitpicker/accuser, or a drunkard, or an extortioner/fraud/dupe: how should other Christians deal with them?

161.   According to **1 Corinthians 5:9-11 (KJV)**, as long as you claim to be a Christians, then, those people should NOT be your friends and they should NOT be the kind of people that you frequent and fraternize with!

162.   That is how to judge fornicators and other sinners in the congregation! You must put away from among yourselves that wicked person so that he/she does not corrupt the rest of the congregation and drag them into Hell!

   i.   **1 Corinthians 5:12 (KJV)** For what have I to do to judge them also that are without? do not ye judge them that are within?

   ii. **1 Corinthians 5:13 (KJV)** But them that are without God judgeth. Therefore put away from among yourselves that wicked person.

163.   One of the demonic reasons why the Roman Catholic Church has become the Hell that it is today for all its ignorant followers is that whereas its Pope Francis in 2023 has ordered all Roman Catholic Bishops to welcome, encourage, and bless homosexuals and lesbians in the Holy Name of the LORD Jesus Christ and the LORD God Almighty, that insane demon-possessed Pope Francis is coming from a very long line of evil deeds of the Roman Catholic Church especially, its tradition of hiding, covering up, and shielding its Priests and Bishops who abused and sodomized already vulnerable children, boys and girls, that were in their care, and they did this evil and hiding of the criminal Bishops for more than 100 years at the same time when the LORD God said: "put away from among yourselves that wicked person/Bishop"!

164.   How can such an evil Roman Catholic Church help and guide you to become saved and go to Heaven?

CHAPTER 6: THE PASTOR WHO REFUSES MEDIATION IN THE HOLY SCRIPTURES IS A SINNER

165.   The LORD God has already concluded all Court Judges and Lawyers to be corrupt, evil beasts, vile, and not worthy for the Kingdom of Heaven, because they are all liars!

    i. **1 Corinthians 6:1 (KJV)** Dare any of you, having a matter against another, go to law before the unjust, and not before the saints?

    ii. **Micah 7:2 (KJV)** The good *man* is perished out of the earth: and *there is* none upright among men: they all lie in wait for blood; they hunt every man his brother with a net.

    iii. **Micah 7:3 (KJV)** That they may do evil with both hands earnestly, the prince asketh, and the judge *asketh* for a reward; and the great *man*, he uttereth his mischievous desire: so they wrap it up.

    iv. **Micah 7:4 (KJV)** The best of them *is* as a brier: the most upright *is sharper* than a thorn hedge: the day of thy watchmen *and* thy visitation cometh; now shall be their perplexity.

    v. **Luke 11:46 (KJV)** And he said, Woe unto you also, *ye* lawyers! for ye lade men with burdens grievous to be borne, and ye yourselves touch not the burdens with one of your fingers.

    vi. **Luke 11:52 (KJV)** Woe unto you, lawyers! for ye have taken away the key of knowledge: ye entered not in yourselves, and them that were entering in ye hindered.

    vii. **Luke 18:6 (KJV)** And the Lord said, Hear what the unjust judge saith.

166.   That is why it is forbidden to Christians in **1 Corinthians 6:1 (KJV)** to go to law before the unjust Judge and the deceitful lawyer!

167.   The superiority of the Church of Christ makes it that the Ministers of Christ are over and above all Court Judges and Lawyers hence, it is anathema and an abomination for true Men of God to go and stand before evil corrupt Court Judges and Lawyers to be tried for their cases!

168.   A Pastor or a Man of God who does that is clearly NOT a child of God!

169.   Yet, when the so-called Man of God will NOT obey the Word of God during a crisis time to do what is right before God, then, know that he is NOT a Man of God and, therefore, if he has broken the Law and offended, then, treat him as the sinner that he is just as the LORD Jesus Christ said in **Matthew 18:15-17 (KJV)**, and you must summon him before the corrupt Court Judges and Lawyers to whom he belongs since that is the only language that he understands!

      i. **Matthew 18:15 (KJV)** Moreover if thy brother shall trespass against thee, go and tell him his fault between thee and him alone: if he shall hear thee, thou hast gained thy brother.

      ii. **Matthew 18:16 (KJV)** But if he will not hear *thee, then* take with thee one or two more, that in the mouth of two or three witnesses every word may be established.

      iii. **Matthew 18:17 (KJV)** And if he shall neglect to hear them, tell *it* unto the church: but if he neglect to hear the church, let him be unto thee as an heathen man and a publican.

170.   An "heathen man and a publican" is NOT a child of God but rather a sinner on his way to Hell, and in **Matthew 18:15-17 (KJV)**, the LORD Jesus Christ is showing you that when a man will NOT receive the Word of God to obey it, then know that he is surely "an heathen man and a publican", meaning that he is NOT a child of God, he is a sinner, and you should therefore treat him as a sinner hence, if before the corrupt Court Judges and Lawyers is the only place where you can seek and obtain justice, then, so do!

171.   Take note very carefully, that the LORD God is speaking to true children of God to NOT go before the corrupt Court Judges and Lawyers! Therefore, if the person that you are dealing with is NOT a true child of God, then, the provisions of this Law of God in **1 Corinthians 6:1-2 (KJV)** does NOT apply to him or her!

      i. **1 Corinthians 6:1 (KJV)** Dare any of you, having a matter against another, go to law before the unjust, and not before the saints?

      ii. **1 Corinthians 6:2 (KJV)** Do ye not know that the saints shall judge the world? and if the world shall be judged by you, are ye unworthy to judge the smallest matters?

172.   Based on the same Law of God in **1 Corinthians 6:1-2 (KJV)**, it is wrong for corrupt Government Agencies to accredit, regulate, and direct the churches in terms of spiritual education and doctrine!

173.   That is why all over the world, there are laws of Separation of Church and State in the Constitutions that say that say that the Governments has no power to accredit religious schools, and the main reason is that the Church is superior to the State!

174.   The superiority of the Church and of the Ministers of Christ is also enshrined in the Law of God that these same Ministers of Christ will not only judge the whole world, but they shall also judge Angels on the Last Day!

      i. **1 Corinthians 6:3 (KJV)** Know ye not that we shall judge angels? how much more things that pertain to this life?

175.   Furthermore, the true Man of God is also a Judge, a Superior Judge of God!

     i. **Numbers 35:24 (KJV)** Then the congregation shall judge between the slayer and the revenger of blood according to these judgments:

    ii. **Deuteronomy 16:18 (KJV)** Judges and officers shalt thou make thee in all thy gates, which the LORD thy God giveth thee, throughout thy tribes: and they shall judge the people with just judgment.

   iii. **Deuteronomy 17:9 (KJV)** And thou shalt come unto the priests the Levites, and unto the judge that shall be in those days, and inquire; and they shall shew thee the sentence of judgment:

   iv. **John 7:24 (KJV)** Judge not according to the appearance, but judge righteous judgment.

    v. **1 Corinthians 6:4 (KJV)** If then ye have judgments of things pertaining to this life, set them to judge who are least esteemed in the church.

   vi. **1 Corinthians 6:5 (KJV)** I speak to your shame. Is it so, that there is not a wise man among you? no, not one that shall be able to judge between his brethren?

  vii. **1 Corinthians 14:29 (KJV)** Let the prophets speak two or three, and let the other judge.

176.   So, now, you can see the blasphemy and the abomination when a Superior Judge of God goes to stand before corrupt Court Judges and Lawyers to be judged when he the Superior Judge of God should rather be the one sitting in the Judge's seat!

     i. **Isaiah 29:16 (KJV)** Surely your turning of things upside down shall be esteemed as the potter's clay: for shall the work say of him that made it, He made me not? or shall the thing framed say of him that framed it, He had no understanding?

177.   The Word of God is the Foremost Lawbook and the Foremost Wisdom Book on Earth hence, when a Man of God has become mighty in the Scriptures, then, he is both a Superior Judge and a Wiseman!

     i. **1 Corinthians 6:4 (KJV)** If then ye have judgments of things pertaining to this life, set them to judge who are least esteemed in the church.

    ii. **1 Corinthians 6:5 (KJV)** I speak to your shame. Is it so, that there is not a wise man among you? no, not one that shall be able to judge between his brethren?

   iii. **Deuteronomy 17:18 (KJV)** And it shall be, when he sitteth upon the throne of his kingdom, that he shall write him a copy of this law in a book out of *that which is* before the priests the Levites:

iv. **Deuteronomy 28:58 (KJV)** If thou wilt not observe to do all the words of this law that are written in this book, that thou mayest fear this glorious and fearful name, THE LORD THY GOD;

v. **Deuteronomy 30:10 (KJV)** If thou shalt hearken unto the voice of the LORD thy God, to keep his commandments and his statutes which are written in this book of the law, *and* if thou turn unto the LORD thy God with all thine heart, and with all thy soul.

vi. **Deuteronomy 31:26 (KJV)** Take this book of the law, and put it in the side of the ark of the covenant of the LORD your God, that it may be there for a witness against thee.

vii. **Joshua 1:8 (KJV)** This book of the law shall not depart out of thy mouth; but thou shalt meditate therein day and night, that thou mayest observe to do according to all that is written therein: for then thou shalt make thy way prosperous, and then thou shalt have good success.

viii. **Joshua 23:6 (KJV)** Be ye therefore very courageous to keep and to do all that is written in the book of the law of Moses, that ye turn not aside therefrom *to* the right hand or *to* the left;

ix. **Joshua 24:26 (KJV)** And Joshua wrote these words in the book of the law of God, and took a great stone, and set it up there under an oak, that *was* by the sanctuary of the LORD.

x. **Nehemiah 8:3 (KJV)** And he read therein before the street that *was* before the water gate from the morning until midday, before the men and the women, and those that could understand; and the ears of all the people *were attentive* unto the book of the law.

xi. **Nehemiah 8:8 (KJV)** So they read in the book in the law of God distinctly, and gave the sense, and caused *them* to understand the reading.

xii. **Nehemiah 9:3 (KJV)** And they stood up in their place, and read in the book of the law of the LORD their God *one* fourth part of the day; and *another* fourth part they confessed, and worshipped the LORD their God.

xiii. **Galatians 3:10 (KJV)** For as many as are of the works of the law are under the curse: for it is written, Cursed *is* every one that continueth not in all things which are written in the book of the law to do them.

xiv. **Acts 18:24 (KJV)** And a certain Jew named Apollos, born at Alexandria, an eloquent man, *and* mighty in the scriptures, came to Ephesus.

178.   Two Brethren shall NOT stand before corrupt Court Judges and Lawyers to be judged of anything! When this happens, the Brother who wanted to solve the matter with the Holy Scriptures but was shunned and rather dragged to Cout against his will remains innocent of **1 Corinthians 6:6-8 (KJV)** while the Brother who refused to listen to the Word of God but preferred to stand before corrupt Court Judges and Lawyers remains guilty of **1 Corinthians 6:6-8 (KJV)**!

      i.   **1 Corinthians 6:6 (KJV)** But brother goeth to law with brother, and that before the unbelievers.

      ii.   **1 Corinthians 6:7 (KJV)** Now therefore there is utterly a fault among you, because ye go to law one with another. Why do ye not rather take wrong? why do ye not rather *suffer yourselves to* be defrauded?

      iii.   **1 Corinthians 6:8 (KJV)** Nay, ye do wrong, and defraud, and that *your* brethren.

179.   A Pastor whose first choice is to stand before corrupt Court Judges and Lawyers, and a Pastor who refuses mediation through the Holy Scriptures, that man is surely "an heathen man and a publican" and remains guilty of **1 Corinthians 6:6-8 (KJV)**, meaning that he is NOT a child of God, he is a sinner, he is NOT a Pastor, and he is on his way to Hell!

180.   The Pastor who of guilty of **1 Corinthians 6:6-8 (KJV)**, the Pastor whose first choice is to stand before corrupt Court Judges and Lawyers, the Pastor who refuses mediation through the Holy Scriptures, that man is also condemned as a fornicator, an idolater, an adulterer, an effeminate person, a homosexual, a thief, a greedy person, a drunkard, a reviler, and an extortionist, and their reward is clear: they shall go to Hell!

      i.   **1 Corinthians 6:9 (KJV)** Know ye not that the unrighteous shall not inherit the kingdom of God? Be not deceived: neither fornicators, nor idolaters, nor adulterers, nor effeminate, nor abusers of themselves with mankind,

      ii.   **1 Corinthians 6:10 (KJV)** Nor thieves, nor covetous, nor drunkards, nor revilers, nor extortioners, shall inherit the kingdom of God.

      iii.   **1 Corinthians 6:11 (KJV)** And such were some of you: but ye are washed, but ye are sanctified, but ye are justified in the name of the Lord Jesus, and by the Spirit of our God.

181.   Such as described here of "an heathen man and a publican" is Prophet Frank Dwomoh Sarpong who rejected mediation through the Holy Scriptures and sued Rev. Prof. Peter Pryce in Court in Maryland from 2020 to 2022 in his futile attempt to suppress the exposure of this thefts, fraud, public collection of money using lies, immigration fraud, money transactions outside the accounting books and banks, fraudulent arranged marriages in his church for USA immigration benefits, etc.

[FRANK SARPONG, ET AL. Plaintiffs, v. PETER PRYCE, ET AL. Defendants, IN THE CIRCUIT COURT FOR PRINCE GEORGE'S COUNTY, Case No. CAL20-10745]

182.   In **1 Corinthians 6:13 (KJV)**, the LORD God gives us to understand that, it becomes a sin when a thing is used for what it was NOT intended at its creation!

     i. **1 Corinthians 6:12 (KJV)** All things are lawful unto me, but all things are not expedient: all things are lawful for me, but I will not be brought under the power of any.

     ii. **1 Corinthians 6:13 (KJV)** Meats for the belly, and the belly for meats: but God shall destroy both it and them. Now the body *is* not for fornication, but for the Lord; and the Lord for the body.

183.   Furthermore, there is a power in all things and the exercise thereof is the door that brings one under the power in it! Hence, just as one can be brought under the power of the Word of God when you exercise yourself therein to read it and to obey it, so also shall a man be brought under the power of meats/food to destroy him when he abuses it! The same power and destruction await any man who abuses the body for fornication and adultery!

184.   If it is truly the spirit that is saved and not the flesh, is that then a license to abuse and corrupt the flesh even more?

     i. **1 Corinthians 5:5 (KJV)** To deliver such an one unto Satan for the destruction of the flesh, that the spirit may be saved in the day of the Lord Jesus.

     ii. **1 Corinthians 6:15 (KJV)** Know ye not that your bodies are the members of Christ? shall I then take the members of Christ, and make *them* the members of an harlot? God forbid.

185.   The uniqueness of the sin of fornication and adultery is without comparison seeing that it has a double edge and a double effect, because it is the only sin on Earth that cannot be executed without the presence of a second person hence, its double application and double effect!

     i. **1 Corinthians 6:16 (KJV)** What? know ye not that he which is joined to an harlot is one body? for two, saith he, shall be one flesh.

     ii. **1 Corinthians 6:17 (KJV)** But he that is joined unto the Lord is one spirit.

     iii. **1 Corinthians 6:18 (KJV)** Flee fornication. Every sin that a man doeth is without the body; but he that committeth fornication sinneth against his own body.

    iv. **1 Corinthians 6:19 (KJV)** What? know ye not that your body is the temple of the Holy Ghost *which is* in you, which ye have of God, and ye are not your own?

    v. **1 Corinthians 6:20 (KJV)** For ye are bought with a price: therefore glorify God in your body, and in your spirit, which are God's.

186.   Just as in **1 Corinthians 6:17 (KJV)** we see that "he that is joined unto the Lord is one spirit", same way, he that is joined to the harlot in fornication and adultery equally acquires the evil spirit of harlotry as well as all the other demons that are in her/him! The successful Christian life requires also a preservation in holiness of the Temple/Body in which lives the Holy Spirit of God!

187.   Finally, all these sins that we have identified and described here in this chapter, should be outside the realm of the true child of God who is truly saved by the Holy Spirit! Do NOT do any of them if you want to enter Heaven!

    i. **1 Corinthians 6:11 (KJV)** And such were some of you: but ye are washed, but ye are sanctified, but ye are justified in the name of the Lord Jesus, and by the Spirit of our God.

    ii. **John 1:12 (KJV)** But as many as received him, to them gave he power to become the sons of God, *even* to them that believe on his name:

    iii. **John 1:13 (KJV)** Which were born, not of blood, nor of the will of the flesh, nor of the will of man, but of God.

    iv. **John 3:8 (KJV)** The wind bloweth where it listeth, and thou hearest the sound thereof, but canst not tell whence it cometh, and whither it goeth: so is every one that is born of the Spirit.

188.   Furthermore, take note very carefully, how the LORD God reveals in **1 Corinthians 6:11 (KJV)** that it is God Himself who does the washing and sanctification in Water Baptism, NOT man!

189.   Now, see again **1 Corinthians 6:11 (KJV)** and notice carefully where the New Spiritual Waterless Baptism takes place:

    i. "in the name of the Lord Jesus, and by the Spirit of our God."

190.   Have you seen in **1 Corinthians 6:11 (KJV)** that in this New Spiritual Waterless Baptism, THERE IS NO PHYSICAL WATER even as John the Baptist testified?

    i. **Matthew 3:11 (KJV)** I indeed baptize you with water unto repentance: but he that cometh after me is mightier than I, whose shoes I am not worthy to bear: he shall baptize you with the Holy Ghost, and *with* fire:

    ii. **Mark 1:8 (KJV)** I indeed have baptized you with water: but he shall baptize you with the Holy Ghost.

      iii. **Luke 3:16 (KJV)** John answered, saying unto *them* all, I indeed baptize you with water; but one mightier than I cometh, the latchet of whose shoes I am not worthy to unloose: he shall baptize you with the Holy Ghost and with fire:

      iv. **John 13:3 (KJV)** Jesus knowing that the Father had given all things into his hands, and that he was come from God, and went to God;

      v. **John 13:4 (KJV)** He riseth from supper, and laid aside his garments; and took a towel, and girded himself.

      vi. **John 13:5 (KJV)** After that he poureth water into a bason, and began to wash the disciples' feet, and to wipe *them* with the towel wherewith he was girded.

191.   Brother, Sister, all Physical Water Baptism is wrong, is evil, is a sin!

Tuesday 9ᵗʰ January 2023 @ 6:11 AM – 9:12 AM

CHAPTER 7: AS A PASTOR, HOW DO I PREPARE A SERMON/TEACHING FOR A MARRIAGE COUNSELING CLASS?

192.   Here are 17 Marriage Counseling Lessons that you must deliver to your Marriage Counseling Class!

193.   The first point that you must tell them is this:

194.   **ONE** – BROTHER, SISTER, YOU WOULD BE BETTER OFF IF YOU HAD NOT DECIDED TO MARRY!

    i. **1 Corinthians 7:1 (KJV)** Now concerning the things whereof ye wrote unto me: *It is* good for a man not to touch a woman.

195.   **TWO** – Marriage is for one man and one woman, and polygamy is outlawed in Christianity! Also, fornication and adultery are forbidden in a true Christian marriage!

    i. **1 Corinthians 7:2 (KJV)** Nevertheless, *to avoid* fornication, let every man have his own wife, and let every woman have her own husband.

196.   **THREE** – In a true Christian marriage, there is equality in spousal kindness, goodwill, good heartedness, charitable, helpful, benevolent, generous, morally upright, kindheartedness, compassionate, well mannered, altruistic, conjugally dutiful, giving, well intentioned, not deceitful, humanistic, selflessness, loving, to each other!

    i. **1 Corinthians 7:3 (KJV)** Let the husband render unto the wife due benevolence: and likewise also the wife unto the husband.

197.   **FOUR** – Each of you the couple will lose and yield the power of his or her body to the other spouse! Meaning that, in a true Christian marriage, the husband has no power or right to refuse his conjugal duty of copulation to the wife, and the wife likewise has no power or right to refuse sex to the husband! The wife has the power and right in the LORD to probe the husband's body and the husband has the power and right in the LORD to probe the wife's body!

    i. **1 Corinthians 7:4 (KJV)** The wife hath not power of her own body, but the husband: and likewise also the husband hath not power of his own body, but the wife.

198.   **FIVE** – In a true Christian marriage, the very day that any of the couple will deny conjugal duty of copulation to the other spouse is the same day that you invited Satan into your marriage! In a true Christian marriage, the denial of conjugal duty of copulation is allowed ONLY by the consent of both spouses, and even that one time consent is for the ONLY reason of fasting and prayer! Meaning that you cannot copulate while fasting and while praying, and you cannot pray or attend to God Almighty while in your period of conjugal duty of copulation! Truly, truly, marriage

compels you to cast off your faith in Christ in order to fully satisfy the demands of marriage and that is the reality of marriage!

    i. **1 Corinthians 7:5 (KJV)** Defraud ye not one the other, except *it be* with consent for a time, that ye may give yourselves to fasting and prayer; and come together again, that Satan tempt you not for your incontinency.

    ii. **1 Corinthians 7:6 (KJV)** But I speak this by permission, *and* not of commandment.

199.   This revelation about marriage that you cannot pray or attend to God Almighty while in your period of conjugal duty of copulation is the reason why marriage is trouble, why marriage is a spiritual distraction, why marriage is a wanton rebellion against Christ because you must cast off your faith in Christ in order to fully satisfy the demands of marriage! Nevertheless, this sin of wanton rebellion against Christ is NOT unto death, and is forgivable!

    i. **Isaiah 3:16 (KJV)** Moreover the LORD saith, Because the daughters of Zion are haughty, and walk with stretched forth necks and wanton eyes, walking and mincing *as* they go, and making a tinkling with their feet:

    ii. **1 Timothy 5:11 (KJV)** But the younger widows refuse: for when they have begun to wax wanton against Christ, they will marry;

    iii. **1 Timothy 5:12 (KJV)** Having damnation, because they have cast off their first faith.

    iv. **James 5:5 (KJV)** Ye have lived in pleasure on the earth, and been wanton; ye have nourished your hearts, as in a day of slaughter.

    v. **1 Corinthians 7:28 (KJV)** But and if thou marry, thou hast not sinned; and if a virgin marry, she hath not sinned. Nevertheless such shall have trouble in the flesh: but I spare you.

    vi. **1 Corinthians 7:35 (KJV)** And this I speak for your own profit; not that I may cast a snare upon you, but for that which is comely, and that ye may attend upon the Lord without distraction.

    vii. **1 John 5:16 (KJV)** If any man see his brother sin a sin *which is* not unto death, he shall ask, and he shall give him life for them that sin not unto death. There is a sin unto death: I do not say that he shall pray for it.

200.   **SIX** – The best solution to banish the demons of marriage that generate marriage troubles, that generate spiritual distractions in marriage, that generate wanton rebellion against Christ, that generate casting off your faith in Christ in order to fully satisfy the demands of marriage, is to remain single, not married!

    i. **1 Corinthians 7:7 (KJV)** For I would that all men were even as I myself. But every man hath his proper gift of God, one after this manner, and another after that.

    ii. **1 Corinthians 7:8 (KJV)** I say therefore to the unmarried and widows, It is good for them if they abide even as I.

    iii. **1 Corinthians 7:9 (KJV)** But if they cannot contain, let them marry: for it is better to marry than to burn.

201.   Nevertheless, this best solution to remain single for the sole purpose of serving God Almighty fully, completely, and without distraction, is NOT for everyone as the LORD Jesus Christ revealed! This best solution to remain single for the sole purpose of serving God Almighty fully is there for those who are able to take it! For those who are NOT able to take it because they are weak and have no power over their flesh, and they desire to have their flesh touch a female flesh, they do NOT sin even when they choose to marry!

    i. **Matthew 19:1 (KJV)** And it came to pass, *that* when Jesus had finished these sayings, he departed from Galilee, and came into the coasts of Judaea beyond Jordan;

    ii. **Matthew 19:2 (KJV)** And great multitudes followed him; and he healed them there.

    iii. **Matthew 19:3 (KJV)** The Pharisees also came unto him, tempting him, and saying unto him, Is it lawful for a man to put away his wife for every cause?

    iv. **Matthew 19:4 (KJV)** And he answered and said unto them, Have ye not read, that he which made *them* at the beginning made them male and female,

    v. **Matthew 19:5 (KJV)** And said, For this cause shall a man leave father and mother, and shall cleave to his wife: and they twain shall be one flesh?

    vi. **Matthew 19:6 (KJV)** Wherefore they are no more twain, but one flesh. What therefore God hath joined together, let not man put asunder.

    vii. **Matthew 19:7 (KJV)** They say unto him, Why did Moses then command to give a writing of divorcement, and to put her away?

    viii. **Matthew 19:8 (KJV)** He saith unto them, Moses because of the hardness of your hearts suffered you to put away your wives: but from the beginning it was not so.

    ix. **Matthew 19:9 (KJV)** And I say unto you, Whosoever shall put away his wife, except *it be* for fornication, and shall marry another, committeth adultery: and whoso marrieth her which is put away doth commit adultery.

    x. **Matthew 19:10 (KJV)** His disciples say unto him, If the case of the man be so with *his* wife, it is not good to marry.

    xi. **Matthew 19:11 (KJV)** But he said unto them, All *men* cannot receive this saying, save *they* to whom it is given.

    xii. **Matthew 19:12 (KJV)** For there are some eunuchs, which were so born from *their* mother's womb: and there are some eunuchs, which were made eunuchs of men: and there be eunuchs, which have made themselves eunuchs for the kingdom of heaven's sake. He that is able to receive *it*, let him receive *it*.

202.   According to the LORD Jesus Christ, it must be given you from Heaven before you can choose the best solution of remaining single to serve God that I have mentioned here above: "All *men* cannot receive this saying, save *they* to whom it is given."!

203.   SEVEN – In a true Christian marriage, divorce is forbidden for both spouses! Also, in a true Christian marriage, divorce is allowed ONLY when the person seeking the divorce will remain unmarried during the entire period of the separation/divorce! Also, in a true Christian marriage, remarriage is allowed but ONLY to the same spouse from whom you divorced!

    i. **1 Corinthians 7:10 (KJV)** And unto the married I command, *yet* not I, but the Lord, Let not the wife depart from *her* husband:

    ii. **1 Corinthians 7:11 (KJV)** But and if she depart, let her remain unmarried, or be reconciled to *her* husband: and let not the husband put away *his* wife.

204.   EIGHT – In a true Christian marriage, one of the spouses may be an unbeliever, unsaved, not born again, in fact quite bluntly, one of the spouses may be a Devil, and when that is the case, then, the Sentence of Judgment is this: Brother, Sister, even though you know that your husband/wife is a Devil, are you still happy to live with him/her? If the answer is, yes, then, there is NO cause for divorce! In that case, you just continue to accept the demonic behavior of your spouse and live with him/her and continue to love him/her just the same way as you will continue to love and help your evil recalcitrant wicked disobedient son/daughter and refuse to throw him/her away!

    i. **1 Corinthians 7:12 (KJV)** But to the rest speak I, not the Lord: If any brother hath a wife that believeth not, and she be pleased to dwell with him, let him not put her away.

      ii. **1 Corinthians 7:13 (KJV)** And the woman which hath an husband that believeth not, and if he be pleased to dwell with her, let her not leave him.

205.   Here is the reason why, in a Christian marriage, you MAY accept to live with a spouse who is a Devil!

      i. **1 Corinthians 7:14 (KJV)** For the unbelieving husband is sanctified by the wife, and the unbelieving wife is sanctified by the husband: else were your children unclean; but now are they holy.

206.   **1 Corinthians 7:14 (KJV)** means that the sanctification/cleansing/washing that you get as a true child of God, some of it rubs off on your unsaved unbelieving wicked wife/husband to make your children also clean before God Almighty!

207.   NINE – In a true Christian marriage, in the case where it is the unsaved unbelieving wicked spouse who decided to divorce, then, let him/her go, and when that is the case, then, you the peaceful God-fearing spouse that is left, you are no longer under the marriage bondage/rule/law of: "bound by the law as long as her husband/wife liveth"!

      i. **1 Corinthians 7:15 (KJV)** But if the unbelieving depart, let him depart. A brother or a sister is not under bondage in such *cases*: but God hath called us to peace.

      ii. **1 Corinthians 7:16 (KJV)** For what knowest thou, O wife, whether thou shalt save *thy* husband? or how knowest thou, O man, whether thou shalt save *thy* wife?

      iii. **Romans 7:2 (KJV)** For the woman which hath an husband is bound by the law to *her* husband so long as he liveth; but if the husband be dead, she is loosed from the law of *her* husband.

      iv. **1 Corinthians 7:39 (KJV)** The wife is bound by the law as long as her husband liveth; but if her husband be dead, she is at liberty to be married to whom she will; only in the Lord.

208.   Then, in this particular case of having become loosed from this marriage bondage/rule/law in **Romans 7:2 (KJV)** and in **1 Corinthians 7:39 (KJV)**, then, you are free to remarry, but ONLY in the LORD, not any more to another unbelieving person!

209.   TEN – Just as the LORD Jesus Christ said, so say I also to you, that, to every man his different calling in the LORD! If you have the capacity to withstand the troubles of marriage, then, do it! If not, then forebear!

      i. **1 Corinthians 7:17 (KJV)** But as God hath distributed to every man, as the Lord hath called every one, so let him walk. And so ordain I in all churches.

    ii. **Matthew 19:9 (KJV)** And I say unto you, Whosoever shall put away his wife, except *it be* for fornication, and shall marry another, committeth adultery: and whoso marrieth her which is put away doth commit adultery.

    iii. **Matthew 19:10 (KJV)** His disciples say unto him, If the case of the man be so with *his* wife, it is not good to marry.

    iv. **Matthew 19:11 (KJV)** But he said unto them, All *men* cannot receive this saying, save *they* to whom it is given.

    v. **Matthew 19:12 (KJV)** For there are some eunuchs, which were so born from *their* mother's womb: and there are some eunuchs, which were made eunuchs of men: and there be eunuchs, which have made themselves eunuchs for the kingdom of heaven's sake. He that is able to receive *it*, let him receive *it*.

210.   ELEVEN – Now, what about those who became saved after they were married, what shall they do? Did your calling come to you while you were still married? Care not about it but go on and serve the LORD with all your heart, with all your mind, with all your soul, and with all your strength and the LORD will reward you for the percentage of work that you are able to accomplish!

    i. **1 Corinthians 7:18 (KJV)** Is any man called being circumcised? let him not become uncircumcised. Is any called in uncircumcision? let him not be circumcised.

    ii. **1 Corinthians 7:19 (KJV)** Circumcision is nothing, and uncircumcision is nothing, but the keeping of the commandments of God.

    iii. **1 Corinthians 3:12 (KJV)** Now if any man build upon this foundation gold, silver, precious stones, wood, hay, stubble;

    iv. **1 Corinthians 3:13 (KJV)** Every man's work shall be made manifest: for the day shall declare it, because it shall be revealed by fire; and the fire shall try every man's work of what sort it is.

    v. **1 Corinthians 3:14 (KJV)** If any man's work abide which he hath built thereupon, he shall receive a reward.

    vi. **1 Corinthians 3:15 (KJV)** If any man's work shall be burned, he shall suffer loss: but he himself shall be saved; yet so as by fire.

211.   The LORD God called Abraham when he was already married, and the LORD God called Isaac before he became married, and the LORD God called Jacob on his way to seek a wife, and the LORD God called Moses after he was married with two sons! So, whatever your marital situation is, whether married or single, it is NOT the status that matters, but your obedience to all the Commandments of God Almighty!

You receive the reward for what you do in Ministry whether married or single and whether good or evil! Therefore, let every man abide in the same calling wherein he was called!

    i. **1 Corinthians 7:20 (KJV)** Let every man abide in the same calling wherein he was called.

    ii. **1 Corinthians 7:21 (KJV)** Art thou called *being* a servant? care not for it: but if thou mayest be made free, use *it* rather.

    iii. **1 Corinthians 7:22 (KJV)** For he that is called in the Lord, *being* a servant, is the Lord's freeman: likewise also he that is called, *being* free, is Christ's servant.

    iv. **1 Corinthians 7:23 (KJV)** Ye are bought with a price; be not ye the servants of men.

    v. **1 Corinthians 7:24 (KJV)** Brethren, let every man, wherein he is called, therein abide with God.

212.   TWELVE – Now, what about if a man or a woman is a virgin, what shall they also do regarding marriage? The answer is that it is "good for a man so to be", meaning that it is good to remain a virgin and serve the LORD God in your flesh purity!

    i. **1 Corinthians 7:25 (KJV)** Now concerning virgins I have no commandment of the Lord: yet I give my judgment, as one that hath obtained mercy of the Lord to be faithful.

    ii. **1 Corinthians 7:26 (KJV)** I suppose therefore that this is good for the present distress, *I say*, that *it is* good for a man so to be.

213.   Remember what I said in the previous chapter that:

    i. The uniqueness of the sin of fornication and adultery is without comparison seeing that it has a double edge and a double effect, because it is the only sin on Earth that cannot be executed without the presence of a second person hence, its double application and double effect!

214.   Therefore, if you are an adult and you have been able to keep yourself pure from the spiritual filthiness of sex that even when it is done within a lawful marriage, it still has the power to displease God as unclean and filthy, if you have been able to keep yourself pure, then, I strongly counsel you to keep it that way even as Paul also counsels you in **1 Corinthians 7:26 (KJV)** saying: "it is good for a man so to be"!

    i. **1 Corinthians 7:37 (KJV)** Nevertheless he that standeth stedfast in his heart, having no necessity, but hath power over his own will, and hath so decreed in his heart that he will keep his virgin, doeth well.

215.   Here is the evidence that, even in a lawful marriage, the conjugal duty of copulation is still a spiritual defilement that cannot be done side by side with the spiritual duty of prayer, whereas the Word of God says: Pray without ceasing!

    i. **1 Corinthians 7:5 (KJV)** Defraud ye not one the other, except *it be* with consent for a time, that ye may give yourselves to fasting and prayer; and come together again, that Satan tempt you not for your incontinency.

    ii. **1 Thessalonians 5:17 (KJV)** Pray without ceasing.

    iii. **Revelation 14:1 (KJV)** And I looked, and, lo, a Lamb stood on the mount Sion, and with him an hundred forty *and* four thousand, having his Father's name written in their foreheads.

    iv. **Revelation 14:2 (KJV)** And I heard a voice from heaven, as the voice of many waters, and as the voice of a great thunder: and I heard the voice of harpers harping with their harps:

    v. **Revelation 14:3 (KJV)** And they sung as it were a new song before the throne, and before the four beasts, and the elders: and no man could learn that song but the hundred *and* forty *and* four thousand, which were redeemed from the earth.

    vi. **Revelation 14:4 (KJV)** These are they which were not defiled with women; for they are virgins. These are they which follow the Lamb whithersoever he goeth. These were redeemed from among men, *being* the firstfruits unto God and to the Lamb.

216.   Remember also that when the LORD God was looking for a person through whom to be born into the world, HE did NOT choose a person who was already stained with sex, but HE chose a Virgin! Furthermore, God never came into the world through sex, but HE completely excluded sex as a means for procreation!

    i. **Luke 1:34 (KJV)** Then said Mary unto the angel, How shall this be, seeing I know not a man?

    ii. **Luke 1:35 (KJV)** And the angel answered and said unto her, The Holy Ghost shall come upon thee, and the power of the Highest shall overshadow thee: therefore also that holy thing which shall be born of thee shall be called the Son of God.

    iii. **Matthew 1:19 (KJV)** Then Joseph her husband, being a just *man*, and not willing to make her a publick example, was minded to put her away privily.

    iv. **Matthew 1:20 (KJV)** But while he thought on these things, behold, the angel of the Lord appeared unto him in a dream, saying, Joseph, thou son of David, fear not to take unto thee Mary thy wife: for that which is conceived in her is of the Holy Ghost.

    v. **Matthew 1:21 (KJV)** And she shall bring forth a son, and thou shalt call his name JESUS: for he shall save his people from their sins.

    vi. **Matthew 1:22 (KJV)** Now all this was done, that it might be fulfilled which was spoken of the Lord by the prophet, saying,

    vii. **Matthew 1:23 (KJV)** Behold, a virgin shall be with child, and shall bring forth a son, and they shall call his name Emmanuel, which being interpreted is, God with us.

    viii. **Matthew 1:24 (KJV)** Then Joseph being raised from sleep did as the angel of the Lord had bidden him, and took unto him his wife:

    ix. **Matthew 1:25 (KJV)** And knew her not till she had brought forth her firstborn son: and he called his name JESUS.

217.   Remember also that marriage and sex are ONLY for lesser creation such as humans and animals, because Angels are higher than humans and there is NO marriage in Heaven!

    i. **Psalm 8:4 (KJV)** What is man, that thou art mindful of him? and the son of man, that thou visitest him?

    ii. **Psalm 8:5 (KJV)** For thou hast made him a little lower than the angels, and hast crowned him with glory and honour.

    iii. **Matthew 22:30 (KJV)** For in the resurrection they neither marry, nor are given in marriage, but are as the angels of God in heaven.

    iv. **Mark 12:25 (KJV)** For when they shall rise from the dead, they neither marry, nor are given in marriage; but are as the angels which are in heaven.

218.   Remember also and ask yourself why you need purification if sex, menstruation, and childbirth are clean and holy?

    i. **2 Samuel 11:4 (KJV)** And David sent messengers, and took her; and she came in unto him, and he lay with her; for she was purified from her uncleanness: and she returned unto her house.

    ii. **Luke 2:22 (KJV)** And when the days of her purification according to the law of Moses were accomplished, they brought him to Jerusalem, to present *him* to the Lord;

    iii. **Leviticus 12:1 (KJV)** And the LORD spake unto Moses, saying,

    iv. **Leviticus 12:2 (KJV)** Speak unto the children of Israel, saying, If a woman have conceived seed, and born a man child: then she shall be unclean seven days; according to the days of the separation for her infirmity shall she be unclean.

    v. **Leviticus 12:3 (KJV)** And in the eighth day the flesh of his foreskin shall be circumcised.

    vi. **Leviticus 12:4 (KJV)** And she shall then continue in the blood of her purifying three and thirty days; she shall touch no hallowed thing, nor come into the sanctuary, until the days of her purifying be fulfilled.

    vii. **Leviticus 12:5 (KJV)** But if she bear a maid child, then she shall be unclean two weeks, as in her separation: and she shall continue in the blood of her purifying threescore and six days.

    viii. **Leviticus 12:6 (KJV)** And when the days of her purifying are fulfilled, for a son, or for a daughter, she shall bring a lamb of the first year for a burnt offering, and a young pigeon, or a turtledove, for a sin offering, unto the door of the tabernacle of the congregation, unto the priest:

    ix. **Leviticus 12:7 (KJV)** Who shall offer it before the LORD, and make an atonement for her; and she shall be cleansed from the issue of her blood. This *is* the law for her that hath born a male or a female.

    x. **Leviticus 12:8 (KJV)** And if she be not able to bring a lamb, then she shall bring two turtles, or two young pigeons; the one for the burnt offering, and the other for a sin offering: and the priest shall make an atonement for her, and she shall be clean.

219. Let all those Truths speak to you as you seek to satisfy your flesh and your lust!

220. Again, after you have come to know all these things, if you still decide to marry, it is NOT a sin!

    i. **1 Corinthians 7:36 (KJV)** But if any man think that he behaveth himself uncomely toward his virgin, if she pass the flower of *her* age, and need so require, let him do what he will, he sinneth not: let them marry.

221. THIRTEEN – Now, what about those who are engaged to be married in the future, what shall they also do regarding marriage?

    i. **1 Corinthians 7:27 (KJV)** Art thou bound unto a wife? seek not to be loosed. Art thou loosed from a wife? seek not a wife.

    ii. **1 Corinthians 7:28 (KJV)** But and if thou marry, thou hast not sinned; and if a virgin marry, she hath not sinned. Nevertheless such shall have trouble in the flesh: but I spare you.

222. Here is the answer!

223. Are you engaged: "Art thou bound unto a wife"?

224. Then, seek not to be loosed from that engagement, meaning that do not break that vow/promise/engagement to marry!

225. Did you just lose your wife or husband because he/she died?

226.   Then, seek no more to marry any other woman/man but serve God with the rest of your life!

227.   Do you feel weak and helpless such that you really need an help meet for your physical needs, because your lawful wife or your lawful husband died?

228.   Then, go ahead and marry again because it is better to serve God without moaning and weeping for yourself! Remember **1 Corinthians 7:28 (KJV)** though, that as you go ahead and get yourself a new wife or a new husband: "Nevertheless ye shall have trouble in the flesh"!

    i.   **Numbers 11:18 (KJV)** And say thou unto the people, Sanctify yourselves against to morrow, and ye shall eat flesh: for ye have wept in the ears of the LORD, saying, Who shall give us flesh to eat? for *it was* well with us in Egypt: therefore the LORD will give you flesh, and ye shall eat.

    ii.   **Jeremiah 31:18 (KJV)** I have surely heard Ephraim bemoaning himself *thus*; Thou hast chastised me, and I was chastised, as a bullock unaccustomed *to the yoke*: turn thou me, and I shall be turned; for thou *art* the LORD my God.

    iii.   **Jeremiah 31:19 (KJV)** Surely after that I was turned, I repented; and after that I was instructed, I smote upon *my* thigh: I was ashamed, yea, even confounded, because I did bear the reproach of my youth.

    iv.   **Jeremiah 31:20 (KJV)** *Is* Ephraim my dear son? *is he* a pleasant child? for since I spake against him, I do earnestly remember him still: therefore my bowels are troubled for him; I will surely have mercy upon him, saith the LORD.

229.   FOURTEEN – Now, how can I succeed in Ministry when I have a wife, and the Word of God says about marriage that I cannot pray or attend to God Almighty while in my period of conjugal duty of copulation, and that marriage is trouble, and that marriage is a spiritual distraction, and that marriage is a wanton rebellion against Christ because you must cast off your faith in Christ in order to fully satisfy the demands of marriage?

230.   Here is the answer: "the time *is* short: it remaineth, that both they that have wives be as though they had none"!

    i.   **1 Corinthians 7:29 (KJV)** But this I say, brethren, the time *is* short: it remaineth, that both they that have wives be as though they had none;

    ii.   **1 Corinthians 7:30 (KJV)** And they that weep, as though they wept not; and they that rejoice, as though they rejoiced not; and they that buy, as though they possessed not;

    iii. **1 Corinthians 7:31 (KJV)** And they that use this world, as not abusing *it*: for the fashion of this world passeth away.

231.   It means that even though you have a wife, you must attend to your Ministry as though you were single!

    i. **Exodus 18:1 (KJV)** When Jethro, the priest of Midian, Moses' father in law, heard of all that God had done for Moses, and for Israel his people, *and* that the LORD had brought Israel out of Egypt;

    ii. **Exodus 18:2 (KJV)** Then Jethro, Moses' father in law, took Zipporah, Moses' wife, after he had sent her back,

    iii. **Exodus 18:3 (KJV)** And her two sons; of which the name of the one *was* Gershom; for he said, I have been an alien in a strange land:

    iv. **Exodus 18:4 (KJV)** And the name of the other *was* Eliezer; for the God of my father, *said he, was* mine help, and delivered me from the sword of Pharaoh:

    v. **Exodus 18:5 (KJV)** And Jethro, Moses' father in law, came with his sons and his wife unto Moses into the wilderness, where he encamped at the mount of God:

    vi. **Exodus 18:6 (KJV)** And he said unto Moses, I thy father in law Jethro am come unto thee, and thy wife, and her two sons with her.

    vii. **Exodus 18:7 (KJV)** And Moses went out to meet his father in law, and did obeisance, and kissed him; and they asked each other of *their* welfare; and they came into the tent.

    viii. **Exodus 18:8 (KJV)** And Moses told his father in law all that the LORD had done unto Pharaoh and to the Egyptians for Israel's sake, *and* all the travail that had come upon them by the way, and *how* the LORD delivered them.

    ix. **Exodus 18:9 (KJV)** And Jethro rejoiced for all the goodness which the LORD had done to Israel, whom he had delivered out of the hand of the Egyptians.

    x. **Exodus 18:10 (KJV)** And Jethro said, Blessed *be* the LORD, who hath delivered you out of the hand of the Egyptians, and out of the hand of Pharaoh, who hath delivered the people from under the hand of the Egyptians.

    xi. **Exodus 18:11 (KJV)** Now I know that the LORD *is* greater than all gods: for in the thing wherein they dealt proudly *he was* above them.

    xii. **Exodus 18:12 (KJV)** And Jethro, Moses' father in law, took a burnt offering and sacrifices for God: and Aaron came, and all the elders of Israel, to eat bread with Moses' father in law before God.

232.   The specific meaning of that command is that you should remove your wife completely from anything that the LORD God has commanded you to do in Ministry! You wife was never called together with you! Your children were never called together with you! The Ministry of Christ is NOT a family business! Do NOT give your wife a prominent seat among the Pastors in front of the congregation! Do NOT make your wife the money-keeper of the church! Do NOT make your wide your special advisor in church matters! That was whet Moses the Man of God did and he succeeded! That was what Apostle Peter did and he succeeded! That was what Apostle Paul did and he succeeded!

233.   FIFTEEN – In a true Christian marriage, marriage is ALWAYS a distraction from the LORD, and the best of the Ministers of Christ serves God ONLY 50%, never with all his/her heart!

    i.   **1 Corinthians 7:32 (KJV)** But I would have you without carefulness. He that is unmarried careth for the things that belong to the Lord, how he may please the Lord:

    ii.   **1 Corinthians 7:33 (KJV)** But he that is married careth for the things that are of the world, how he may please *his* wife.

    iii.   **1 Corinthians 7:34 (KJV)** There is difference *also* between a wife and a virgin. The unmarried woman careth for the things of the Lord, that she may be holy both in body and in spirit: but she that is married careth for the things of the world, how she may please *her* husband.

    iv.   **1 Corinthians 7:35 (KJV)** And this I speak for your own profit; not that I may cast a snare upon you, but for that which is comely, and that ye may attend upon the Lord without distraction.

234.   Here is what the LORD Jesus Christ said about seeking the things of the world that every married couple seek!

    i.   **Luke 12:29 (KJV)** And seek not ye what ye shall eat, or what ye shall drink, neither be ye of doubtful mind.

    ii.   **Luke 12:30 (KJV)** For all these things do the nations of the world seek after: and your Father knoweth that ye have need of these things.

    iii.   **Luke 12:31 (KJV)** But rather seek ye the kingdom of God; and all these things shall be added unto you.

235.   Brother, Sister, did you hear what the LORD Jesus Christ said?

236.   HE said that it is "the nations of the world that seek after the things of the world", meaning that, in a true Christian marriage, you and your husband/wife are considered the same as unsaved people of the world who chase after money and properties daily, why? Because it is impossible serve God halfheartedly!

    i. **Deuteronomy 6:5 (KJV)** And thou shalt love the LORD thy God with all thine heart, and with all thy soul, and with all thy might.

    ii. **Matthew 22:37 (KJV)** Jesus said unto him, Thou shalt love the Lord thy God with all thy heart, and with all thy soul, and with all thy mind.

    iii. **Mark 12:30 (KJV)** And thou shalt love the Lord thy God with all thy heart, and with all thy soul, and with all thy mind, and with all thy strength: this *is* the first commandment.

    iv. **Luke 10:27 (KJV)** And he answering said, Thou shalt love the Lord thy God with all thy heart, and with all thy soul, and with all thy strength, and with all thy mind; and thy neighbour as thyself.

    v. **Luke 10:28 (KJV)** And he said unto him, Thou hast answered right: this do, and thou shalt live.

237.   Brother, Sister, when I tell you that it is impossible to serve God halfheartedly, I am even being too kind with you, because Apostle John the Beloved says it very plainly and more sharply to tell you plainly that, when you seek the things of the world and therefore you serve God halfheartedly, THEN, YOU ARE NOT EVEN SAVED!

    i. **1 John 2:15 (KJV)** Love not the world, neither the things *that are* in the world. If any man love the world, the love of the Father is not in him.

238.   Then, someone will say:

    i. What about if I can stay in marriage and also worship and "love the Lord my God with all my heart, and with all my soul, and with all my mind"?

239.   Alright, Brother, Sister, I hear your question, but between you and the LORD God Almighty, who is the liar? Must I believe you and leave aside what God has said in **1 Corinthians 7:32-35 (KJV)**? God forbid!

    i. **Romans 3:4 (KJV)** God forbid: yea, let God be true, but every man a liar; as it is written, That thou mightest be justified in thy sayings, and mightest overcome when thou art judged.

240.   If God Almighty told me in **1 Corinthians 7:32-35 (KJV)** that every married couple seeks the things of the world and the two spouses also serve God halfheartedly, and here, you are trying to get me to disbelieve God and rather believe you, then tell me, between you and God, who is the Devil?

    i. **Matthew 16:22 (KJV)** Then Peter took him, and began to rebuke him, saying, Be it far from thee, Lord: this shall not be unto thee.

    ii. **Matthew 16:23 (KJV)** But he turned, and said unto Peter, Get thee behind me, Satan: thou art an offence unto me: for thou savourest not the things that be of God, but those that be of men.

    iii. **Matthew 4:6 (KJV)** And saith unto him, If thou be the Son of God, cast thyself down: for it is written, He shall give his angels charge concerning thee: and in *their* hands they shall bear thee up, lest at any time thou dash thy foot against a stone.

    iv. **Matthew 4:7 (KJV)** Jesus said unto him, It is written again, Thou shalt not tempt the Lord thy God.

241.   SIXTEEN – Is it then good to marry, or, is it not good to marry?

242.   Brother, Sister, you are asking a two thousand year old question whose answer has never changed, and it is found in **Matthew 19:10-12 (KJV)**!

    i. **Matthew 19:10 (KJV)** His disciples say unto him, If the case of the man be so with *his* wife, it is not good to marry.

    ii. **Matthew 19:11 (KJV)** But he said unto them, All *men* cannot receive this saying, save *they* to whom it is given.

    iii. **Matthew 19:12 (KJV)** For there are some eunuchs, which were so born from *their* mother's womb: and there are some eunuchs, which were made eunuchs of men: and there be eunuchs, which have made themselves eunuchs for the kingdom of heaven's sake. He that is able to receive *it*, let him receive *it*.

243.   So then, if marriage is with such a guilt and 50% condemnation, then why should I marry?

244.   Again, the LORD God has already said, that if you do this thing called marriage, God will NOT count it as a sin against you, so what is your problem?

    i. **1 Corinthians 7:36 (KJV)** But if any man think that he behaveth himself uncomely toward his virgin, if she pass the flower of *her* age, and need so require, let him do what he will, he sinneth not: let them marry.

    ii. **1 Corinthians 7:37 (KJV)** Nevertheless he that standeth stedfast in his heart, having no necessity, but hath power over his own will, and hath so decreed in his heart that he will keep his virgin, doeth well.

    iii. **1 Corinthians 7:38 (KJV)** So then he that giveth *her* in marriage doeth well; but he that giveth *her* not in marriage doeth better.

245.   SEVENTEEN – In conclusion, so, then, if you want to marry, please do, and as you do that, please remember that this man and this woman that you never know the spirit that is sitting inside him or her, whether good or evil, but you have decided to marry him/her anyway, whatever he or she reveals himself or herself to be after the marriage, in the future, maybe 10 years down the road, the Marriage Law in Christ is this: "The wife/husband is bound by the law as long as her husband/his wife liveth"!

    i. **1 Corinthians 7:39 (KJV)** The wife is bound by the law as long as her husband liveth; but if her husband be dead, she is at liberty to be married to whom she will; only in the Lord.

    ii. **1 Corinthians 7:40 (KJV)** But she is happier if she so abide, after my judgment: and I think also that I have the Spirit of God.

246.   In other words, you, Madam Christian, you have decided and you make a sacred vow before God and men that, when this your husband turns out in the future to be a monster, you will NOT seek divorce but you will still keep him and live with your decision and choice that you have made today!

247.   In other words, you, Mr. Christian, you have decided and you make a sacred vow before God and men that, when this your wife turns out in the future to be a monster, you will NOT seek divorce but you will still keep her and live with your decision and choice that you have made today!

248.   The LORD be witness then!

    i. **Jeremiah 32:10 (KJV)** And I subscribed the evidence, and sealed *it*, and took witnesses, and weighed *him* the money in the balances.

    ii. **Nehemiah 9:38 (KJV)** And because of all this we make a sure *covenant*, and write *it*; and our princes, Levites, *and* priests, seal *unto it*.

Tuesday 9ᵗʰ January 2024 @ 5:35 PM – 10:37 PM

CHAPTER 8: DOES FOOD POSSESS ANY SPIRITUAL PROPERTIES OR POWER? WHERE IS THE COMMAND TO OFFER HOLY COMMUNION WAFERS, WINE, AND BREAD?

249.   In other words, when we eat certain foods and meats, does that observance enhance, prolong, advance, or improve our spiritual standing?

250.   The short answer is, NO!

251.   The potency or the spirituality of any food, meat, or drink that are served unto idols derive their potency and spirituality from the knowledge and belief that the worshippers thereof invest in those same foods, drinks, and meats!

252.   In other words, the food, meat, or drink becomes evil when you so think, and the food, meat, or drink is nothing when you so think!

      i. **1 Corinthians 8:1 (KJV)** Now as touching things offered unto idols, we know that we all have knowledge. Knowledge puffeth up, but charity edifieth.

      ii. **1 Corinthians 8:2 (KJV)** And if any man think that he knoweth any thing, he knoweth nothing yet as he ought to know.

      iii. **1 Corinthians 8:4 (KJV)** As concerning therefore the eating of those things that are offered in sacrifice unto idols, we know that an idol *is* nothing in the world, and that *there is* none other God but one.

253.   So that concerning foods and meats that are offered unto idols, and asking whether they assume any spiritual potency or importance: they do not, because those foods and meats are as dumb as the lifeless idols themselves that have no power to consume these same foods and drinks that are offered unto them?

254.   But, our God is different because our God is the Living God and the Consuming Fire and this attribute of God Almighty, none of the dumb gods and lords is able to do!

      i. **Deuteronomy 5:26 (KJV)** For who *is there of* all flesh, that hath heard the voice of the living God speaking out of the midst of the fire, as we *have*, and lived?

      ii. **Joshua 3:10 (KJV)** And Joshua said, Hereby ye shall know that the living God *is* among you, and *that* he will without fail drive out from before you the Canaanites, and the Hittites, and the Hivites, and the Perizzites, and the Girgashites, and the Amorites, and the Jebusites.

      iii. **Psalm 42:2 (KJV)** My soul thirsteth for God, for the living God: when shall I come and appear before God?

iv. **Jeremiah 10:10 (KJV)** But the LORD *is* the true God, he *is* the living God, and an everlasting king: at his wrath the earth shall tremble, and the nations shall not be able to abide his indignation.

v. **Daniel 6:26 (KJV)** I make a decree, That in every dominion of my kingdom men tremble and fear before the God of Daniel: for he *is* the living God, and stedfast for ever, and his kingdom *that* which shall not be destroyed, and his dominion *shall be even* unto the end.

vi. **Hosea 1:10 (KJV)** Yet the number of the children of Israel shall be as the sand of the sea, which cannot be measured nor numbered; and it shall come to pass, *that* in the place where it was said unto them, Ye *are* not my people, *there* it shall be said unto them, *Ye are* the sons of the living God.

vii. **Matthew 16:16 (KJV)** And Simon Peter answered and said, Thou art the Christ, the Son of the living God.

255. Here is God Almighty as a Consuming Fire!

i. **Deuteronomy 4:24 (KJV)** For the LORD thy God *is* a consuming fire, *even* a jealous God.

ii. **Deuteronomy 9:3 (KJV)** Understand therefore this day, that the LORD thy God *is* he which goeth over before thee; *as* a consuming fire he shall destroy them, and he shall bring them down before thy face: so shalt thou drive them out, and destroy them quickly, as the LORD hath said unto thee.

iii. **Hebrews 12:29 (KJV)** For our God *is* a consuming fire.

iv. **Exodus 24:12 (KJV)** And the LORD said unto Moses, Come up to me into the mount, and be there: and I will give thee tables of stone, and a law, and commandments which I have written; that thou mayest teach them.

v. **Exodus 24:13 (KJV)** And Moses rose up, and his minister Joshua: and Moses went up into the mount of God.

vi. **Exodus 24:14 (KJV)** And he said unto the elders, Tarry ye here for us, until we come again unto you: and, behold, Aaron and Hur *are* with you: if any man have any matters to do, let him come unto them.

vii. **Exodus 24:15 (KJV)** And Moses went up into the mount, and a cloud covered the mount.

viii. **Exodus 24:16 (KJV)** And the glory of the LORD abode upon mount Sinai, and the cloud covered it six days: and the seventh day he called unto Moses out of the midst of the cloud.

    ix. **Exodus 24:17 (KJV)** And the sight of the glory of the LORD *was* like devouring fire on the top of the mount in the eyes of the children of Israel.

256.   Now, here is one of the most important differences between the dumb idols and the LORD God Almighty whereby the LORD God can receive meat/food and drink offerings but the dumb idols cannot!

    i. **Leviticus 9:23 (KJV)** And Moses and Aaron went into the tabernacle of the congregation, and came out, and blessed the people: and the glory of the LORD appeared unto all the people.

    ii. **Leviticus 9:24 (KJV)** And there came a fire out from before the LORD, and consumed upon the altar the burnt offering and the fat: *which* when all the people saw, they shouted, and fell on their faces.

    iii. **1 Kings 18:36 (KJV)** And it came to pass at *the time of* the offering of the *evening* sacrifice, that Elijah the prophet came near, and said, LORD God of Abraham, Isaac, and of Israel, let it be known this day that thou *art* God in Israel, and *that* I *am* thy servant, and *that* I have done all these things at thy word.

    iv. **1 Kings 18:37 (KJV)** Hear me, O LORD, hear me, that this people may know that thou *art* the LORD God, and *that* thou hast turned their heart back again.

    v. **1 Kings 18:38 (KJV)** Then the fire of the LORD fell, and consumed the burnt sacrifice, and the wood, and the stones, and the dust, and licked up the water that *was* in the trench.

    vi. **1 Kings 18:39 (KJV)** And when all the people saw *it*, they fell on their faces: and they said, The LORD, he *is* the God; the LORD, he *is* the God.

257.   Therefore, the most important thing is to love God and keep HIS commandments! The dumb idols might call themselves gods and deities and lords, yet they are dumb and have no power over the true child of God who loves God and is known of God as **1 Corinthians 8:3 (KJV)** reveals!

    i. **1 Corinthians 8:3 (KJV)** But if any man love God, the same is known of him.

    ii. **1 Corinthians 8:5 (KJV)** For though there be that are called gods, whether in heaven or in earth, (as there be gods many, and lords many,)

    iii. **1 Corinthians 8:6 (KJV)** But to us *there is but* one God, the Father, of whom *are* all things, and we in him; and one Lord Jesus Christ, by whom *are* all things, and we by him.

258.   Agan, it is the knowledge from the worshippers that is invested in the food, drinks, and meats that defiles the man and NOT the food, drinks, and meats themselves! That is why "meat commendeth us not to God", meaning that there is zero spiritual significance in any food, including the useless Holy Communion foods and drinks!

    i. **1 Corinthians 8:7 (KJV)** Howbeit *there is* not in every man that knowledge: for some with conscience of the idol unto this hour eat *it* as a thing offered unto an idol; and their conscience being weak is defiled.

    ii. **1 Corinthians 8:8 (KJV)** But meat commendeth us not to God: for neither, if we eat, are we the better; neither, if we eat not, are we the worse.

    iii. **Mark 7:14 (KJV)** And when he had called all the people *unto him*, he said unto them, Hearken unto me every one *of you*, and understand:

    iv. **Mark 7:15 (KJV)** There is nothing from without a man, that entering into him can defile him: but the things which come out of him, those are they that defile the man.

    v. **Mark 7:16 (KJV)** If any man have ears to hear, let him hear.

    vi. **Matthew 15:15 (KJV)** Then answered Peter and said unto him, Declare unto us this parable.

    vii. **Matthew 15:16 (KJV)** And Jesus said, Are ye also yet without understanding?

    viii. **Matthew 15:17 (KJV)** Do not ye yet understand, that whatsoever entereth in at the mouth goeth into the belly, and is cast out into the draught?

    ix. **Matthew 15:18 (KJV)** But those things which proceed out of the mouth come forth from the heart; and they defile the man.

    x. **Matthew 15:19 (KJV)** For out of the heart proceed evil thoughts, murders, adulteries, fornications, thefts, false witness, blasphemies:

    xi. **Matthew 15:20 (KJV)** These are *the things* which defile a man: but to eat with unwashen hands defileth not a man.

259.   Consequently, the Word of God considers any person who places any spiritual importance into physical food, meat, and drink, as a weak person!

    i. **1 Corinthians 8:9 (KJV)** But take heed lest by any means this liberty of yours become a stumblingblock to them that are weak.

260.   All Holy Communion Pastors, Bishops, and Church Leaders are spiritually weak people since they believe that the idolatry of Holy Communion that they perform

every Sunday in their churches is able to procure them some spiritual benefit, which it does NOT!

261.   If pagans offer foods and drinks to their dumb gods and deities and the dumb gods and deities have no power to eat the food and meat, and then, you who claim to be Christians also offer foods and drinks to your God and your God does not receive nor accept them from your hands hence, you have to eat these same foods and meats by yourselves just as the idol worshippers also consume by themselves the foods and meats that they offer to their idols, then, what is the difference between you two worshippers when both of you do the same thing and both of your gods also do the same thing by NOT accepting the foods and meats at your hands?

    i. **Isaiah 1:10 (KJV)** Hear the word of the LORD, ye rulers of Sodom; give ear unto the law of our God, ye people of Gomorrah.

    ii. **Isaiah 1:11 (KJV)** To what purpose *is* the multitude of your sacrifices unto me? saith the LORD: I am full of the burnt offerings of rams, and the fat of fed beasts; and I delight not in the blood of bullocks, or of lambs, or of he goats.

    iii. **Isaiah 1:12 (KJV)** When ye come to appear before me, who hath required this at your hand, to tread my courts?

    iv. **Isaiah 1:13 (KJV)** Bring no more vain oblations; incense is an abomination unto me; the new moons and sabbaths, the calling of assemblies, I cannot away with; *it is* iniquity, even the solemn meeting.

262.   All you Holy Communion Pastors, Bishops, and Church Leaders, is it true that the LORD Jesus Christ said this?

    i. **Matthew 5:17 (KJV)** Think not that I am come to destroy the law, or the prophets: I am not come to destroy, but to fulfil.

    ii. **Matthew 5:18 (KJV)** For verily I say unto you, Till heaven and earth pass, one jot or one tittle shall in no wise pass from the law, till all be fulfilled.

263.   All you Holy Communion Pastors, Bishops, and Church Leaders, is it true that the LORD God Almighty said this?

    i. **Psalm 50:7 (KJV)** Hear, O my people, and I will speak; O Israel, and I will testify against thee: I *am* God, *even* thy God.

    ii. **Psalm 50:8 (KJV)** I will not reprove thee for thy sacrifices or thy burnt offerings, *to have been* continually before me.

    iii. **Psalm 50:9 (KJV)** I will take no bullock out of thy house, *nor* he goats out of thy folds.

    iv. **Psalm 50:10 (KJV)** For every beast of the forest *is* mine, *and* the cattle upon a thousand hills.

> v. **Psalm 50:11 (KJV)** I know all the fowls of the mountains: and the wild beasts of the field *are* mine.
>
> vi. **Psalm 50:12 (KJV)** If I were hungry, I would not tell thee: for the world *is* mine, and the fulness thereof.
>
> vii. **Psalm 50:13 (KJV)** Will I eat the flesh of bulls, or drink the blood of goats?

264.   So, then, why would the LORD Jesus Christ fulfil **Psalm 50:7-13 (KJV)** by telling you to do exactly the opposite of what the LORD God commanded there?

265.   When the LORD God removed all your food, meat, and drink offerings in **Psalm 50:7-13 (KJV)**, what did God replace them with? God replaced them with words, just words, the Words of God ONLY!

> i. **Psalm 50:14 (KJV)** Offer unto God thanksgiving; and pay thy vows unto the most High:
>
> ii. **Psalm 50:15 (KJV)** And call upon me in the day of trouble: I will deliver thee, and thou shalt glorify me.

266.   Therefore, when the LORD Jesus Christ fulfilled **Psalm 50:7-13 (KJV)** by telling you to eat bread and drink from the cup, HE never commanded you to make an offering out of them unto God since that would have been a blatant disobedience to **Psalm 50:7-13 (KJV**!

267.   Here is exactly what the LORD Jesus Christ commanded!

> i. **Luke 22:14 (KJV)** And when the hour was come, he sat down, and the twelve apostles with him.
>
> ii. **Luke 22:15 (KJV)** And he said unto them, With desire I have desired to eat this passover with you before I suffer:
>
> iii. **Luke 22:16 (KJV)** For I say unto you, I will not any more eat thereof, until it be fulfilled in the kingdom of God.
>
> iv. **Luke 22:17 (KJV)** And he took the cup, and gave thanks, and said, Take this, and divide *it* among yourselves:
>
> v. **Luke 22:18 (KJV)** For I say unto you, I will not drink of the fruit of the vine, until the kingdom of God shall come.
>
> vi. **Luke 22:19 (KJV)** And he took bread, and gave thanks, and brake *it*, and gave unto them, saying, This is my body which is given for you: this do in remembrance of me.
>
> vii. **Luke 22:20 (KJV)** Likewise also the cup after supper, saying, This cup *is* the new testament in my blood, which is shed for you.

268.   Now, all you Holy Communion Pastors, Bishops, and Church Leaders, I have reproduced your Holy Communion Law in **Luke 22:14-20 (KJV)**, so, now, show me the exact words that says "OFFERING or SACRIFICE"!

269.   Second, when you have finished showing me the "offering" in the command of the LORD Jesus Christ in **Luke 22:14-20 (KJV)**, then also, show me the worship service that is in **Luke 22:14-20 (KJV)** that empowers you also to do Holy Communion in a church worship service!

270.   Third, when you have finished showing me the "offering" in the command of the LORD Jesus Christ in **Luke 22:14-20 (KJV)**, then also, show me the Altar that the LORD Jesus Christ was using to make HIS "sacrifice and offerings" at the Last Supper!

271.   Fourth, when you have finished showing me the "offering" in the command of the LORD Jesus Christ in **Luke 22:14-20 (KJV)**, then also, show me the many wine cups in those verses that empower you to "offer" your Holy Communion in many cups!

272.   Fifth, when you have finished showing me the "offering" in the command of the LORD Jesus Christ in **Luke 22:14-20 (KJV)**, then also, show me in those same verses the many different pieces of bread that the LORD Jesus Christ used that empowers you also to use all those many different pieces of bread instead of the only one bread that the LORD Jesus Christ broke and gave to the Apostles!

273.   Holy Communion Pastors, Bishops, and Church Leaders, do you now see what despicable filthy fraudsters you have been?

274.   Do you now see how very stupid and most ignorant bastards that you are?

275.   Do you now see how many millions of innocent equally foolish people like you that you have successfully sent to Hell?

276.   Holy Communion Pastors, Bishops, and Church Leaders, do you now see how you are NOT fit to stand in the Pulpit and even to be in the Ministry at all?

277.   Shame on you and may the curse of Sodom and Gomorrah be on you forever!

     i.   **Jeremiah 23:14 (KJV)** I have seen also in the prophets of Jerusalem an horrible thing: they commit adultery, and walk in lies: they strengthen also the hands of evildoers, that none doth return from his wickedness: they are all of them unto me as Sodom, and the inhabitants thereof as Gomorrah.

278.   Again, when the LORD God removed all your food, meat, and drink offerings in **Psalm 50:7-13 (KJV)**, what did God replace them with? God replaced them with words, just words, the Words of God ONLY!

     i.   **Psalm 50:14 (KJV)** Offer unto God thanksgiving; and pay thy vows unto the most High:

     ii.   **Psalm 50:15 (KJV)** And call upon me in the day of trouble: I will deliver thee, and thou shalt glorify me.

279.   Therefore, since the LORD Jesus Christ said in **Matthew 5:17-18 (KJV)** that HE came to fulfill the Law and the Prophets, then, the Holy Communion Law of the LORD Jesus Christ in **Luke 22:14-20 (KJV)** can NEVER mean a command for you to disobey **Psalm 50:7-13 (KJV)**, but rather, and specifically, **Luke 22:14-20 (KJV)** is a command to do and obey **Psalm 50:14-15 (KJV)**!

280.   How is it that this plain language is in plain sight: "But meat commendeth us not to God", and yet all the Holy Communion Pastors, Bishops, and Church Leaders are so blind that they cannot see it?

 i.   **1 Corinthians 8:8 (KJV)** But meat commendeth us not to God: for neither, if we eat, are we the better; neither, if we eat not, are we the worse.

281.   The revelation that meat (meaning foods, meats, and drinks) DOES NOT COMMEND US TO GOD means that:

 i.   Foods, meats, and drinks, even when offered in sacrifice as Holy Communion, DO NOT commend, approve, entrust, preserve, make us worthy, praise, dedicate, commit, confide, consign, endear, esteem, congratulate, applaud, compliment, endorse, extol, hail, nor justify us before God Almighty!

282.   So, then, what is so hard in this sentence: "But meat commendeth us not to God", that educated illiterates and Doctors such as all these Holy Communion Pastors, Bishops, and Church Leaders are NOT able to understand?

 i.   **1 Corinthians 8:9 (KJV)** But take heed lest by any means this liberty of yours become a stumblingblock to them that are weak.

283.   This particular idolatry and pagan worship in **1 Corinthians 8:10 (KJV)**, is exactly what you have imported into your Holy Communion, and yet it was abolished already in **Psalm 50:7-13 (KJV)**!

 i.   **1 Corinthians 8:10 (KJV)** For if any man see thee which hast knowledge sit at meat in the idol's temple, shall not the conscience of him which is weak be emboldened to eat those things which are offered to idols;

284.   And this your knowledge and practise of idolatrous Holy Communion has already caused millions of so-called Christians to perish!

 i.   **1 Corinthians 8:11 (KJV)** And through thy knowledge shall the weak brother perish, for whom Christ died?

285.   You cannot deny that your idolatrous Holy Communion has already caused millions of so-called Christians to perish because the practise of offering and sacrificing food, meat, and drinks before the LORD God Almighty, is NOT even

found as a commandment in your own Holy Communion Law of the LORD Jesus Christ in **Luke 22:14-20 (KJV)**!

      i.   **1 Corinthians 8:12 (KJV)** But when ye sin so against the brethren, and wound their weak conscience, ye sin against Christ.

     ii.   **1 Corinthians 8:13 (KJV)** Wherefore, if meat make my brother to offend, I will eat no flesh while the world standeth, lest I make my brother to offend.

286.   Or, if you comprehend the sentence, then what is it that informs your stupidity to continue doing it against the LORD God Almighty?

287.   I counsel you by the Holy Ghost, that you do NOT gain access to the LORD or to Heaven through food, meat, and wine!

288.   Food/meat is NOT a medium by which you reach or connect the Kingdom of God in Heaven!

289.   The LORD God Almighty does NOT operate through food/meat, but ONLY through the Word of God!

290.   Food/meat are products fit for the dunghill and for the toilet, but the Words of God are the Keys to open Heaven!

291.   Food/meat are oblations for sacrifice unto Devils but the Word of God is the correct sacrifice and offering unto God!

292.   The Word of God is the correct sacrifice and offering unto God!

293.   You approach the LORD God Almighty with words, the Words of God, NOT with food/meat/drinks!

Wednesday 10th January 2024 @ 9:04 AM – 2:03 PM

CHAPTER 9: SHALL THE MAN OF GOD BE PAID?

294.   When you talk about payment, reward, remuneration, wages, hire, or compensation, then you first want to know if any work has been done!

295.   In other words, what the Man of God does usually, is it work? Can it be called work? Is it labor? Does the LORD God Almighty pay HIS workers for the work done, or is it for free? How does God Almighty determine work?

296.   Yes the occupation of the Man of God is work! It is labour! Time is spent on it to do the work of God and time is a paid commodity, NOT a free commodity!

     i. **Ecclesiastes 2:21 (KJV)** For there is a man whose labour *is* in wisdom, and in knowledge, and in equity; yet to a man that hath not laboured therein shall he leave it *for* his portion. This also *is* vanity and a great evil.

     ii. **Exodus 21:19 (KJV)** If he rise again, and walk abroad upon his staff, then shall he that smote *him* be quit: only he shall pay *for* the loss of his time, and shall cause *him* to be thoroughly healed.

     iii. **Jeremiah 22:13 (KJV)** Woe unto him that buildeth his house by unrighteousness, and his chambers by wrong; *that* useth his neighbour's service without wages, and giveth him not for his work;

     iv. **Ezekiel 29:20 (KJV)** I have given him the land of Egypt *for* his labour wherewith he served against it, because they wrought for me, saith the Lord GOD.

297.   All those are questions that seek to examine the occupation of the Man of God and to determine whether what he is doing is work and, if so, whether he deserves any wages or not!

298.   Here is the answer!

299.   ONE – The first point or item that you need to consider in order to answer all those questions is: Was the Man of God called into the Ministry? What then is his title? If he was called and sent, then, his title is: Apostle!

     i. **1 Corinthians 9:1 (KJV)** Am I not an apostle? am I not free? have I not seen Jesus Christ our Lord? are not ye my work in the Lord?

300.   TWO – Is the Man of God free in accepting to do the work of a Man of God, or was he forced as a slave, or was he under any obligation to do the work of a Man of God! Was he forced to do the work, or does he believe in what he is doing?

301.   THREE – Was it the LORD Jesus Christ who called him into Ministry, or, did he call himself because he sees money in the Ministry? If he says that it was the LORD Jesus Christ who called him into Ministry, then how does he reveal the LORD

Jesus Christ in his thoughts, in his speech, and in this actions? Do you perceive a deep knowledge of the Word of God in him when you speak with him, or does he come across as an ignorant fool who does not know the Word of God? Does he know how to correctly divide/teach the Word of God?

    i. **Proverbs 14:7 (KJV)** Go from the presence of a foolish man, when thou perceivest not *in him* the lips of knowledge.

    ii. **Jeremiah 3:15 (KJV)** And I will give you pastors according to mine heart, which shall feed you with knowledge and understanding.

    iii. **Jeremiah 9:23 (KJV)** Thus saith the LORD, Let not the wise *man* glory in his wisdom, neither let the mighty *man* glory in his might, let not the rich *man* glory in his riches:

    iv. **Jeremiah 9:24 (KJV)** But let him that glorieth glory in this, that he understandeth and knoweth me, that I *am* the LORD which exercise lovingkindness, judgment, and righteousness, in the earth: for in these *things* I delight, saith the LORD.

    v. **Malachi 2:7 (KJV)** For the priest's lips should keep knowledge, and they should seek the law at his mouth: for he *is* the messenger of the LORD of hosts.

    vi. **2 Timothy 2:15 (KJV)** Study to shew thyself approved unto God, a workman that needeth not to be ashamed, rightly dividing the word of truth.

302.   FOUR – The last point in **1 Corinthians 9:1 (KJV)** that you can use to examine the Man of God is: "are not ye my work in the Lord?", meaning that you need to find out whether the Man of God has already preached, taught, or written any books where he is expounding the Word of God very eloquently and quite persuasively to his audience such that they believe what he is teaching concerning the LORD Jesus Christ!

    i. **Acts 18:9 (KJV)** Then spake the Lord to Paul in the night by a vision, Be not afraid, but speak, and hold not thy peace:

    ii. **Acts 18:10 (KJV)** For I am with thee, and no man shall set on thee to hurt thee: for I have much people in this city.

    iii. **Acts 18:11 (KJV)** And he continued *there* a year and six months, teaching the word of God among them.

    iv. **Acts 18:24 (KJV)** And a certain Jew named Apollos, born at Alexandria, an eloquent man, *and* mighty in the scriptures, came to Ephesus.

    v.   **Acts 18:25 (KJV)** This man was instructed in the way of the Lord; and being fervent in the spirit, he spake and taught diligently the things of the Lord, knowing only the baptism of John.

    vi.   **Acts 18:26 (KJV)** And he began to speak boldly in the synagogue: whom when Aquila and Priscilla had heard, they took him unto *them*, and expounded unto him the way of God more perfectly.

    vii.   **Acts 18:27 (KJV)** And when he was disposed to pass into Achaia, the brethren wrote, exhorting the disciples to receive him: who, when he was come, helped them much which had believed through grace:

    viii.   **Acts 18:28 (KJV)** For he mightily convinced the Jews, *and that* publickly, shewing by the scriptures that Jesus was Christ.

    ix.   **Acts 23:11 (KJV)** And the night following the Lord stood by him, and said, Be of good cheer, Paul: for as thou hast testified of me in Jerusalem, so must thou bear witness also at Rome.

303.   FIVE – An Apostle of the LORD Jesus Christ is someone who can show evidence that some people have become Christians or have become strengthened as Christians as a direct result of his teachings in the Ministry!

    i.   **1 Corinthians 9:2 (KJV)** If I be not an apostle unto others, yet doubtless I am to you: for the seal of mine apostleship are ye in the Lord.

304.   SIX – When you are examining the Man of God to know whether you should pay him anything for his work or not, you need to ask yourself this question: Does the Man of God also have the right to eat and to drink just as you do?

    i.   **1 Corinthians 9:3 (KJV)** Mine answer to them that do examine me is this,

    ii.   **1 Corinthians 9:4 (KJV)** Have we not power to eat and to drink?

305.   If the answer is, yes, then, why are you such a fool to be even thinking whether he should be paid or not? If you have a right to eat and to drink, then why are you such a demon to even hesitate to reward the Man of God for his work so that he can also eat and drink?

306.   SEVEN – According to **1 Corinthians 9:5-6 (KJV)**, when the Man of God does the work of Ministry full time, then, the Word of God grants him authority to stop doing side work and to focus full time on the Word of God whereby, in that case, the congregation feeds and shelters the Man of God for feeding them with knowledge and understanding!

    i.   **Jeremiah 3:15 (KJV)** And I will give you pastors according to mine heart, which shall feed you with knowledge and understanding.

     ii. **1 Corinthians 9:5 (KJV)** Have we not power to lead about a sister, a wife, as well as other apostles, and *as* the brethren of the Lord, and Cephas?

     iii. **1 Corinthians 9:6 (KJV)** Or I only and Barnabas, have not we power to forbear working?

307.   EIGHT – According to **1 Corinthians 9:7 (KJV)**, when you are examining the Man of God to know whether you should pay him anything for his work or not, you need to ask yourself the following questions:

     i. **1 Corinthians 9:7 (KJV)** Who goeth a warfare any time at his own charges? who planteth a vineyard, and eateth not of the fruit thereof? or who feedeth a flock, and eateth not of the milk of the flock?

     ii. Who goeth a warfare any time at his own charges?

     iii. Who planteth a vineyard, and eateth not of the fruit thereof?

     iv. Who feedeth a flock, and eateth not of the milk of the flock?

308.   All the three questions are one and they reveal that the Man of God is engaged in warfare, planting a vineyard, and feeding a flock, all on the behalf of the flock/congregation, and the rhetorical nature of the three questions is that: You the person who is examining whether the Man of God deserved to be paid:

     i. Will you yourself accept to engaged in warfare for a people free of charge?

     ii. Will you yourself accept to plant a vineyard for a people free of charge?

     iii. Will you yourself accept to feed a flock of sheep and goats for another person free of charge?

     iv. Will you yourself accept to raise a flock, or feed sheep and goats for someone, and then say that you will not eat of the milk and the meat of the flock of sheep and goats?

309.   So, Brother, Sister, you see that all the above four questions in **1 Corinthians 9:7 (KJV)** are supposed to reveal to you how much stupid you are for thinking that someone should work for free when you yourself will refuse to do the same thing that you are asking someone to do for free?

310.   Is that fair in your own eyes? Will you be able to employ a teacher for your daughter and son and then tell the teacher that Jesus Christ said all Christians should work for free?

311.   Will you able to visit a Doctor or a Lawyer and share this your free work ideas with him or her and he will accept you and give you free work?

312.   Does that kind of thinking make you a good Christian, or does it reveal you to be a Devil? Does that kind of thinking reveal you to be a fraudster? Does that kind of thinking reveal you to be a thief? Does that kind of thinking reveal you to be a robber?

Does that kind of thinking reveal that you were never saved, never born again, and never a Christian? Is this not the curse that the LORD God put in you because you are a thief and you have been stealing your Pastor's wages and refusing to pay him?

      i. **Jeremiah 22:13 (KJV)** Woe unto him that buildeth his house by unrighteousness, and his chambers by wrong; *that* useth his neighbour's service without wages, and giveth him not for his work;

313.   NINE – All those questions that I am asking you, am I asking you because I want your money, or am I asking you because the Word of God said so?

      i. **1 Corinthians 9:8 (KJV)** Say I these things as a man? or saith not the law the same also?

      ii. **1 Corinthians 9:9 (KJV)** For it is written in the law of Moses, Thou shalt not muzzle the mouth of the ox that treadeth out the corn. Doth God take care for oxen?

      iii. **1 Corinthians 9:10 (KJV)** Or saith he *it* altogether for our sakes? For our sakes, no doubt, *this* is written: that he that ploweth should plow in hope; and that he that thresheth in hope should be partaker of his hope.

314.   Here is what the Word of God said: "Thou shalt not muzzle the mouth of the ox that treadeth out the corn"! Meaning that even when the cow works for you, that animal deserves wages in the form of feeding!

315.   So, now, the LORD God is asking you whether you are such a Devil that you are ready to give food to your dogs and cattle who help you to stay on the Earth, but you are ready to starve the Man of God who helps you to go to Heaven?

316.   So, as you call yourself a Christian and a child of God, in your heart, you consider animals to be more important than the Man of God!

317.   Is this not what the Word of God said in **1 Corinthians 9:10 (KJV)** that "he that thresheth in hope should be partaker of his hope"?

318.   Does that command not mean that if the Man of God is helping you to grow spiritually, then he is also authorized to hope to partake of the material and financial growth that come to you?

319.   You know all these things and you still want to be a robber and be able to enter Heaven as a thief?

320.   TEN – You are asking if the Man of God should be paid wages for his labour. Here is the plain answer form God Almighty to you!

      i. **1 Corinthians 9:11 (KJV)** If we have sown unto you spiritual things, *is it* a great thing if we shall reap your carnal things?

ii.   **1 Corinthians 9:12 (KJV)** If others be partakers of *this* power over you, *are* not we rather? Nevertheless we have not used this power; but suffer all things, lest we should hinder the gospel of Christ.

iii.   **1 Corinthians 9:13 (KJV)** Do ye not know that they which minister about holy things live *of the things* of the temple? and they which wait at the altar are partakers with the altar?

iv.   **1 Corinthians 9:14 (KJV)** Even so hath the Lord ordained that they which preach the gospel should live of the gospel.

321.   Brother, Sister, did you see the word "carnal" in **1 Corinthians 9:11 (KJV)**?

322.   Well, the Word of God says in **1 Corinthians 9:11 (KJV)**, that you have done nothing great if you reciprocate a Man of God's spiritual giving with your material carnal giving!

323.   So, already, even the wages that you should give to the Man of God is seen as "carnal" in Heaven, but what does "carnal" mean?

324.   Here is the answer! The word "carnal" does NOT mean anything good!

i.   "Carnal" means something related to physical, sexual, sensual, flesh, things that satisfy animal needs, spiritually deficient, uncovered flesh and nakedness like the half-naked choir women in the churches, something that is enmity against God, worldly, lustful, impure, beastly, unchristian, earthly, lewd, wanton, corporal genital, lascivious, lacking Holy Spirit, unbelieving, temporal, something that is not subject to the law of God, selfishness, self-willed, self-focused and self-seeking, legal term for sexual intercourse, crudity, etc.

325.   Brother, Sister, are you listening?

326.   The Man of God gives you knowledge and understanding to help you enter Heaven, and then the filthy carnal money that you should give him to buy simple food, lodging, and transportation, you are refusing to give, and yet still you want to take his teaching to improve your spiritual situation so that you can go to Heaven? Did you think that God is a thief as you are, to allow you to enter Heaven after stealing the wages of a Man of God? Jesus Christ said: NO WAY!

i.   **Luke 16:10 (KJV)** He that is faithful in that which is least is faithful also in much: and he that is unjust in the least is unjust also in much.

ii.   **Luke 16:11 (KJV)** If therefore ye have not been faithful in the unrighteous mammon, who will commit to your trust the true *riches*?

iii.   **Luke 16:12 (KJV)** And if ye have not been faithful in that which is another man's, who shall give you that which is your own?

327.   ELEVEN – You are asking if the Man of God should be paid wages for his labour.

328.   Brother, Sister, the LORD God is asking you again:

  i. **1 Corinthians 9:12 (KJV)** If others be partakers of *this* power over you, *are* not we rather? Nevertheless we have not used this power; but suffer all things, lest we should hinder the gospel of Christ.

329.   This phrase: "If others be partakers of *this* power over you,", do you know what it means?

330.   It is referring to all the worldly evil wicked unsaved men and women of the world who render work and services to you, such as your University Professors, your Medical Doctors, your evil lying Lawyers and Judges, your Drivers, your dog-walkers, and so on and so forth, do you pay them when they work for you?

331.   The answer is, yes, and the LORD God is saying in **1 Corinthians 9:12 (KJV)** that, compared to all other workers in the world, the Man of God is rather the first person that you should be paying, helping, and taking care of!

332.   This Word: "Nevertheless we have not used this power; but suffer all things, lest we should hinder the gospel of Christ", means that there are some Men of God who are shy and will NOT ask any money from you or dupe you, yet, the fact that they say nothing to you as you continue to cheat them, to rob them, and to steal their wages, that does not mean that you will escape the curse of God on you, no, you will Not escape it, and that was why the LORD Jesus Christ said this Word to you: "And if ye have not been faithful in that which is another man's, who shall give you that which is your own?"!

333.   TWELVE – You are asking if the Man of God should be paid wages for his labour.

334.   Here is the third answer from God to your question on whether the Man of God should be paid!

  i. **1 Corinthians 9:13 (KJV)** Do ye not know that they which minister about holy things live *of the things* of the temple? and they which wait at the altar are partakers with the altar?

335.   Here, the LORD God Almighty is saying it plainly that:

  i. Every Man of God who is ministering the Holy Word of God to people MUST be able to earn his living form the work of God!

336.   This revelation in **1 Corinthians 9:13 (KJV)** is not only against the congregation or Christians who give nothing to the Man of God for his work! It is also against all the Head Pastors and all Church Leaders who also steal the wages of their Assistant Pastors, make them work many hours, and then give them stupid money that is just enough for their transportation back home! To go and do what at home? To starve and then to return the next day to serve you the criminal robber General

Overseer? Woe unto you also, all you Church Leaders who exploit Assistant Pastors and refuse to share the church money equally with them!

337.   THIRTEEN – You are asking if the Man of God should be paid wages for his labour.

338.   Here is the fourth answer from God to your question on whether the Man of God should be paid! Thus, in **1 Corinthians 9:11-14 (KJV)** alone, we have seen four answers already from the LORD God, added to all the many answers from the beginning of this chapter!

     i. **1 Corinthians 9:14 (KJV)** Even so hath the Lord ordained that they which preach the gospel should live of the gospel.

339.   So, your question was: should the Man of God be paid for his work, or shall we apply the "freely ye have received freely give" law!

340.   Then, the LORD God gives you an answer saying: "the Lord hath ordained that they which preach the gospel should live of the gospel"!

341.   Is that language plain enough for you? Does that language sound to you that the LORD God is telling Men of God to work for free? Or, does it sound to you that the LORD God is saying that Men of God should be able to earn a living from their work?

     i. **Luke 10:7 (KJV)** And in the same house remain, eating and drinking such things as they give: for the labourer is worthy of his hire. Go not from house to house.

     ii. **Matthew 10:8 (KJV)** Heal the sick, cleanse the lepers, raise the dead, cast out devils: freely ye have received, freely give.

     iii. **Matthew 10:9 (KJV)** Provide neither gold, nor silver, nor brass in your purses,

     iv. **Matthew 10:10 (KJV)** Nor scrip for *your* journey, neither two coats, neither shoes, nor yet staves: for the workman is worthy of his meat.

342.   FOURTEEN – You are asking if the Man of God should be paid wages for his labour.

343.   To those of you evil Christians who quote **Matthew 10:8 (KJV)**: "freely ye have received, freely give", does **Matthew 10:10 (KJV)** sound to you that the LORD Jesus Christ is teaching free work here?

344.   If "the workman is worthy of his meat", then who will pay it? Who will pay this workman his hire/meat that the LORD Jesus said should be paid?

345.   It is you the audience members of the Man of God who benefit form his teachings who are supposed to pay the Man of God his living, and it is NOT a personal choice, but it is an obligation and a Christian duty as God Almighty commanded in **Romans 15:27 (KJV)**!

    i. **Romans 15:27 (KJV)** It hath pleased them verily; and their debtors they are. For if the Gentiles have been made partakers of their spiritual things, their duty is also to minister unto them in carnal things.

    ii. **1 Corinthians 9:11 (KJV)** If we have sown unto you spiritual things, *is it* a great thing if we shall reap your carnal things?

    iii. **Matthew 10:11 (KJV)** And into whatsoever city or town ye shall enter, inquire who in it is worthy; and there abide till ye go thence.

    iv. **1 Timothy 5:17 (KJV)** Let the elders that rule well be counted worthy of double honour, especially they who labour in the word and doctrine.

    v. **1 Timothy 5:18 (KJV)** For the scripture saith, Thou shalt not muzzle the ox that treadeth out the corn. And, The labourer *is* worthy of his reward.

346.   FIFTEEN – You are asking if the Man of God should be paid wages for his labour.

347.   Now, the LORD God Almighty that I know in **Numbers 18:31 (KJV)** does not dupe HIS workers but pays them immediately when they have worked for him!

    i. **Numbers 18:31 (KJV)** And ye shall eat it in every place, ye and your households: for it *is* your reward for your service in the tabernacle of the congregation.

348.   Furthermore, the LORD Jesus Christ that I know in **Matthew 20:1-16 (KJV)** does not dupe HIS workers but pays them immediately when they have worked for him!

    i. **Matthew 20:1 (KJV)** For the kingdom of heaven is like unto a man *that is* an householder, which went out early in the morning to hire labourers into his vineyard.

    ii. **Matthew 20:2 (KJV)** And when he had agreed with the labourers for a penny a day, he sent them into his vineyard.

    iii. **Matthew 20:3 (KJV)** And he went out about the third hour, and saw others standing idle in the marketplace,

    iv. **Matthew 20:4 (KJV)** And said unto them; Go ye also into the vineyard, and whatsoever is right I will give you. And they went their way.

    v. **Matthew 20:5 (KJV)** Again he went out about the sixth and ninth hour, and did likewise.

    vi. **Matthew 20:6 (KJV)** And about the eleventh hour he went out, and found others standing idle, and saith unto them, Why stand ye here all the day idle?

    vii. **Matthew 20:7 (KJV)** They say unto him, Because no man hath hired us. He saith unto them, Go ye also into the vineyard; and whatsoever is right, *that* shall ye receive.

    viii. **Matthew 20:8 (KJV)** So when even was come, the lord of the vineyard saith unto his steward, Call the labourers, and give them *their* hire, beginning from the last unto the first.

    ix. **Matthew 20:9 (KJV)** And when they came that *were hired* about the eleventh hour, they received every man a penny.

349.   So, I have shown you my God Almighty and my Jesus Christ, that they dso pay their workers promptly and immediately, therefore, now, you show me your Jesus Christ who does not pay HIS workers but tells them: "Thank you for working for me whole day, now, go home and be warm because "freely ye have received, freely give"!

    i. **1 John 3:17 (KJV)** But whoso hath this world's good, and seeth his brother have need, and shutteth up his bowels *of compassion* from him, how dwelleth the love of God in him?

    ii. **1 John 3:18 (KJV)** My little children, let us not love in word, neither in tongue; but in deed and in truth.

    iii. **1 John 3:19 (KJV)** And hereby we know that we are of the truth, and shall assure our hearts before him.

350.   SIXTEEN – You are asking if the Man of God should be paid wages for his labour.

351.   Now ye Men of God, do NOT abuse this divine power to earn a living from the Gospel! Do NOT use this power to exploit, to dupe, and to abuse your congregations because you will go to Hell just as those who refuse to pay you will go to Hell!

    i. **1 Corinthians 9:15 (KJV)** But I have used none of these things: neither have I written these things, that it should be so done unto me: for *it were* better for me to die, than that any man should make my glorying void.

    ii. **1 Corinthians 9:16 (KJV)** For though I preach the gospel, I have nothing to glory of: for necessity is laid upon me; yea, woe is unto me, if I preach not the gospel!

    iii. **1 Corinthians 9:17 (KJV)** For if I do this thing willingly, I have a reward: but if against my will, a dispensation *of the gospel* is committed unto me.

    iv. **1 Corinthians 9:18 (KJV)** What is my reward then? *Verily* that, when I preach the gospel, I may make the gospel of Christ without charge, that I abuse not my power in the gospel.

352.　　　Here are Apostle Paul and Bishop Timothy receiving funding for the poor saints in Jerusalem and for their work for the LORD Jesus Christ!

   i. **1 Corinthians 16:1 (KJV)** Now concerning the collection for the saints, as I have given order to the churches of Galatia, even so do ye.

   ii. **1 Corinthians 16:2 (KJV)** Upon the first *day* of the week let every one of you lay by him in store, as *God* hath prospered him, that there be no gatherings when I come.

   iii. **1 Corinthians 16:3 (KJV)** And when I come, whomsoever ye shall approve by *your* letters, them will I send to bring your liberality unto Jerusalem.

   iv. **1 Corinthians 16:4 (KJV)** And if it be meet that I go also, they shall go with me.

   v. **1 Corinthians 16:5 (KJV)** Now I will come unto you, when I shall pass through Macedonia: for I do pass through Macedonia.

   vi. **1 Corinthians 16:6 (KJV)** And it may be that I will abide, yea, and winter with you, that ye may bring me on my journey whithersoever I go.

   vii. **1 Corinthians 16:7 (KJV)** For I will not see you now by the way; but I trust to tarry a while with you, if the Lord permit.

   viii. **1 Corinthians 16:8 (KJV)** But I will tarry at Ephesus until Pentecost.

   ix. **1 Corinthians 16:9 (KJV)** For a great door and effectual is opened unto me, and *there are* many adversaries.

   x. **1 Corinthians 16:10 (KJV)** Now if Timotheus come, see that he may be with you without fear: for he worketh the work of the Lord, as I also *do*.

   xi. **1 Corinthians 16:11 (KJV)** Let no man therefore despise him: but conduct him forth in peace, that he may come unto me: for I look for him with the brethren.

353.　　　SEVENTEEN – You are asking if the Man of God should be paid wages for his labour.

354.　　　Now, to be able to have a clear conscience before God from the wages that I receive as a Man of God, how shall I do my work?

355.　　　Here is the answer!

   i. **1 Corinthians 9:19 (KJV)** For though I be free from all *men*, yet have I made myself servant unto all, that I might gain the more.

   ii. **1 Corinthians 9:20 (KJV)** And unto the Jews I became as a Jew, that I might gain the Jews; to them that are under the law, as under the law, that I might gain them that are under the law;

iii.   **1 Corinthians 9:21 (KJV)** To them that are without law, as without law, (being not without law to God, but under the law to Christ,) that I might gain them that are without law.

iv.   **1 Corinthians 9:22 (KJV)** To the weak became I as weak, that I might gain the weak: I am made all things to all *men*, that I might by all means save some.

v.   **1 Corinthians 9:23 (KJV)** And this I do for the gospel's sake, that I might be partaker thereof with *you*.

vi.   **1 Corinthians 9:24 (KJV)** Know ye not that they which run in a race run all, but one receiveth the prize? So run, that ye may obtain.

vii.   **1 Corinthians 9:25 (KJV)** And every man that striveth for the mastery is temperate in all things. Now they *do it* to obtain a corruptible crown; but we an incorruptible.

viii.   **1 Corinthians 9:26 (KJV)** I therefore so run, not as uncertainly; so fight I, not as one that beateth the air:

ix.   **1 Corinthians 9:27 (KJV)** But I keep under my body, and bring *it* into subjection: lest that by any means, when I have preached to others, I myself should be a castaway.

356.   In conclusion, you asked if the Man of God should be paid wages for his labour. Behold, I have given you seventeen Bible lessons why you should give wages to the Man of God for his work!

Wednesday 10ᵗʰ January 2024 @ 3:55 PM – 11:11 PM

CHAPTER 10: CHRISTIAN IDOLATRY IN WATER BAPTISM AND IN HOLY COMMUNION

357.   Is it possible for Christianity and idolatry to walk together?

358.   Yes, and the consequence for that is Hell!

    i.   **1 Samuel 15:23 (KJV)** For rebellion *is as* the sin of witchcraft, and stubbornness *is as* iniquity and idolatry. Because thou hast rejected the word of the LORD, he hath also rejected thee from *being* king.

    ii.   **Acts 17:16 (KJV)** Now while Paul waited for them at Athens, his spirit was stirred in him, when he saw the city wholly given to idolatry.

    iii.   **Acts 17:21 (KJV)** (For all the Athenians and strangers which were there spent their time in nothing else, but either to tell, or to hear some new thing.)

    iv.   **1 Corinthians 10:14 (KJV)** Wherefore, my dearly beloved, flee from idolatry.

    v.   **Galatians 5:19 (KJV)** Now the works of the flesh are manifest, which are *these*; Adultery, fornication, uncleanness, lasciviousness,

    vi.   **Galatians 5:20 (KJV)** Idolatry, witchcraft, hatred, variance, emulations, wrath, strife, seditions, heresies,

    vii.   **Galatians 5:21 (KJV)** Envyings, murders, drunkenness, revellings, and such like: of the which I tell you before, as I have also told *you* in time past, that they which do such things shall not inherit the kingdom of God.

    viii.   **Colossians 3:5 (KJV)** Mortify therefore your members which are upon the earth; fornication, uncleanness, inordinate affection, evil concupiscence, and covetousness, which is idolatry:

    ix.   **Colossians 3:6 (KJV)** For which things' sake the wrath of God cometh on the children of disobedience:

359.   So, as you can see from the evidence, the LORD God reveals to us in **1 Samuel 15:23 (KJV)** that rebellion, stubbornness, and rejection/refusal of the Word of God, they are all both witchcraft and idolatry!

360.   Then, in **Acts 17:16-21 (KJV)**, you can see that debating politics as a passion and journalism are also idolatry and you know that there are many so-called Christians who love politics more than the Word of God!

361.   Then, in **1 Corinthians 10:14 (KJV)**, you can see that Apostle Paul was writing to already saved Brethren and yet he was accusing them of idolatry, and so, yes, Christianity and idolatry can walk together!

362.   Then, in **Galatians 5:19-21 (KJV)**, you can see that when people claim to be Christians and they still do the works of the flesh instead of focusing only on the Word of God, such as Water baptism and Holy Communion and Feet Washing, then, they are not only idolaters, but they are also practising witchcraft!

363.   Then, in **Colossians 3:5 (KJV)**, you can see that even the very common sin of covetousness/greediness, is also known as idolatry in the spiritual realm!

364.   Then, finally in **Colossians 3:6 (KJV)**, you see that anyone who practices idolatry and is therefore a witch and wizard, also has the wrath of God on him, meaning that he/she will go to Hell!

365.   Why is 1 Corinthians chapter 10 about idolatry, but already in the second verse, it is talking about Baptism?

        i. **1 Corinthians 10:1 (KJV)** Moreover, brethren, I would not that ye should be ignorant, how that all our fathers were under the cloud, and all passed through the sea;

        ii. **1 Corinthians 10:2 (KJV)** And were all baptized unto Moses in the cloud and in the sea;

366.   Because it is possible to commit idolatry with Water baptism!

367.   Look again at **1 Corinthians 10:1-2 (KJV)** and tell me what you see God Almighty revealing to you over there!

368.   **ONE** – You see that this expression: "and they all passed through the sea" takes you straight to **Exodus 14:15-22 (KJV)**:

        i. **Exodus 14:15 (KJV)** And the LORD said unto Moses, Wherefore criest thou unto me? speak unto the children of Israel, that they go forward:

        ii. **Exodus 14:16 (KJV)** But lift thou up thy rod, and stretch out thine hand over the sea, and divide it: and the children of Israel shall go on dry *ground* through the midst of the sea.

        iii. **Exodus 14:17 (KJV)** And I, behold, I will harden the hearts of the Egyptians, and they shall follow them: and I will get me honour upon Pharaoh, and upon all his host, upon his chariots, and upon his horsemen.

        iv. **Exodus 14:18 (KJV)** And the Egyptians shall know that I *am* the LORD, when I have gotten me honour upon Pharaoh, upon his chariots, and upon his horsemen.

        v. **Exodus 14:19 (KJV)** And the angel of God, which went before the camp of Israel, removed and went behind them; and the pillar of the cloud went from before their face, and stood behind them:

     vi. **Exodus 14:20 (KJV)** And it came between the camp of the Egyptians and the camp of Israel; and it was a cloud and darkness *to them*, but it gave light by night *to these*: so that the one came not near the other all the night.

     vii. **Exodus 14:21 (KJV)** And Moses stretched out his hand over the sea; and the LORD caused the sea to go *back* by a strong east wind all that night, and made the sea dry *land*, and the waters were divided.

     viii. **Exodus 14:22 (KJV)** And the children of Israel went into the midst of the sea upon the dry *ground*: and the waters *were* a wall unto them on their right hand, and on their left.

369.   TWO – Then, this Word: "And they were all baptized unto Moses" is evidence that God Almighty is talking about "Baptism"!

370.   THREE – Then, now look again at **1 Corinthians 10:2 (KJV)**, and then, tell me how the people were baptized, or, with what did Moses baptize the people?

371.   FOUR – Here is the answer: "And they were all baptized unto Moses in the cloud"!

372.   SIX – Now, tell me, did you see any water there in **1 Corinthians 10:1-2 (KJV)**?

373.   SEVEN – The correct answer is, no, and yet, the LORD God says that, even without water, the people still were baptized, meaning that, originally, the very first time that baptism took place in the entire Holy Bible, it was Waterless Baptism! Can you see that?

374.   That revelation of Waterless Baptism that I have just shown you means that the true and correct baptism is NOT with water but waterless, and here is further evidence!

     i. "and the children of Israel shall go on dry *ground* through the midst of the sea" – **Exodus 14:16 (KJV)**

     ii. "and made the sea dry *land*, and the waters were divided" – **Exodus 14:21 (KJV)**

     iii. "And the children of Israel went into the midst of the sea upon the dry *ground*: and the waters *were* a wall unto them on their right hand, and on their left" – **Exodus 14:22 (KJV)**

375.   Here is the third evidence that the true and correct baptism is NOT with water but waterless!

     i. **Matthew 3:11 (KJV)** I indeed baptize you with water unto repentance: but he that cometh after me is mightier than I, whose shoes I am not worthy to bear: he shall baptize you with the Holy Ghost, and *with* fire:

    ii. **Mark 1:8 (KJV)** I indeed have baptized you with water: but he shall baptize you with the Holy Ghost.

    iii. **Luke 3:16 (KJV)** John answered, saying unto *them* all, I indeed baptize you with water; but one mightier than I cometh, the latchet of whose shoes I am not worthy to unloose: he shall baptize you with the Holy Ghost and with fire:

376.   Here is the fourth evidence that the true and correct baptism is NOT with water but waterless!

    i. **Acts 1:4 (KJV)** And, being assembled together with *them*, commanded them that they should not depart from Jerusalem, but wait for the promise of the Father, which, *saith he*, ye have heard of me.

    ii. **Acts 1:5 (KJV)** For John truly baptized with water; but ye shall be baptized with the Holy Ghost not many days hence.

377.   Now, here is the idolatry part that is connected to Water Baptism!

    i. When you move away from the true and correct Waterless Baptism to do the inferior Water Baptism of John the Baptist, then, that water part of your baptism is your idolatry!

    ii. Meaning that you are using a thing as a medium to reach the LORD God Almighty!

378.   Now, is it correct Christianity to use things to worship God Almighty? NO!

    i. **John 4:23 (KJV)** But the hour cometh, and now is, when the true worshippers shall worship the Father in spirit and in truth: for the Father seeketh such to worship him.

    ii. **John 4:24 (KJV)** God *is* a Spirit: and they that worship him must worship *him* in spirit and in truth.

379.   Do you remember what the LORD Jesus Christ did to all the people who were using things in God-worship in the Temple?

    i. **John 2:12 (KJV)** After this he went down to Capernaum, he, and his mother, and his brethren, and his disciples: and they continued there not many days.

    ii. **John 2:13 (KJV)** And the Jews' passover was at hand, and Jesus went up to Jerusalem,

    iii. **John 2:14 (KJV)** And found in the temple those that sold oxen and sheep and doves, and the changers of money sitting:

    iv. **John 2:15 (KJV)** And when he had made a scourge of small cords, he drove them all out of the temple, and the sheep, and the oxen; and poured out the changers' money, and overthrew the tables;

    v. **John 2:16 (KJV)** And said unto them that sold doves, Take these things hence; make not my Father's house an house of merchandise.

    vi. **John 2:17 (KJV)** And his disciples remembered that it was written, The zeal of thine house hath eaten me up.

380.   In summary so far, we have two baptisms:

    i. The Physical Water Baptism, and

    ii. The Spiritual Waterless Baptism

381.   But, the LORD God Almighty is emphasizing the spiritual over the physical, because it is the physical that creates the link to the idolatry!

    i. **Romans 3:27 (KJV)** Where *is* boasting then? It is excluded. By what law? of works? Nay: but by the law of faith.

    ii. **Romans 9:32 (KJV)** Wherefore? Because *they sought it* not by faith, but as it were by the works of the law. For they stumbled at that stumblingstone;

    iii. **Galatians 2:16 (KJV)** Knowing that a man is not justified by the works of the law, but by the faith of Jesus Christ, even we have believed in Jesus Christ, that we might be justified by the faith of Christ, and not by the works of the law: for by the works of the law shall no flesh be justified.

    iv. **Galatians 3:5 (KJV)** He therefore that ministereth to you the Spirit, and worketh miracles among you, *doeth he it* by the works of the law, or by the hearing of faith?

    v. **Galatians 3:10 (KJV)** For as many as are of the works of the law are under the curse: for it is written, Cursed *is* every one that continueth not in all things which are written in the book of the law to do them.

    vi. **Romans 8:13 (KJV)** For if ye live after the flesh, ye shall die: but if ye through the Spirit do mortify the deeds of the body, ye shall live.

382.   Idolatry simply means anything that you use to stand in the place of God Almighty! Anything material that represents God is idolatry! Anything or any thought that can draw you away from focusing ONLY on the LORD Jesus Christ is an idol!

383.   In other words, when you have any item such as beads, rosary, scarf, mantle, oil, water, cross, graven image, nature, that you claim to need to worship God, then, that thing becomes the idol that replaces God Almighty, why?

384.   Because, the Word of God alone is enough to represent God Almighty!

    i. **John 1:1 (KJV)** In the beginning was the Word, and the Word was with God, and the Word was God.

    ii. **John 1:2 (KJV)** The same was in the beginning with God.

    iii. **John 15:7 (KJV)** If ye abide in me, and my words abide in you, ye shall ask what ye will, and it shall be done unto you.

385.   So, as you can see from the above two evidences, the ONLY thing that is between you and God Almighty is the Word of God, NOT beads, rosary, scarf, mantle, oil, or water, cross, graven image, nature, etc.!

    i. **John 14:6 (KJV)** Jesus saith unto him, I am the way, the truth, and the life: no man cometh unto the Father, but by me.

    ii. **1 Timothy 2:5 (KJV)** For *there is* one God, and one mediator between God and men, the man Christ Jesus;

386.   It is for the sake of removing idolatry, that is why you no longer need a physical temple or a physical House of God before you can worship God Almighty!

387.   That is why you no longer need to repeat the Physical Crucifixion before you can worship God Almighty!

388.   That is why you no longer need to repeat the Physical Circumcision before you can worship God Almighty!

389.   That is why you no longer need to repeat the Physical Water Baptism before you can worship God Almighty!

390.   That is why you no longer need to repeat the Physical Holy Communion/Last Supper before you can worship God Almighty!

391.   As you can see, the LORD God is emphasizing the spiritual over the physical, here in these verses! Though it was the LORD God Almighty who gave them the physical water to drink, yet what matters most to God Almighty is the spiritual water and NOT the physical water, is the Spirit behind the water and NOT the physical water, is the thought behind the water and NOT the physical water!

    i. **1 Corinthians 10:3 (KJV)** And did all eat the same spiritual meat;

    ii. **1 Corinthians 10:4 (KJV)** And did all drink the same spiritual drink: for they drank of that spiritual Rock that followed them: and that Rock was Christ.

392.   Now, see why the LORD God was angry with them and killed many of them in the wilderness!

    i. **1 Corinthians 10:5 (KJV)** But with many of them God was not well pleased: for they were overthrown in the wilderness.

    ii. **1 Corinthians 10:6 (KJV)** Now these things were our examples, to the intent we should not lust after evil things, as they also lusted.

    iii. **1 Corinthians 10:7 (KJV)** Neither be ye idolaters, as *were* some of them; as it is written, The people sat down to eat and drink, and rose up to play.

393.   The LORD God killed those who died because they were idolaters!

394.   Now, check again very carefully how they practiced their idolatry!

    i. **Exodus 32:1 (KJV)** And when the people saw that Moses delayed to come down out of the mount, the people gathered themselves together unto Aaron, and said unto him, Up, make us gods, which shall go before us; for *as for* this Moses, the man that brought us up out of the land of Egypt, we wot not what is become of him.

    ii. **Exodus 32:2 (KJV)** And Aaron said unto them, Break off the golden earrings, which *are* in the ears of your wives, of your sons, and of your daughters, and bring *them* unto me.

    iii. **Exodus 32:3 (KJV)** And all the people brake off the golden earrings which *were* in their ears, and brought *them* unto Aaron.

    iv. **Exodus 32:4 (KJV)** And he received *them* at their hand, and fashioned it with a graving tool, after he had made it a molten calf: and they said, These *be* thy gods, O Israel, which brought thee up out of the land of Egypt.

    v. **Exodus 32:5 (KJV)** And when Aaron saw *it*, he built an altar before it; and Aaron made proclamation, and said, To morrow *is* a feast to the LORD.

    vi. **Exodus 32:6 (KJV)** And they rose up early on the morrow, and offered burnt offerings, and brought peace offerings; and the people sat down to eat and to drink, and rose up to play.

    vii. **Exodus 32:7 (KJV)** And the LORD said unto Moses, Go, get thee down; for thy people, which thou broughtest out of the land of Egypt, have corrupted *themselves*:

    viii. **1 Corinthians 10:7 (KJV)** Neither be ye idolaters, as *were* some of them; as it is written, The people sat down to eat and drink, and rose up to play.

395.   Did you see in **Exodus 32:1-7 (KJV)** that the people committed idolatry by introducing a physical tangible object in their worship? That was their idolatry, and that is the same way that when you also introduce a physical thing into your worship, then, for them as well as for you, it also becomes idolatry, no matter what that physical thing is, whether water as in Water Baptism, or wafers, wine, bread as in Holy Communion!

396.   Even fornication and adultery, did you know that they are also forms of idolatry? Yes, they are when you love flesh more than the Word of God, or when you love your wife more than the Word of God!

    i. **1 Corinthians 10:8 (KJV)** Neither let us commit fornication, as some of them committed, and fell in one day three and twenty thousand.

    ii. **1 Corinthians 10:9 (KJV)** Neither let us tempt Christ, as some of them also tempted, and were destroyed of serpents.

    iii. **1 Corinthians 10:10 (KJV)** Neither murmur ye, as some of them also murmured, and were destroyed of the destroyer.

397.   Someone will say: But we are in the New testament and our form of worship is different.

398.   Well, they are not dot different rather, the Old Testament is fulfilled in the New Testament!

    i. **Matthew 5:17 (KJV)** Think not that I am come to destroy the law, or the prophets: I am not come to destroy, but to fulfil.

    ii. **1 Corinthians 10:11 (KJV)** Now all these things happened unto them for ensamples: and they are written for our admonition, upon whom the ends of the world are come.

    iii. **1 Corinthians 10:12 (KJV)** Wherefore let him that thinketh he standeth take heed lest he fall.

399.   Here is the connection between the Old and the New Testaments for us, meaning that, the idolatry that the LORD God is showing us in the Old Testament also applies to us in the New Testament!

    i. **1 Corinthians 10:13 (KJV)** There hath no temptation taken you but such as is common to man: but God *is* faithful, who will not suffer you to be tempted above that ye are able; but will with the temptation also make a way to escape, that ye may be able to bear *it*.

    ii. **1 Corinthians 10:14 (KJV)** Wherefore, my dearly beloved, flee from idolatry.

    iii. **1 Corinthians 10:15 (KJV)** I speak as to wise men; judge ye what I say.

400.   Thus far, we have finished with the following levels of idolatry:

    i. Christian idolatry in Water Baptism

    ii. Idolatry pertaining to spiritual drink from the Spiritual Rock

    iii. Idolatry pertaining to physical items in worship

    iv. Idolatry pertaining to fornication and adultery

401.   Now, we are going to the question of Christian idolatry in Holy Communion!

    i. **1 Corinthians 10:16 (KJV)** The cup of blessing which we bless, is it not the communion of the blood of Christ? The bread which we break, is it not the communion of the body of Christ?

    ii. **1 Corinthians 10:17 (KJV)** For we *being* many are one bread, *and* one body: for we are all partakers of that one bread.

402.   Now, when you read **1 Corinthians 10:16-17 (KJV)**, what is the level or the realm that you see the LORD God referring to?

403.   There are many, even a majority Christians who will say that **1 Corinthians 10:16-17 (KJV)** is talking about the Physical Water Baptism that we do in our churches, but that will be a false answer!

404.   What is physical about "the communion of the blood of Christ" in **1 Corinthians 10:16 (KJV)**?

405.   The answer is zero, NONE!

406.   Are you able to communicate the Blood of Christ through physical wafers, wine, and bread? NO!

  i. **Hebrews 9:13 (KJV)** For if the blood of bulls and of goats, and the ashes of an heifer sprinkling the unclean, sanctifieth to the purifying of the flesh:

  ii. **Hebrews 9:14 (KJV)** How much more shall the blood of Christ, who through the eternal Spirit offered himself without spot to God, purge your conscience from dead works to serve the living God?

407.   Did you see in **Hebrews 9:14 (KJV)** the specific Person who is able to communicate the Blood of Christ? It is the Holy Spirit alone, not you the foolish ignorant filthy Holy Communion Pastor!

408.   Are your filthy physical wafers, wine, and bread enough good representations of Christ? NO!

  i. **Luke 1:76 (KJV)** And thou, child, shalt be called the prophet of the Highest: for thou shalt go before the face of the Lord to prepare his ways;

  ii. **Matthew 3:11 (KJV)** I indeed baptize you with water unto repentance: but he that cometh after me is mightier than I, whose shoes I am not worthy to bear: he shall baptize you with the Holy Ghost, and *with* fire:

  iii. **Mark 1:7 (KJV)** And preached, saying, There cometh one mightier than I after me, the latchet of whose shoes I am not worthy to stoop down and unloose.

  iv. **Luke 3:16 (KJV)** John answered, saying unto *them* all, I indeed baptize you with water; but one mightier than I cometh, the latchet of whose shoes I am not worthy to unloose: he shall baptize you with the Holy Ghost and with fire:

  v. **Acts 13:25 (KJV)** And as John fulfilled his course, he said, Whom think ye that I am? I am not *he*. But, behold, there cometh one after me, whose shoes of *his* feet I am not worthy to loose.

409.   If John the Baptist who was sent by God from Heaven as the Prophet of the Highest, to introduce the LORD Jesus Christ, said himself that, despite all his holiness, he was still not worthy to even pick up the shoe laces of the LORD Jesus Christ, then

how very stupid can you be to think and suppose that your filthy physical wafers, wine, and bread can stand in the place of Christ?

410.   We are still on the spirituality of Holy Communion in **1 Corinthians 10:16-17 (KJV)**!

      i.   **1 Corinthians 10:16 (KJV)** The cup of blessing which we bless, is it not the communion of the blood of Christ? The bread which we break, is it not the communion of the body of Christ?

      ii. **1 Corinthians 10:17 (KJV)** For we *being* many are one bread, *and* one body: for we are all partakers of that one bread.

411.   The LORD God says over there that "The bread which we break, it is the body of Christ"! – **1 Corinthians 10:16 (KJV)**

412.   Now, look at the spirituality of the Holy Communion in **1 Corinthians 10:17 (KJV)**!

413.   The LORD God says over there, that the same bread which is the body of Christ, that "we *being* many are one bread, *and* one body"!

414.   So, the LORD God is saying that both we and the LORD Jesus Christ are eating and drinking this Bread!

415.   YES, you got that right: "until that day when I drink it new with you in my Father's kingdom"!

      i.   **Matthew 26:26 (KJV)** And as they were eating, Jesus took bread, and blessed *it*, and brake *it*, and gave *it* to the disciples, and said, Take, eat; this is my body.

      ii. **Matthew 26:27 (KJV)** And he took the cup, and gave thanks, and gave *it* to them, saying, Drink ye all of it;

      iii. **Matthew 26:28 (KJV)** For this is my blood of the new testament, which is shed for many for the remission of sins.

      iv. **Matthew 26:29 (KJV)** But I say unto you, I will not drink henceforth of this fruit of the vine, until that day when I drink it new with you in my Father's kingdom.

416.   See again what the LORD God said over there: "for we are all partakers of that one bread" – **1 Corinthians 10:17 (KJV)**

417.   So, the LORD Jesus Christ is also partaking/eating of this same Bread with us while HE is in Heaven?

418.   YES, and the evidence is **Matthew 26:29 (KJV)** and **1 Corinthians 10:17 (KJV)**!

      i.   **Matthew 26:29 (KJV)** But I say unto you, I will not drink henceforth of this fruit of the vine, until that day when I drink it new with you in my Father's kingdom.

ii. **1 Corinthians 10:17 (KJV)** For we *being* many are one bread, *and* one body: for we are all partakers of that one bread.

419.   Now, Brethren, that is a very interesting revelation that raises a very serious question!

420.   If, according to **Matthew 26:29 (KJV)** and **1 Corinthians 10:17**, the LORD Jesus Christ is eating the same Bread and drinking the same wine with us as we are doing in our Holy Communion in all the churches, then how did those filthy physical wafers, wine, and bread get to the LORD Jesus Christ in Heaven?

421.   Now, Brethren, first of all, is it even possible for those filthy physical wafers, wine, and bread to get to the LORD Jesus Christ in Heaven? Since when did physical items start entering Heaven?

i. **1 Corinthians 15:50 (KJV)** Now this I say, brethren, that flesh and blood cannot inherit the kingdom of God; neither doth corruption inherit incorruption.

422.   Brother, are you now beginning to see the stupidity of you Holy Communion doctrine?

423.   Brother, let us consider it again. Here is the condition that the LORD Jesus Christ gave for the Holy Communion that HE commanded us to do: "when I drink it new with you in my Father's kingdom"!

424.   But, the truth is that, you know very well that the Holy Communion that you are doing right now in all your churches does NOT meet his spiritual condition, and yet you are still doing it?

425.   Or, are you ready to show me what part of those filthy physical wafers, wine, and bread is spiritual and is able to enter Heaven? None of them!

426.   If none of them, then, why are you doing it?

427.   The simple answer is because you are very stupid! You have no understanding of the Word of God! You do NOT have the Holy Spirit hence you have that carnal Holy Communion doctrine!

428.   Or, are you even worse than stupid to tell me that those filthy physical wafers, wine, and bread are not carnal?

429.   Are you even aware at all what the word "carnal" means? Here is the meaning of your carnal filthy physical Holy Communion wafers, wine, and bread!

i. "Carnal" means something related to physical, sexual, sensual, flesh, things that satisfy animal needs, spiritually deficient, uncovered flesh and nakedness like the half-naked choir women in the churches, something that is enmity against God, worldly, lustful, impure, beastly, unchristian, earthly, lewd, wanton, corporal genital, lascivious, lacking Holy Spirit, unbelieving, temporal, something that is not subject to the law of God, selfishness, self-willed, self-focused and self-seeking, legal term for sexual intercourse, crudity, etc."

430. Well, we have come to the point now where, if you had any sense at all, then you would asking:

i. So, after we have removed this carnal filthy physical Holy Communion wafers, wine, and bread, then what shall we do then?

431. See, the LORD God already gave you the answer in the same **1 Corinthians 10:17 (KJV)** that we have already read several times!

i. **1 Corinthians 10:17 (KJV)** For we *being* many are one bread, *and* one body: for we are all partakers of that one bread.

432. So, as you read **1 Corinthians 10:17 (KJV)**, where do you think the revelation is, since you claim to be a Pastor, a Bishop, a General Overseer, and you also claim that it was the LORD Jesus Christ who called you into the Ministry, and you also claim that you have the Holy Spirit?

i. **Jeremiah 3:15 (KJV)** And I will give you pastors according to mine heart, which shall feed you with knowledge and understanding.

ii. **Malachi 2:7 (KJV)** For the priest's lips should keep knowledge, and they should seek the law at his mouth: for he *is* the messenger of the LORD of hosts.

433. That is the work of the true Man of God, so tell us what the LORD God is saying in **1 Corinthians 10:17 (KJV)** concerning Holy Communion!

434. In answer to your question on what we shall do after we have removed this carnal filthy physical Holy Communion wafers, wine, and bread, here is where the revelation is located: "for we are all partakers of that one bread"!

435. Brother, that is the ONLY ONE BREAD that when you eat it here on the Earth, the LORD Jesus Christ will be eating with you same time in the Kingdom of Heaven as HE promised!

i. **Matthew 26:29 (KJV)** But I say unto you, I will not drink henceforth of this fruit of the vine, until that day when I drink it new with you in my Father's kingdom.

436. Now, I can hear someone asking: So where is the Bread?

437. Thou fool! Here is the ONLY ONE BREAD!

i. **John 6:27 (KJV)** Labour not for the meat which perisheth, but for that meat which endureth unto everlasting life, which the Son of man shall give unto you: for him hath God the Father sealed.

ii. **John 6:32 (KJV)** Then Jesus said unto them, Verily, verily, I say unto you, Moses gave you not that bread from heaven; but my Father giveth you the true bread from heaven.

       iii. **John 6:58 (KJV)** This is that bread which came down from heaven: not as your fathers did eat manna, and are dead: he that eateth of this bread shall live for ever.

438.   So, in **John 6:27 (KJV)**, the LORD Jesus Christ said:

       i. Throw away your carnal filthy physical Holy Communion wafers, wine, and bread, because if you refuse and you continue to eat them, you will die!

439.   Now, read again **John 6:32 (KJV)**, and tell me: the true Holy Communion Bread, where does it come from?

440.   From Heaven, NOT from your filthy sweat-stained polluted bread shop!

441.   See here: "my Father giveth you the true bread from heaven"!

       i. **John 6:33 (KJV)** For the bread of God is he which cometh down from heaven, and giveth life unto the world.

442.   So, then who will go to Heaven and bring us this Bread?

443.   Thou fool again and again! The Bread is already in your mouth according to **Deuteronomy 30:11-14 (KJV)** and confirmed in **Romans 10:8 (KJV)**!

       i. **Deuteronomy 30:11 (KJV)** For this commandment which I command thee this day, it is not hidden from thee, neither is it far off.

       ii. **Deuteronomy 30:11 (KJV)** For this commandment which I command thee this day, it is not hidden from thee, neither is it far off.

       iii. **Deuteronomy 30:12 (KJV)** It is not in heaven, that thou shouldest say, Who shall go up for us to heaven, and bring it unto us, that we may hear it, and do it?

       iv. **Deuteronomy 30:13 (KJV)** Neither is it beyond the sea, that thou shouldest say, Who shall go over the sea for us, and bring it unto us, that we may hear it, and do it?

       v. **Deuteronomy 30:14 (KJV)** But the word is very nigh unto thee, in thy mouth, and in thy heart, that thou mayest do it.

       vi. **Romans 10:8 (KJV)** But what saith it? The word is nigh thee, even in thy mouth, and in thy heart: that is, the word of faith, which we preach;

444.   Here is another evidence that the proper Spiritual Holy Communing Bread is in your mouth and it is the Word of Faith that we preach!

       i. **John 1:1 (KJV)** In the beginning was the Word, and the Word was with God, and the Word was God.

       ii. **John 1:2 (KJV)** The same was in the beginning with God.

445.   Here is another evidence that the proper Spiritual Holy Communing Bread is in your mouth and it is the Word of Faith that we preach!

       i. **Revelation 19:11 (KJV)** And I saw heaven opened, and behold a white horse; and he that sat upon him *was* called Faithful and True, and in righteousness he doth judge and make war.

446. Here is another evidence that the proper Spiritual Holy Communing Bread is in your mouth and it is the Word of Faith that we preach!

       i. **Revelation 19:13 (KJV)** And he *was* clothed with a vesture dipped in blood: and his name is called The Word of God.

447. What then is the idolatry in the Holy Communion that we do in the churches?

448. It is the physical oblations, tokens, and elements that we use as representing Christ…they are all works of the flesh and they can never be the point of contact between Heaven and any human being on Earth!

       i. **1 Corinthians 10:18 (KJV)** Behold Israel after the flesh: are not they which eat of the sacrifices partakers of the altar?

       ii. **1 Corinthians 10:19 (KJV)** What say I then? that the idol is any thing, or that which is offered in sacrifice to idols is any thing?

       iii. **1 Corinthians 10:20 (KJV)** But *I say*, that the things which the Gentiles sacrifice, they sacrifice to devils, and not to God: and I would not that ye should have fellowship with devils.

449. As you can from **1 Corinthians 10:18-20 (KJV)**, anything that is after the flesh, or food items that you offer as sacrifice to deities, to devils, and to gods, that is idolatry, except you want to tell me that your carnal filthy physical Holy Communion wafers, wine, and bread, are not of the flesh?

450. Which one is the table of devils and which one is the table of the LORD?

       i. **1 Corinthians 10:21 (KJV)** Ye cannot drink the cup of the Lord, and the cup of devils: ye cannot be partakers of the Lord's table, and of the table of devils.

       ii. **1 Corinthians 10:22 (KJV)** Do we provoke the Lord to jealousy? are we stronger than he?

       iii. **1 Corinthians 10:23 (KJV)** All things are lawful for me, but all things are not expedient: all things are lawful for me, but all things edify not.

451. When the Holy Communion is done with your carnal filthy physical Holy Communion wafers, wine, and bread, then, it is "the table of devils, but when the Holy Communion is done with ONLY the Word of God, then, it is the table of the LORD!

452. Brother, are you able to show me how your carnal filthy physical Holy Communion wafers, wine, and bread are able to edify me spiritually as **1 Corinthians 10:23 (KJV)** requires?

453.   The answer is, NO, and you know that very well hence, your Holy Communion is evil and for devils since it cannot edify anyone unto righteousness nor unto the Kingdom of Heaven!

454.   There is no record anywhere in the entire Word of God from Genesis to Revelation where food and wine were able to edify and sanctify a people unto righteousness or unto the Kingdom of Heaven! Look at **Micah 6:8 (KJV)** to see what has power to edify worshippers unto Christ!

      i. **Micah 6:6 (KJV)** Wherewith shall I come before the LORD, *and* bow myself before the high God? shall I come before him with burnt offerings, with calves of a year old?

      ii. **Micah 6:7 (KJV)** Will the LORD be pleased with thousands of rams, *or* with ten thousands of rivers of oil? shall I give my firstborn *for* my transgression, the fruit of my body *for* the sin of my soul?

      iii. **Micah 6:8 (KJV)** He hath shewed thee, O man, what *is* good; and what doth the LORD require of thee, but to do justly, and to love mercy, and to walk humbly with thy God?

455.   Here is an example of unbelievers who worship using food oblations, so, both you the Christian and the unbelieving Devil worshipper are one, as long as you both use food items that you falsely consider holy oblations!

      i. **1 Corinthians 10:25 (KJV)** Whatsoever is sold in the shambles, *that* eat, asking no question for conscience sake:

      ii. **1 Corinthians 10:26 (KJV)** For the earth *is* the Lord's, and the fulness thereof.

      iii. **1 Corinthians 10:27 (KJV)** If any of them that believe not bid you *to a feast*, and ye be disposed to go; whatsoever is set before you, eat, asking no question for conscience sake.

      iv. **1 Corinthians 10:28 (KJV)** But if any man say unto you, This is offered in sacrifice unto idols, eat not for his sake that shewed it, and for conscience sake: for the earth *is* the Lord's, and the fulness thereof:

      v. **1 Corinthians 10:29 (KJV)** Conscience, I say, not thine own, but of the other: for why is my liberty judged of another *man's* conscience?

      vi. **1 Corinthians 10:30 (KJV)** For if I by grace be a partaker, why am I evil spoken of for that for which I give thanks?

      vii. **1 Corinthians 10:31 (KJV)** Whether therefore ye eat, or drink, or whatsoever ye do, do all to the glory of God.

Thursday 11ᵗʰ January 2024 @ 11:02 PM – Friday 12ᵗʰ January 2024 @ 3:13 AM

CHAPTER 11: THE DOCTRINE OF THE HEAD COVERING

456.   There are four levels of spiritual authority in the Church hierarchy!
      i. **1 Corinthians 11:1 (KJV)** Be ye followers of me, even as I also *am* of Christ.
      ii. **1 Corinthians 11:2 (KJV)** Now I praise you, brethren, that ye remember me in all things, and keep the ordinances, as I delivered *them* to you.
      iii. **1 Corinthians 11:3 (KJV)** But I would have you know, that the head of every man is Christ; and the head of the woman *is* the man; and the head of Christ *is* God.

457.   The four levels of spiritual authority in the Church hierarchy are:
      i. The LORD God Almighty
      ii. The LORD Jesus Christ
      iii. The Man
      iv. The Woman

458.   Therefore, in ascending or, the head of the woman is the man, the head of the man is Christ, the Head of Christ is God Almighty!

459.   Now, the head covering is a symbol of communication of the spiritual level of the person who is wearing the head covering.

460.   The LORD God Almighty has ordained that the man should NOT wear a head covering, because that will communicate/mean a sign of dishonor/disrespect to his Head the Christ of God!
      i. **1 Corinthians 11:4 (KJV)** Every man praying or prophesying, having *his* head covered, dishonoureth his head.

461.   The LORD God Almighty has also ordained that the woman should wear a head covering, because that will communicate/mean a sign of honor/respect to her Head who is the Man!
      i. **1 Corinthians 11:5 (KJV)** But every woman that prayeth or prophesieth with *her* head uncovered dishonoureth her head: for that is even all one as if she were shaven.

462.   When the Woman has no head covering but her hair only while praying or prophesying, the dishonor/disrespect that she communicates by that absence of head covering rises to the level of shaming her head who is the Man!

463.   It is the same shame that a woman feels when she has no hair on her head at all and is therefore completely bald like a man!

464.   Pertaining to the woman's head covering, the LORD God gives three choices:

        i. **1 Corinthians 11:6 (KJV)** For if the woman be not covered, let her also be shorn: but if it be a shame for a woman to be shorn or shaven, let her be covered.

465.   Choice #1:

        i. Have a head covering as the Word of God commands, and keep your hair on your head!

466.   Choice #2:

        i. Reject the head covering against the Word of God, and have all your hair on your head, shaved off!

467.   Choice #3:

        i. If the woman feels shame to have all her hair on her head shaven off, and looking bald as a man, then the solution is to have a head covering when praying or prophesying unto God!

468.   According to the Word of God in **1 Corinthians 11:5-6 (KJV)**, baldness in a woman is a shame, and a woman who has hair on her head, but praying or prophesying unto God Almighty, with her head uncovered with a scarf or shawl, that woman is a bald woman who should feel shame for her baldness!

469.   You mean that a woman can have full hair on her head, but when she prays or prophesies unto God with her head uncovered, then, in the spiritual realm, she is seen as a completely bald woman, distorting nature? YES!

470.   In the case of the man, the LORD God has ordained that he should NOT cover his head when praying or prophesying!

        i. **1 Corinthians 11:7 (KJV)** For a man indeed ought not to cover *his* head, forasmuch as he is the image and glory of God: but the woman is the glory of the man.

471.   In **1 Corinthians 11:7 (KJV)**, the LORD God gives us the spiritual reason for the head covering!

472.   The LORD God ordained for the man NOT to cover his head when praying or prophesying "forasmuch as he is the image and glory of God"!

473.   The LORD God ordained for the woman to cover her head when praying or prophesying "because the woman is the glory of the man"!

474.   There is yet two very profound revelations in **1 Corinthians 11:7 (KJV)** that will certainly shock many Christians, Pastors, Bishops, and Church Leaders when they hear them, and the revelation are these:

        i. The man has the image and the glory of God, but the woman does NOT have them!

        ii. The woman's image and glory come from the man, NOT from God!

    iii. **Genesis 2:21 (KJV)** And the LORD God caused a deep sleep to fall upon Adam, and he slept: and he took one of his ribs, and closed up the flesh instead thereof;

    iv. **Genesis 2:22 (KJV)** And the rib, which the LORD God had taken from man, made he a woman, and brought her unto the man.

    v. **Genesis 2:23 (KJV)** And Adam said, This *is* now bone of my bones, and flesh of my flesh: she shall be called Woman, because she was taken out of Man.

475. Those are the two very profound revelations in **1 Corinthians 11:7 (KJV)** that explain the command for the head covering for the woman!

476. In other words, the head covering for the woman is serving the same purpose and role as:

    i. "the ribband of blue upon fringes in the borders of the garments of the children of Israel that ye may look upon it, and remember all the commandments of the LORD, and do them; and be holy, and that ye seek not after your own heart and your own eyes, after which ye use to go a whoring"!

    ii. **Numbers 15:37 (KJV)** And the LORD spake unto Moses, saying,

    iii. **Numbers 15:38 (KJV)** Speak unto the children of Israel, and bid them that they make them fringes in the borders of their garments throughout their generations, and that they put upon the fringe of the borders a ribband of blue:

    iv. **Numbers 15:39 (KJV)** And it shall be unto you for a fringe, that ye may look upon it, and remember all the commandments of the LORD, and do them; and that ye seek not after your own heart and your own eyes, after which ye use to go a whoring:

    v. **Numbers 15:40 (KJV)** That ye may remember, and do all my commandments, and be holy unto your God.

    vi. **Numbers 15:41 (KJV)** I *am* the LORD your God, which brought you out of the land of Egypt, to be your God: I *am* the LORD your God.

477. Here is the second spiritual reason for the head covering for the Christian woman!

    i. **1 Corinthians 11:8 (KJV)** For the man is not of the woman; but the woman of the man.

    ii. **1 Corinthians 11:9 (KJV)** Neither was the man created for the woman; but the woman for the man.

478. In other words, the fact that the LORD God created the woman second after the man is indicative of the spiritual hierarchy and spiritual superiority of the man over

the woman, which spiritual hierarchy and spiritual superiority are communicated through the woman's head covering, communicated not only the Body of Christ the Church, but also to the Angels of God who recognize the power dynamics and the hierarchy that the woman is communicating through the symbol of her head covering!

     i. **1 Corinthians 11:10 (KJV)** For this cause ought the woman to have power on *her* head because of the angels.

479.   Nevertheless, these spiritual hierarchy and spiritual superiority of the man do NOT bestow on the man any physical superiority over the woman, because those spiritual hierarchy and spiritual superiority are applicable ONLY in the spiritual realm and NOT in the physical realm! In the physical realm, what is ordained is equality even as **1 Corinthians 11:11-12 (KJV)** reveal!

     i. **1 Corinthians 11:11 (KJV)** Nevertheless neither is the man without the woman, neither the woman without the man, in the Lord.

     ii. **1 Corinthians 11:12 (KJV)** For as the woman *is* of the man, even so *is* the man also by the woman; but all things of God.

480.   Now we come to the human natural side of this doctrine of women's head covering!

     i. **1 Corinthians 11:13 (KJV)** Judge in yourselves: is it comely that a woman pray unto God uncovered?

     ii. **1 Corinthians 11:14 (KJV)** Doth not even nature itself teach you, that, if a man have long hair, it is a shame unto him?

481.   In **1 Corinthians 11:13-14 (KJV)**, the LORD God Almighty is reminding us that this requirement for women to cover their head when praying or prophesying unto God is not new at all, but that it is also a human requirement hence, there is no strangeness about it at all since humans already have it so!

482.   Therefore, whereas when it comes to the spirituality of praying and prophesying, the woman ought to cover her hair-covered head, in the human realm, the same hair/head does NOT need to be covered because the hair is already a covering while she is NOT doing any spiritual work such as praying and prophesying!

     i. **1 Corinthians 11:14 (KJV)** Doth not even nature itself teach you, that, if a man have long hair, it is a shame unto him?

     ii. **1 Corinthians 11:15 (KJV)** But if a woman have long hair, it is a glory to her: for *her* hair is given her for a covering.

483.   So, then, when you compare the spiritual realm requirement for women's head covering to the natural realm requirement for women's head covering, they are both the same even as you see in the following Old Testament evidence!

    i. **Numbers 5:17 (KJV)** And the priest shall take holy water in an earthen vessel; and of the dust that is in the floor of the tabernacle the priest shall take, and put *it* into the water:

    ii. **Numbers 5:18 (KJV)** And the priest shall set the woman before the LORD, and uncover the woman's head, and put the offering of memorial in her hands, which *is* the jealousy offering: and the priest shall have in his hand the bitter water that causeth the curse:

484.   In other words, both in the Old and New Testaments, this requirement for the women's head covering is there, but if a person calling herself a Christian decides to do contrary to both the Old and New Testament requirement for the women's head covering, and actually goes ahead to pray and to prophesy unto God with her head uncovered, then, that is NOT the way or the custom of both nature and the Church!

    i. **1 Corinthians 11:16 (KJV)** But if any man seem to be contentious, we have no such custom, neither the churches of God.

Friday 12th January 2024 @ 2:14 PM – 4:55 PM

CHAPTER 12: THE CHURCH ASSEMBLY IS NOT FOR THE EATING OF HOLY COMMUNION

485.   We now go to the second main idea or the second theme in 1 Corinthians chapter 11, which is Holy Communion! The first theme is the women's head covering, which we have just finished teaching!

     i. **1 Corinthians 11:20 (KJV)** When ye come together therefore into one place, *this* is not to eat the Lord's supper.

     ii. **1 Corinthians 11:21 (KJV)** For in eating every one taketh before *other* his own supper: and one is hungry, and another is drunken.

     iii. **1 Corinthians 11:22 (KJV)** What? have ye not houses to eat and to drink in? or despise ye the church of God, and shame them that have not? What shall I say to you? shall I praise you in this? I praise *you* not.

486.   As you can see in the evidence in **1 Corinthians 11:20 (KJV)**, the church assembly is NOT for the eating of Holy Communion/the Lord's supper!

487.   This evidence alone in **1 Corinthians 11:20 (KJV)** is enough to make you stop your Holy Communion eating and drinking in all your churches!

488.   The command is as clear as water, saying:

     i. The church assembly is NOT for the eating of Holy Communion/the Lord's supper!

489.   Yet, the very opposite of that command is what we see Christians, Pastors, Bishops, and Church Leaders doing Sunday after Sunday after Sunday!

490.   If you asked the same Christians, Pastors, Bishops, and Church Leaders to tell you the meaning of: "the body *is* not for fornication", they would tell you correctly, that you cannot be a Christian and still engage in fornication and adultery!

     i. **1 Corinthians 6:13 (KJV)** Meats for the belly, and the belly for meats: but God shall destroy both it and them. Now the body *is* not for fornication, but for the Lord; and the Lord for the body.

491.   Do you why they will give you that correct answer?

492.   It is because of this negative phrase in the verse:

     i. "the body (**noun**) *is* (**auxiliary verb**) not (**negative**) for fornication (**main verb**)"!

493.   Now, read also this verse again!

     i. **1 Corinthians 11:20 (KJV)** When ye come together therefore into one place, *this* is not to eat the Lord's supper.

494.   Now, compare the same thing that we have just done above to this:

     i. "when ye (**noun**) come together therefore into one place, *this* is (**auxiliary verb**) not (**negative**) to eat (**main verb**) the Lord's supper"!

495.   Now, ask yourself: where is the difference?

496.   There is NONE, ZERO!

497.   So, then, the question is:

    i. Why would the same Christians, Pastors, Bishops, and Church Leaders answer correctly in **1 Corinthians 6:13 (KJV)**, but lie in **1 Corinthians 11:20 (KJV)** when both verses have the same properties?

    ii. **1 Corinthians 6:13 (KJV)** Meats for the belly, and the belly for meats: but God shall destroy both it and them. Now the body *is* not for fornication, but for the Lord; and the Lord for the body.

    iii. **1 Corinthians 11:20 (KJV)** When ye come together therefore into one place, *this* is not to eat the Lord's supper.

498.   The reason why they the same Christians, Pastors, Bishops, and Church Leaders will lie is that they are Devils! They were never born again! They are NOT saved! They are on their way to Hell! They serve Satan and are Ministers of Satan in the Pulpit! They serve the same role as Judas Iscariot who served in the Pulpit but was a Devil!

    i. **Matthew 10:4 (KJV)** Simon the Canaanite, and Judas Iscariot, who also betrayed him.

    ii. **John 6:70 (KJV)** Jesus answered them, Have not I chosen you twelve, and one of you is a devil?

    iii. **John 12:4 (KJV)** Then saith one of his disciples, Judas Iscariot, Simon's *son*, which should betray him,

    iv. **John 12:5 (KJV)** Why was not this ointment sold for three hundred pence, and given to the poor?

    v. **John 12:6 (KJV)** This he said, not that he cared for the poor; but because he was a thief, and had the bag, and bare what was put therein.

    vi. **Matthew 15:9 (KJV)** But in vain they do worship me, teaching *for* doctrines the commandments of men.

    vii. **Mark 7:7 (KJV)** Howbeit in vain do they worship me, teaching *for* doctrines the commandments of men.

    viii. **1 Timothy 4:1 (KJV)** Now the Spirit speaketh expressly, that in the latter times some shall depart from the faith, giving heed to seducing spirits, and doctrines of devils;

499.   If we were still in the physical Old Testament and practiced the carnal ordinances thereof, then we should still be eating and drinking physical Holy Communion food as the Corinthians were doing in **1 Corinthians 11:20 (KJV)**!

    i. **1 Corinthians 11:20 (KJV)** When ye come together therefore into one place, *this* is not to eat the Lord's supper.

ii. **1 Corinthians 11:23 (KJV)** For I have received of the Lord that which also I delivered unto you, That the Lord Jesus the *same* night in which he was betrayed took bread:

iii. **1 Corinthians 11:24 (KJV)** And when he had given thanks, he brake *it*, and said, Take, eat: this is my body, which is broken for you: this do in remembrance of me.

iv. **1 Corinthians 11:25 (KJV)** After the same manner also *he took* the cup, when he had supped, saying, This cup is the new testament in my blood: this do ye, as oft as ye drink *it*, in remembrance of me.

v. **1 Corinthians 11:26 (KJV)** For as often as ye eat this bread, and drink this cup, ye do shew the Lord's death till he come.

vi. **Hebrews 9:10 (KJV)** *Which stood* only in meats and drinks, and divers washings, and carnal ordinances, imposed *on them* until the time of reformation.

500.   However, because we are NO MORE in the Old Testament of works, but now in the New Testament of Faith, and all the Old Testament physical forms of God-worship have passed away, therefore, to continue to practise the physical works of Holy Communion/the LORD'S Supper that the LORD Jesus Christ accomplished when HE fulfilled HIS Ministry under the Old Testament Laws, it is a sin because of **John 4:23-24 (KJV)** and many other such verses!

i. **Matthew 5:17 (KJV)** Think not that I am come to destroy the law, or the prophets: I am not come to destroy, but to fulfil.

ii. **John 4:23 (KJV)** But the hour cometh, and now is, when the true worshippers shall worship the Father in spirit and in truth: for the Father seeketh such to worship him.

iii. **John 4:24 (KJV)** God *is* a Spirit: and they that worship him must worship *him* in spirit and in truth.

iv. **Romans 3:20 (KJV)** Therefore by the deeds of the law there shall no flesh be justified in his sight: for by the law *is* the knowledge of sin.

v. **Galatians 3:23 (KJV)** But before faith came, we were kept under the law, shut up unto the faith which should afterwards be revealed.

vi. **Galatians 3:24 (KJV)** Wherefore the law was our schoolmaster *to bring us* unto Christ, that we might be justified by faith.

vii. **Galatians 3:25 (KJV)** But after that faith is come, we are no longer under a schoolmaster.

501.   Therefore, because we are now in the New Testament of Faith, we need to, and we should be seeking the Faith/Spiritual meanings of "my body, broken for you, the new testament, my blood, in remembrance of me"!

      i. **1 Corinthians 11:24 (KJV)** And when he had given thanks, he brake *it*, and said, Take, eat: this is my body, which is broken for you: this do in remembrance of me.

     ii. **1 Corinthians 11:25 (KJV)** After the same manner also *he took* the cup, when he had supped, saying, This cup is the new testament in my blood: this do ye, as oft as ye drink *it*, in remembrance of me.

502.   And when you search the Scriptures for the correct Faith/Spiritual meanings of "my body, broken for you, the new testament, my blood, in remembrance of me", what you get is this: THE WORD OF GOD!

503.   In other words, the Word of God was the real and actual "my body, broken for you, the new testament, my blood, in remembrance of me" that the LORD Jesus Christ was giving to the Apostles!

504.   Now, let us test the doctrine that the Word of God is the real and actual "my body, broken for you, the new testament, my blood, in remembrance of me" that the LORD Jesus Christ was giving to the Apostles!

505.   The Word of God is the real and actual "my body"!

      i. **John 1:1 (KJV)** In the beginning was the Word, and the Word was with God, and the Word was God.

     ii. **John 1:2 (KJV)** The same was in the beginning with God.

    iii. **John 1:14 (KJV)** And the Word was made flesh, and dwelt among us, (and we beheld his glory, the glory as of the only begotten of the Father,) full of grace and truth.

    iv. **John 6:32 (KJV)** Then Jesus said unto them, Verily, verily, I say unto you, Moses gave you not that bread from heaven; but my Father giveth you the true bread from heaven.

     v. **John 6:33 (KJV)** For the bread of God is he which cometh down from heaven, and giveth life unto the world.

    vi. **John 6:48 (KJV)** I am that bread of life.

   vii. **John 6:51 (KJV)** I am the living bread which came down from heaven: if any man eat of this bread, he shall live for ever: and the bread that I will give is my flesh, which I will give for the life of the world.

506.   The Word of God is the real and actual "broken for you", meaning, "rightly dividing the word of truth"!

      i. **Ezekiel 3:1 (KJV)** Moreover he said unto me, Son of man, eat that thou findest; eat this roll, and go speak unto the house of Israel.

     ii. **Ezekiel 3:2 (KJV)** So I opened my mouth, and he caused me to eat that roll.

    iii. **Ezekiel 3:3 (KJV)** And he said unto me, Son of man, cause thy belly to eat, and fill thy bowels with this roll that I give thee. Then did I eat *it*; and it was in my mouth as honey for sweetness.

    iv. **Jeremiah 15:16 (KJV)** Thy words were found, and I did eat them; and thy word was unto me the joy and rejoicing of mine heart: for I am called by thy name, O LORD God of hosts.

    v. **John 5:46 (KJV)** For had ye believed Moses, ye would have believed me: for he wrote of me.

    vi. **2 Timothy 2:15 (KJV)** Study to shew thyself approved unto God, a workman that needeth not to be ashamed, rightly dividing the word of truth.

507.   The Word of God is the real and actual "the new testament"!

    i. **Hebrews 9:13 (KJV)** For if the blood of bulls and of goats, and the ashes of an heifer sprinkling the unclean, sanctifieth to the purifying of the flesh:

    ii. **Hebrews 9:14 (KJV)** How much more shall the blood of Christ, who through the eternal Spirit offered himself without spot to God, purge your conscience from dead works to serve the living God?

    iii. **Hebrews 9:15 (KJV)** And for this cause he is the mediator of the new testament, that by means of death, for the redemption of the transgressions *that were* under the first testament, they which are called might receive the promise of eternal inheritance.

    iv. **Hebrews 9:16 (KJV)** For where a testament *is*, there must also of necessity be the death of the testator.

    v. **Hebrews 9:17 (KJV)** For a testament *is* of force after men are dead: otherwise it is of no strength at all while the testator liveth.

508.   The Word of God is the real and actual "my blood"!

    i. **Luke 22:20 (KJV)** Likewise also the cup after supper, saying, This cup *is* the new testament in my blood, which is shed for you.

    ii. **Hebrews 9:14 (KJV)** How much more shall the blood of Christ, who through the eternal Spirit offered himself without spot to God, purge your conscience from dead works to serve the living God?

    iii. **Hebrews 9:15 (KJV)** And for this cause he is the mediator of the new testament, that by means of death, for the redemption of the transgressions *that were* under the first testament, they which are called might receive the promise of eternal inheritance.

509.   The Word of God is the real and actual "in remembrance of me", meaning that, the Holy Communion wafers, wine, and bread, and all physical food and drinks

themselves being dung, excreta, feces, and filthy physical perishable items, they have no power at all to connect into the spiritual, neither do they have any ability at all to cause or to compel the remembrance of the LORD Jesus Christ in any human being by reason of their presence and their eating!

    i. **Mark 7:15 (KJV)** There is nothing from without a man, that entering into him can defile him: but the things which come out of him, those are they that defile the man.

    ii. **Matthew 15:16 (KJV)** And Jesus said, Are ye also yet without understanding?

    iii. **Matthew 15:17 (KJV)** Do not ye yet understand, that whatsoever entereth in at the mouth goeth into the belly, and is cast out into the draught?

    iv. **Mark 7:18 (KJV)** And he saith unto them, Are ye so without understanding also? Do ye not perceive, that whatsoever thing from without entereth into the man, *it* cannot defile him;

    v. **Mark 7:19 (KJV)** Because it entereth not into his heart, but into the belly, and goeth out into the draught, purging all meats?

510.   There is no food on Earth that possesses any spiritual properties, therefore, to use physical food to bring the presence of Christ to a physical scene by way of remembrance into the human mind, whether it be in a Holy Communion setting in a church, or whether it be in a voodoo seance as many do in the Akwasidae festival and in the Aboakyer festival of Ghana, both of them are demonic idolatry!

    i. **John 6:27 (KJV)** Labour not for the meat which perisheth, but for that meat which endureth unto everlasting life, which the Son of man shall give unto you: for him hath God the Father sealed.

    ii. **Micah 6:6 (KJV)** Wherewith shall I come before the LORD, *and* bow myself before the high God? shall I come before him with burnt offerings, with calves of a year old?

    iii. **Micah 6:7 (KJV)** Will the LORD be pleased with thousands of rams, *or* with ten thousands of rivers of oil? shall I give my firstborn *for* my transgression, the fruit of my body *for* the sin of my soul?

    iv. **Micah 6:8 (KJV)** He hath shewed thee, O man, what *is* good; and what doth the LORD require of thee, but to do justly, and to love mercy, and to walk humbly with thy God?

511.   Finally, as you can see, we have tested all the five parts and key phrases in the doctrine that the Word of God is the true, the real, and the actual oblation that has power to cause the remembrance of the LORD Jesus Christ in Christians, and we

found out from the testing that the doctrine is perfect and there is not even one single part lacking! I have demonstrated the doctrine to you fully!

512.   Therefore, you should continue to use your physical filthy Holy Communion wafers, wine and bread at your own peril in Hell!

513.   How is it that the LORD Jesus Christ is God, and HE said that HE came to fulfill the Law, and the Law says that what God gives HIS Servants to eat are words, NOT physical food, and yet you are able to conclude that the same Jesus Christ gave food to HIS Servants and not words! How does that reasoning match up to you if you are not a fool?

  i.   **Isaiah 9:6 (KJV)** For unto us a child is born, unto us a son is given: and the government shall be upon his shoulder: and his name shall be called Wonderful, Counseller, The mighty God, The everlasting Father, The Prince of Peace.

  ii. **Jeremiah 32:18 (KJV)** Thou shewest lovingkindness unto thousands, and recompensest the iniquity of the fathers into the bosom of their children after them: the Great, the Mighty God, the LORD of hosts, *is* his name,

  iii. **Matthew 5:17 (KJV)** Think not that I am come to destroy the law, or the prophets: I am not come to destroy, but to fulfil.

  iv. **Jeremiah 15:16 (KJV)** Thy words were found, and I did eat them; and thy word was unto me the joy and rejoicing of mine heart: for I am called by thy name, O LORD God of hosts.

  v.   **Ezekiel 3:1 (KJV)** Moreover he said unto me, Son of man, eat that thou findest; eat this roll, and go speak unto the house of Israel.

  vi. **Ezekiel 3:2 (KJV)** So I opened my mouth, and he caused me to eat that roll.

  vii. **John 17:8 (KJV)** For I have given unto them the words which thou gavest me; and they have received *them*, and have known surely that I came out from thee, and they have believed that thou didst send me.

514.   Since the world began, is it recorded anywhere that a man became guilty before God because of some food that he did not eat and drink, or, is it rather recorded that a man became guilty before God because of the words of the Covenant of God that he did not obey?

  i.   **1 Corinthians 11:27 (KJV)** Wherefore whosoever shall eat this bread, and drink *this* cup of the Lord, unworthily, shall be guilty of the body and blood of the Lord.

  ii. **1 Corinthians 11:28 (KJV)** But let a man examine himself, and so let him eat of *that* bread, and drink of *that* cup.

    iii. **1 Corinthians 11:29 (KJV)** For he that eateth and drinketh unworthily, eateth and drinketh damnation to himself, not discerning the Lord's body.

    iv. **1 Corinthians 10:31 (KJV)** Whether therefore ye eat, or drink, or whatsoever ye do, do all to the glory of God.

515.   You know certainly that a man's spirituality, holiness or guilt is never derived from some food that he ate or failed to eat and drink, but instead, a man became guilty before God because of the words of the Covenant of God that he did not obey!

    i. **Matthew 15:10 (KJV)** And he called the multitude, and said unto them, Hear, and understand:

    ii. **Matthew 15:11 (KJV)** Not that which goeth into the mouth defileth a man; but that which cometh out of the mouth, this defileth a man.

    iii. **Mark 7:15 (KJV)** There is nothing from without a man, that entering into him can defile him: but the things which come out of him, those are they that defile the man.

516.   How could you know all this and still be that very stupid not to know that you have the wrong doctrine of Holy Communion which derives holiness from perishable food and drink and NOT from the Covenant of God?

    i. **Luke 22:20 (KJV)** Likewise also the cup after supper, saying, This cup *is* the new testament in my blood, which is shed for you.

    ii. **1 Corinthians 11:25 (KJV)** After the same manner also *he took* the cup, when he had supped, saying, This cup is the new testament in my blood: this do ye, as oft as ye drink *it*, in remembrance of me.

517.   If the cup is inside the New Testament, and you being the Pastor and Bishop of the church, you are always going outside the New Testament in order to procure holiness, spirituality, worship, remembrance of Christ, and blessings from outside the New Testament, then where are your senses Brother?

518.   Can you be that incorrigibly stupid and perpetually cursed unto Satan, that the LORD Jesus Christ has told you plainly that the bread and the cup are inside the New Testament, but yet still you decided to seek the same bread and the cup from OUTSIDE the New Testament?

519.   Here is another evidence of your incorrigible stupidity and your perpetual curse unto Satan!

    i. **1 Corinthians 11:30 (KJV)** For this cause many *are* weak and sickly among you, and many sleep.

520.   Now, after you have read **1 Corinthians 11:30 (KJV)**, can you show me any evidence from Genesis to Revelation where a man or many people became weak, sickly, and died because they failed to eat some physical food?

521.   Do not weakness, sickness, and death actually and truly come from NOT eating the spiritual food of the Word of God, the same as Jesus Christ told you in **Luke 22:20 (KJV)** and **1 Corinthians 11:25 (KJV)**?

522.   How very stupid can you be Brother, Sister?

      i.   **1 Corinthians 11:31 (KJV)** For if we would judge ourselves, we should not be judged.

      ii. **1 Corinthians 11:32 (KJV)** But when we are judged, we are chastened of the Lord, that we should not be condemned with the world.

523.   Brother, Sister, are you under any illusion at all that there are two types of eating in 1 Corinthians chapter 11, and that one of them is the physical useless eating of physical foods whereas the other is the preferred spiritual eating as I have showed you many times in the very chapter?

      i.   **1 Corinthians 11:33 (KJV)** Wherefore, my brethren, when ye come together to eat, tarry one for another.

      ii. **1 Corinthians 11:34 (KJV)** And if any man hunger, let him eat at home; that ye come not together unto condemnation. And the rest will I set in order when I come.

Friday 12ᵗʰ January 2024 @ 4:55 PM – 7:27 PM

CHAPTER 13: DIFFERENT LEVELS OF SPIRITUAL GIFTS

524.   It is very important to notice the record here in 1 Corinthians chapter 12.
   i.   **1 Corinthians 12:1 (KJV)** Now concerning spiritual *gifts*, brethren, I would not have you ignorant.
   ii. **1 Corinthians 12:2 (KJV)** Ye know that ye were Gentiles, carried away unto these dumb idols, even as ye were led.

525.   The chapter opens with a revelation that white people are the Gentiles and they were idol worshippers!

526.   I have already published several research findings showing that Gentiles are the white people of the world! Here is the LORD Jesus Christ identifying the white European Roman colonizers in Jerusalem as Gentiles!
   i.   **Matthew 20:25 (KJV)** But Jesus called them *unto him*, and said, Ye know that the princes of the Gentiles exercise dominion over them, and they that are great exercise authority upon them.
   ii. **Mark 10:33 (KJV)** *Saying*, Behold, we go up to Jerusalem; and the Son of man shall be delivered unto the chief priests, and unto the scribes; and they shall condemn him to death, and shall deliver him to the Gentiles:
   iii. **Luke 18:32 (KJV)** For he shall be delivered unto the Gentiles, and shall be mocked, and spitefully entreated, and spitted on:
   iv. **Acts 9:15 (KJV)** But the Lord said unto him, Go thy way: for he is a chosen vessel unto me, to bear my name before the Gentiles, and kings, and the children of Israel:
   v.   **Acts 22:21 (KJV)** And he said unto me, Depart: for I will send thee far hence unto the Gentiles.
   vi. **Acts 23:11 (KJV)** And the night following the Lord stood by him, and said, Be of good cheer, Paul: for as thou hast testified of me in Jerusalem, so must thou bear witness also at Rome.
   vii. **Acts 26:17 (KJV)** Delivering thee from the people, and *from* the Gentiles, unto whom now I send thee,

527.   Now, if **1 Corinthians 12:2 (KJV)** confirms that white people Gentiles were idol worshippers, how then say some ignorant Pastors and foolish Christians that it was white people who brought Christianity to Black People in Africa?

528.   The lie of the white people to steal Black People's superior spiritual record is evident when you see that the LORD Jesus Christ sent Apostle Paul to bring the Word

of God to the barbaric unsaved unchristian ungodly uncivilized white people in Europe!

    i. **Acts 9:15 (KJV)** But the Lord said unto him, Go thy way: for he is a chosen vessel unto me, to bear my name before the Gentiles, and kings, and the children of Israel:

    ii. **Acts 22:21 (KJV)** And he said unto me, Depart: for I will send thee far hence unto the Gentiles.

    iii. **Acts 23:11 (KJV)** And the night following the Lord stood by him, and said, Be of good cheer, Paul: for as thou hast testified of me in Jerusalem, so must thou bear witness also at Rome.

529.   All spiritual gifts devolve from the Holy Spirit, from the LORD Jesus Christ, and from God the Father yet all Three are One!

    i. **1 Corinthians 12:3 (KJV)** Wherefore I give you to understand, that no man speaking by the Spirit of God calleth Jesus accursed: and *that* no man can say that Jesus is the Lord, but by the Holy Ghost.

    ii. **1 Corinthians 12:4 (KJV)** Now there are diversities of gifts, but the same Spirit.

    iii. **1 Corinthians 12:5 (KJV)** And there are differences of administrations, but the same Lord.

    iv. **1 Corinthians 12:6 (KJV)** And there are diversities of operations, but it is the same God which worketh all in all.

530.   Spiritual Gifts may come in three categories namely:

    i. Spiritual gifts for Ministry!

    ii. Spiritual gifts for church administration!

    iii. Spiritual gifts for one-time special spiritual operations!

531.   According to **1 Corinthians 12:7 (KJV)**, all spiritual gifts are for the benefit of the congregation and NOT for personal benefit! This means that you can have a Man of God who has the spiritual gift of healing other people yet he himself is sick!

    i. **1 Corinthians 12:7 (KJV)** But the manifestation of the Spirit is given to every man to profit withal.

    ii. **2 Corinthians 12:7 (KJV)** And lest I should be exalted above measure through the abundance of the revelations, there was given to me a thorn in the flesh, the messenger of Satan to buffet me, lest I should be exalted above measure.

    iii. **2 Corinthians 12:8 (KJV)** For this thing I besought the Lord thrice, that it might depart from me.

    iv. **2 Corinthians 12:9 (KJV)** And he said unto me, My grace is sufficient for thee: for my strength is made perfect in weakness. Most gladly therefore will I rather glory in my infirmities, that the power of Christ may rest upon me.

    v. **Galatians 4:14 (KJV)** And my temptation which was in my flesh ye despised not, nor rejected; but received me as an angel of God, *even* as Christ Jesus.

    vi. **Galatians 4:15 (KJV)** Where is then the blessedness ye spake of? for I bear you record, that, if *it had been* possible, ye would have plucked out your own eyes, and have given them to me.

532.   All these spiritual gifts are for the edifying of the Body of Christ!

    i. **1 Corinthians 12:8 (KJV)** For to one is given by the Spirit the word of wisdom; to another the word of knowledge by the same Spirit;

    ii. **1 Corinthians 12:9 (KJV)** To another faith by the same Spirit; to another the gifts of healing by the same Spirit;

    iii. **1 Corinthians 12:10 (KJV)** To another the working of miracles; to another prophecy; to another discerning of spirits; to another *divers* kinds of tongues; to another the interpretation of tongues:

    iv. **1 Corinthians 12:11 (KJV)** But all these worketh that one and the selfsame Spirit, dividing to every man severally as he will.

533.   Tongues must benefit others, NOT the speaker!

534.   Tongues-speaking must give knowledge., NOT ignorance and confusion!

535.   Tongues must edify the Body of Christ through interpretation, NOT oneself!

536.   Every true Man of God has a spiritual gift or a talent!

    i. **Matthew 25:14 (KJV)** For *the kingdom of heaven is* as a man travelling into a far country, *who* called his own servants, and delivered unto them his goods.

    ii. **Matthew 25:15 (KJV)** And unto one he gave five talents, to another two, and to another one; to every man according to his several ability; and straightway took his journey.

537.   While every true Man of God is different, yet all the spiritual gifts of all the Men of God in the world are interdependently operational to complement each other in order to attain fullness, and the glue that binds all of them together across all the continents of the Earth is called the Holy Spirit!

    i. **1 Corinthians 12:12 (KJV)** For as the body is one, and hath many members, and all the members of that one body, being many, are one body: so also *is* Christ.

    ii. **1 Corinthians 12:13 (KJV)** For by one Spirit are we all baptized into one body, whether *we be* Jews or Gentiles, whether *we be* bond or free; and have been all made to drink into one Spirit.

      iii. **1 Corinthians 12:14 (KJV)** For the body is not one member, but many.

      iv. **1 Corinthians 12:23 (KJV)** And those *members* of the body, which we think to be less honourable, upon these we bestow more abundant honour; and our uncomely *parts* have more abundant comeliness.

538.   I do not need to know the spiritual gift that a Man of God has, but I can discern the Spirit who is behind your gift by means of your obedience to the Word of God and your daily life in Truth and Righteousness!

539.   Where a Man of God deviates from Truth and Righteousness, then, I know immediately that the spirit who is behind his gift is Satan, and that he is NOT a true Man of God but a Minister of Satan!

540.   Another way through which I can discern a false Man of God is the absence of Christ-love in him, and the presence of greed and selfishness!

      i. **1 Corinthians 12:25 (KJV)** That there should be no schism in the body; but *that* the members should have the same care one for another.

      ii. **1 Corinthians 12:26 (KJV)** And whether one member suffer, all the members suffer with it; or one member be honoured, all the members rejoice with it.

      iii. **1 Corinthians 12:27 (KJV)** Now ye are the body of Christ, and members in particular.

      iv. **John 13:34 (KJV)** A new commandment I give unto you, That ye love one another; as I have loved you, that ye also love one another.

      v. **John 13:35 (KJV)** By this shall all *men* know that ye are my disciples, if ye have love one to another.

      vi. **John 17:23 (KJV)** I in them, and thou in me, that they may be made perfect in one; and that the world may know that thou hast sent me, and hast loved them, as thou hast loved me.

541.   The spiritual gifts that are needed to successfully operate the entire Church of Christ in the whole world are these:

      i. **1 Corinthians 12:28 (KJV)** And God hath set some in the church, first apostles, secondarily prophets, thirdly teachers, after that miracles, then gifts of healings, helps, governments, diversities of tongues.

      ii. **1 Corinthians 12:29 (KJV)** *Are* all apostles? *are* all prophets? *are* all teachers? *are* all workers of miracles?

      iii. **1 Corinthians 12:30 (KJV)** Have all the gifts of healing? do all speak with tongues? do all interpret?

542.   So that, in one church, you may find it headed by an Apostle. In another church, you may find it headed by a Prophet. In yet another church or a bible School, you may find only a Bible Teacher. Then, in some church, you may find only a Miracle

Worker. Another Man of God may also be only a Healer and he is heading one church. Somebody's Ministry may also only be a Ministry or an NGO of Helps of Christian churches or Helps for Christian Organizations. In yet another instance, you can find a Ministry or a School that is only dedicated to Church Administration. Then, finally, you can also come across a Ministry that is dedicated to only the interpretation of diversities of tongues.

543.　　　Those are not all the different Ministries in the Body of Christ! There is also the Ministry of the Scribe of the Law of the God of Heaven, or the Ministry of the Scholar of the Word of God!

i. **1 Chronicles 25:8 (KJV)** And they cast lots, ward against *ward*, as well the small as the great, the teacher as the scholar.

ii. **Malachi 2:12 (KJV)** The LORD will cut off the man that doeth this, the master and the scholar, out of the tabernacles of Jacob, and him that offereth an offering unto the LORD of hosts.

iii. **Ezra 7:12 (KJV)** Artaxerxes, king of kings, unto Ezra the priest, a scribe of the law of the God of heaven, perfect *peace*, and at such a time.

iv. **Ezra 7:21 (KJV)** And I, *even* I Artaxerxes the king, do make a decree to all the treasurers which *are* beyond the river, that whatsoever Ezra the priest, the scribe of the law of the God of heaven, shall require of you, it be done speedily,

Saturday 13th January 2024 @ 12:20 PM – 6:21 PM

CHAPTER 14: TONGUES OF ANGELS

544. There be many who have pointed to "Tongues of Angels" saying that there be any such thing that itself translates into one of the spiritual gifts of the Holy Ghost!

545. Is that true, and what does it mean: "Tongues of Angels"? what languages/tongues do Angels speak?

  i. **1 Corinthians 13:1 (KJV)** Though I speak with the tongues of men and of angels, and have not charity, I am become *as* sounding brass, or a tinkling cymbal.

546. The language in **1 Corinthians 13:1-4 (KJV)** is a Figure of Speech called "Exaggeration", meaning that those references and descriptions do NOT exist in real human life! So, therefore, the specific meaning of **1 Corinthians 13:1 (KJV)** is this:

  i. There is nothing in the human realm or spiritual realms called "Tongues of Angels"!

547. Moreover, if you claim that "tongues of men and of angels" in **1 Corinthians 13:1 (KJV)** means that there is a real language/tongue different and specific to the Angels, then, you must also accept to give your body to be burned just as **1 Corinthians 13:3 (KJV)** says! Thou fool!

  i. **1 Corinthians 13:3 (KJV)** And though I bestow all my goods to feed *the poor*, and though I give my body to be burned, and have not charity, it profiteth me nothing.

548. The two words: "languages/tongues" are the same and interchangeable!

549. The LORD God uses the word "Angel" 194 times in the entire Holy Bible from Genesis to Revelation, and the LORD God uses the word "Angels" 92 times in the entire Holy Bible, and here is the very first time that the word Angle is used in the Holy Bible:

550. Here is evidence #1 showing that both Angels and humans speak the same languages/tongues!

  i. **Genesis 16:7 (KJV)** And the angel of the LORD found her by a fountain of water in the wilderness, by the fountain in the way to Shur.

  ii. **Genesis 16:8 (KJV)** And he said, Hagar, Sarai's maid, whence camest thou? and whither wilt thou go? And she said, I flee from the face of my mistress Sarai.!

  iii. **Genesis 16:9 (KJV)** And the angel of the LORD said unto her, Return to thy mistress, and submit thyself under her hands.

    iv. **Genesis 16:10 (KJV)** And the angel of the LORD said unto her, I will multiply thy seed exceedingly, that it shall not be numbered for multitude.

    v. **Genesis 16:11 (KJV)** And the angel of the LORD said unto her, Behold, thou *art* with child, and shalt bear a son, and shalt call his name Ishmael; because the LORD hath heard thy affliction.

    vi. **Genesis 16:12 (KJV)** And he will be a wild man; his hand *will be* against every man, and every man's hand against him; and he shall dwell in the presence of all his brethren.

    vii. **Genesis 16:13 (KJV)** And she called the name of the LORD that spake unto her, Thou God seest me: for she said, Have I also here looked after him that seeth me?

    viii. **Genesis 16:14 (KJV)** Wherefore the well was called Beer-lahai-roi; behold, *it is* between Kadesh and Bered.

    ix. **Genesis 16:15 (KJV)** And Hagar bare Abram a son: and Abram called his son's name, which Hagar bare, Ishmael.

551.   As you can see from the evidence in **Genesis 16:7-15 (KJV)** above, Angels speak human languages/tongues!

552.   Therefore, this phrase: "Though I speak with the tongues of men and of angels" in **1 Corinthians 13:1 (KJV)**, does NOT mean two different languages/tongues where one language belongs to men and the other tongue belongs to Angels!

553.   No, that is NOT what **1 Corinthians 13:1 (KJV)** means!

554.   Rather, that phrase means: "the same languages/tongues belonging to both men and Angels"!

555.   That is why you see both the Angel of the LORD and Hagar speaking the same tongue/language in **Genesis 16:7-15 (KJV)** above!

556.   Here is evidence #2 showing that even when Angels speak directly from Heaven, they do speak human languages!

    i. **Genesis 21:17 (KJV)** And God heard the voice of the lad; and the angel of God called to Hagar out of heaven, and said unto her, What aileth thee, Hagar? fear not; for God hath heard the voice of the lad where he *is*.

    ii. **Genesis 22:11 (KJV)** And the angel of the LORD called unto him out of heaven, and said, Abraham, Abraham: and he said, Here *am* I.

    iii. **Genesis 22:15 (KJV)** And the angel of the LORD called unto Abraham out of heaven the second time,

557.　　　Here is evidence #3 showing that even when God Almighty appears as an Angel to speak to humans in dreams, God does speak human languages!

      i.　**Genesis 31:11 (KJV)** And the angel of God spake unto me in a dream, *saying*, Jacob: And I said, Here *am* I.

      ii.　**Genesis 31:12 (KJV)** And he said, Lift up now thine eyes, and see, all the rams which leap upon the cattle *are* ringstraked, speckled, and grisled: for I have seen all that Laban doeth unto thee.

      iii.　**Genesis 31:13 (KJV)** I *am* the God of Beth-el, where thou anointedst the pillar, *and* where thou vowedst a vow unto me: now arise, get thee out from this land, and return unto the land of thy kindred.

558.　　　Here is evidence #4 showing that both Angels and the LORD God Almighty speak in human languages/tongues!

      i.　**Exodus 3:1 (KJV)** Now Moses kept the flock of Jethro his father in law, the priest of Midian: and he led the flock to the backside of the desert, and came to the mountain of God, *even* to Horeb.

      ii.　**Exodus 3:2 (KJV)** And the angel of the LORD appeared unto him in a flame of fire out of the midst of a bush: and he looked, and, behold, the bush burned with fire, and the bush *was* not consumed.

      iii.　**Exodus 3:3 (KJV)** And Moses said, I will now turn aside, and see this great sight, why the bush is not burnt.

      iv.　**Exodus 3:4 (KJV)** And when the LORD saw that he turned aside to see, God called unto him out of the midst of the bush, and said, Moses, Moses. And he said, Here *am* I.

      v.　**Exodus 3:5 (KJV)** And he said, Draw not nigh hither: put off thy shoes from off thy feet, for the place whereon thou standest *is* holy ground.

      vi.　**Exodus 3:6 (KJV)** Moreover he said, I *am* the God of thy father, the God of Abraham, the God of Isaac, and the God of Jacob. And Moses hid his face; for he was afraid to look upon God.

559.　　　Here is evidence #5 showing that the Angels of God speak to Prophets in human languages!

      i.　**Numbers 22:21 (KJV)** And Balaam rose up in the morning, and saddled his ass, and went with the princes of Moab.

      ii.　**Numbers 22:22 (KJV)** And God's anger was kindled because he went: and the angel of the LORD stood in the way for an adversary against him. Now he was riding upon his ass, and his two servants *were* with him.

iii. **Numbers 22:23 (KJV)** And the ass saw the angel of the LORD standing in the way, and his sword drawn in his hand: and the ass turned aside out of the way, and went into the field: and Balaam smote the ass, to turn her into the way.

iv. **Numbers 22:24 (KJV)** But the angel of the LORD stood in a path of the vineyards, a wall *being* on this side, and a wall on that side.

v. **Numbers 22:25 (KJV)** And when the ass saw the angel of the LORD, she thrust herself unto the wall, and crushed Balaam's foot against the wall: and he smote her again.

vi. **Numbers 22:26 (KJV)** And the angel of the LORD went further, and stood in a narrow place, where *was* no way to turn either to the right hand or to the left.

vii. **Numbers 22:27 (KJV)** And when the ass saw the angel of the LORD, she fell down under Balaam: and Balaam's anger was kindled, and he smote the ass with a staff.

viii. **Numbers 22:28 (KJV)** And the LORD opened the mouth of the ass, and she said unto Balaam, What have I done unto thee, that thou hast smitten me these three times?

ix. **Numbers 22:29 (KJV)** And Balaam said unto the ass, Because thou hast mocked me: I would there were a sword in mine hand, for now would I kill thee.

x. **Numbers 22:30 (KJV)** And the ass said unto Balaam, *Am* not I thine ass, upon which thou hast ridden ever since *I was* thine unto this day? was I ever wont to do so unto thee? And he said, Nay.

xi. **Numbers 22:31 (KJV)** Then the LORD opened the eyes of Balaam, and he saw the angel of the LORD standing in the way, and his sword drawn in his hand: and he bowed down his head, and fell flat on his face.

xii. **Numbers 22:32 (KJV)** And the angel of the LORD said unto him, Wherefore hast thou smitten thine ass these three times? behold, I went out to withstand thee, because *thy* way is perverse before me:

xiii. **Numbers 22:33 (KJV)** And the ass saw me, and turned from me these three times: unless she had turned from me, surely now also I had slain thee, and saved her alive.

xiv. **Numbers 22:34 (KJV)** And Balaam said unto the angel of the LORD, I have sinned; for I knew not that thou stoodest in the way against me: now therefore, if it displease thee, I will get me back again.

xv. **Numbers 22:35 (KJV)** And the angel of the LORD said unto Balaam, Go with the men: but only the word that I shall speak unto thee, that thou shalt speak. So Balaam went with the princes of Balak.

560.   Here is evidence #6 showing that Angels preach the Word of God NOT in any Heavenly language/tongue, but only in human languages/tongues!

        i. **Judges 2:1 (KJV)** And an angel of the LORD came up from Gilgal to Bochim, and said, I made you to go up out of Egypt, and have brought you unto the land which I sware unto your fathers; and I said, I will never break my covenant with you.

        ii. **Judges 2:2 (KJV)** And ye shall make no league with the inhabitants of this land; ye shall throw down their altars: but ye have not obeyed my voice: why have ye done this?

        iii. **Judges 2:3 (KJV)** Wherefore I also said, I will not drive them out from before you; but they shall be *as thorns* in your sides, and their gods shall be a snare unto you.

        iv. **Judges 2:4 (KJV)** And it came to pass, when the angel of the LORD spake these words unto all the children of Israel, that the people lifted up their voice, and wept.

        v. **Judges 2:5 (KJV)** And they called the name of that place Bochim: and they sacrificed there unto the LORD.

561.   Here is evidence #7 showing that even when Angels take part in human offerings and sacrifices unto God Almighty, they still speak human languages/tongues to God Almighty, NOT Heavenly tongue of Angels!

        i. **Judges 6:17 (KJV)** And he said unto him, If now I have found grace in thy sight, then shew me a sign that thou talkest with me.

        ii. **Judges 6:18 (KJV)** Depart not hence, I pray thee, until I come unto thee, and bring forth my present, and set *it* before thee. And he said, I will tarry until thou come again.

        iii. **Judges 6:19 (KJV)** And Gideon went in, and made ready a kid, and unleavened cakes of an ephah of flour: the flesh he put in a basket, and he put the broth in a pot, and brought *it* out unto him under the oak, and presented *it*.

        iv. **Judges 6:20 (KJV)** And the angel of God said unto him, Take the flesh and the unleavened cakes, and lay *them* upon this rock, and pour out the broth. And he did so.

        v. **Judges 6:21 (KJV)** Then the angel of the LORD put forth the end of the staff that *was* in his hand, and touched the flesh and the unleavened cakes; and there rose up fire out of the rock, and consumed the flesh and the unleavened cakes. Then the angel of the LORD departed out of his sight.

vi. **Judges 6:22 (KJV)** And when Gideon perceived that he *was* an angel of the LORD, Gideon said, Alas, O Lord GOD! for because I have seen an angel of the LORD face to face.

vii. **Judges 6:23 (KJV)** And the LORD said unto him, Peace *be* unto thee; fear not: thou shalt not die.

562.   Here is evidence #8 showing that humans pray to God in human languages/tongues, NOT in any false Heavenly tongue/language!

i. **Judges 13:8 (KJV)** Then Manoah intreated the LORD, and said, O my Lord, let the man of God which thou didst send come again unto us, and teach us what we shall do unto the child that shall be born.

ii. **Judges 13:9 (KJV)** And God hearkened to the voice of Manoah; and the angel of God came again unto the woman as she sat in the field: but Manoah her husband *was* not with her.

iii. **1 Kings 8:38 (KJV)** What prayer and supplication soever be *made* by any man, *or* by all thy people Israel, which shall know every man the plague of his own heart, and spread forth his hands toward this house:

iv. **Acts 4:23 (KJV)** And being let go, they went to their own company, and reported all that the chief priests and elders had said unto them.

v. **Acts 4:24 (KJV)** And when they heard that, they lifted up their voice to God with one accord, and said, Lord, thou *art* God, which hast made heaven, and earth, and the sea, and all that in them is:

vi. **Acts 4:25 (KJV)** Who by the mouth of thy servant David hast said, Why did the heathen rage, and the people imagine vain things?

vii. **Acts 4:26 (KJV)** The kings of the earth stood up, and the rulers were gathered together against the Lord, and against his Christ.

viii. **Acts 4:27 (KJV)** For of a truth against thy holy child Jesus, whom thou hast anointed, both Herod, and Pontius Pilate, with the Gentiles, and the people of Israel, were gathered together,

ix. **Acts 4:28 (KJV)** For to do whatsoever thy hand and thy counsel determined before to be done.

x. **Acts 4:29 (KJV)** And now, Lord, behold their threatenings: and grant unto thy servants, that with all boldness they may speak thy word,

xi. **Acts 4:30 (KJV)** By stretching forth thine hand to heal; and that signs and wonders may be done by the name of thy holy child Jesus.

xii. **Acts 4:31 (KJV)** And when they had prayed, the place was shaken where they were assembled together; and they were all filled with the Holy Ghost, and they spake the word of God with boldness.

563.	Here is evidence #9 showing that in Heaven, the LORD God Almighty speaks to Angels in human languages/tongues!

i. **2 Samuel 24:15 (KJV)** So the LORD sent a pestilence upon Israel from the morning even to the time appointed: and there died of the people from Dan even to Beer-sheba seventy thousand men.

ii. **2 Samuel 24:16 (KJV)** And when the angel stretched out his hand upon Jerusalem to destroy it, the LORD repented him of the evil, and said to the angel that destroyed the people, It is enough: stay now thine hand. And the angel of the LORD was by the threshingplace of Araunah the Jebusite.

iii. **1 Chronicles 21:27 (KJV)** And the LORD commanded the angel; and he put up his sword again into the sheath thereof.

iv. **Hebrews 1:5 (KJV)** For unto which of the angels said he at any time, Thou art my Son, this day have I begotten thee? And again, I will be to him a Father, and he shall be to me a Son?

v. **Hebrews 1:6 (KJV)** And again, when he bringeth in the firstbegotten into the world, he saith, And let all the angels of God worship him.

vi. **Hebrews 1:13 (KJV)** But to which of the angels said he at any time, Sit on my right hand, until I make thine enemies thy footstool?

564.	Here is evidence #10 showing that when Angels help humans in their Ministry, they communicate to them in human languages/tongues, NOT in other unknown incomprehensible languages/tongues!

i. **1 Kings 19:5 (KJV)** And as he lay and slept under a juniper tree, behold, then an angel touched him, and said unto him, Arise *and* eat.

ii. **1 Kings 19:7 (KJV)** And the angel of the LORD came again the second time, and touched him, and said, Arise *and* eat; because the journey *is* too great for thee.

iii. **2 Kings 1:3 (KJV)** But the angel of the LORD said to Elijah the Tishbite, Arise, go up to meet the messengers of the king of Samaria, and say unto them, *Is it* not because *there is* not a God in Israel, *that* ye go to inquire of Baal-zebub the god of Ekron?

iv. **2 Kings 1:15 (KJV)** And the angel of the LORD said unto Elijah, Go down with him: be not afraid of him. And he arose, and went down with him unto the king.

    v. **1 Chronicles 21:18 (KJV)** Then the angel of the LORD commanded Gad to say to David, that David should go up, and set up an altar unto the LORD in the threshingfloor of Ornan the Jebusite.

    vi. **Acts 5:19 (KJV)** But the angel of the Lord by night opened the prison doors, and brought them forth, and said,

    vii. **Acts 5:20 (KJV)** Go, stand and speak in the temple to the people all the words of this life.

    viii. **Hebrews 2:2 (KJV)** For if the word spoken by angels was stedfast, and every transgression and disobedience received a just recompence of reward;

565.   Here is evidence #11 showing that when humans go to Heaven, the language/tongue that they speak with Angeles and with God Almighty in Heaven are human languages/tongues, NOT other unknown incomprehensible languages/tongues!

    i. **Zechariah 1:8 (KJV)** I saw by night, and behold a man riding upon a red horse, and he stood among the myrtle trees that *were* in the bottom; and behind him *were there* red horses, speckled, and white.

    ii. **Zechariah 1:8 (KJV)** I saw by night, and behold a man riding upon a red horse, and he stood among the myrtle trees that *were* in the bottom; and behind him *were there* red horses, speckled, and white.

    iii. **Zechariah 1:9 (KJV)** Then said I, O my lord, what *are* these? And the angel that talked with me said unto me, I will shew thee what these *be*.

    iv. **Zechariah 1:10 (KJV)** And the man that stood among the myrtle trees answered and said, These *are they* whom the LORD hath sent to walk to and fro through the earth.

    v. **Zechariah 1:11 (KJV)** And they answered the angel of the LORD that stood among the myrtle trees, and said, We have walked to and fro through the earth, and, behold, all the earth sitteth still, and is at rest.

    vi. **Zechariah 1:12 (KJV)** Then the angel of the LORD answered and said, O LORD of hosts, how long wilt thou not have mercy on Jerusalem and on the cities of Judah, against which thou hast had indignation these threescore and ten years?

    vii. **Zechariah 1:13 (KJV)** And the LORD answered the angel that talked with me *with* good words *and* comfortable words.

    viii. **Zechariah 1:14 (KJV)** So the angel that communed with me said unto me, Cry thou, saying, Thus saith the LORD of hosts; I am jealous for Jerusalem and for Zion with a great jealousy.

ix. **Zechariah 1:15 (KJV)** And I am very sore displeased with the heathen *that are* at ease: for I was but a little displeased, and they helped forward the affliction.

x. **Revelation 7:9 (KJV)** After this I beheld, and, lo, a great multitude, which no man could number, of all nations, and kindreds, and people, and tongues, stood before the throne, and before the Lamb, clothed with white robes, and palms in their hands;

566.　　Here is evidence #12 showing that the LORD God Almighty speaks human languages/tongues with Satan, NOT other unknown incomprehensible languages/tongues!

i. **Zechariah 3:1 (KJV)** And he shewed me Joshua the high priest standing before the angel of the LORD, and Satan standing at his right hand to resist him.

ii. **Zechariah 3:2 (KJV)** And the LORD said unto Satan, The LORD rebuke thee, O Satan; even the LORD that hath chosen Jerusalem rebuke thee: *is* not this a brand plucked out of the fire?

iii. **Zechariah 3:3 (KJV)** Now Joshua was clothed with filthy garments, and stood before the angel.

iv. **Zechariah 3:4 (KJV)** And he answered and spake unto those that stood before him, saying, Take away the filthy garments from him. And unto him he said, Behold, I have caused thine iniquity to pass from thee, and I will clothe thee with change of raiment.

v. **Zechariah 3:5 (KJV)** And I said, Let them set a fair mitre upon his head. So they set a fair mitre upon his head, and clothed him with garments. And the angel of the LORD stood by.

vi. **Zechariah 3:6 (KJV)** And the angel of the LORD protested unto Joshua, saying,

vii. **Zechariah 3:7 (KJV)** Thus saith the LORD of hosts; If thou wilt walk in my ways, and if thou wilt keep my charge, then thou shalt also judge my house, and shalt also keep my courts, and I will give thee places to walk among these that stand by.

viii. **Zechariah 3:8 (KJV)** Hear now, O Joshua the high priest, thou, and thy fellows that sit before thee: for they *are* men wondered at: for, behold, I will bring forth my servant the BRANCH.

ix. **Zechariah 3:9 (KJV)** For behold the stone that I have laid before Joshua; upon one stone *shall be* seven eyes: behold, I will engrave the graving thereof, saith the LORD of hosts, and I will remove the iniquity of that land in one day.

        x. **Zechariah 3:10 (KJV)** In that day, saith the LORD of hosts, shall ye call every man his neighbour under the vine and under the fig tree.

567.   Here is evidence #13 showing that when Angels from Heaven speak to humans in dreams, they use human languages/tongues, NOT other unknown incomprehensible languages/tongues!

        i. **Matthew 1:20 (KJV)** But while he thought on these things, behold, the angel of the Lord appeared unto him in a dream, saying, Joseph, thou son of David, fear not to take unto thee Mary thy wife: for that which is conceived in her is of the Holy Ghost.

        ii. **Matthew 2:13 (KJV)** And when they were departed, behold, the angel of the Lord appeareth to Joseph in a dream, saying, Arise, and take the young child and his mother, and flee into Egypt, and be thou there until I bring thee word: for Herod will seek the young child to destroy him.

        iii. **Matthew 2:19 (KJV)** But when Herod was dead, behold, an angel of the Lord appeareth in a dream to Joseph in Egypt,

568.   The above 13 evidences are for the singular use of the name: Angel, in the entire Holy Bible from Genesis to Revelation. We shall now see the record for the plural form (Angels) in the entire Holy Bible from Genesis to Revelation!

569.   Here is evidence #14 showing that when Angels come to the Earth for a destructive assignment, they always speak human languages/tongues, NOT other unknown incomprehensible languages/tongues!

        i. **Genesis 19:1 (KJV)** And there came two angels to Sodom at even; and Lot sat in the gate of Sodom: and Lot seeing *them* rose up to meet them; and he bowed himself with his face toward the ground;

        ii. **Genesis 19:2 (KJV)** And he said, Behold now, my lords, turn in, I pray you, into your servant's house, and tarry all night, and wash your feet, and ye shall rise up early, and go on your ways. And they said, Nay; but we will abide in the street all night.

        iii. **Genesis 19:3 (KJV)** And he pressed upon them greatly; and they turned in unto him, and entered into his house; and he made them a feast, and did bake unleavened bread, and they did eat.

        iv. **Hebrews 13:2 (KJV)** Be not forgetful to entertain strangers: for thereby some have entertained angels unawares.

570.   Here is evidence #15 showing that Angels in Heaven do bless and praise the LORD God Almighty speaking human languages/tongues, NOT other unknown incomprehensible languages/tongues!

     i.   **Psalm 103:20 (KJV)** Bless the LORD, ye his angels, that excel in strength, that do his commandments, hearkening unto the voice of his word.

     ii.   **Psalm 148:2 (KJV)** Praise ye him, all his angels: praise ye him, all his hosts.

571.   Here is evidence #16 showing that the LORD Jesus Christ has Angels and HE communicates with them speaking human languages/tongues, NOT other unknown incomprehensible languages/tongues!

     i.   **Matthew 13:39 (KJV)** The enemy that sowed them is the devil; the harvest is the end of the world; and the reapers are the angels.

     ii.   **Matthew 13:41 (KJV)** The Son of man shall send forth his angels, and they shall gather out of his kingdom all things that offend, and them which do iniquity;

     iii.   **Matthew 24:31 (KJV)** And he shall send his angels with a great sound of a trumpet, and they shall gather together his elect from the four winds, from one end of heaven to the other.

     iv.   **Mark 13:27 (KJV)** And then shall he send his angels, and shall gather together his elect from the four winds, from the uttermost part of the earth to the uttermost part of heaven.

572.   Here is evidence #17 showing that the LORD Jesus Christ speaks human languages/tongues with God the father, NOT other unknown incomprehensible languages/tongues!

     i.   **Luke 12:8 (KJV)** Also I say unto you, Whosoever shall confess me before men, him shall the Son of man also confess before the angels of God:

     ii.   **Luke 12:9 (KJV)** But he that denieth me before men shall be denied before the angels of God.

     iii.   **Luke 23:46 (KJV)** And when Jesus had cried with a loud voice, he said, Father, into thy hands I commend my spirit: and having said thus, he gave up the ghost.

573.   Here is evidence #18 showing that the Angels in the Old Testament communicated the Law of God to the Prophets using human languages/tongues, NOT other unknown incomprehensible languages/tongues!

     i.   **Acts 7:52 (KJV)** Which of the prophets have not your fathers persecuted? and they have slain them which shewed before of the coming of the Just One; of whom ye have been now the betrayers and murderers:

ii. **Acts 7:53 (KJV)** Who have received the law by the disposition of angels, and have not kept *it*.

iii. **1 Corinthians 6:3 (KJV)** Know ye not that we shall judge angels? how much more things that pertain to this life?

iv. **Galatians 3:19 (KJV)** Wherefore then *serveth* the law? It was added because of transgressions, till the seed should come to whom the promise was made; *and it was* ordained by angels in the hand of a mediator.

574.   Here is evidence #19 showing that all the above 18 evidences reveal that "tongues of men" are "tongues of Angels" and that there is no difference at all between the two!

i. **1 Corinthians 13:1 (KJV)** Though I speak with the tongues of men and of angels, and have not charity, I am become *as* sounding brass, or a tinkling cymbal.

575.   Here is evidence #20 showing that in Heaven, they all speak human languages/tongues, NOT other unknown incomprehensible languages/tongues!

i. **Revelation 5:11 (KJV)** And I beheld, and I heard the voice of many angels round about the throne and the beasts and the elders: and the number of them was ten thousand times ten thousand, and thousands of thousands;

ii. **Revelation 7:2 (KJV)** And I saw another angel ascending from the east, having the seal of the living God: and he cried with a loud voice to the four angels, to whom it was given to hurt the earth and the sea,

iii. **Revelation 7:11 (KJV)** And all the angels stood round about the throne, and *about* the elders and the four beasts, and fell before the throne on their faces, and worshipped God,

iv. **Revelation 8:13 (KJV)** And I beheld, and heard an angel flying through the midst of heaven, saying with a loud voice, Woe, woe, woe, to the inhabiters of the earth by reason of the other voices of the trumpet of the three angels, which are yet to sound!

v. **Revelation 9:14 (KJV)** Saying to the sixth angel which had the trumpet, Loose the four angels which are bound in the great river Euphrates.

vi. **Revelation 16:1 (KJV)** And I heard a great voice out of the temple saying to the seven angels, Go your ways, and pour out the vials of the wrath of God upon the earth.

vii. **Revelation 17:1 (KJV)** And there came one of the seven angels which had the seven vials, and talked with me, saying unto me, Come hither;

I will shew unto thee the judgment of the great whore that sitteth upon many waters:

viii. **Revelation 21:9 (KJV)** And there came unto me one of the seven angels which had the seven vials full of the seven last plagues, and talked with me, saying, Come hither, I will shew thee the bride, the Lamb's wife.

ix. **Revelation 21:12 (KJV)** And had a wall great and high, *and* had twelve gates, and at the gates twelve angels, and names written thereon, which are *the names* of the twelve tribes of the children of Israel:

576. In summary, we researched the words: "Angel" and "Angels" in the entire Holy Bible from Genesius to Revelation, and we found a total of 286 times when the LORD God used both words.

577. Upon further research, we did not find even one time when either "Angel" or "Angels" spoke any language that was different from human languages/tongues!

578. Therefore, the phrases: "tongues of men" and "tongues of Angels" are both one and the same thing!

i. **1 Corinthians 13:1 (KJV)** Though I speak with the tongues of men and of angels, and have not charity, I am become *as* sounding brass, or a tinkling cymbal.

579. Furthermore, we conclude that there is nothing called "other tongues/languages" that are different from human languages!

580. When a tongue/language deviates from any known human language, and yet it comes with no interpretation, then know now, that it is from Satan, and it was called "Ecstatic Language" in established pagan temples in Ancient Byblos in 1100 BC, which demonic phenomenon Palto (429-347 BC also mentions it in his writings some one thousand one hundred years before Pentecost, and Plato calls it "Divine Possession" accompanied with "utterances and visions" that the speaker DID NOT UNDERSTAND!

581. Even in the Akan and Ewe native traditional religions of the Okomfo (the original name of the Prophet in the Twi language of Ghana is Okomfo and Okomfo means Fetish Priest), it was a very normal phenomenon to see the shrine priest and priestesses, with their body and faces painted with white powder, and adorned with many talismans and amulets, wearing the same skirt and girdle as Prophet Elijah and Prophet Samuel wore, dancing to frenetic drumming and tambourine display, turning and twirling around for up to one hour, until this same Okomfo becomes fully possessed with the devils of the shrine, and then, he or she begins to speak the linguistically structureless gibberish unintelligible meaningless mumbo jumbo language, with his or her assistant Okomfo standing close by him or her, interpreting

and telling the worshippers what the strange other tongues meant! Brethren and true Christians, this is the satanic practise that has been imported into Christianity as "speaking in tongues"!

    i. **1 Samuel 15:27 (KJV)** And as Samuel turned about to go away, he laid hold upon the skirt of his mantle, and it rent.

    ii. **2 Kings 1:8 (KJV)** And they answered him, *He was* an hairy man, and girt with a girdle of leather about his loins. And he said, It *is* Elijah the Tishbite.

    iii. **Haggai 2:12 (KJV)** If one bear holy flesh in the skirt of his garment, and with his skirt do touch bread, or pottage, or wine, or oil, or any meat, shall it be holy? And the priests answered and said, No.

582.   See also Virgil (70-19 BC) who also wrote about Sibylline priestesses who spoke in strange other tongues and conducted physical healings of people present!

583.   See also the writings of Irenaeus (114-202 AD) in his book: ***Against Heresies*** where he condemns "Ecstatic Utterances" of violent emotions in the early churches!

    i. **1 Corinthians 14:26 (KJV)** How is it then, brethren? when ye come together, every one of you hath a psalm, hath a doctrine, hath a tongue, hath a revelation, hath an interpretation. Let all things be done unto edifying.

584.   Many white people Gentiles, such as Nicolas of "the Nicolaitans, which I also hate", who became Christians but who were once practising pagans occultists and ritualists, shrine priests and priestesses, they imported their pagan practices into the new Christianity that they had embraced even as Apostle Paul correctly testified in **1 Corinthians 14:26 (KJV)**!

    i. **Acts 6:5 (KJV)** And the saying pleased the whole multitude: and they chose Stephen, a man full of faith and of the Holy Ghost, and Philip, and Prochorus, and Nicanor, and Timon, and Parmenas, and Nicolas a proselyte of Antioch:

    ii. **Revelation 2:6 (KJV)** But this thou hast, that thou hatest the deeds of the Nicolaitans, which I also hate.

    iii. **Revelation 2:15 (KJV)** So hast thou also them that hold the doctrine of the Nicolaitans, which thing I hate.

    iv. **Acts 19:13 (KJV)** Then certain of the vagabond Jews, exorcists, took upon them to call over them which had evil spirits the name of the Lord Jesus, saying, We adjure you by Jesus whom Paul preacheth.

    v. **Acts 19:14 (KJV)** And there were seven sons of *one* Sceva, a Jew, *and* chief of the priests, which did so.

vi. **Acts 19:15 (KJV)** And the evil spirit answered and said, Jesus I know, and Paul I know; but who are ye?

vii. **Acts 19:16 (KJV)** And the man in whom the evil spirit was leaped on them, and overcame them, and prevailed against them, so that they fled out of that house naked and wounded.

viii. **Acts 19:17 (KJV)** And this was known to all the Jews and Greeks also dwelling at Ephesus; and fear fell on them all, and the name of the Lord Jesus was magnified.

ix. **Acts 19:18 (KJV)** And many that believed came, and confessed, and shewed their deeds.

x. **Acts 19:19 (KJV)** Many of them also which used curious arts brought their books together, and burned them before all *men*: and they counted the price of them, and found *it* fifty thousand *pieces* of silver.

xi. **Acts 19:20 (KJV)** So mightily grew the word of God and prevailed.

xii. **Acts 19:24 (KJV)** For a certain *man* named Demetrius, a silversmith, which made silver shrines for Diana, brought no small gain unto the craftsmen;

xiii. **Acts 19:25 (KJV)** Whom he called together with the workmen of like occupation, and said, Sirs, ye know that by this craft we have our wealth.

xiv. **Acts 19:26 (KJV)** Moreover ye see and hear, that not alone at Ephesus, but almost throughout all Asia, this Paul hath persuaded and turned away much people, saying that they be no gods, which are made with hands:

xv. **Acts 19:27 (KJV)** So that not only this our craft is in danger to be set at nought; but also that the temple of the great goddess Diana should be despised, and her magnificence should be destroyed, whom all Asia and the world worshippeth.

xvi. **Acts 19:35 (KJV)** And when the townclerk had appeased the people, he said, *Ye* men of Ephesus, what man is there that knoweth not how that the city of the Ephesians is a worshipper of the great goddess Diana, and of the *image* which fell down from Jupiter?

585. The demonic racist Black People hating Mormon Sect under Joseph Smith their founder, who took the apostate name of "Father Smith", also spoke in "other tongues" in the United States of America, just as their other leader Brigham Young also spoke in "other tongues" and interpreted his own tongues, and today, they call themselves a church when the truth is that, they are NOT a church!

i. "Father Smith would call upon some illiterate brother to rise up and speak in tongues in the name of Jesus Christ. The order was given…Arise upon your feet, speak or make some sound, continue to make sounds of some kind, and the LORD will make a tongue or language out of it"

Sunday 14th January 2024 @ 9:00 AM – 3:19 PM

CHAPTER 15: ATTRIBUTES OF CHARITY/LOVE OF GOD

586.　　　If I can communicate with both men and Angels with ease, but I have no charity/love to help the poor/giving for the needy, then, I am nothing!

> i. **1 Corinthians 13:1 (KJV)** Though I speak with the tongues of men and of angels, and have not charity, I am become *as* sounding brass, or a tinkling cymbal.

587.　　　If I possess all physical and spiritual power, but I have no charity/love to help the poor/giving for the needy, then, I am nothing!

> i. **1 Corinthians 13:2 (KJV)** And though I have *the gift of* prophecy, and understand all mysteries, and all knowledge; and though I have all faith, so that I could remove mountains, and have not charity, I am nothing.
>
> ii. **1 Corinthians 13:3 (KJV)** And though I bestow all my goods to feed *the poor*, and though I give my body to be burned, and have not charity, it profiteth me nothing.

588.　　　He has charity he who has the Holy Ghost!

> i. **1 Corinthians 13:4 (KJV)** Charity suffereth long, *and* is kind; charity envieth not; charity vaunteth not itself, is not puffed up,
>
> ii. **1 Corinthians 13:5 (KJV)** Doth not behave itself unseemly, seeketh not her own, is not easily provoked, thinketh no evil;
>
> iii. **1 Corinthians 13:6 (KJV)** Rejoiceth not in iniquity, but rejoiceth in the truth;
>
> iv. **1 Corinthians 13:7 (KJV)** Beareth all things, believeth all things, hopeth all things, endureth all things.
>
> v. **1 Corinthians 13:8 (KJV)** Charity never faileth: but whether *there be* prophecies, they shall fail; whether *there be* tongues, they shall cease; whether *there be* knowledge, it shall vanish away.

589.　　　This word: "but whether *there be* prophecies, they shall fail", DOES NOT apply to the prophecy of the testimony of the LORD Jesus Christ, for, that one WILL NOT fail!

> i. **Matthew 5:18 (KJV)** For verily I say unto you, Till heaven and earth pass, one jot or one tittle shall in no wise pass from the law, till all be fulfilled.
>
> ii. **Matthew 24:35 (KJV)** Heaven and earth shall pass away, but my words shall not pass away.
>
> iii. **Mark 13:31 (KJV)** Heaven and earth shall pass away: but my words shall not pass away.

     iv. **Luke 21:33 (KJV)** Heaven and earth shall pass away: but my words shall not pass away.

     v. **Revelation 19:10 (KJV)** And I fell at his feet to worship him. And he said unto me, See *thou do it* not: I am thy fellowservant, and of thy brethren that have the testimony of Jesus: worship God: for the testimony of Jesus is the spirit of prophecy.

590.   This word: "But when that which is perfect is come": has that "perfect" come already, or, is it yet to come?

     i. **1 Corinthians 13:9 (KJV)** For we know in part, and we prophesy in part.

     ii. **1 Corinthians 13:10 (KJV)** But when that which is perfect is come, then that which is in part shall be done away.

     iii. **1 Corinthians 13:11 (KJV)** When I was a child, I spake as a child, I understood as a child, I thought as a child: but when I became a man, I put away childish things.

     iv. **1 Corinthians 13:12 (KJV)** For now we see through a glass, darkly; but then face to face: now I know in part; but then shall I know even as also I am known.

     v. **1 Corinthians 13:13 (KJV)** And now abideth faith, hope, charity, these three; but the greatest of these *is* charity.

591.   Here is the answer!

592.   The words: "For we know in part, and we prophesy in part" refers to the time of Apostle Paul when the entire written Word of God was not yet complete, and Paul himself was still in the process of writing many of the Books of the New Testament!

593.   Then, once the entire New Testament came and the Holy Bible was complete from Genesis to Revelation, once the Holy Spirit came to perfect all things among the saints of Christ, then that "perfect" in **1 Corinthians 13:10 (KJV)** has come and this prophecy has now, therefore, been fulfilled! He that is perfect is the LORD Jesus Christ and HE has come already!

     i. **1 Corinthians 13:10 (KJV)** But when that which is perfect is come, then that which is in part shall be done away.

594.   Here are evidences that the "perfect" has already come!

     i. **Genesis 6:9 (KJV)** These *are* the generations of Noah: Noah was a just man *and* perfect in his generations, *and* Noah walked with God.

     ii. **Genesis 17:1 (KJV)** And when Abram was ninety years old and nine, the LORD appeared to Abram, and said unto him, I *am* the Almighty God; walk before me, and be thou perfect.

iii. **Deuteronomy 18:13 (KJV)** Thou shalt be perfect with the LORD thy God.

iv. **2 Samuel 22:31 (KJV)** *As for* God, his way *is* perfect; the word of the LORD *is* tried: he *is* a buckler to all them that trust in him.

v. **1 Kings 15:14 (KJV)** But the high places were not removed: nevertheless Asa's heart was perfect with the LORD all his days.

vi. **Job 1:1 (KJV)** There was a man in the land of Uz, whose name *was* Job; and that man was perfect and upright, and one that feared God, and eschewed evil.

vii. **Job 1:8 (KJV)** And the LORD said unto Satan, Hast thou considered my servant Job, that *there is* none like him in the earth, a perfect and an upright man, one that feareth God, and escheweth evil?

viii. **Psalm 18:32 (KJV)** *It is* God that girdeth me with strength, and maketh my way perfect.

ix. **Psalm 19:7 (KJV)** The law of the LORD *is* perfect, converting the soul: the testimony of the LORD *is* sure, making wise the simple.

x. **Isaiah 38:3 (KJV)** And said, Remember now, O LORD, I beseech thee, how I have walked before thee in truth and with a perfect heart, and have done *that which is* good in thy sight. And Hezekiah wept sore.

xi. **Matthew 5:48 (KJV)** Be ye therefore perfect, even as your Father which is in heaven is perfect.

xii. **Luke 6:40 (KJV)** The disciple is not above his master: but every one that is perfect shall be as his master.

xiii. **John 17:23 (KJV)** I in them, and thou in me, that they may be made perfect in one; and that the world may know that thou hast sent me, and hast loved them, as thou hast loved me.

xiv. **1 Corinthians 2:6 (KJV)** Howbeit we speak wisdom among them that are perfect: yet not the wisdom of this world, nor of the princes of this world, that come to nought:

xv. **2 Corinthians 12:9 (KJV)** And he said unto me, My grace is sufficient for thee: for my strength is made perfect in weakness. Most gladly therefore will I rather glory in my infirmities, that the power of Christ may rest upon me.

xvi. **2 Corinthians 13:11 (KJV)** Finally, brethren, farewell. Be perfect, be of good comfort, be of one mind, live in peace; and the God of love and peace shall be with you.

xvii. **Philippians 3:15 (KJV)** Let us therefore, as many as be perfect, be thus minded: and if in any thing ye be otherwise minded, God shall reveal even this unto you.

xviii. **Colossians 4:12 (KJV)** Epaphras, who is *one* of you, a servant of Christ, saluteth you, always labouring fervently for you in prayers, that ye may stand perfect and complete in all the will of God.

xix. **2 Timothy 3:17 (KJV)** That the man of God may be perfect, throughly furnished unto all good works.

xx. **Hebrews 5:9 (KJV)** And being made perfect, he became the author of eternal salvation unto all them that obey him;

xxi. **Hebrews 7:19 (KJV)** For the law made nothing perfect, but the bringing in of a better hope *did*; by the which we draw nigh unto God.

xxii. **Hebrews 9:11 (KJV)** But Christ being come an high priest of good things to come, by a greater and more perfect tabernacle, not made with hands, that is to say, not of this building;

xxiii. **James 1:25 (KJV)** But whoso looketh into the perfect law of liberty, and continueth *therein*, he being not a forgetful hearer, but a doer of the work, this man shall be blessed in his deed.

xxiv. **Revelation 3:2 (KJV)** Be watchful, and strengthen the things which remain, that are ready to die: for I have not found thy works perfect before God.

595.   To be "perfect" means "to walk in his statutes, and to keep his commandments", therefore, when the Statutes/the Commandments of God are not complete, then perfection is rare as in the case of Noah and Job, but once the Statutes/the Commandments of God are now completed, then perfection is widely available and possible!

i. **1 Kings 8:61 (KJV)** Let your heart therefore be perfect with the LORD our God, to walk in his statutes, and to keep his commandments, as at this day.

ii. **Hebrews 1:1 (KJV)** God, who at sundry times and in divers manners spake in time past unto the fathers by the prophets,

iii. **Hebrews 1:2 (KJV)** Hath in these last days spoken unto us by *his* Son, whom he hath appointed heir of all things, by whom also he made the worlds;

Sunday 14ᵗʰ January 2024 @ 3:20 PM – 4:15 PM

CHAPTER 16: THE SIX PRINCIPLES OF THE LAW OF SPEAKING WITH TONGUES

596.   When you have charity, it means that you have the Holy Spirit, and when you have the Holy Spirit, it means that you have the love of God, and when you have the love of God in you, this is what you will always be doing!

     i. **Deuteronomy 5:32 (KJV)** Ye shall observe to do therefore as the LORD your God hath commanded you: ye shall not turn aside to the right hand or to the left.

     ii. **Deuteronomy 6:25 (KJV)** And it shall be our righteousness, if we observe to do all these commandments before the LORD our God, as he hath commanded us.

     iii. **Deuteronomy 8:1 (KJV)** All the commandments which I command thee this day shall ye observe to do, that ye may live, and multiply, and go in and possess the land which the LORD sware unto your fathers.

     iv. **Deuteronomy 11:32 (KJV)** And ye shall observe to do all the statutes and judgments which I set before you this day.

     v. **Deuteronomy 12:32 (KJV)** What thing soever I command you, observe to do it: thou shalt not add thereto, nor diminish from it.

     vi. **Deuteronomy 15:5 (KJV)** Only if thou carefully hearken unto the voice of the LORD thy God, to observe to do all these commandments which I command thee this day.

     vii. **Deuteronomy 17:10 (KJV)** And thou shalt do according to the sentence, which they of that place which the LORD shall choose shall shew thee; and thou shalt observe to do according to all that they inform thee:

     viii. **Matthew 22:37 (KJV)** Jesus said unto him, Thou shalt love the Lord thy God with all thy heart, and with all thy soul, and with all thy mind.

     ix. **Matthew 22:38 (KJV)** This is the first and great commandment.

     x. **Matthew 22:39 (KJV)** And the second *is* like unto it, Thou shalt love thy neighbour as thyself.

     xi. **Matthew 22:40 (KJV)** On these two commandments hang all the law and the prophets.

597.   It is the above foundation that will bring about the spiritual gifts, such as prophecy!

     i. **1 Corinthians 14:1 (KJV)** Follow after charity, and desire spiritual *gifts*, but rather that ye may prophesy.

598.   The Law of Speaking with Tongues derives from the following Law!

      i.   **Isaiah 33:19 (KJV)** Thou shalt not see a fierce people, a people of a deeper speech than thou canst perceive; of a stammering tongue, *that thou canst* not understand.

      ii.   **Ezekiel 3:4 (KJV)** And he said unto me, Son of man, go, get thee unto the house of Israel, and speak with my words unto them.

      iii.   **Ezekiel 3:5 (KJV)** For thou *art* not sent to a people of a strange speech and of an hard language, *but* to the house of Israel;

      iv.   **Ezekiel 3:6 (KJV)** Not to many people of a strange speech and of an hard language, whose words thou canst not understand. Surely, had I sent thee to them, they would have hearkened unto thee.

      v.   **Ezekiel 3:7 (KJV)** But the house of Israel will not hearken unto thee; for they will not hearken unto me: for all the house of Israel *are* impudent and hardhearted.

      vi.   **Hosea 8:12 (KJV)** I have written to him the great things of my law, *but* they were counted as a strange thing.

599.   Now that we have seen the origin of the Law of Speaking with Tongues, we shall identify the Principles inside the Law of Speaking with Tongues, those Principles that govern the act of Speaking with Tongues!

600.   **ONE** – The First Principle of the Law of Speaking with Tongues is that:

      i.   "Thou shalt not see a fierce people, a people of a deeper speech than thou canst perceive", meaning that the Law of Speaking with Tongues outlaws, forbids, and prohibits any language/tongue that is deeper than you know, that is deeper than you can perceive or figure out! **Isaiah 33:19 (KJV)**

601.   **TWO** – The Second Principle of the Law of Speaking with Tongues is that:

      i.   Stammering tongue/language is outlawed, forbidden, and prohibited, meaning that tongue/language shall not falter, hesitate, or flow in stuttering/stammering fits! **Isaiah 33:19 (KJV)**

602.   **THREE** – The Third Principle of the Law of Speaking with Tongues is that:

      i.   The LORD God Almighty does NOT speak to a people in a language/tongue that they do NOT understand! **Isaiah 33:19 (KJV)**

603.   **FOUR** – The Fourth Principle of the Law of Speaking with Tongues is that:

      i.   The LORD commands you the Christian and the Minister of Christ "to speak with my words unto them", meaning that you cannot go outside from Genesis to Revelation to bring any words from outside the Word of God and call those strange words "tongues", and here is the evidence! **Ezekiel 3:4 (KJV)**

      ii.   **Hebrews 1:1 (KJV)** God, who at sundry times and in divers manners spake in time past unto the fathers by the prophets,

      iii.   **Hebrews 1:2 (KJV)** Hath in these last days spoken unto us by *his* Son, whom he hath appointed heir of all things, by whom also he made the worlds;

      iv.   **Revelation 19:10 (KJV)** And I fell at his feet to worship him. And he said unto me, See *thou do it* not: I am thy fellowservant, and of thy brethren that have the testimony of Jesus: worship God: for the testimony of Jesus is the spirit of prophecy.

604.   As you can see from **Revelation 19:10 (KJV)**, if you are a true Prophet of God, and if you have the Holy Spirit, then, everything that you will speak in your entire Ministry for the rest of your life is contained in the Testimony of Jesus Christ, meaning that, the moment that you go outside of the Testimony of Jesus to prophecy anything whatsoever, then, that is the same moment that you lost your title as a true Prophet of God and became a Prophet of Satan!

605.   Another reason why you will become a Prophet of Satan the very moment that you step outside of the Word of God to prophecy foolish things such as football, national elections, who will become a millionaire, soccer winners, etc. is because of **Hebrews 1:1-2 (KJV)** where the LORD God states clearly that, in the past, God spoke to us through "the prophets", meaning Genesis to John, but today the LORD God speaks to us only through HIS Son the LORD Jesus Christ, meaning from the Book of Matthew through Revelation, just as **Revelation 19:10 (KJV)** said!

606.   So, because of those evidences that I have just shown you, you cannot bring any words from outside of Genesis to Revelation and call them prophecies, tongues, or languages, because they are NOT!

607.   FIVE – The Fifth Principle of the Law of Speaking with Tongues is that:

      i.   The LORD God has set a language boundary to all true Prophets of God, saying: "thou *art* not sent to a people of a strange speech and of an hard language", meaning that the LORD God Almighty DOES NOT send a Prophet to any people when the people do NOT understand the language of the Prophet and the Prophet does NOT understand the language of the people! **Ezekiel 3:6 (KJV)**

608.   That Fifth Principle of the Law of Speaking with Tongues is an abomination in the spirit realm, and so when you see any supposed Christian or Pastor who comes with tongues, languages, or other tongues that both he himself and the church congregation are NOT able to understand, then, that is the sign that God is showing you so you can know immediately that the person speaking in other tongues has a Devil inside of him/her!

609. SIX – The Sixth Principle of the Law of Speaking with Tongues is that:
    i.   There is a very frightening revelation at the end of **Ezekiel 3:6 (KJV)** where we see the LORD God saying that:
    ii.   "Surely, had I sent thee to them, they would have hearkened unto thee" **Ezekiel 3:6 (KJV)**
    iii.   Meaning that, it is ONLY children of Satan, it is only a people who are NOT people of God who will accept, receive, welcome, and hearken unto someone who comes with "strange speech and of an hard language, whose words thou canst not understand!

610. Brethren, Sisters, do you hear what the LORD God revealed over there?
    i.   **Ezekiel 3:4 (KJV)** And he said unto me, Son of man, go, get thee unto the house of Israel, and speak with my words unto them.
    ii.   **Ezekiel 3:5 (KJV)** For thou *art* not sent to a people of a strange speech and of an hard language, *but* to the house of Israel;
    iii.   **Ezekiel 3:6 (KJV)** Not to many people of a strange speech and of an hard language, whose words thou canst not understand. Surely, had I sent thee to them, they would have hearkened unto thee.

611. **Ezekiel 3:4-6 (KJV)** is the Key to expose the demonic Christians and Pastors who claim to speak with other tongues!

612. Here is the summary of what the LORD God is saying in **Ezekiel 3:4-6 (KJV)**!
    i.   Always speak with my words ONLY unto the people of God, and my words are from Genesis to Revelation, and my words are also called The Testimony of Jesus Christ, and I send my words to no other people but my true children, who know my words and my voice and they follow me, and any person who comes with words that are different from my words in Genesis to Revelation, that person is a Devil and from Satan, and finally, when a people give ear to, listen to, hearken to, receive, accept, and welcome the person who came with the strange speech and of an hard language, whose words thou canst not understand, then, know that the same people are NOT the people of God but children of Devils since they are unable to make/know the difference between the words of God and the words of Satan!
    ii.   **John 10:4 (KJV)** And when he putteth forth his own sheep, he goeth before them, and the sheep follow him: for they know his voice.
    iii.   **John 10:5 (KJV)** And a stranger will they not follow, but will flee from him: for they know not the voice of strangers.
    iv.   **John 10:27 (KJV)** My sheep hear my voice, and I know them, and they follow me:

v. **John 10:28 (KJV)** And I give unto them eternal life; and they shall never perish, neither shall any *man* pluck them out of my hand.

vi. **John 17:8 (KJV)** For I have given unto them the words which thou gavest me; and they have received *them*, and have known surely that I came out from thee, and they have believed that thou didst send me.

vii. **Luke 24:44 (KJV)** And he said unto them, These *are* the words which I spake unto you, while I was yet with you, that all things must be fulfilled, which were written in the law of Moses, and *in* the prophets, and *in* the psalms, concerning me.

viii. **1 Timothy 6:3 (KJV)** If any man teach otherwise, and consent not to wholesome words, *even* the words of our Lord Jesus Christ, and to the doctrine which is according to godliness;

ix. **1 Peter 1:25 (KJV)** But the word of the Lord endureth for ever. And this is the word which by the gospel is preached unto you.

x. **Revelation 1:3 (KJV)** Blessed *is* he that readeth, and they that hear the words of this prophecy, and keep those things which are written therein: for the time *is* at hand.

xi. **Revelation 21:5 (KJV)** And he that sat upon the throne said, Behold, I make all things new. And he said unto me, Write: for these words are true and faithful.

xii. **Revelation 22:18 (KJV)** For I testify unto every man that heareth the words of the prophecy of this book, If any man shall add unto these things, God shall add unto him the plagues that are written in this book:

xiii. **Revelation 22:19 (KJV)** And if any man shall take away from the words of the book of this prophecy, God shall take away his part out of the book of life, and out of the holy city, and *from* the things which are written in this book.

613. Brethren, Sisters, I have just shown you The Six Principles of the Law of Speaking with Tongues, and from these Six Principles derive every Bible doctrine on Speaking with Tongues that anyone can find in the entire Holy Bible from Genesis to Revelation!

CHAPTER 17: THE FIVE PROPERTIES OF "UNKNOWN TONGUE/STRANGE LANGUAGE/STRANGE SPEECH"

614. Therefore, we now return to 1 Corinthians chapter 14 to subject that chapter to these Six Principles of the Law of Speaking with Tongues, in order to obtain the correct understanding of Speaking with Tongues!

615. Here is **Point #1**:

    i. **1 Corinthians 14:1 (KJV)** Follow after charity, and desire spiritual *gifts*, but rather that ye may prophesy.

616. You see that there are 2 key words here: Charity and Prophesy, yet, take note very carefully, that both key words have their roots in the Word of God that we already identified in the Six Principles of the Law of Speaking with Tongues, where, in the first sentence of the previous chapter, I wrote that:

    i. When you have charity, it means that you have the Holy Spirit, and when you have the Holy Spirit, it means that you have the love of God, and when you have the love of God in you, then, you will always obey the Word of God starting at **Deuteronomy 5:32 (KJV)**!

617. Then, regarding the key word "prophesy" in **1 Corinthians 14:1 (KJV)**, remember what I wrote still in the previous chapter that, a true Man of God can prophesy only from within the Word of God from Gensis to Revelation!

618. So, you see that, when you use this Template of the Six Principles of the Law of Speaking with Tongues, then, you begin to get a better and correct understanding of 1 Corinthians chapter 14, specifically on the question of Speaking with Tongues?

619. In other words, once you discover the Old Testament foundation (**Isaiah 33:19 (KJV), Ezekiel 3:4-7 (KJV), Hosea 8:12 (KJV)**) on which 1 Corinthians chapter 14 is built, specifically the question of Speaking with Tongues, then, it becomes very easy to understand the subject!

620. Let us use the same strategy for the remaining verses in the same 1 Corinthians chapter 14!

621. Here is **Point #2**:

    i. **1 Corinthians 14:2 (KJV)** For he that speaketh in an *unknown* tongue speaketh not unto men, but unto God: for no man understandeth *him*; howbeit in the spirit he speaketh mysteries.

622. Why is the tongue/language/speech called "unknown tongue/language/speech"?

623. Here is the answer!

624.   A language/tongue/speech, even when you are familiar with it, even when you can speak it, and even when you are able to communicate in it, becomes "unknown tongue/strange language/strange speech" when it has the following five properties:

      i.   ONE – When you do NOT understand it! – **Daniel 5:7 (KJV)**

      ii.   TWO –When you are confused when you hear someone speaking it! – **Acts 2:6 (KJV)**

      iii.   THREE –When there is a mystery in it such as proverbs, parables, and dark sayings! – **1 Corinthians 14:3 (KJV), Psalm 78:2 (KJV), Proverbs 1:6 (KJV), Matthew 13:34 (KJV), Mark 4:34 (KJV)**

      iv.   FOUR –When it must be revealed to you before you can understand what has been said! – **Deuteronomy 29:29 (KJV), 1 Samuel 3:7 (KJV), 1 Samuel 3:21 (KJV), Matthew 11:25 (KJV), Matthew 16:17 (KJV), Luke 2:26 (KJV), 1 Corinthians 2:10 (KJV)**

      v.   FIVE –When it must be interpreted to you before you can understand what has been said! – **Daniel 8:16 (KJV), Genesis 41:8 (KJV), 1 Corinthians 12:30 (KJV), 1 Corinthians 14:27 (KJV)**

625.   Any language/tongue/speech/form of communication that possesses the above 5 language properties is called: "unknown tongue/strange language/strange speech"!

626.   The Word of God possesses the above 5 language properties and that is why the Word of God is "unknown tongue/strange language/strange speech"!

627.   Still on **1 Corinthians 14:2 (KJV)**, when the above five properties are present in a language/tongue/speech/form of communication, such as in the Word of God, and, then, a person is speaking this Word of God WITHOUT INTERPRETATION, then, he "speaketh not unto men, but unto God: for no man understandeth *him*; howbeit in the spirit he speaketh mysteries"!

CHAPTER 18: DEFINITION OF PRAYER, PROPHECY, AND THE PROPHET OF GOD

628.   Here is Point #3:
   i. **1 Corinthians 14:3 (KJV)** But he that prophesieth speaketh unto men *to* edification, and exhortation, and comfort.

629.   Now, when you compare **1 Corinthians 14:3 (KJV)** to **1 Corinthians 14:2 (KJV)**, you can see that there are two interlocutors, namely, God and men:
   i. "speaketh not unto men, but unto God" – **1 Corinthians 14:2 (KJV)**
   ii. "he that prophesieth speaketh unto men" – **1 Corinthians 14:3 (KJV)**

630.   So, therefore, when you "speak with tongues" or when you "pray with tongues", then, the LORD God Almighty is the focus and the objective!

631.   On the other hand, when you "prophesy", then, human beings are the focus and the objective!

632.   So, then, to "speak with tongues" or to "pray with tongues" means that you are speaking to God about the wonderful works of God!
   i. **2 Chronicles 20:7 (KJV)** *Art* not thou our God, *who* didst drive out the inhabitants of this land before thy people Israel, and gavest it to the seed of Abraham thy friend for ever?
   ii. **Nehemiah 9:6 (KJV)** Thou, *even* thou, *art* LORD alone; thou hast made heaven, the heaven of heavens, with all their host, the earth, and all *things* that *are* therein, the seas, and all that *is* therein, and thou preservest them all; and the host of heaven worshippeth thee.
   iii. **Nehemiah 9:7 (KJV)** Thou *art* the LORD the God, who didst choose Abram, and broughtest him forth out of Ur of the Chaldees, and gavest him the name of Abraham;
   iv. **Acts 4:23 (KJV)** And being let go, they went to their own company, and reported all that the chief priests and elders had said unto them.
   v. **Acts 4:24 (KJV)** And when they heard that, they lifted up their voice to God with one accord, and said, Lord, thou *art* God, which hast made heaven, and earth, and the sea, and all that in them is:
   vi. **Acts 4:25 (KJV)** Who by the mouth of thy servant David hast said, Why did the heathen rage, and the people imagine vain things?
   vii. **Acts 4:26 (KJV)** The kings of the earth stood up, and the rulers were gathered together against the Lord, and against his Christ.

633.   On the other hand, to "prophesy" means that you are speaking to people about the wonderful works of God!

      i. **1 Samuel 10:5 (KJV)** After that thou shalt come to the hill of God, where *is* the garrison of the Philistines: and it shall come to pass, when thou art come thither to the city, that thou shalt meet a company of prophets coming down from the high place with a psaltery, and a tabret, and a pipe, and a harp, before them; and they shall prophesy:

      ii. **1 Samuel 10:6 (KJV)** And the Spirit of the LORD will come upon thee, and thou shalt prophesy with them, and shalt be turned into another man.

      iii. **Jeremiah 25:30 (KJV)** Therefore prophesy thou against them all these words, and say unto them, The LORD shall roar from on high, and utter his voice from his holy habitation; he shall mightily roar upon his habitation; he shall give a shout, as they that tread *the grapes*, against all the inhabitants of the earth.

634.   Please, take note very carefully, that in the following verses, the main and only objective of God Almighty is for men "to prophesy"!

      i. **Joel 2:28 (KJV)** And it shall come to pass afterward, *that* I will pour out my spirit upon all flesh; and your sons and your daughters shall prophesy, your old men shall dream dreams, your young men shall see visions:

      ii. **Joel 2:29 (KJV)** And also upon the servants and upon the handmaids in those days will I pour out my spirit.

      iii. **Acts 2:17 (KJV)** And it shall come to pass in the last days, saith God, I will pour out of my Spirit upon all flesh: and your sons and your daughters shall prophesy, and your young men shall see visions, and your old men shall dream dreams:

      iv. **Acts 2:18 (KJV)** And on my servants and on my handmaidens I will pour out in those days of my Spirit; and they shall prophesy:

      v. **Revelation 11:3 (KJV)** And I will give *power* unto my two witnesses, and they shall prophesy a thousand two hundred *and* threescore days, clothed in sackcloth.

635.   Please, again, take note very carefully, that when Men/Women of God prophesy according to the Spirit of God, then, you must "hear them speak in your tongues the wonderful works of God."!

      i. **Acts 2:11 (KJV)** Cretes and Arabians, we do hear them speak in our tongues the wonderful works of God.

636.   Specifically, therefore:

      i. (1) If what is being said is NOT in the language that you understand and also speak, and

ii. (2) If what is being said is NOT the wonderful works of God,

iii. (3) If what is being said does NOT edify, exhort, and comfort people,

iv. Then, know immediately, that IT IS NOT PROPHECY FROM GOD ALMIGHTY, but rather, it is a prophecy from Devils!

637. So, you can define "prophesy" as: The Wonderful Works of God!

i. **Revelation 1:3 (KJV)** Blessed *is* he that readeth, and they that hear the words of this prophecy, and keep those things which are written therein: for the time *is* at hand.

ii. **Revelation 22:18 (KJV)** For I testify unto every man that heareth the words of the prophecy of this book, If any man shall add unto these things, God shall add unto him the plagues that are written in this book:

iii. **Revelation 22:19 (KJV)** And if any man shall take away from the words of the book of this prophecy, God shall take away his part out of the book of life, and out of the holy city, and *from* the things which are written in this book.

638. Specifically, therefore, speaking to God about the wonderful works of God is **Prayer**, and speaking to people about the wonderful works of God, in order to edify, exhort, and comfort people, is **Prophecy**, and the man who does this is called the **Prophet of God**!

Tuesday 16th January 2024 @ 12:51 PM – 1:21 PM

CHAPTER 19: HOW TO EDIFY YOURSELF AND THE BODY OF CHRIST

639.   Here is Point #4:

      i.   **1 Corinthians 14:4 (KJV)** He that speaketh in an *unknown* tongue edifieth himself; but he that prophesieth edifieth the church.

640.   As I wrote in the previous chapter, speaking or praying to God about the wonderful works of God is the same as "speaketh in an *unknown* tongue" since I have also already shown you that the Word of God is "unknown tongue"!

641.   That is why, when you engage in this type of prayer namely, speaking or praying to God about the wonderful works of God, then, it results in "you edifying yourself" before God Almighty!

642.   To edify (someone or yourself) means:

      i.   Instruct in religious knowledge

      ii. Improve

      iii. Uplift

      iv. Enlighten

      v.   Empower with the knowledge of God

      vi. Help someone to understand the Word of God

      vii. Support

      viii. Educate

      ix. Be of benefit to someone

643.   So, as you can see in the evidence in **1 Corinthians 14:4 (KJV)**, the objective of the action of speaking or praying in an unknown tongue is: to edify either yourself or the congregation, and when you do it alone in prayer, it is called "praying or speaking in tongues"!

      i.   **Romans 14:19 (KJV)** Let us therefore follow after the things which make for peace, and things wherewith one may edify another.

      ii. **1 Corinthians 10:23 (KJV)** All things are lawful for me, but all things are not expedient: all things are lawful for me, but all things edify not.

      iii. **1 Thessalonians 5:11 (KJV)** Wherefore comfort yourselves together, and edify one another, even as also ye do.

      iv. **2 Corinthians 12:19 (KJV)** Again, think ye that we excuse ourselves unto you? we speak before God in Christ: but *we do* all things, dearly beloved, for your edifying.

644.   Then, when you do the same thing toward a people, as in a church, then, it is called "prophesying"!

i. **1 Corinthians 14:5 (KJV)** I would that ye all spake with tongues, but rather that ye prophesied: for greater *is* he that prophesieth than he that speaketh with tongues, except he interpret, that the church may receive edifying.

ii. **1 Corinthians 14:26 (KJV)** How is it then, brethren? when ye come together, every one of you hath a psalm, hath a doctrine, hath a tongue, hath a revelation, hath an interpretation. Let all things be done unto edifying.

645.   So, then, you use the Word of God to edify yourself before God and that is "speaking with tongues", and, then, you also use the Word of God to edify the church and that is "prophesying"!

i. **Acts 9:31 (KJV)** Then had the churches rest throughout all Judaea and Galilee and Samaria, and were edified; and walking in the fear of the Lord, and in the comfort of the Holy Ghost, were multiplied.

646.   Either way, for edification to be spiritually correct, you must use ONLY the Word of God or the Faith of Christ which we preach to accomplish the act of edifying, even as **1 Timothy 1:4 (KJV)** says!

i. **Romans 10:8 (KJV)** But what saith it? The word is nigh thee, *even* in thy mouth, and in thy heart: that is, the word of faith, which we preach;

ii. **Ephesians 4:12 (KJV)** For the perfecting of the saints, for the work of the ministry, for the edifying of the body of Christ:

iii. **Ephesians 4:29 (KJV)** Let no corrupt communication proceed out of your mouth, but that which is good to the use of edifying, that it may minister grace unto the hearers.

iv. **1 Timothy 1:4 (KJV)** Neither give heed to fables and endless genealogies, which minister questions, rather than godly edifying which is in faith: *so do.*

647.   Here is Point #5:

i. **1 Corinthians 14:5 (KJV)** I would that ye all spake with tongues, but rather that ye prophesied: for greater *is* he that prophesieth than he that speaketh with tongues, except he interpret, that the church may receive edifying.

648.   Even though speaking in tongues or praying in tongues is a spiritual gift, to be able to prophesy is superior to and better than speaking in tongues or praying in tongues!

649.   I said before that speaking or praying to God about the wonderful works of God is the same as "speaketh in an *unknown* tongue"!

650.   Therefore, someone will ask:

      i. How can the mere reading and reproducing the wonderful works of God back to God be a spiritual gift?

651.   Here is the answer showing that no man can call Jesus Christ LORD except the Holy Spirit has qualified you to do so!

      i. **1 Corinthians 12:3 (KJV)** Wherefore I give you to understand, that no man speaking by the Spirit of God calleth Jesus accursed: and *that* no man can say that Jesus is the Lord, but by the Holy Ghost.

652.   Now, the reason why the person who is prophesying is greater than the person who is speaking in tongues or praying in tongues is that, whereas speaking in tongues or praying in tongues benefits only one person, himself or herself, the person who is prophesying is greater because his work benefits an entire people, an entire congregation, and the entire Body of Christ!

653.   In practical terms, the Bible Teacher who is instructing people in the Word of God unto holiness, unto Truth, and unto Righteousness, through either preaching or writing Christian Theological Research Textbooks unto the world, he is greater than the person who reads the Word of God, obeys it alone, and prays with the Word of God daily!

      i. **Luke 1:76 (KJV)** And thou, child, shalt be called the prophet of the Highest: for thou shalt go before the face of the Lord to prepare his ways;

      ii. **Luke 1:77 (KJV)** To give knowledge of salvation unto his people by the remission of their sins,

      iii. **Matthew 13:52 (KJV)** Then said he unto them, Therefore every scribe *which is* instructed unto the kingdom of heaven is like unto a man *that is* an householder, which bringeth forth out of his treasure *things* new and old.

      iv. **Matthew 11:11 (KJV)** Verily I say unto you, Among them that are born of women there hath not risen a greater than John the Baptist: notwithstanding he that is least in the kingdom of heaven is greater than he.

      v. **Luke 7:28 (KJV)** For I say unto you, Among those that are born of women there is not a greater prophet than John the Baptist: but he that is least in the kingdom of God is greater than he.

      vi. **John 10:41 (KJV)** And many resorted unto him, and said, John did no miracle: but all things that John spake of this man were true.

654.   That is why Apostle Paul revealed by the Holy Ghost that: "greater *is* he that prophesieth than he that speaketh with tongues"!

      i. **1 Corinthians 14:5 (KJV)** I would that ye all spake with tongues, but rather that ye prophesied: for greater *is* he that prophesieth than he that speaketh with tongues, except he interpret, that the church may receive edifying.

655.   Here is Point #6:

656.   Since the Word of God comes ONLY by revelation, the reason being that the entire Word of God from Genesis to Revelation is in parables, proverbs, and in dark sayings, when you speak it (the Word of God) and you have no interpretation, explanation, expounding, doctrine, or instruction to accompany it as Paul says in **1 Corinthians 14:5 (KJV)**, then, it becomes a barbarity, a barbaric tongue, a barbaric speech, and a Word unto curse and unto death!

      i. **1 Samuel 3:19 (KJV)** And Samuel grew, and the LORD was with him, and did let none of his words fall to the ground.

      ii. **1 Samuel 3:20 (KJV)** And all Israel from Dan even to Beer-sheba knew that Samuel *was* established *to be* a prophet of the LORD.

      iii. **1 Samuel 3:21 (KJV)** And the LORD appeared again in Shiloh: for the LORD revealed himself to Samuel in Shiloh by the word of the LORD.

      iv. **Galatians 1:11 (KJV)** But I certify you, brethren, that the gospel which was preached of me is not after man.

      v. **Galatians 1:12 (KJV)** For I neither received it of man, neither was I taught *it*, but by the revelation of Jesus Christ.

      vi. **Mark 4:34 (KJV)** But without a parable spake he not unto them: and when they were alone, he expounded all things to his disciples.

      vii. **Luke 24:27 (KJV)** And beginning at Moses and all the prophets, he expounded unto them in all the scriptures the things concerning himself.

      viii. **Acts 18:26 (KJV)** And he began to speak boldly in the synagogue: whom when Aquila and Priscilla had heard, they took him unto *them*, and expounded unto him the way of God more perfectly.

      ix. **Acts 28:23 (KJV)** And when they had appointed him a day, there came many to him into *his* lodging; to whom he expounded and testified the kingdom of God, persuading them concerning Jesus, both out of the law of Moses, and *out of* the prophets, from morning till evening.

      x. **Matthew 13:3 (KJV)** And he spake many things unto them in parables, saying, Behold, a sower went forth to sow;

      xi. **Matthew 13:10 (KJV)** And the disciples came, and said unto him, Why speakest thou unto them in parables?

xii. **Matthew 13:13 (KJV)** Therefore speak I to them in parables: because they seeing see not; and hearing they hear not, neither do they understand.

xiii. **Matthew 13:34 (KJV)** All these things spake Jesus unto the multitude in parables; and without a parable spake he not unto them:

xiv. **Mark 4:2 (KJV)** And he taught them many things by parables, and said unto them in his doctrine,

xv. **1 Corinthians 14:10 (KJV)** There are, it may be, so many kinds of voices in the world, and none of them *is* without signification.

xvi. **1 Corinthians 14:11 (KJV)** Therefore if I know not the meaning of the voice, I shall be unto him that speaketh a barbarian, and he that speaketh *shall be* a barbarian unto me.

xvii. **Isaiah 28:13 (KJV)** But the word of the LORD was unto them precept upon precept, precept upon precept; line upon line, line upon line; here a little, *and* there a little; that they might go, and fall backward, and be broken, and snared, and taken.

xviii. **2 Corinthians 2:15 (KJV)** For we are unto God a sweet savour of Christ, in them that are saved, and in them that perish:

xix. **2 Corinthians 2:16 (KJV)** To the one *we are* the savour of death unto death; and to the other the savour of life unto life. And who *is* sufficient for these things?

xx. **2 Corinthians 2:17 (KJV)** For we are not as many, which corrupt the word of God: but as of sincerity, but as of God, in the sight of God speak we in Christ.

Tuesday 16th January 2024 @ 1:21 PM – 4:29 PM

CHAPTER 20: SPEAKING WITH TONGUES IS AN EVANGELICAL INSTRUMENT OF SALVATION

657.   Understanding is the #1 principle of Speaking in Tongues or Praying in Tongues!

658.   Here is **Point #7**:

    i. **1 Corinthians 14:6 (KJV)** Now, brethren, if I come unto you speaking with tongues, what shall I profit you, except I shall speak to you either by revelation, or by knowledge, or by prophesying, or by doctrine?

659.   As I said before, so I it again that:

    i. Since the Word of God comes ONLY by revelation, the reason being that the entire Word of God from Genesis to Revelation is in parables, proverbs, and in dark sayings, when you speak it (the Word of God) and you have no interpretation, explanation, expounding, doctrine, or instruction to accompany it as Paul says in **1 Corinthians 14:5 (KJV)**, then, it becomes a barbarity, a barbaric tongue, a barbaric speech, and a Word unto curse and unto death!

660.   The #1 principle of speaking in tongues or praying in tongues is the UNDERSTANDING that you must add to what you are speaking! If you fail to add that understanding, then, you are a dead man, because your lack of understanding of the tongue/language/speech/Word of God that you are speaking is the sure sign that you are of the Devil! That is the Law of Tongues in **1 Corinthians 14:9 (KJV)**!

    i. **1 Corinthians 14:7 (KJV)** And even things without life giving sound, whether pipe or harp, except they give a distinction in the sounds, how shall it be known what is piped or harped?

    ii. **1 Corinthians 14:8 (KJV)** For if the trumpet give an uncertain sound, who shall prepare himself to the battle?

    iii. **1 Corinthians 14:9 (KJV)** So likewise ye, except ye utter by the tongue words easy to be understood, how shall it be known what is spoken? for ye shall speak into the air.

661.   Here is **Point #8**:

662.   Need I remind you that the correct understanding of the Word of God is the principal thing and that the correct understanding of the Word of God that you possess, is your Ticket to Heaven, meaning that when you do NOT correctly understand the Word of God, you will go to Hell!

    i. **Psalm 119:104 (KJV)** Through thy precepts I get understanding: therefore I hate every false way.

ii. **Proverbs 4:7 (KJV)** Wisdom *is* the principal thing; *therefore* get wisdom: and with all thy getting get understanding.

iii. **Matthew 13:15 (KJV)** For this people's heart is waxed gross, and *their* ears are dull of hearing, and their eyes they have closed; lest at any time they should see with *their* eyes, and hear with *their* ears, and should understand with *their* heart, and should be converted, and I should heal them.

iv. **John 12:40 (KJV)** He hath blinded their eyes, and hardened their heart; that they should not see with *their* eyes, nor understand with *their* heart, and be converted, and I should heal them.

v. **Acts 28:27 (KJV)** For the heart of this people is waxed gross, and their ears are dull of hearing, and their eyes have they closed; lest they should see with *their* eyes, and hear with *their* ears, and understand with *their* heart, and should be converted, and I should heal them.

663. Here is Point #9:

664. Furthermore, I remind you that the LORD God never speaks to a people in a language/tongue that they do not understand:

i. **Isaiah 33:19 (KJV)** Thou shalt not see a fierce people, a people of a deeper speech than thou canst perceive; of a stammering tongue, *that thou canst* not understand.

ii. **Ezekiel 3:4 (KJV)** And he said unto me, Son of man, go, get thee unto the house of Israel, and speak with my words unto them.

iii. **Ezekiel 3:5 (KJV)** For thou *art* not sent to a people of a strange speech and of an hard language, *but* to the house of Israel;

iv. **Ezekiel 3:6 (KJV)** Not to many people of a strange speech and of an hard language, whose words thou canst not understand. Surely, had I sent thee to them, they would have hearkened unto thee.

665. And when the LORD does speaks to a people in a language/tongue that they do not understand, then, it is a curse and death is following right after it!

i. **Daniel 5:1 (KJV)** Belshazzar the king made a great feast to a thousand of his lords, and drank wine before the thousand.

ii. **Daniel 5:2 (KJV)** Belshazzar, whiles he tasted the wine, commanded to bring the golden and silver vessels which his father Nebuchadnezzar had taken out of the temple which *was* in Jerusalem; that the king, and his princes, his wives, and his concubines, might drink therein.

iii. **Daniel 5:3 (KJV)** Then they brought the golden vessels that were taken out of the temple of the house of God which *was* at Jerusalem;

and the king, and his princes, his wives, and his concubines, drank in them.

iv. **Daniel 5:4 (KJV)** They drank wine, and praised the gods of gold, and of silver, of brass, of iron, of wood, and of stone.

v. **Daniel 5:5 (KJV)** In the same hour came forth fingers of a man's hand, and wrote over against the candlestick upon the plaister of the wall of the king's palace: and the king saw the part of the hand that wrote.

vi. **Daniel 5:6 (KJV)** Then the king's countenance was changed, and his thoughts troubled him, so that the joints of his loins were loosed, and his knees smote one against another.

vii. **Daniel 5:7 (KJV)** The king cried aloud to bring in the astrologers, the Chaldeans, and the soothsayers. *And* the king spake, and said to the wise *men* of Babylon, Whosoever shall read this writing, and shew me the interpretation thereof, shall be clothed with scarlet, and *have* a chain of gold about his neck, and shall be the third ruler in the kingdom. **Daniel 5:8 (KJV)** Then came in all the king's wise *men*: but they could not read the writing, nor make known to the king the interpretation thereof.

viii. **Daniel 5:9 (KJV)** Then was king Belshazzar greatly troubled, and his countenance was changed in him, and his lords were astonied.

ix. **Daniel 5:30 (KJV)** In that night was Belshazzar the king of the Chaldeans slain.

666. Here is Point #10:

667. Your barbarity and your sentence of death are determined by your failure to add understanding to the tongues that you are speaking!

i. **1 Corinthians 14:10 (KJV)** There are, it may be, so many kinds of voices in the world, and none of them *is* without signification.

ii. **1 Corinthians 14:11 (KJV)** Therefore if I know not the meaning of the voice, I shall be unto him that speaketh a barbarian, and he that speaketh *shall be* a barbarian unto me.

iii. **1 Corinthians 14:12 (KJV)** Even so ye, forasmuch as ye are zealous of spiritual *gifts*, seek that ye may excel to the edifying of the church.

iv. **1 Corinthians 14:13 (KJV)** Wherefore let him that speaketh in an *unknown* tongue pray that he may interpret.

v. **1 Corinthians 14:14 (KJV)** For if I pray in an *unknown* tongue, my spirit prayeth, but my understanding is unfruitful.

668.   Brethren, I say to you again, that under the penalty of curse and death, speaking with tongues and the instruction to add understanding to what you are saying MUST go together, if not, then, it is from Devils!

    i. **1 Corinthians 14:15 (KJV)** What is it then? I will pray with the spirit, and I will pray with the understanding also: I will sing with the spirit, and I will sing with the understanding also.

    ii. **1 Corinthians 14:16 (KJV)** Else when thou shalt bless with the spirit, how shall he that occupieth the room of the unlearned say Amen at thy giving of thanks, seeing he understandeth not what thou sayest?

    iii. **1 Corinthians 14:17 (KJV)** For thou verily givest thanks well, but the other is not edified.

    iv. **1 Corinthians 14:18 (KJV)** I thank my God, I speak with tongues more than ye all:

    v. **1 Corinthians 14:19 (KJV)** Yet in the church I had rather speak five words with my understanding, that *by my voice* I might teach others also, than ten thousand words in an *unknown* tongue.

    vi. **1 Corinthians 14:20 (KJV)** Brethren, be not children in understanding: howbeit in malice be ye children, but in understanding be men.

669.   Here is Point #11:

670.   As I wrote before, the New Testament Law of Speaking with Tongues or Praying with Tongues in 1 Corinthians chapter 14, has its roots in the Old Testament Law of Tongues, in **Isaiah 33:19 (KJV)** and in **Ezekiel 3:4-6 (KJV)**!

    i. **Isaiah 33:19 (KJV)** Thou shalt not see a fierce people, a people of a deeper speech than thou canst perceive; of a stammering tongue, *that thou canst* not understand.

    ii. **Ezekiel 3:4 (KJV)** And he said unto me, Son of man, go, get thee unto the house of Israel, and speak with my words unto them.

    iii. **Ezekiel 3:5 (KJV)** For thou *art* not sent to a people of a strange speech and of an hard language, *but* to the house of Israel;

    iv. **Ezekiel 3:6 (KJV)** Not to many people of a strange speech and of an hard language, whose words thou canst not understand. Surely, had I sent thee to them, they would have hearkened unto thee.

    v. **1 Corinthians 14:21 (KJV)** In the law it is written, With *men of* other tongues and other lips will I speak unto this people; and yet for all that will they not hear me, saith the Lord.

671.   Here is Point #12:

672.   Now, take note very carefully of this word: "With *men of* other tongues and other lips will I speak"!

673.   That word means that the tongues belong to men, humans!

674.   That word means that the tongues are NOT the tongues of Angels!

675.   That word means that the tongues are ordinary languages of people, just as it was with the 17 languages on the Day of Pentecost!

676.   That word means that the tongues that you speak in your churches that no one understands, they come from Devils!

677.   That word means that the tongues are ordinary languages of people and that is why those same tongues are a sign/linguistic symbols/phonemic signs and symbols, to UNBELIEVERS who need the instruction and the interpretation of the tongues in order to become saved, edified, and sanctified in Christ!

    i.   **1 Corinthians 14:22 (KJV)** Wherefore tongues are for a sign, not to them that believe, but to them that believe not: but prophesying *serveth* not for them that believe not, but for them which believe.

    ii.   **1 Corinthians 14:23 (KJV)** If therefore the whole church be come together into one place, and all speak with tongues, and there come in *those that are* unlearned, or unbelievers, will they not say that ye are mad?

    iii.   **1 Corinthians 14:24 (KJV)** But if all prophesy, and there come in one that believeth not, or *one* unlearned, he is convinced of all, he is judged of all:

    iv.   **1 Corinthians 14:25 (KJV)** And thus are the secrets of his heart made manifest; and so falling down on *his* face he will worship God, and report that God is in you of a truth.

    v.   **1 Corinthians 14:31 (KJV)** For ye may all prophesy one by one, that all may learn, and all may be comforted.

678.   In other words, **1 Corinthians 14:22 (KJV)** is showing you plainly that speaking with tongues and praying with tongues are both evangelical instruments of Salvation hence, when you fail to add the correct understanding to the tongues that you are speaking, for the benefit of the UNBELIEVERS to become saved, then, what you are actually doing in the Spirit realm is that, you are hindering Salvation, you are obstructing Salvation, by your incomprehensible gibberish speaking with tongues, you are surely blocking sinners from becoming saved, and that is why the LORD God Almighty has decreed curses and death to anyone who speaks with tongues to a people as in the church, without any explanation or interpretation!

679.   Here is Point #13:

680.   Moreover, see how in **1 Corinthians 14:22 (KJV)**, the LORD God is revealing the demonology in the present fraud of speaking with tongues and praying with tongues in all the churches!

681.   As you can see in the evidence of **1 Corinthians 14:22 (KJV)**, whereas the LORD God said that you should ONLY speak with tongues, WITH INTERPRETATION, to the unbelievers, today, in all the churches, the evil Christians, the bastard cursed Pastors, and the demon-possessed Prophets speak with tongues, NOT to the unbelievers as God commanded, but to the believers!

682.   Then, on the other hand, today, in all the churches, the evil Christians, the bastard cursed Pastors, and the demon-possessed Prophets prophesy, NOT to the believers as God commanded, but to the unbelievers, after they have deceived them to sow money seed at their filthy demonic pagan altar!

683.   Brother, go to every church that you know where they speak with tongues, and see how so-called Christians have turned **1 Corinthians 14:22 (KJV)** on its head, upside down, to the complete joy of Satan, and then those same filthy Christian will come and be lecturing you on "speaking in tongues and praying in tongues"! Woe unto them! May the fire and destruction of Sodom and Gomorrah be too little for them and to all their family!

     i.   **1 Corinthians 14:22 (KJV)** Wherefore tongues are for a sign, not to them that believe, but to them that believe not: but prophesying *serveth* not for them that believe not, but for them which believe.

     ii.   **1 Corinthians 14:26 (KJV)** How is it then, brethren? when ye come together, every one of you hath a psalm, hath a doctrine, hath a tongue, hath a revelation, hath an interpretation. Let all things be done unto edifying.

684.   Here is Point #14:

685.   Again, if you are not able to add understanding and interpretation to your speaking in tongues where people can hear you, then, for Christ sake: SHUT UP!

     i.   **1 Corinthians 14:27 (KJV)** If any man speak in an *unknown* tongue, *let it be* by two, or at the most *by* three, and *that* by course; and let one interpret.

     ii.   **1 Corinthians 14:28 (KJV)** But if there be no interpreter, let him keep silence in the church; and let him speak to himself, and to God.

686.   And now, you the so-called Christians who stand by and watch and listen to all the demonic speaking with tongues and praying with tongues, you are participants in their evil, in their curse, and in their death, EXCEPT YOU JUDGE THEM AND COMDEN THEM!

        i. **1 Corinthians 14:29 (KJV)** Let the prophets speak two or three, and let the other judge.

        ii. **1 Corinthians 14:30 (KJV)** If *any thing* be revealed to another that sitteth by, let the first hold his peace.

687.   Why am I cursing you evil Christians to death?

688.   I am cursing you to death because speaking with tongues, praying with tongues, and prophesying are all for understanding of unbelievers and for the saints, for instruction, for learning, and for edification as I have said already many many times, and so if you defy the Word of God and insist on doing the opposite of what God Almighty has commanded and thereby help Satan, then, my cursing you is even a great favor unto you, because it were even better that you were never born by that woman that you call your mother!

        i. **1 Corinthians 14:31 (KJV)** For ye may all prophesy one by one, that all may learn, and all may be comforted.

        ii. **Matthew 18:5 (KJV)** And whoso shall receive one such little child in my name receiveth me.

        iii. **Matthew 18:6 (KJV)** But whoso shall offend one of these little ones which believe in me, it were better for him that a millstone were hanged about his neck, and *that* he were drowned in the depth of the sea.

        iv. **Matthew 18:7 (KJV)** Woe unto the world because of offences! for it must needs be that offences come; but woe to that man by whom the offence cometh!

        v. **Mark 14:21 (KJV)** The Son of man indeed goeth, as it is written of him: but woe to that man by whom the Son of man is betrayed! good were it for that man if he had never been born.

689.   Here is **Point #15**:

690.   Brother, how is it that the prophetic Ministry of Christ is for learning and for comforting, and yet all your Prophets in Ghana and all over the world engage in prophesying to frighten, to scare, to cause to panic, and to cause to fear?

        i. **1 Corinthians 14:31 (KJV)** For ye may all prophesy one by one, that all may learn, and all may be comforted.

691.   Brother, Sister, when you receive a prophecy from any Prophet, and these two pillars, these two characteristics, and these two markers of true prophecy "all may learn, and all may be comforted" are NOT in the prophecy, then, know immediately that you are talking to a Minister of Satan!

692.   Furthermore, when you receive a prophecy from any Prophet, or speaking with tongues, or praying with tongues, or prophesying, and you are confused because what you heard, because what you heard does not match with the Word of God the

Testimony of Christ, then know immediately that you are talking with a Minister of Satan!

    i. **1 Corinthians 14:33 (KJV)** For God is not *the author* of confusion, but of peace, as in all churches of the saints.

    ii. **Revelation 19:10 (KJV)** And I fell at his feet to worship him. And he said unto me, See *thou do it* not: I am thy fellowservant, and of thy brethren that have the testimony of Jesus: worship God: for the testimony of Jesus is the spirit of prophecy.

693.   The Word in **1 Corinthians 14:32 (KJV)** means that the Word of God is ONE and the Spirit is ONE and the meaning is ONE, therefore the revelation is ONE, but the spirit of the Man of God or the Prophet of God is different and is limited to his personal development, talent, and ability hence, after the Holy Spirit has revealed the Word of God to the Man of God, the dividing of the Word is subject to the personal and spiritual limitations of the Man of God!

    i. **1 Corinthians 14:32 (KJV)** And the spirits of the prophets are subject to the prophets.

694.   Hence, Paul is different because of his personal background, and Apollos is different because of his personal background, and Peter is different because of his personal background, and Moses is different because of his personal background, each man according to his several ability!

    i. **Matthew 25:15 (KJV)** And unto one he gave five talents, to another two, and to another one; to every man according to his several ability; and straightway took his journey.

    ii. **Luke 19:15 (KJV)** And it came to pass, that when he was returned, having received the kingdom, then he commanded these servants to be called unto him, to whom he had given the money, that he might know how much every man had gained by trading.

    iii. **Romans 12:3 (KJV)** For I say, through the grace given unto me, to every man that is among you, not to think *of himself* more highly than he ought to think; but to think soberly, according as God hath dealt to every man the measure of faith.

    iv. **1 Corinthians 3:4 (KJV)** For while one saith, I am of Paul; and another, I *am* of Apollos; are ye not carnal?

    v. **1 Corinthians 3:5 (KJV)** Who then is Paul, and who *is* Apollos, but ministers by whom ye believed, even as the Lord gave to every man?

    vi. **1 Corinthians 3:6 (KJV)** I have planted, Apollos watered; but God gave the increase.

vii. **1 Corinthians 3:7 (KJV)** So then neither is he that planteth any thing, neither he that watereth; but God that giveth the increase.

viii. **1 Corinthians 3:8 (KJV)** Now he that planteth and he that watereth are one: and every man shall receive his own reward according to his own labour.

ix. **1 Corinthians 3:9 (KJV)** For we are labourers together with God: ye are God's husbandry, *ye are* God's building.

x. **1 Corinthians 3:10 (KJV)** According to the grace of God which is given unto me, as a wise masterbuilder, I have laid the foundation, and another buildeth thereon. But let every man take heed how he buildeth thereupon.

xi. **1 Corinthians 12:7 (KJV)** But the manifestation of the Spirit is given to every man to profit withal.

xii. **Matthew 19:11 (KJV)** But he said unto them, All *men* cannot receive this saying, save *they* to whom it is given.

xiii. **Matthew 19:12 (KJV)** For there are some eunuchs, which were so born from *their* mother's womb: and there are some eunuchs, which were made eunuchs of men: and there be eunuchs, which have made themselves eunuchs for the kingdom of heaven's sake. He that is able to receive *it*, let him receive *it*.

695.   Likewise, all my writings are different from another Man of God, and every revelation that the Holy Spirit has given me and which I have written in many books for the edification of the churches in the world, they are unique and they are specifically the style of Rev. Prof. Peter Pryce even as the LORD Jesus Christ and the LORD Holy Spirit give me utterance and I write with my own hand all these many years!

i. **Revelation 1:9 (KJV)** I John, who also am your brother, and companion in tribulation, and in the kingdom and patience of Jesus Christ, was in the isle that is called Patmos, for the word of God, and for the testimony of Jesus Christ.

ii. **Revelation 1:10 (KJV)** I was in the Spirit on the Lord's day, and heard behind me a great voice, as of a trumpet,

iii. **Revelation 1:11 (KJV)** Saying, I am Alpha and Omega, the first and the last: and, What thou seest, write in a book, and send *it* unto the seven churches which are in Asia; unto Ephesus, and unto Smyrna, and unto Pergamos, and unto Thyatira, and unto Sardis, and unto Philadelphia, and unto Laodicea.

Tuesday 16th January 2024 @ 4:29 PM – 7:07 PM

CHAPTER 21: LET YOUR WOMEN KEEP SILENCE IN THE CHURCHES

696.   Here is Point #16:

    i. **1 Corinthians 14:34 (KJV)** Let your women keep silence in the churches: for it is not permitted unto them to speak; but *they are commanded* to be under obedience, as also saith the law.

697.   The LORD God Almighty never appointed a woman Priest!

698.   The LORD Jesus Christ never appointed a woman Apostle!

699.   The Apostles of the LORD Jesus Christ never appointed a woman Minister!

700.   We are in the year 2024 and the phenomenon of women Pastors and women church leaders began some 50 years ago!

701.   So, in the thousands of years before the last 50 years, was the LORD God Almighty wrong that God did NOT appoint any woman Priest at all?

702.   Was the LORD Jesus Christ wrong that HE did NOT appoint any woman Apostle at all?

703.   Were the Apostles of the LORD Jesus Christ also wrong that they did NOT appoint any woman Minister at all?

704.   Is the entire Holy Bible wrong that there is not even one single record of a woman who had a Teaching Priest Ministry?

705.   Is the New Testament wrong to specify that "Let your women keep silence in the churches"?

706.   Is the Old Testament wrong to specify that women are not permitted to speak in the churches but "they are commanded to be under obedience, as also saith the law"?

707.   Was the LORD God wrong when God commanded this in the Law of God?

    i. **Numbers 30:1 (KJV)** And Moses spake unto the heads of the tribes concerning the children of Israel, saying, This *is* the thing which the LORD hath commanded.

    ii. **Numbers 30:2 (KJV)** If a man vow a vow unto the LORD, or swear an oath to bind his soul with a bond; he shall not break his word, he shall do according to all that proceedeth out of his mouth.

    iii. **Numbers 30:3 (KJV)** If a woman also vow a vow unto the LORD, and bind *herself* by a bond, *being* in her father's house in her youth;

    iv. **Numbers 30:4 (KJV)** And her father hear her vow, and her bond wherewith she hath bound her soul, and her father shall hold his peace at her: then all her vows shall stand, and every bond wherewith she hath bound her soul shall stand.

v. **Numbers 30:5 (KJV)** But if her father disallow her in the day that he heareth; not any of her vows, or of her bonds wherewith she hath bound her soul, shall stand: and the LORD shall forgive her, because her father disallowed her.

vi. **Numbers 30:6 (KJV)** And if she had at all an husband, when she vowed, or uttered ought out of her lips, wherewith she bound her soul;

vii. **Numbers 30:7 (KJV)** And her husband heard *it,* and held his peace at her in the day that he heard *it:* then her vows shall stand, and her bonds wherewith she bound her soul shall stand.

viii. **Numbers 30:8 (KJV)** But if her husband disallowed her on the day that he heard *it;* then he shall make her vow which she vowed, and that which she uttered with her lips, wherewith she bound her soul, of none effect: and the LORD shall forgive her.

ix. **Numbers 30:9 (KJV)** But every vow of a widow, and of her that is divorced, wherewith they have bound their souls, shall stand against her.

x. **Numbers 30:10 (KJV)** And if she vowed in her husband's house, or bound her soul by a bond with an oath;

xi. **Numbers 30:11 (KJV)** And her husband heard *it,* and held his peace at her, *and* disallowed her not: then all her vows shall stand, and every bond wherewith she bound her soul shall stand.

xii. **Numbers 30:12 (KJV)** But if her husband hath utterly made them void on the day he heard *them; then* whatsoever proceeded out of her lips concerning her vows, or concerning the bond of her soul, shall not stand: her husband hath made them void; and the LORD shall forgive her.

xiii. **Numbers 30:13 (KJV)** Every vow, and every binding oath to afflict the soul, her husband may establish it, or her husband may make it void.

xiv. **Numbers 30:14 (KJV)** But if her husband altogether hold his peace at her from day to day; then he establisheth all her vows, or all her bonds, which *are* upon her: he confirmeth them, because he held his peace at her in the day that he heard *them.*

xv. **Numbers 30:15 (KJV)** But if he shall any ways make them void after that he hath heard *them;* then he shall bear her iniquity.

xvi. **Numbers 30:16 (KJV)** These *are* the statutes, which the LORD commanded Moses, between a man and his wife, between the father and his daughter, *being yet* in her youth in her father's house.

708.   **Numbers 30:1-16 (KJV)** is the Old Testament Law that that the LORD God reaffirmed in the New Testament that Apostle Paul was referring to in **1 Corinthians 14:34 (KJV)**! Was it wrong?

709.   All these questions are for the women Pastors, women church leaders, and all their male backers of today to answer!

710.   Also in the same Law of the Old Testament that Apostle Paul quoted from, there is a Law that anyone who came to minister before the LORD God Almighty when that person was NOT called, the only reward for that person was death! Shall this death be applied today to all these women Pastors, women church leaders, and all their male backers of today?

    i. **Leviticus 10:1 (KJV)** And Nadab and Abihu, the sons of Aaron, took either of them his censer, and put fire therein, and put incense thereon, and offered strange fire before the LORD, which he commanded them not.

    ii. **Leviticus 10:2 (KJV)** And there went out fire from the LORD, and devoured them, and they died before the LORD.

    iii. **Leviticus 10:3 (KJV)** Then Moses said unto Aaron, This *is it* that the LORD spake, saying, I will be sanctified in them that come nigh me, and before all the people I will be glorified. And Aaron held his peace.

    iv. **Leviticus 10:4 (KJV)** And Moses called Mishael and Elzaphan, the sons of Uzziel the uncle of Aaron, and said unto them, Come near, carry your brethren from before the sanctuary out of the camp.

    v. **Leviticus 10:5 (KJV)** So they went near, and carried them in their coats out of the camp; as Moses had said.

711.   I call on Heaven and Earth to witness against all these women Pastors, women Ministers, women church leaders, every woman who is standing in the Pulpit today to minister anything whatsoever, and all their evil male backers of today, for the LORD God Almighty to bring the curse and the death of **Leviticus 10:1-5 (KJV)** upon all of them!

712.   If it is true that the LORD Jesus Christ came to fulfill the Law of the Old Testament, then let the curse and the death of **Leviticus 10:1-5 (KJV)** come upon all these women Pastors, women Ministers, women church leaders, every woman who is standing in the Pulpit today to minister anything whatsoever, and all their evil male backers of today!

713.   Now, did the LORD God give women any teaching Mistry at all? YES, and let women stay in their Ministry and in their lane!

    i. **Titus 2:1 (KJV)** But speak thou the things which become sound doctrine:

    ii. **Titus 2:2 (KJV)** That the aged men be sober, grave, temperate, sound in faith, in charity, in patience.

    iii. **Titus 2:3 (KJV)** The aged women likewise, that *they be* in behaviour as becometh holiness, not false accusers, not given to much wine, teachers of good things;

    iv. **Titus 2:4 (KJV)** That they may teach the young women to be sober, to love their husbands, to love their children,

    v. **Titus 2:5 (KJV)** *To be* discreet, chaste, keepers at home, good, obedient to their own husbands, that the word of God be not blasphemed.

714.   That is the Women's Ministry in **Titus 2:3-5 (KJV)**, where women teach women, NOT men, NOT in the church, and NOT in the Pulpit!

715.   Here is Point #17:

    i. **Numbers 12:2 (KJV)** And they said, Hath the LORD indeed spoken only by Moses? hath he not spoken also by us? And the LORD heard *it*.

    ii. **1 Corinthians 14:35 (KJV)** And if they will learn any thing, let them ask their husbands at home: for it is a shame for women to speak in the church.

    iii. **1 Corinthians 14:36 (KJV)** What? came the word of God out from you? or came it unto you only?

    iv. **1 Corinthians 14:37 (KJV)** If any man think himself to be a prophet, or spiritual, let him acknowledge that the things that I write unto you are the commandments of the Lord.

    v. **1 Corinthians 14:38 (KJV)** But if any man be ignorant, let him be ignorant.

716.   What! The LORD God said that it is a shame for women to speak in the church, and you are challenging God to say that, NO, women can speak in the church?

717.   The LORD God put a shame on all women who speak in the church and you a mere filthy woman and man you came and took off the shame?

718.   Has anyone ever challenged God and lived?

    i. **Jeremiah 2:22 (KJV)** For though thou wash thee with nitre, and take thee much soap, *yet* thine iniquity is marked before me, saith the Lord GOD.

    ii. **Isaiah 1:20 (KJV)** But if ye refuse and rebel, ye shall be devoured with the sword: for the mouth of the LORD hath spoken *it*.

iii. **Psalm 138:2 (KJV)** I will worship toward thy holy temple, and praise thy name for thy lovingkindness and for thy truth: for thou hast magnified thy word above all thy name.

iv. **Job 38:1 (KJV)** Then the LORD answered Job out of the whirlwind, and said,

v. **Job 38:2 (KJV)** Who *is* this that darkeneth counsel by words without knowledge?

vi. **Job 40:8 (KJV)** Wilt thou also disannul my judgment? wilt thou condemn me, that thou mayest be righteous?

vii. **Job 40:9 (KJV)** Hast thou an arm like God? or canst thou thunder with a voice like him?

719.   To all the women Pastors and women Apostles who claim that it was the LORD Jesus Christ who called them and told them to go and preach and establish a church, the Holy Spirit is asking you in **1 Corinthians 14:36 (KJV)** whether the LORD Jesus Christ is in the business of contradicting HIS own Word? Is this your rebellion against the Word of God not the same evil witchcraft spirit of rebellion that was in Miriam in **Numbers 12:2 (KJV)**?

i. **Numbers 12:2 (KJV)** And they said, Hath the LORD indeed spoken only by Moses? hath he not spoken also by us? And the LORD heard *it*.

ii. **Isaiah 45:23 (KJV)** I have sworn by myself, the word is gone out of my mouth *in* righteousness, and shall not return, That unto me every knee shall bow, every tongue shall swear.

iii. **Psalm 138:2 (KJV)** I will worship toward thy holy temple, and praise thy name for thy lovingkindness and for thy truth: for thou hast magnified thy word above all thy name.

iv. **Matthew 5:18 (KJV)** For verily I say unto you, Till heaven and earth pass, one jot or one tittle shall in no wise pass from the law, till all be fulfilled.

v. **Matthew 24:35 (KJV)** Heaven and earth shall pass away, but my words shall not pass away.

vi. **Mark 13:31 (KJV)** Heaven and earth shall pass away: but my words shall not pass away.

Wednesday 17th January 2024 @ 9:10 AM – 11:37 AM

CHAPTER 22: THE GOSPEL BY WHICH YE ARE SAVED

720.　　You have noticed that the Holy Scriptures begin at Genesis and ends with Revelation hence, someone will ask: which part of it is the Salvation Gospel of Christ?

721.　　Here is the answer!

i. **1 Corinthians 15:1 (KJV)** Moreover, brethren, I declare unto you the gospel which I preached unto you, which also ye have received, and wherein ye stand;

ii. **1 Corinthians 15:2 (KJV)** By which also ye are saved, if ye keep in memory what I preached unto you, unless ye have believed in vain.

iii. **1 Corinthians 15:3 (KJV)** For I delivered unto you first of all that which I also received, how that Christ died for our sins according to the scriptures;

iv. **1 Corinthians 15:4 (KJV)** And that he was buried, and that he rose again the third day according to the scriptures:

v. **1 Corinthians 15:5 (KJV)** And that he was seen of Cephas, then of the twelve:

vi. **1 Corinthians 15:6 (KJV)** After that, he was seen of above five hundred brethren at once; of whom the greater part remain unto this present, but some are fallen asleep.

vii. **1 Corinthians 15:7 (KJV)** After that, he was seen of James; then of all the apostles.

viii. **1 Corinthians 15:8 (KJV)** And last of all he was seen of me also, as of one born out of due time.

ix. **1 Corinthians 15:9 (KJV)** For I am the least of the apostles, that am not meet to be called an apostle, because I persecuted the church of God.

x. **1 Corinthians 15:10 (KJV)** But by the grace of God I am what I am: and his grace which *was bestowed* upon me was not in vain; but I laboured more abundantly than they all: yet not I, but the grace of God which was with me.

xi. **1 Corinthians 15:11 (KJV)** Therefore whether *it were* I or they, so we preach, and so ye believed.

722.　　So, when you want to focus on Salvation in your Ministry, this is the specific Gospel of Christ that you should be teaching for the people to believe and become born again!

723.　　　As you can see from **1 Corinthians 15:3 (KJV)**, the. evidence of a true Man of God is that he repeats what is already written in the Holy Scriptures!

724.　　　It is most essential that you retain that revelation, because the same revelation also shows you that a false Man of God is he who deviates from the Holy Scriptures!

725.　　　In fact, any member of the five-fold Ministers of Christ who preaches or teaches or prophesies from outside the written Holy Scriptures, that same man of false, is demon-possessed, and he words for Satan!

> i. **1 Corinthians 12:27 (KJV)** Now ye are the body of Christ, and members in particular.
>
> ii. **1 Corinthians 12:28 (KJV)** And God hath set some in the church, first apostles, secondarily prophets, thirdly teachers, after that miracles, then gifts of healings, helps, governments, diversities of tongues.

726.　　　Here is the evidence that every revelation from God Almighty comes from the written Holy Scriptures!

> i. **1 Samuel 3:19 (KJV)** And Samuel grew, and the LORD was with him, and did let none of his words fall to the ground.
>
> ii. **1 Samuel 3:20 (KJV)** And all Israel from Dan even to Beer-sheba knew that Samuel *was* established *to be* a prophet of the LORD.
>
> iii. **1 Samuel 3:21 (KJV)** And the LORD appeared again in Shiloh: for the LORD revealed himself to Samuel in Shiloh by the word of the LORD.

727.　　　Here is the evidence that every true prophecy from Heaven and from God Almighty comes from the written Holy Scriptures, specifically, from the Testimony of Christ!

> i. **Revelation 19:10 (KJV)** And I fell at his feet to worship him. And he said unto me, See *thou do it* not: I am thy fellowservant, and of thy brethren that have the testimony of Jesus: worship God: for the testimony of Jesus is the spirit of prophecy.

728.　　　Here is the evidence that there is nothing that the Holy Ghost will say to anyone that can come from outside the written Holy Scriptures!

> i. **John 14:26 (KJV)** But the Comforter, *which is* the Holy Ghost, whom the Father will send in my name, he shall teach you all things, and bring all things to your remembrance, whatsoever I have said unto you.
>
> ii. **John 16:13 (KJV)** Howbeit when he, the Spirit of truth, is come, he will guide you into all truth: for he shall not speak of himself; but whatsoever he shall hear, *that* shall he speak: and he will shew you things to come.

729. So, again, I remind you that everything that Prophet Samuel and Apostle Paul received, they received them through the Scriptures!

    i. **1 Samuel 3:21 (KJV)** And the LORD appeared again in Shiloh: for the LORD revealed himself to Samuel in Shiloh by the word of the LORD.

    ii. **1 Corinthians 15:3 (KJV)** For I delivered unto you first of all that which I also received, how that Christ died for our sins according to the scriptures;

730. I ask you therefore, your Prophet, your Pastor, your church, where you go to worship, where does he receive his prophecies from?

731. I have shown you the evidence, so, all that you need to do is to make the judgment and decisively say where your Pastor, your Prophet, and your Bishop get their doctrines, their power, their prophecies, and all their knowledge from?

    i. **1 Corinthians 10:15 (KJV)** I speak as to wise men; judge ye what I say.

732. Bible Teaching, the teaching of the Testimony of Christ, that is the greatest of all the Ministries in the entire Holy Bible! The LORD Jesus Christ did not commend any of the workers in the five-fold Ministries, but ONLY the Bible Teacher Paul! Furthermore, Paul did many miracles, but the LORD Jesus Christ did NOT commend Paul for miracles, signs, and wonders in his Ministry, but ONLY for his teaching the Gospel of Christ the Word of God!

    i. **Acts 18:9 (KJV)** Then spake the Lord to Paul in the night by a vision, Be not afraid, but speak, and hold not thy peace:

    ii. **Acts 18:10 (KJV)** For I am with thee, and no man shall set on thee to hurt thee: for I have much people in this city.

    iii. **Acts 18:11 (KJV)** And he continued *there* a year and six months, teaching the word of God among them.

    iv. **Acts 23:11 (KJV)** And the night following the Lord stood by him, and said, Be of good cheer, Paul: for as thou hast testified of me in Jerusalem, so must thou bear witness also at Rome.

733. Minister Paul uses the doctrine of the Death, Burial, and Resurrection of the LORD Jesus Christ to teach a very important Bible Teaching Methodology, which is: Zero Contradiction by means of comparing spiritual with spiritual!

    i. **1 Corinthians 15:12 (KJV)** Now if Christ be preached that he rose from the dead, how say some among you that there is no resurrection of the dead?

    ii. **1 Corinthians 15:13 (KJV)** But if there be no resurrection of the dead, then is Christ not risen:

    iii. **1 Corinthians 15:14 (KJV)** And if Christ be not risen, then *is* our preaching vain, and your faith *is* also vain.

    iv. **1 Corinthians 15:15 (KJV)** Yea, and we are found false witnesses of God; because we have testified of God that he raised up Christ: whom he raised not up, if so be that the dead rise not.

    v. **1 Corinthians 15:16 (KJV)** For if the dead rise not, then is not Christ raised:

    vi. **1 Corinthians 15:17 (KJV)** And if Christ be not raised, your faith *is* vain; ye are yet in your sins.

    vii. **1 Corinthians 15:18 (KJV)** Then they also which are fallen asleep in Christ are perished.

    viii. **1 Corinthians 15:19 (KJV)** If in this life only we have hope in Christ, we are of all men most miserable.

734.   Here is where the Bible Teaching Methodology derives from!

    i. **1 Corinthians 2:1 (KJV)** And I, brethren, when I came to you, came not with excellency of speech or of wisdom, declaring unto you the testimony of God.

    ii. **1 Corinthians 2:2 (KJV)** For I determined not to know any thing among you, save Jesus Christ, and him crucified.

    iii. **1 Corinthians 2:3 (KJV)** And I was with you in weakness, and in fear, and in much trembling.

    iv. **1 Corinthians 2:4 (KJV)** And my speech and my preaching *was* not with enticing words of man's wisdom, but in demonstration of the Spirit and of power:

    v. **1 Corinthians 2:5 (KJV)** That your faith should not stand in the wisdom of men, but in the power of God.

    vi. **1 Corinthians 2:6 (KJV)** Howbeit we speak wisdom among them that are perfect: yet not the wisdom of this world, nor of the princes of this world, that come to nought:

    vii. **1 Corinthians 2:7 (KJV)** But we speak the wisdom of God in a mystery, *even* the hidden *wisdom*, which God ordained before the world unto our glory:

    viii. **1 Corinthians 2:8 (KJV)** Which none of the princes of this world knew: for had they known *it*, they would not have crucified the Lord of glory.

    ix. **1 Corinthians 2:9 (KJV)** But as it is written, Eye hath not seen, nor ear heard, neither have entered into the heart of man, the things which God hath prepared for them that love him.

     x.   **1 Corinthians 2:10 (KJV)** But God hath revealed *them* unto us by his Spirit: for the Spirit searcheth all things, yea, the deep things of God.

     xi.   **1 Corinthians 2:11 (KJV)** For what man knoweth the things of a man, save the spirit of man which is in him? even so the things of God knoweth no man, but the Spirit of God.

     xii.   **1 Corinthians 2:12 (KJV)** Now we have received, not the spirit of the world, but the spirit which is of God; that we might know the things that are freely given to us of God.

     xiii.   **1 Corinthians 2:13 (KJV)** Which things also we speak, not in the words which man's wisdom teacheth, but which the Holy Ghost teacheth; comparing spiritual things with spiritual.

     xiv.   **1 Corinthians 2:14 (KJV)** But the natural man receiveth not the things of the Spirit of God: for they are foolishness unto him: neither can he know *them*, because they are spiritually discerned.

     xv.   **1 Corinthians 2:15 (KJV)** But he that is spiritual judgeth all things, yet he himself is judged of no man.

     xvi.   **1 Corinthians 2:16 (KJV)** For who hath known the mind of the Lord, that he may instruct him? But we have the mind of Christ.

735.   Here is the LORD Jesus Christ teaching the same Bible Teaching Methodology!

     i.   **Matthew 22:41 (KJV)** While the Pharisees were gathered together, Jesus asked them,

     ii.   **Matthew 22:42 (KJV)** Saying, What think ye of Christ? whose son is he? They say unto him, *The Son* of David.

     iii.   **Matthew 22:43 (KJV)** He saith unto them, How then doth David in spirit call him Lord, saying,

     iv.   **Matthew 22:44 (KJV)** The LORD said unto my Lord, Sit thou on my right hand, till I make thine enemies thy footstool?

     v.   **Matthew 22:45 (KJV)** If David then call him Lord, how is he his son?

     vi.   **Matthew 22:46 (KJV)** And no man was able to answer him a word, neither durst any *man* from that day forth ask him any more *questions*.

736.   Here is Apostle Paul again emphasizing the same correct Bible Teaching Methodology!

     i.   **Romans 12:16 (KJV)** *Be* of the same mind one toward another. Mind not high things, but condescend to men of low estate. Be not wise in your own conceits.

     ii.   **Romans 15:6 (KJV)** That ye may with one mind *and* one mouth glorify God, even the Father of our Lord Jesus Christ.

   iii. **2 Corinthians 13:11 (KJV)** Finally, brethren, farewell. Be perfect, be of good comfort, be of one mind, live in peace; and the God of love and peace shall be with you.

   iv. **Philippians 1:27 (KJV)** Only let your conversation be as it becometh the gospel of Christ: that whether I come and see you, or else be absent, I may hear of your affairs, that ye stand fast in one spirit, with one mind striving together for the faith of the gospel;

   v. **Philippians 2:2 (KJV)** Fulfil ye my joy, that ye be likeminded, having the same love, *being* of one accord, of one mind.

   vi. **1 Peter 3:8 (KJV)** Finally, *be ye* all of one mind, having compassion one of another, love as brethren, *be* pitiful, *be* courteous:

737.   Here is the LORD Jesus Christ again teaching the same correct Bible Teaching Methodology!

   i. **John 17:11 (KJV)** And now I am no more in the world, but these are in the world, and I come to thee. Holy Father, keep through thine own name those whom thou hast given me, that they may be one, as we *are*.

   ii. **John 17:21 (KJV)** That they all may be one; as thou, Father, *art* in me, and I in thee, that they also may be one in us: that the world may believe that thou hast sent me.

   iii. **John 17:22 (KJV)** And the glory which thou gavest me I have given them; that they may be one, even as we are one:

   iv. **John 17:23 (KJV)** I in them, and thou in me, that they may be made perfect in one; and that the world may know that thou hast sent me, and hast loved them, as thou hast loved me.

Wednesday 17ᵗʰ January 2024 @ 11:37 AM – 6:40 PM

CHAPTER 23: BODY RESURRECTION VERSUS SPIRIT RESURRECTION

738. It is important to make the difference between body resurrection and spirit resurrection!

   i. **1 Corinthians 15:12 (KJV)** Now if Christ be preached that he rose from the dead, how say some among you that there is no resurrection of the dead?

   ii. **1 Corinthians 15:13 (KJV)** But if there be no resurrection of the dead, then is Christ not risen:

   iii. **1 Corinthians 15:14 (KJV)** And if Christ be not risen, then *is* our preaching vain, and your faith *is* also vain.

   iv. **1 Corinthians 15:15 (KJV)** Yea, and we are found false witnesses of God; because we have testified of God that he raised up Christ: whom he raised not up, if so be that the dead rise not.

   v. **1 Corinthians 15:16 (KJV)** For if the dead rise not, then is not Christ raised:

   vi. **1 Corinthians 15:17 (KJV)** And if Christ be not raised, your faith *is* vain; ye are yet in your sins.

   vii. **1 Corinthians 15:18 (KJV)** Then they also which are fallen asleep in Christ are perished.

   viii. **1 Corinthians 15:19 (KJV)** If in this life only we have hope in Christ, we are of all men most miserable.

   ix. **1 Corinthians 15:20 (KJV)** But now is Christ risen from the dead, *and* become the firstfruits of them that slept.

739. The LORD Jesus Christ died in HIS Flesh, as **1 Peter 3:18 (KJV)** reveals, and NOT in HIS Spirit, for, it was into HIS Flesh that HE took all the sins of the world and NOT into HIS Spirit! That was why HE revealed that HIS Spirit was willing but HIS Flesh was weak!

   i. **Matthew 26:41 (KJV)** Watch and pray, that ye enter not into temptation: the spirit indeed *is* willing, but the flesh *is* weak.

   ii. **Mark 14:38 (KJV)** Watch ye and pray, lest ye enter into temptation. The spirit truly *is* ready, but the flesh *is* weak.

   iii. **John 10:17 (KJV)** Therefore doth my Father love me, because I lay down my life, that I might take it again.

   iv. **John 10:18 (KJV)** No man taketh it from me, but I lay it down of myself. I have power to lay it down, and I have power to take it again. This commandment have I received of my Father.

v. **Philippians 2:7 (KJV)** But made himself of no reputation, and took upon him the form of a servant, and was made in the likeness of men:

vi. **Hebrews 4:15 (KJV)** For we have not an high priest which cannot be touched with the feeling of our infirmities; but was in all points tempted like as *we are, yet* without sin.

vii. **Matthew 8:17 (KJV)** That it might be fulfilled which was spoken by Esaias the prophet, saying, Himself took our infirmities, and bare *our* sicknesses.

740. **John 10:17-18 (KJV)** is the evidence that while the LORD Jesus Christ was dead in the Flesh, HE was still alive in HIS Spirit still meeting people and preaching them!

i. **1 Peter 3:18 (KJV)** For Christ also hath once suffered for sins, the just for the unjust, that he might bring us to God, being put to death in the flesh, but quickened by the Spirit:

ii. **1 Peter 3:19 (KJV)** By which also he went and preached unto the spirits in prison;

iii. **1 Peter 3:20 (KJV)** Which sometime were disobedient, when once the longsuffering of God waited in the days of Noah, while the ark was a preparing, wherein few, that is, eight souls were saved by water.

741. As I have written already, the first, the correct, and the original Water Baptism with Moses the Man of God, was without water! It was a Waterless Baptism and that is the true and correct baptism!

i. **1 Corinthians 15:29 (KJV)** Else what shall they do which are baptized for the dead, if the dead rise not at all? why are they then baptized for the dead?

ii. **Exodus 14:16 (KJV)** But lift thou up thy rod, and stretch out thine hand over the sea, and divide it: and the children of Israel shall go on dry *ground* through the midst of the sea.

iii. **Exodus 14:22 (KJV)** And the children of Israel went into the midst of the sea upon the dry *ground*: and the waters *were* a wall unto them on their right hand, and on their left.

iv. **1 Corinthians 10:1 (KJV)** Moreover, brethren, I would not that ye should be ignorant, how that all our fathers were under the cloud, and all passed through the sea;

v. **1 Corinthians 10:2 (KJV)** And were all baptized unto Moses in the cloud and in the sea;

742.	Hence, anytime that you pray upon anyone, or, anytime that you yourself pray and say: In the Name of the LORD Jesus Christ, when you speak those words, you are effecting Waterless Baptism using the pure water of the Word!

   i.	**Matthew 28:18 (KJV)** And Jesus came and spake unto them, saying, All power is given unto me in heaven and in earth.

   ii.	**Matthew 28:19 (KJV)** Go ye therefore, and teach all nations, baptizing them in the name of the Father, and of the Son, and of the Holy Ghost:

   iii.	**Matthew 28:20 (KJV)** Teaching them to observe all things whatsoever I have commanded you: and, lo, I am with you alway, *even* unto the end of the world. Amen.

   iv.	**John 4:13 (KJV)** Jesus answered and said unto her, Whosoever drinketh of this water shall thirst again:

   v.	**John 4:14 (KJV)** But whosoever drinketh of the water that I shall give him shall never thirst; but the water that I shall give him shall be in him a well of water springing up into everlasting life.

   vi.	**John 7:37 (KJV)** In the last day, that great *day* of the feast, Jesus stood and cried, saying, If any man thirst, let him come unto me, and drink.

   vii.	**Ephesians 5:26 (KJV)** That he might sanctify and cleanse it with the washing of water by the word,

743.	Take note here how the Holy Spirit, by the hands of Paul, reveals that "shame and insult" are spiritual instruments of Gospel Impartation!

   i.	**1 Corinthians 15:34 (KJV)** Awake to righteousness, and sin not; for some have not the knowledge of God: I speak *this* to your shame.

744.	That is why they are cursed all those who seek to strip the Word of God of its shameful language, its pornographic language, it violent language, its whorish language, and seek to correct God and polish the Word of God because they bethink their corrupt filthy selves as highly more civilized than the LORD God Almighty who deemed it good and correct to put all that language in there in the Word of God! Woe unto them and great shame upon them!

745.	The flash body is different from the spirit body and each of them has it lifespan! While the flesh may live for about 120 years, the spirit lives forever, either in Hell or in Heaven!

   i.	**1 Corinthians 15:35 (KJV)** But some *man* will say, How are the dead raised up? and with what body do they come?

   ii.	**1 Corinthians 15:36 (KJV)** *Thou* fool, that which thou sowest is not quickened, except it die:

   iii. **1 Corinthians 15:37 (KJV)** And that which thou sowest, thou sowest not that body that shall be, but bare grain, it may chance of wheat, or of some other *grain*:

   iv. **1 Corinthians 15:38 (KJV)** But God giveth it a body as it hath pleased him, and to every seed his own body.

   v. **1 Corinthians 15:39 (KJV)** All flesh *is* not the same flesh: but *there is* one *kind of* flesh of men, another flesh of beasts, another of fishes, *and* another of birds.

   vi. **1 Corinthians 15:40 (KJV)** *There are* also celestial bodies, and bodies terrestrial: but the glory of the celestial *is* one, and the *glory* of the terrestrial *is* another.

   vii. **1 Corinthians 15:41 (KJV)** *There is* one glory of the sun, and another glory of the moon, and another glory of the stars: for *one* star differeth from *another* star in glory.

   viii. **1 Corinthians 15:42 (KJV)** So also *is* the resurrection of the dead. It is sown in corruption; it is raised in incorruption:

746.   The revelation in **1 Corinthians 15:40 (KJV)** saying that "*There are* also celestial bodies, and bodies terrestrial: but the glory of the celestial *is* one, and the *glory* of the terrestrial *is* another", is a condemnation of all those who misuse **Galatians 3:28 (KJV)** to falsely preach that women can stand in the Pulpit in the church and preach, conduct service, and even be ordained as a Pastor and Bishop!

   i. **Galatians 3:28 (KJV)** There is neither Jew nor Greek, there is neither bond nor free, there is neither male nor female: for ye are all one in Christ Jesus.

   ii. **1 Corinthians 15:23 (KJV)** But every man in his own order: Christ the firstfruits; afterward they that are Christ's at his coming.

747.   Yet, as you can see in **1 Corinthians 15:40 (KJV)**, "you need to drop your terrestrial body in order to take up your celestial body", just as the LORD Jesus Christ demonstrated at HIS Resurrection, before you can qualify to implement the genderless spiritual provision in **Galatians 3:28 (KJV)**!

748.   The second confirmation for the doctrine that "you need to drop your terrestrial body in order to take up your celestial body" is in **1 Corinthians 15:23 (KJV)** where the LORD God refers to Christ and the order of how Christ dropped HIS Flesh before HE took up HIS Spirit Body, as an example, saying that "But every man in his own order", again, meaning the same thing as: "you need to drop your terrestrial body in order to take up your celestial body"!

749.   The same doctrine that "you need to drop your terrestrial body in order to take up your celestial body", which I have shown you with evidence twice already right here

above, has yet a third confirmation! Now, watch very carefully, as you read the following eight evidences from **1 Corinthians 15:42-49 (KJV)**, and see how each of them emphasizes and re-emphasizes the same doctrine that "you need to drop your terrestrial body in order to take up your celestial body"! Take note how one (the flesh/the physical) must die before the other (the unseen/ the spiritual) can appear!

    i. **1 Corinthians 15:42 (KJV)** So also *is* the resurrection of the dead. It is sown in corruption; it is raised in incorruption:

    ii. **1 Corinthians 15:43 (KJV)** It is sown in dishonour; it is raised in glory: it is sown in weakness; it is raised in power:

    iii. **1 Corinthians 15:44 (KJV)** It is sown a natural body; it is raised a spiritual body. There is a natural body, and there is a spiritual body.

    iv. **1 Corinthians 15:45 (KJV)** And so it is written, The first man Adam was made a living soul; the last Adam *was made* a quickening spirit.

    v. **1 Corinthians 15:46 (KJV)** Howbeit that *was* not first which is spiritual, but that which is natural; and afterward that which is spiritual.

    vi. **1 Corinthians 15:47 (KJV)** The first man *is* of the earth, earthy: the second man *is* the Lord from heaven.

    vii. **1 Corinthians 15:48 (KJV)** As *is* the earthy, such *are* they also that are earthy: and as *is* the heavenly, such *are* they also that are heavenly.

    viii. **1 Corinthians 15:49 (KJV)** And as we have borne the image of the earthy, we shall also bear the image of the heavenly.

750.   So, again on this third round of examining **Galatians 3:28 (KJV)** in the light of the Scriptures, all those ignorant fools who make a false justification for female ordination, and the cursed equality of the sexes, and the demonic doctrine of feminism in the churches, they have again failed, as the evidence in **1 Corinthians 15:42-49 (KJV)** reveals!

751.   The final stage of the spirit resurrection is the change from a flesh body into a spirit body in an instant. This is the exact moment when **Galatians 3:28 (KJV)** begins!

    i. **Galatians 3:28 (KJV)** There is neither Jew nor Greek, there is neither bond nor free, there is neither male nor female: for ye are all one in Christ Jesus.

    ii. **1 Corinthians 15:51 (KJV)** Behold, I shew you a mystery; We shall not all sleep, but we shall all be changed,

    iii. **1 Corinthians 15:52 (KJV)** In a moment, in the twinkling of an eye, at the last trump: for the trumpet shall sound, and the dead shall be raised incorruptible, and we shall be changed.

    iv. **1 Corinthians 15:53 (KJV)** For this corruptible must put on incorruption, and this mortal *must* put on immortality.

v. **1 Corinthians 15:54 (KJV)** So when this corruptible shall have put on incorruption, and this mortal shall have put on immortality, then shall be brought to pass the saying that is written, Death is swallowed up in victory.

vi. **1 Corinthians 15:55 (KJV)** O death, where *is* thy sting? O grave, where *is* thy victory?

vii. **1 Corinthians 15:56 (KJV)** The sting of death *is* sin; and the strength of sin *is* the law.

viii. **1 Corinthians 15:57 (KJV)** But thanks *be* to God, which giveth us the victory through our Lord Jesus Christ.

ix. **1 Corinthians 15:58 (KJV)** Therefore, my beloved brethren, be ye stedfast, unmoveable, always abounding in the work of the Lord, forasmuch as ye know that your labour is not in vain in the Lord.

752. In other words, as long as you still have the sentence of death still working in you, then, **Galatians 3:28 (KJV)** is NOT operable!

i. **2 Corinthians 1:9 (KJV)** But we had the sentence of death in ourselves, that we should not trust in ourselves, but in God which raiseth the dead:

ii. **Romans 7:22 (KJV)** For I delight in the law of God after the inward man:

iii. **Romans 7:23 (KJV)** But I see another law in my members, warring against the law of my mind, and bringing me into captivity to the law of sin which is in my members.

iv. **Romans 7:24 (KJV)** O wretched man that I am! who shall deliver me from the body of this death?

v. **Romans 7:25 (KJV)** I thank God through Jesus Christ our Lord. So then with the mind I myself serve the law of God; but with the flesh the law of sin.

753. Therefore, as **1 Corinthians 15:57 (KJV)** says, "through our Lord Jesus Christ", following in the steps of HIS Resurrection, we shall also obtain the spirit resurrection in the order of when we shall have completed the flesh life and then graduated into the spirit life of Christ!

i. **2 Peter 1:13 (KJV)** Yea, I think it meet, as long as I am in this tabernacle, to stir you up by putting *you* in remembrance;

ii. **2 Peter 1:14 (KJV)** Knowing that shortly I must put off *this* my tabernacle, even as our Lord Jesus Christ hath shewed me.

Thursday 18th January 2024 @ 11:00 AM – 1:25 PM

CHAPTER 24: THE CORRUPTION IN THE OFFERING OF HOLY COMMUNION AND WATER BAPTISM

754.   Now, here in **1 Corinthians 15:50 (KJV)** is a revelation that has a very profound meaning for many things that we do in the churches!

      i. **1 Corinthians 15:50 (KJV)** Now this I say, brethren, that flesh and blood cannot inherit the kingdom of God; neither doth corruption inherit incorruption.

755.   The revelation in **1 Corinthians 15:50 (KJV)** is a confirmation of the Truth of Christ that God Almighty is Spirit, therefore, God-worship must always be conducted at the spirit level and NOT at the physical level to which many Christians are often accustomed, howbeit in error!

      i. **John 4:23 (KJV)** But the hour cometh, and now is, when the true worshippers shall worship the Father in spirit and in truth: for the Father seeketh such to worship him.

      ii. **John 4:24 (KJV)** God *is* a Spirit: and they that worship him must worship *him* in spirit and in truth.

      iii. **1 Corinthians 2:12 (KJV)** Now we have received, not the spirit of the world, but the spirit which is of God; that we might know the things that are freely given to us of God.

      iv. **1 Corinthians 2:13 (KJV)** Which things also we speak, not in the words which man's wisdom teacheth, but which the Holy Ghost teacheth; comparing spiritual things with spiritual.

      v. **Deuteronomy 30:14 (KJV)** But the word *is* very nigh unto thee, in thy mouth, and in thy heart, that thou mayest do it.

      vi. **Romans 10:8 (KJV)** But what saith it? The word is nigh thee, *even* in thy mouth, and in thy heart: that is, the word of faith, which we preach;

756.   If "flesh and blood cannot inherit the Kingdom of God", and the Kingdom of God is in your mouth, and the Kingdom of God is the Word of Faith which we preach, then how do you not understand that the fleshly-produced wafers, wine, and bread of your Holy Communion cannot inherit the kingdom of God since you agree that your wafers, wine, and bread are flesh, your wafers, wine, and bread are blood, and your wafers, wine, and bread are corruption, as condemned in **1 Corinthians 15:50 (KJV)**?

757.   How also do you not understand that your flesh-based Water Baptism cannot inherit the Kingdom of God since you agree that your Water Baptism is flesh, your Water Baptism is blood, and your Water Baptism is corruption, as condemned in **1 Corinthians 15:50 (KJV)**?

758.   How also do you not understand that any part of your God-worship that is accomplished through the works of flesh, blood, and corruption are all disqualified by the same **1 Corinthians 15:50 (KJV)** which says that "flesh and blood cannot inherit the kingdom of God; neither doth corruption inherit incorruption"?

759.   Or, are you able to contradict the Word of God in **John 4:23-24 (KJV)** and in **1 Corinthians 15:50 (KJV)** to show me that your Holy Communion wafers, wine, and bread, and your Water Baptism, and all your physical worship man-made items, do not come from corruption and are not done with corrupt filthy human hands?

  i.   **Leviticus 22:25 (KJV)** Neither from a stranger's hand shall ye offer the bread of your God of any of these; because their corruption *is* in them, *and* blemishes *be* in them: they shall not be accepted for you.

  ii.   **Romans 8:21 (KJV)** Because the creature itself also shall be delivered from the bondage of corruption into the glorious liberty of the children of God.

  iii. **1 Corinthians 15:42 (KJV)** So also *is* the resurrection of the dead. It is sown in corruption; it is raised in incorruption:

  iv.   **Galatians 6:8 (KJV)** For he that soweth to his flesh shall of the flesh reap corruption; but he that soweth to the Spirit shall of the Spirit reap life everlasting.

  v.   **Haggai 2:10 (KJV)** In the four and twentieth *day* of the ninth *month*, in the second year of Darius, came the word of the LORD by Haggai the prophet, saying,

  vi.   **Haggai 2:11 (KJV)** Thus saith the LORD of hosts; Ask now the priests *concerning* the law, saying,

  vii. **Haggai 2:12 (KJV)** If one bear holy flesh in the skirt of his garment, and with his skirt do touch bread, or pottage, or wine, or oil, or any meat, shall it be holy? And the priests answered and said, No.

  viii. **Haggai 2:13 (KJV)** Then said Haggai, If *one that is* unclean by a dead body touch any of these, shall it be unclean? And the priests answered and said, It shall be unclean.

  ix.   **Haggai 2:14 (KJV)** Then answered Haggai, and said, So *is* this people, and so *is* this nation before me, saith the LORD; and so *is* every work of their hands; and that which they offer there *is* unclean.

760.   If you agree that there is no good thing dwelling in your flesh, then how do you presume that God Almighty will be pleased to take Holy Communion offering and Water Baptism offering from your dirty hands?

i. **Romans 7:18 (KJV)** For I know that in me (that is, in my flesh,) dwelleth no good thing: for to will is present with me; but *how* to perform that which is good I find not.

761.   Brother Bishop, in both the Old and New Testaments of Christ, the LORD God has identified for you, clearly and very plainly, the specific part and spot of your human flesh that all God-worship should come from, should proceed, and should be accomplished, and that place is YOUR MOUTH!

i. **Deuteronomy 30:14 (KJV)** But the word *is* very nigh unto thee, in thy mouth, and in thy heart, that thou mayest do it.

ii. **Romans 10:8 (KJV)** But what saith it? The word is nigh thee, *even* in thy mouth, and in thy heart: that is, the word of faith, which we preach;

iii. **Micah 6:8 (KJV)** He hath shewed thee, O man, what *is* good; and what doth the LORD require of thee, but to do justly, and to love mercy, and to walk humbly with thy God?

iv. **Joshua 1:7 (KJV)** Only be thou strong and very courageous, that thou mayest observe to do according to all the law, which Moses my servant commanded thee: turn not from it *to* the right hand or *to* the left, that thou mayest prosper whithersoever thou goest.

v. **Joshua 1:8 (KJV)** This book of the law shall not depart out of thy mouth; but thou shalt meditate therein day and night, that thou mayest observe to do according to all that is written therein: for then thou shalt make thy way prosperous, and then thou shalt have good success.

vi. **1 Corinthians 5:8 (KJV)** Therefore let us keep the feast, not with old leaven, neither with the leaven of malice and wickedness; but with the unleavened *bread* of sincerity and truth.

vii. **Hebrews 13:15 (KJV)** By him therefore let us offer the sacrifice of praise to God continually, that is, the fruit of *our* lips giving thanks to his name.

762.   So, I have shown you only seven evidences (there are many) why your worship to Godward should proceed from your mouth and NOT from corruptible things such as Holy Communion wafers, wine, bread, and filthy Water Baptism river waters!

Thursday 18th January 2024 @ 11:00 AM – 1:25 PM

CHAPTER 25: A TEMPLATE FOR HOW TO FINANCE THE MINISTRY OF CHRIST

763.   In this last chapter of 1 Corinthians, the LORD God is revealing to us Thirteen (13) Lessons on Church collection and Gospel Financing, a Template for how to finance the Ministry of Christ!

   i.   **1 Corinthians 16:1 (KJV)** Now concerning the collection for the saints, as I have given order to the churches of Galatia, even so do ye.

764.   Gospel Fiancing Lesson #1:

765.   The first lesson that we learn on Gospel Fiancing is that its proper name is:

   i.   "the collection for the saints"!

766.   You can see, therefore, that church money is NOT for the Head Pastor only, as many criminal Pastors and Bishops do these days? Neither is church money for the Pastor's wife, no, that is NOT her calling, and churches who do that, making the Pastor's wife the church money collector or the church treasurer, all such churches and Pastors are thieves, robbers, criminals, and robbers of churches!

   i.   **Acts 19:37 (KJV)** For ye have brought hither these men, which are neither robbers of churches, nor yet blasphemers of your goddess.

767.   Gospel Fiancing Lesson #2:

   i.   **1 Corinthians 16:2 (KJV)** Upon the first *day* of the week let every one of you lay by him in store, as *God* hath prospered him, that there be no gatherings when I come.

768.   Church collection is to be done weekly!

769.   Gospel Fiancing Lesson #2:

770.   Church collection and Gospel Financing are voluntary, according to your financial ability, NOT by force, NOT by 10% tithing, and NOT by fraudulent first fruit money!

   i.   **Exodus 25:2 (KJV)** Speak unto the children of Israel, that they bring me an offering: of every man that giveth it willingly with his heart ye shall take my offering.

   ii.   **Ezra 1:1 (KJV)** Now in the first year of Cyrus king of Persia, that the word of the LORD by the mouth of Jeremiah might be fulfilled, the LORD stirred up the spirit of Cyrus king of Persia, that he made a proclamation throughout all his kingdom, and *put it* also in writing, saying,

   iii. **Ezra 1:2 (KJV)** Thus saith Cyrus king of Persia, The LORD God of heaven hath given me all the kingdoms of the earth; and he hath charged me to build him an house at Jerusalem, which *is* in Judah.

     iv. **Ezra 1:3 (KJV)** Who *is there* among you of all his people? his God be with him, and let him go up to Jerusalem, which *is* in Judah, and build the house of the LORD God of Israel, (he *is* the God,) which *is* in Jerusalem.

     v. **Ezra 1:4 (KJV)** And whosoever remaineth in any place where he sojourneth, let the men of his place help him with silver, and with gold, and with goods, and with beasts, beside the freewill offering for the house of God that *is* in Jerusalem.

771.   Gospel Fiancing Lesson #3:

772.   The next lesson in **1 Corinthians 16:2 (KJV)** is that Church collection and Gospel Financing are for a pre-determined specific time and for a pre-determined specific purpose and need!

773.   Gospel Fiancing Lesson #4:

774.   The next lesson in **1 Corinthians 16:2 (KJV)** is that Church collection and Gospel Financing money should NOT be collected in perpetuity forever by the church! That is illegal, crooked, and against God Almighty!

775.   Gospel Fiancing Lesson #5:

     i. **1 Corinthians 16:3 (KJV)** And when I come, whomsoever ye shall approve by *your* letters, them will I send to bring your liberality unto Jerusalem.

     ii. **1 Corinthians 16:4 (KJV)** And if it be meet that I go also, they shall go with me.

776.   In **1 Corinthians 16:3-4 (KJV)**, we learn that Church collection and Gospel Financing money should be documented and very penny accounted for diligently, not by the Pastor alone, but also by lay Christians chosen freely from among the congregation!

777.   Gospel Fiancing Lesson #6:

778.   Church collection and Gospel Financing money are for the poor, the needy, the widows, the strangers, the fatherless, and the destitute in the church!

     i. **Deuteronomy 15:11 (KJV)** For the poor shall never cease out of the land: therefore I command thee, saying, Thou shalt open thine hand wide unto thy brother, to thy poor, and to thy needy, in thy land.

     ii. **Deuteronomy 10:18 (KJV)** He doth execute the judgment of the fatherless and widow, and loveth the stranger, in giving him food and raiment.

     iii. **Deuteronomy 14:29 (KJV)** And the Levite, (because he hath no part nor inheritance with thee,) and the stranger, and the fatherless, and the widow, which *are* within thy gates, shall come, and shall eat and be satisfied; that the LORD thy God may bless thee in all the work of thine hand which thou doest.

    iv. **Deuteronomy 16:11 (KJV)** And thou shalt rejoice before the LORD thy God, thou, and thy son, and thy daughter, and thy manservant, and thy maidservant, and the Levite that *is* within thy gates, and the stranger, and the fatherless, and the widow, that *are* among you, in the place which the LORD thy God hath chosen to place his name there.

    v. **Galatians 2:8 (KJV)** (For he that wrought effectually in Peter to the apostleship of the circumcision, the same was mighty in me toward the Gentiles:)

    vi. **Galatians 2:9 (KJV)** And when James, Cephas, and John, who seemed to be pillars, perceived the grace that was given unto me, they gave to me and Barnabas the right hands of fellowship; that we *should go* unto the heathen, and they unto the circumcision.

    vii. **Galatians 2:10 (KJV)** Only *they would* that we should remember the poor; the same which I also was forward to do.

779.   Gospel Fiancing Lesson #7:

780.   Church collection and Gospel Financing money are what is used to also pay for the travel, lodging, and feeding expenses of poor Pastors who is doing the work of God! Church collection and Gospel Financing money are NOT for rich peole! There is a curse attched to it whenever you give church money to any rich person!

    i. **1 Corinthians 16:5 (KJV)** Now I will come unto you, when I shall pass through Macedonia: for I do pass through Macedonia.

    ii. **1 Corinthians 16:6 (KJV)** And it may be that I will abide, yea, and winter with you, that ye may bring me on my journey whithersoever I go.

    iii. **1 Corinthians 16:7 (KJV)** For I will not see you now by the way; but I trust to tarry a while with you, if the Lord permit.

    iv. **1 Corinthians 16:8 (KJV)** But I will tarry at Ephesus until Pentecost.

781.   Gospel Fiancing Lesson #8:

    i. **1 Corinthians 16:10 (KJV)** Now if Timotheus come, see that he may be with you without fear: for he worketh the work of the Lord, as I also *do*.

    ii. **1 Corinthians 16:11 (KJV)** Let no man therefore despise him: but conduct him forth in peace, that he may come unto me: for I look for him with the brethren.

    iii. **1 Corinthians 16:12 (KJV)** As touching *our* brother Apollos, I greatly desired him to come unto you with the brethren: but his will was not at all to come at this time; but he will come when he shall have convenient time.

782.   In addition to Church collection and Gospel Financing money, established churches and Pastors should also give letters of recommendation to fellow Servants of Christ on their journey, not so much for themselves, but so that the work of the LORD Jesus Christ should NOT be hindered because of lack of funding!

    i. **Ezra 1:2 (KJV)** Thus saith Cyrus king of Persia, The LORD God of heaven hath given me all the kingdoms of the earth; and he hath charged me to build him an house at Jerusalem, which *is* in Judah.

    ii. **Ezra 1:3 (KJV)** Who *is there* among you of all his people? his God be with him, and let him go up to Jerusalem, which *is* in Judah, and build the house of the LORD God of Israel, (he *is* the God,) which *is* in Jerusalem.

    iii. **Ezra 1:4 (KJV)** And whosoever remaineth in any place where he sojourneth, let the men of his place help him with silver, and with gold, and with goods, and with beasts, beside the freewill offering for the house of God that *is* in Jerusalem.

783.   Gospel Fiancing Lesson #9:

784.   Now, what do I get for helping the poor and the poor man of God? Here is the answer!

    i. **Matthew 10:40 (KJV)** He that receiveth you receiveth me, and he that receiveth me receiveth him that sent me.

    ii. **Matthew 10:41 (KJV)** He that receiveth a prophet in the name of a prophet shall receive a prophet's reward; and he that receiveth a righteous man in the name of a righteous man shall receive a righteous man's reward.

    iii. **Matthew 10:42 (KJV)** And whosoever shall give to drink unto one of these little ones a cup of cold *water* only in the name of a disciple, verily I say unto you, he shall in no wise lose his reward.

785.   Gospel Fiancing Lesson #10:

786.   Now, all those Men of God who receive support and funding from Church collection and Gospel Financing money, how shall they comport themselves in order to merit this financial help? Here is the answer!

    i. **1 Corinthians 16:13 (KJV)** Watch ye, stand fast in the faith, quit you like men, be strong.

    ii. **1 Corinthians 16:14 (KJV)** Let all your things be done with charity.

787.   Gospel Fiancing Lesson #11:

788.   In addition to doing Church collection and Gospel Financing from time to time for the sole purpose of financing a specific church need, the Holy Spirit shows us in **1 Corinthians 16:15-16 (KJV)** that Brethren and Sisters can also enter the Ministry of Helps, whose only task will be to seek out true Men of God, identify their calling, scrutinize their Ministry in the Light of the Word of God, and then, fund them to accomplish the work of the LORD Jesus Chreist!

    i.   **1 Corinthians 16:15 (KJV)** I beseech you, brethren, (ye know the house of Stephanas, that it is the firstfruits of Achaia, and *that* they have addicted themselves to the ministry of the saints,)

    ii.   **1 Corinthians 16:16 (KJV)** That ye submit yourselves unto such, and to every one that helpeth with *us*, and laboureth.

    iii.   **1 Corinthians 16:17 (KJV)** I am glad of the coming of Stephanas and Fortunatus and Achaicus: for that which was lacking on your part they have supplied.

    iv.   **1 Corinthians 16:18 (KJV)** For they have refreshed my spirit and yours: therefore acknowledge ye them that are such.

789.   **Gospel Fiancing Lesson #12:**

790.   Finally, all such true Men of God who receive help and funding from good Christians to advance the work of the LORD, they should also pray for those who fund them with a clean hand and heart, so that it shall be well with them, and for the LORD to remember HIS promise unto them in good measure!

    i.   **Matthew 10:41 (KJV)** He that receiveth a prophet in the name of a prophet shall receive a prophet's reward; and he that receiveth a righteous man in the name of a righteous man shall receive a righteous man's reward.

    ii.   **Matthew 10:42 (KJV)** And whosoever shall give to drink unto one of these little ones a cup of cold *water* only in the name of a disciple, verily I say unto you, he shall in no wise lose his reward.

    iii.   **1 Corinthians 16:19 (KJV)** The churches of Asia salute you. Aquila and Priscilla salute you much in the Lord, with the church that is in their house.

    iv.   **1 Corinthians 16:20 (KJV)** All the brethren greet you. Greet ye one another with an holy kiss.

    v.   **1 Corinthians 16:21 (KJV)** The salutation of *me* Paul with mine own hand.

    vi.   **1 Corinthians 16:23 (KJV)** The grace of our Lord Jesus Christ *be* with you.

vii. **1 Corinthians 16:24 (KJV)** My love *be* with you all in Christ Jesus. Amen. The first *epistle* to the Corinthians was written from Philippi by Stephanas, and Fortunatus, and Achaicus, and Timotheus.

791.   Gospel Fiancing Lesson #13:

792.   Finally, all such true Men of God who do NOT receive help and funding from bad Christians, whose churlishness therefore hinder the advancement of the work of the LORD Jesus Christ, let the same true Men of God also pray against them, that it should ill and evil with them all the days of their lives, for being thus evil-minded against the work of the LORD Jesus Christ!

i. **Matthew 10:14 (KJV)** And whosoever shall not receive you, nor hear your words, when ye depart out of that house or city, shake off the dust of your feet.

ii. **Matthew 10:15 (KJV)** Verily I say unto you, It shall be more tolerable for the land of Sodom and Gomorrha in the day of judgment, than for that city.

iii. **Matthew 11:24 (KJV)** But I say unto you, That it shall be more tolerable for the land of Sodom in the day of judgment, than for thee.

iv. **Luke 9:5 (KJV)** And whosoever will not receive you, when ye go out of that city, shake off the very dust from your feet for a testimony against them.

v. **1 Corinthians 16:22 (KJV)** If any man love not the Lord Jesus Christ, let him be Anathema Maran-atha.

Thursday 18th January 2024 @ 11:00 AM – 7:44 PM

CHAPTER 3
THE BOOK OF 2 CORINTHIANS

AKOFENA
"Sword of war"
Asante philosophical symbol of Courage, Valor

CHAPTER 1: HOW TO COMFORT THOSE IN TROUBLE, IN AFFLICTION, AND IN TRIBULATION

1. A saint is a true child of God! A saint is NOT appointed by corrupt men in cassock as the corrupt Roman Catholic Popes do! A person becomes a saint when he is born again by the Holy Spirit of God!

    i. **2 Corinthians 1:1 (KJV)** Paul, an apostle of Jesus Christ by the will of God, and Timothy *our* brother, unto the church of God which is at Corinth, with all the saints which are in all Achaia:

2. Step #1:

3. Tell the person in trouble, tell the afflicted, and tell the one going through any tribulation, that God the Father of mercies, is the God of all comfort!

    i. **2 Corinthians 1:3 (KJV)** Blessed *be* God, even the Father of our Lord Jesus Christ, the Father of mercies, and the God of all comfort;

4. Step #2:

5. Tell the person in trouble, tell the afflicted, and tell the one going through any tribulation, that we are partakers of the sufferings of Christ even as much as equal and more consolation also abound in Christ for that suffering!

    i. **2 Corinthians 1:5 (KJV)** For as the sufferings of Christ abound in us, so our consolation also aboundeth by Christ.

6. The revelation in **2 Corinthians 1:5 (KJV)** is a condemnation of all the property preachers who preach that Christian suddering is over because Jesus Christ did all the suffering for all Christians and so a suffering person is not a Christian!

7. The truth of Christ is that Christian suffering is one of the requirements of true Christianity, therefore, those who teach that suffering is not Christian are all Ministers of Satan!

8. Step #3:

9. Tell the person in trouble, tell the afflicted, and tell the one going through any tribulation, that the enduring of Christian affliction and suffering is actually a good thing because affliction and suffering are spiritual instruments to generate consolation and salvation unto others!

    i. **2 Corinthians 1:6 (KJV)** And whether we be afflicted, *it is* for your consolation and salvation, which is effectual in the enduring of the same sufferings which we also suffer: or whether we be comforted, *it is* for your consolation and salvation.

10. Step #4:

11. Tell the person in trouble, tell the afflicted, and tell the one going through any tribulation, that there is no Christian consolation without a prior Christian suffering!

       i. **2 Corinthians 1:7 (KJV)** And our hope of you *is* stedfast, knowing, that as ye are partakers of the sufferings, so *shall ye be* also of the consolation.

12. Step #5:

13. Tell the person in trouble, tell the afflicted, and tell the one going through any tribulation, that you share in his/her trouble, affliction, suffering, and tribulation because you yourself once came close to death, and your suffering was too painful insomuch that you even despaired even of life, but once you came into the knowledge of God which raiseth the dead, you began to trust in that God for help, and this same God delivered us from so great a death, and doth deliver: in whom we trust that he will yet deliver us again!

       i. **2 Corinthians 1:8 (KJV)** For we would not, brethren, have you ignorant of our trouble which came to us in Asia, that we were pressed out of measure, above strength, insomuch that we despaired even of life:

      ii. **2 Corinthians 1:9 (KJV)** But we had the sentence of death in ourselves, that we should not trust in ourselves, but in God which raiseth the dead:

     iii. **2 Corinthians 1:10 (KJV)** Who delivered us from so great a death, and doth deliver: in whom we trust that he will yet deliver *us*;

14. Step #6:

15. Tell the person in trouble, tell the afflicted, and tell the one going through any tribulation, that prayer unto this God who is able to deliver is one very potent instrument of consolation and salvation to all those who are suffering and are in despair!

       i. **2 Corinthians 1:11 (KJV)** Ye also helping together by prayer for us, that for the gift *bestowed* upon us by the means of many persons thanks may be given by many on our behalf.

16. Step #7:

17. Tell the person in trouble, tell the afflicted, and tell the one going through any tribulation, that another instrument of consolation and salvation from the suffering is to hold regular conversations with those whose presence you acknowledge as capable of bringing you joy, laughter, and good fond memories of the past that glorify the Lord Jesus!

       i. **2 Corinthians 1:12 (KJV)** For our rejoicing is this, the testimony of our conscience, that in simplicity and godly sincerity, not with fleshly wisdom, but by the grace of God, we have had our conversation in the world, and more abundantly to you-ward.

    ii. **2 Corinthians 1:13 (KJV)** For we write none other things unto you, than what ye read or acknowledge; and I trust ye shall acknowledge even to the end;

    iii. **2 Corinthians 1:14 (KJV)** As also ye have acknowledged us in part, that we are your rejoicing, even as ye also *are* ours in the day of the Lord Jesus.

18. Step #8:

19. Tell the person in trouble, tell the afflicted, and tell the one going through any tribulation, that you are ready to undertake personal visits with him/her that generate mutual benefits to both of you!

    i. **2 Corinthians 1:15 (KJV)** And in this confidence I was minded to come unto you before, that ye might have a second benefit;

    ii. **2 Corinthians 1:16 (KJV)** And to pass by you into Macedonia, and to come again out of Macedonia unto you, and of you to be brought on my way toward Judaea.

20. Step #9:

21. Tell the person in trouble, tell the afflicted, and tell the one going through any tribulation, that "truth speaking" is another very potent spiritual instrument for healing! "Truth speaking" to the acknowledgelent of the Truth of the Gospel of Christ is a very potent spiritual instrument for healing!

    i. **2 Corinthians 1:17 (KJV)** When I therefore was thus minded, did I use lightness? or the things that I purpose, do I purpose according to the flesh, that with me there should be yea yea, and nay nay?

    ii. **2 Corinthians 1:18 (KJV)** But *as* God *is* true, our word toward you was not yea and nay.

    iii. **2 Corinthians 1:19 (KJV)** For the Son of God, Jesus Christ, who was preached among you by us, *even* by me and Silvanus and Timotheus, was not yea and nay, but in him was yea.

    iv. **2 Corinthians 1:20 (KJV)** For all the promises of God in him *are* yea, and in him Amen, unto the glory of God by us.

22. Step #10:

23. Tell the person in trouble, tell the afflicted, and tell the one going through any tribulation, that the person who is qualified to administer comfort unto the Christian or unto any person who is in affliction, in suffering, in trouble, and in tribulation, is the person who is already established in Christ, the person who has the anointing of God, and the person who has the Holy Spirit by reason of his deep knowledge in the Word of God, and by reason of his/her daily walk in Truth and in Righteousness!

    i.   **2 Corinthians 1:21 (KJV)** Now he which stablisheth us with you in Christ, and hath anointed us, *is* God;

    ii.   **2 Corinthians 1:22 (KJV)** Who hath also sealed us, and given the earnest of the Spirit in our hearts.

    iii.   **2 Corinthians 1:23 (KJV)** Moreover I call God for a record upon my soul, that to spare you I came not as yet unto Corinth.

24. Then, finally, on the other hand, the whole exercise of Christian crisis intervention and administration of comfort to the afflicted will work when the afflicted also, on his/her part, stands/believes in the Faith of Christ!

    i.   **2 Corinthians 1:24 (KJV)** Not for that we have dominion over your faith, but are helpers of your joy: for by faith ye stand.

Friday 19th January 2024 @ 10:14 AM – 12:19 PM

CHAPTER 2: HOW TO RESTORE A SINNER BACK INTO FELLOWSHIP

25. When one has sinned in the congregation, the punishment is to put out that person so that he or she does not corrupt the rest of the people!
    i. **1 Corinthians 5:1 (KJV)** It is reported commonly *that there is* fornication among you, and such fornication as is not so much as named among the Gentiles, that one should have his father's wife.
    ii. **1 Corinthians 5:2 (KJV)** And ye are puffed up, and have not rather mourned, that he that hath done this deed might be taken away from among you.
    iii. **1 Corinthians 5:13 (KJV)** But them that are without God judgeth. Therefore put away from among yourselves that wicked person.
26. Now, after a while, what shall the church do?
27. The curch will need to confirm the sinner back into faith and establish him or her in the faith, and then receive him or her again into fellowship!
28. Here is how to establish brethren in the faith!
    i. **Acts 16:4 (KJV)** And as they went through the cities, they delivered them the decrees for to keep, that were ordained of the apostles and elders which were at Jerusalem.
    ii. **Acts 16:5 (KJV)** And so were the churches established in the faith, and increased in number daily.
    iii. **2 Corinthians 1:24 (KJV)** Not for that we have dominion over your faith, but are helpers of your joy: for by faith ye stand.
29. Here is how to receive the sinner back into fellowship!
    i. **2 Corinthians 2:1 (KJV)** But I determined this with myself, that I would not come again to you in heaviness.
    ii. **2 Corinthians 2:2 (KJV)** For if I make you sorry, who is he then that maketh me glad, but the same which is made sorry by me?
    iii. **2 Corinthians 2:3 (KJV)** And I wrote this same unto you, lest, when I came, I should have sorrow from them of whom I ought to rejoice; having confidence in you all, that my joy is *the joy* of you all.
    iv. **2 Corinthians 2:4 (KJV)** For out of much affliction and anguish of heart I wrote unto you with many tears; not that ye should be grieved, but that ye might know the love which I have more abundantly unto you.
    v. **2 Corinthians 2:5 (KJV)** But if any have caused grief, he hath not grieved me, but in part: that I may not overcharge you all.

      vi. **2 Corinthians 2:6 (KJV)** Sufficient to such a man *is* this punishment, which *was inflicted* of many.

30. After the punishment of putting the sinner out of the church comes a time to receive him or her back into fellowship through forgiveness, when it is confirmed that he or she has returned to the Faith of Christ and is obedient to the Word of God!

      i. **2 Corinthians 2:7 (KJV)** So that contrariwise ye *ought* rather to forgive *him*, and comfort *him*, lest perhaps such a one should be swallowed up with overmuch sorrow.

      ii. **2 Corinthians 2:8 (KJV)** Wherefore I beseech you that ye would confirm *your* love toward him.

      iii. **2 Corinthians 2:9 (KJV)** For to this end also did I write, that I might know the proof of you, whether ye be obedient in all things.

      iv. **2 Corinthians 2:10 (KJV)** To whom ye forgive any thing, I *forgive* also: for if I forgave any thing, to whom I forgave *it*, for your sakes *forgave I it* in the person of Christ;

31. The risk of not forgiving the sinner after that he or she has repented and forsaken the sin is that Satan will then take advantage of the believers who refuse to forgive!

      i. **2 Corinthians 2:11 (KJV)** Lest Satan should get an advantage of us: for we are not ignorant of his devices.

      ii. **John 8:7 (KJV)** So when they continued asking him, he lifted up himself, and said unto them, He that is without sin among you, let him first cast a stone at her.

      iii. **John 8:8 (KJV)** And again he stooped down, and wrote on the ground.

      iv. **John 8:9 (KJV)** And they which heard *it*, being convicted by *their own* conscience, went out one by one, beginning at the eldest, *even* unto the last: and Jesus was left alone, and the woman standing in the midst.

      v. **John 8:10 (KJV)** When Jesus had lifted up himself, and saw none but the woman, he said unto her, Woman, where are those thine accusers? hath no man condemned thee?

      vi. **John 8:11 (KJV)** She said, No man, Lord. And Jesus said unto her, Neither do I condemn thee: go, and sin no more.

      vii. **Matthew 6:15 (KJV)** But if ye forgive not men their trespasses, neither will your Father forgive your trespasses.

      viii. **Matthew 18:35 (KJV)** So likewise shall my heavenly Father do also unto you, if ye from your hearts forgive not every one his brother their trespasses.

      ix. **Mark 11:26 (KJV)** But if ye do not forgive, neither will your Father which is in heaven forgive your trespasses.

32. Furthermore, one of the most serious reasons why we need to forgive after one has repented and forsaken the sin is because of the power of the Gospel of Christ in every true Man of God, either to kill or to save alive! The truth is that, when a person lives in sin, then, the words of a true Man of God leads him to death! On the other hand, when a person lives in obedience to the Word of God, then, the words of a true Man of God leads him to life!

     i. **2 Corinthians 2:14 (KJV)** Now thanks *be* unto God, which always causeth us to triumph in Christ, and maketh manifest the savour of his knowledge by us in every place.

     ii. **2 Corinthians 2:15 (KJV)** For we are unto God a sweet savour of Christ, in them that are saved, and in them that perish:

     iii. **2 Corinthians 2:16 (KJV)** To the one *we are* the savour of death unto death; and to the other the savour of life unto life. And who *is* sufficient for these things?

     iv. **2 Corinthians 2:17 (KJV)** For we are not as many, which corrupt the word of God: but as of sincerity, but as of God, in the sight of God speak we in Christ.

     v. **John 20:19 (KJV)** Then the same day at evening, being the first *day* of the week, when the doors were shut where the disciples were assembled for fear of the Jews, came Jesus and stood in the midst, and saith unto them, Peace *be* unto you.

     vi. **John 20:20 (KJV)** And when he had so said, he shewed unto them *his* hands and his side. Then were the disciples glad, when they saw the Lord.

     vii. **John 20:21 (KJV)** Then said Jesus to them again, Peace *be* unto you: as *my* Father hath sent me, even so send I you.

     viii. **John 20:22 (KJV)** And when he had said this, he breathed on *them,* and saith unto them, Receive ye the Holy Ghost:

     ix. **John 20:23 (KJV)** Whose soever sins ye remit, they are remitted unto them; *and* whose soever *sins* ye retain, they are retained.

Saturday 20th January 2024 @ 12:01 AM – 12:57 AM

CHAPTER 3: SEVEN STEPS ON HOW TO CORRECTLY TEACH THE WORD OF GOD

33. It is inconceivable that the LORD God should give us such an imeasurably powerful instrument of Salvation, which is the Gospel of Christ, and not also give us any methodology to administer it!
    i. **Romans 1:16 (KJV)** For I am not ashamed of the gospel of Christ: for it is the power of God unto salvation to every one that believeth; to the Jew first, and also to the Greek.
    ii. **2 Corinthians 4:7 (KJV)** But we have this treasure in earthen vessels, that the excellency of the power may be of God, and not of us.

34. Therefore, thinking along the lines of the error of a lack of a Bible Interpretation Methodology in the Holy Scriptures, many humans have come up with several theories for Bible Translation and Interpretation without reasoning whether it makes any sense that God would call all human wisdom *foolishness* and then, the same God would return and hand over the translation and interpretation of what God calls *wisdom* to the same humans whom God has already condemned as foolish!
    i. **1 Corinthians 1:21 (KJV)** For after that in the wisdom of God the world by wisdom knew not God, it pleased God by the foolishness of preaching to save them that believe.
    ii. **1 Corinthians 3:19 (KJV)** For the wisdom of this world is foolishness with God. For it is written, He taketh the wise in their own craftiness.

35. How can foolish human beings exercise the power of correct understanding and interpretation of that which is NOT foolish but pure wisdom?
    i. **Deuteronomy 4:5 (KJV)** Behold, I have taught you statutes and judgments, even as the LORD my God commanded me, that ye should do so in the land whither ye go to possess it.
    ii. **Deuteronomy 4:6 (KJV)** Keep therefore and do *them*; for this *is* your wisdom and your understanding in the sight of the nations, which shall hear all these statutes, and say, Surely this great nation *is* a wise and understanding people.
    iii. **Psalm 119:140 (KJV)** Thy word *is* very pure: therefore thy servant loveth it.
    iv. **Proverbs 30:5 (KJV)** Every word of God *is* pure: he *is* a shield unto them that put their trust in him.
    v. **Jeremiah 4:22 (KJV)** For my people *is* foolish, they have not known me; they *are* sottish children, and they have none understanding: they *are* wise to do evil, but to do good they have no knowledge.

     vi.   **Haggai 2:14 (KJV)** Then answered Haggai, and said, So *is* this people, and so *is* this nation before me, saith the LORD; and so *is* every work of their hands; and that which they offer there *is* unclean.

36. If sinful men, and NOT God, shall decide on the correct meaning of the instrument (Word of God) that takes men to Heaven, then where is the need for the LORD God to write the Word of God Himself and not rather leave it to men to do so?

     i.   **Exodus 34:28 (KJV)** And he was there with the LORD forty days and forty nights; he did neither eat bread, nor drink water. And he wrote upon the tables the words of the covenant, the ten commandments.

     ii.   **Exodus 31:18 (KJV)** And he gave unto Moses, when he had made an end of communing with him upon mount Sinai, two tables of testimony, tables of stone, written with the finger of God.

     iii.   **Deuteronomy 9:10 (KJV)** And the LORD delivered unto me two tables of stone written with the finger of God; and on them *was written* according to all the words, which the LORD spake with you in the mount out of the midst of the fire in the day of the assembly.

     iv.   **Exodus 34:1 (KJV)** And the LORD said unto Moses, Hew thee two tables of stone like unto the first: and I will write upon *these* tables the words that were in the first tables, which thou brakest.

     v.   **Deuteronomy 10:2 (KJV)** And I will write on the tables the words that were in the first tables which thou brakest, and thou shalt put them in the ark.

     vi.   **Jeremiah 31:33 (KJV)** But this *shall be* the covenant that I will make with the house of Israel; After those days, saith the LORD, I will put my law in their inward parts, and write it in their hearts; and will be their God, and they shall be my people.

     vii.   **Hebrews 8:10 (KJV)** For this *is* the covenant that I will make with the house of Israel after those days, saith the Lord; I will put my laws into their mind, and write them in their hearts: and I will be to them a God, and they shall be to me a people:

     viii.   **Hebrews 10:16 (KJV)** This *is* the covenant that I will make with them after those days, saith the Lord, I will put my laws into their hearts, and in their minds will I write them;

     ix.   **Revelation 3:12 (KJV)** Him that overcometh will I make a pillar in the temple of my God, and he shall go no more out: and I will write upon him the name of my God, and the name of the city of my God, *which is* new Jerusalem, which cometh down out of heaven from my God: and *I will write upon him* my new name.

37. That is why every Theory for Bible Translation and Interpretation, and every Methodology for Bible Translation and Interpretation, and every Approach to Bible Translation and Interpretation, that was devised by humans, is condemned as foolishness even before it sees the light of day, because man is the sum product of all his error thoughts, of all his error words, and of all his error deeds, which triple levels of error are also transferred into every Theory for Bible Translation and Interpretation that he devises!

      i. **Matthew 12:37 (KJV)** For by thy words thou shalt be justified, and by thy words thou shalt be condemned.

      ii. **John 3:18 (KJV)** He that believeth on him is not condemned: but he that believeth not is condemned already, because he hath not believed in the name of the only begotten Son of God.

      iii. **Hebrews 11:7 (KJV)** By faith Noah, being warned of God of things not seen as yet, moved with fear, prepared an ark to the saving of his house; by the which he condemned the world, and became heir of the righteousness which is by faith.

      iv. **Romans 11:32 (KJV)** For God hath concluded them all in unbelief, that he might have mercy upon all.

      v. **Galatians 3:22 (KJV)** But the scripture hath concluded all under sin, that the promise by faith of Jesus Christ might be given to them that believe.

      vi. **Romans 7:18 (KJV)** For I know that in me (that is, in my flesh,) dwelleth no good thing: for to will is present with me; but *how* to perform that which is good I find not.

      vii. **2 Corinthians 2:17 (KJV)** For we are not as many, which corrupt the word of God: but as of sincerity, but as of God, in the sight of God speak we in Christ.

38. STEP #1:

39. In order to correctly teach or preach the Word of God, the first step is to learn how to "speak in Christ" as **2 Corinthians 2:17 (KJV)** reveals!

40. What does it mean to "speak in Christ"?

41. It simply means to speak ONLY what the Gospel of Christ speaks, permits, directs, and allows!

      i. **Numbers 22:20 (KJV)** And God came unto Balaam at night, and said unto him, If the men come to call thee, rise up, *and* go with them; but yet the word which I shall say unto thee, that shalt thou do.

      ii. **Ezekiel 3:4 (KJV)** And he said unto me, Son of man, go, get thee unto the house of Israel, and speak with my words unto them.

    iii. **John 3:34 (KJV)** For he whom God hath sent speaketh the words of God: for God giveth not the Spirit by measure *unto him*.

    iv. **Numbers 22:35 (KJV)** And the angel of the LORD said unto Balaam, Go with the men: but only the word that I shall speak unto thee, that thou shalt speak. So Balaam went with the princes of Balak.

    v. **Numbers 22:36 (KJV)** And when Balak heard that Balaam was come, he went out to meet him unto a city of Moab, which *is* in the border of Arnon, which *is* in the utmost coast.

    vi. **Numbers 22:37 (KJV)** And Balak said unto Balaam, Did I not earnestly send unto thee to call thee? wherefore camest thou not unto me? am I not able indeed to promote thee to honour?

    vii. **Numbers 22:38 (KJV)** And Balaam said unto Balak, Lo, I am come unto thee: have I now any power at all to say any thing? the word that God putteth in my mouth, that shall I speak.

    viii. **Revelation 19:10 (KJV)** And I fell at his feet to worship him. And he said unto me, See *thou do it* not: I am thy fellowservant, and of thy brethren that have the testimony of Jesus: worship God: for the testimony of Jesus is the spirit of prophecy.

42. In other words, if the power to speak is given to you by God according to **John 12:49 (KJV)**, and if the words that you are speaking are NOT yours but were given to you by God according to **John 17:8 (KJV)**, then you have zero entitlement to profess any meanings to those same words that do NOT belong to you in the first place!

    i. **Jeremiah 23:30 (KJV)** Therefore, behold, I *am* against the prophets, saith the LORD, that steal my words every one from his neighbour.

    ii. **John 14:10 (KJV)** Believest thou not that I am in the Father, and the Father in me? the words that I speak unto you I speak not of myself: but the Father that dwelleth in me, he doeth the works.

    iii. **John 12:49 (KJV)** For I have not spoken of myself; but the Father which sent me, he gave me a commandment, what I should say, and what I should speak.

    iv. **John 17:8 (KJV)** For I have given unto them the words which thou gavest me; and they have received *them*, and have known surely that I came out from thee, and they have believed that thou didst send me.

43. The real Owner of the words, being God Almighty, retains the right to define what HIS Words mean hence, all human Theories for Bible Translation and Interpretation are nonsense, void, and excluded!

44. STEP #2:

45. The second step to correctly teach or preach the Word of God is to measure the efficacy of the teaching, NOT in terms of pastoral commendation and approval one of the other, but in terms of actual men and women who have received the teachings of Christ from you, and, being led of the Holy Spirit, are actually walking in Truth and Righteousness daily!

    i. **2 Corinthians 3:1 (KJV)** Do we begin again to commend ourselves? or need we, as some *others*, epistles of commendation to you, or *letters* of commendation from you?

    ii. **2 Corinthians 3:2 (KJV)** Ye are our epistle written in our hearts, known and read of all men:

    iii. **2 Corinthians 3:3 (KJV)** *Forasmuch as ye are* manifestly declared to be the epistle of Christ ministered by us, written not with ink, but with the Spirit of the living God; not in tables of stone, but in fleshy tables of the heart.

    iv. **2 Corinthians 10:12 (KJV)** For we dare not make ourselves of the number, or compare ourselves with some that commend themselves: but they measuring themselves by themselves, and comparing themselves among themselves, are not wise.

46. STEP #3:

47. The third step to correctly teach or preach the Word of God is to acknowledge our own insufficiency and yield our insufficiency to the sufficiency of God who owns the words that we are preaching and teaching!

    i. **2 Corinthians 3:4 (KJV)** And such trust have we through Christ to God-ward:

    ii. **2 Corinthians 3:5 (KJV)** Not that we are sufficient of ourselves to think any thing as of ourselves; but our sufficiency *is* of God;

48. STEP #4:

49. The fourth step to correctly teach or preach the Word of God is to identify and to recognize the two-prong meanings in the Word of God, which are "the letter of the text" (the physical meaning) and "the spirit of the text" (the spiritual meaning), and, then, in your preaching or teaching, to emphasize and focus on "the spirit of the text", because God is Spirit and never physical!

    i. **2 Corinthians 3:6 (KJV)** Who also hath made us able ministers of the new testament; not of the letter, but of the spirit: for the letter killeth, but the spirit giveth life.

    ii. **John 4:23 (KJV)** But the hour cometh, and now is, when the true worshippers shall worship the Father in spirit and in truth: for the Father seeketh such to worship him.

iii. **John 4:24 (KJV)** God *is* a Spirit: and they that worship him must worship *him* in spirit and in truth.

iv. **Acts 7:48 (KJV)** Howbeit the most High dwelleth not in temples made with hands; as saith the prophet,

v. **Acts 17:24 (KJV)** God that made the world and all things therein, seeing that he is Lord of heaven and earth, dwelleth not in temples made with hands;

vi. **Acts 17:25 (KJV)** Neither is worshipped with men's hands, as though he needed any thing, seeing he giveth to all life, and breath, and all things;

50. STEP #5:

51. The fifth step to correctly teach or preach the Word of God is to recognize the consequence of dwelling on the physical in God-worship, which consequence is death! That form of preaching and teaching the Word of God that considers the physical meaning of the Word of God as essential is called "the ministration of death"! In other words, all the Old Testament physical forms of God-worship were NOT unto life but into death!

i. **2 Corinthians 3:7 (KJV)** But if the ministration of death, written *and* engraven in stones, was glorious, so that the children of Israel could not stedfastly behold the face of Moses for the glory of his countenance; which *glory* was to be done away:

ii. **Romans 3:20 (KJV)** Therefore by the deeds of the law there shall no flesh be justified in his sight: for by the law *is* the knowledge of sin.

iii. **Romans 8:13 (KJV)** For if ye live after the flesh, ye shall die: but if ye through the Spirit do mortify the deeds of the body, ye shall live.

iv. **Romans 3:20 (KJV)** Therefore by the deeds of the law there shall no flesh be justified in his sight: for by the law *is* the knowledge of sin.

v. **Galatians 2:16 (KJV)** Knowing that a man is not justified by the works of the law, but by the faith of Jesus Christ, even we have believed in Jesus Christ, that we might be justified by the faith of Christ, and not by the works of the law: for by the works of the law shall no flesh be justified.

52. Hence, for example, it is called "the ministration of death", or, it is understood that you the Pastor or Bishop, you are administering death to the congregation when you read **Luke 22:19-20 (KJV)** and then you proceed to think and to preach that the LORD Jesus Christ wants you to eat and drink physical bread, wafers, and wine!

     i. **Luke 22:19 (KJV)** And he took bread, and gave thanks, and brake *it*, and gave unto them, saying, This is my body which is given for you: this do in remembrance of me.

     ii. **Luke 22:20 (KJV)** Likewise also the cup after supper, saying, This cup *is* the new testament in my blood, which is shed for you.

53. The moment that you choose to stay with the physical meaning of **Luke 22:19-20 (KJV)**, that is the same moment that you fell into the condemnation of **2 Corinthians 3:6 (KJV)**, and also, are in violation of the same!

54. The same doctrine of "the ministration of death" is applicable in all instances of the Word of God where you choose to present/minister the physical instead of the spiriual side of the same, why? Because the physical is already done away with! When was that? The physical was abolished in **John 4:23-24 (KJV)**!

     i. **2 Corinthians 3:8 (KJV)** How shall not the ministration of the spirit be rather glorious?

     ii. **2 Corinthians 3:9 (KJV)** For if the ministration of condemnation *be* glory, much more doth the ministration of righteousness exceed in glory.

     iii. **2 Corinthians 3:10 (KJV)** For even that which was made glorious had no glory in this respect, by reason of the glory that excelleth.

     iv. **2 Corinthians 3:11 (KJV)** For if that which is done away *was* glorious, much more that which remaineth *is* glorious.

     v. **John 4:23 (KJV)** But the hour cometh, and now is, when the true worshippers shall worship the Father in spirit and in truth: for the Father seeketh such to worship him.

     vi. **John 4:24 (KJV)** God *is* a Spirit: and they that worship him must worship *him* in spirit and in truth.

55. **STEP #6:**

56. The sixth step to correctly teach or preach the Word of God is to be fully convinced that the greatness of dropping the physical aspects of God-worship and placing all hope in the "ministration of the Spirit", or, in the act of "speaking in Christ", lies in the fact that you assume zero responsibility for all things spiritual, because it is then the Holy Spirit who is in control and responsible for the words of the LORD God Almighty, and not you!

     i. **2 Corinthians 3:12 (KJV)** Seeing then that we have such hope, we use great plainness of speech:

     ii. **2 Corinthians 3:13 (KJV)** And not as Moses, *which* put a vail over his face, that the children of Israel could not stedfastly look to the end of that which is abolished:

57. STEP #7:

58. The seventh step to correctly teach or preach the Word of God is to learn that all the physical blindness that the LORD Jesus Christ healed were nothing in themselves since all of the healed people were going to die again anyway!

59. The reason being that the most precious healing of their blindness was NOT in their ability to physically see the world and the things in the world, but, rather, that the blindness of their minds hindering their ability to correctly understand the Word of God was taken away by Jesus Christ, and this is the same spiritual healing of the blind that you the Pastor and the Bishop should be practising and ministring in your preaching and teaching of the Word of God!

     i. **2 Corinthians 3:14 (KJV)** But their minds were blinded: for until this day remaineth the same vail untaken away in the reading of the old testament; which *vail* is done away in Christ.

60. Therefore, I testify to you by the Holy Ghost, that blindness is in the mind and in the head, and this is the real blindness that you are commanded to heal, given the fact that the eyes of man are in his head and NOT on his face!

     i. **Ecclesiastes 2:14 (KJV)** The wise man's eyes *are* in his head; but the fool walketh in darkness: and I myself perceived also that one event happeneth to them all.

     ii. **Matthew 10:8 (KJV)** Heal the sick, cleanse the lepers, raise the dead, cast out devils: freely ye have received, freely give.

     iii. **Isaiah 42:6 (KJV)** I the LORD have called thee in righteousness, and will hold thine hand, and will keep thee, and give thee for a covenant of the people, for a light of the Gentiles;

     iv. **Isaiah 42:7 (KJV)** To open the blind eyes, to bring out the prisoners from the prison, *and* them that sit in darkness out of the prison house.

     v. **Acts 26:17 (KJV)** Delivering thee from the people, and *from* the Gentiles, unto whom now I send thee,

     vi. **Acts 26:18 (KJV)** To open their eyes, *and* to turn *them* from darkness to light, and *from* the power of Satan unto God, that they may receive forgiveness of sins, and inheritance among them which are sanctified by faith that is in me.

     vii. **Isaiah 61:1 (KJV)** The Spirit of the Lord GOD *is* upon me; because the LORD hath anointed me to preach good tidings unto the meek; he hath sent me to bind up the brokenhearted, to proclaim liberty to the captives, and the opening of the prison to *them that are* bound;

     viii. **Luke 4:18 (KJV)** The Spirit of the Lord *is* upon me, because he hath anointed me to preach the gospel to the poor; he hath sent me to heal

> the brokenhearted, to preach deliverance to the captives, and recovering of sight to the blind, to set at liberty them that are bruised,

61. How very stupid are you as a Man of God teaching the physical meaning of the Word of God, when you claim that it was the LORD Jesus Christ who called you into Ministry, and yet you are blind in the spiritual meaning of the Word of God, not knowing what the Word of God means, NOT having the Holy Spirit who is The Teacher of Truth, and therefore, you go about teaching the Word of God in error and in corruption, alas, to the utter destruction of your own soul in Hell

      i. **2 Corinthians 3:15 (KJV)** But even unto this day, when Moses is read, the vail is upon their heart.

      ii. **2 Corinthians 3:16 (KJV)** Nevertheless when it shall turn to the Lord, the vail shall be taken away.

      iii. **2 Corinthians 2:17 (KJV)** For we are not as many, which corrupt the word of God: but as of sincerity, but as of God, in the sight of God speak we in Christ.

      iv. **Acts 13:10 (KJV)** And said, O full of all subtilty and all mischief, *thou* child of the devil, *thou* enemy of all righteousness, wilt thou not cease to pervert the right ways of the Lord?

      v. **Galatians 1:7 (KJV)** Which is not another; but there be some that trouble you, and would pervert the gospel of Christ.

62. In conclusion, the Man of God who focuses on the spiritual side of the Word of God is demonstrating liberty in Chirst! Liberty from what? Liberty, or breaking away, from the physical and entering into one accord with the Spirit of the Lord, to manifest the spiritual, by means of daily beholding ourselves in the mirror and glass of the Gospel of Christ, to read the Word, to meditate in the Word, and to observe diligently to do all the commandments of the LORD God Almighty, so deeply and so intently that we end by becoming like the same Christ image whom we behold in the glass of the perfect Law of Liberty!

      i. **2 Corinthians 3:17 (KJV)** Now the Lord is that Spirit: and where the Spirit of the Lord *is*, there *is* liberty.

      ii. **2 Corinthians 3:18 (KJV)** But we all, with open face beholding as in a glass the glory of the Lord, are changed into the same image from glory to glory, *even* as by the Spirit of the Lord.

      iii. **Job 37:18 (KJV)** Hast thou with him spread out the sky, *which is* strong, *and* as a molten looking glass?

      iv. **James 1:25 (KJV)** But whoso looketh into the perfect law of liberty, and continueth *therein*, he being not a forgetful hearer, but a doer of the work, this man shall be blessed in his deed.

v. **Philippians 2:5 (KJV)** Let this mind be in you, which was also in Christ Jesus:

Saturday 20th January 2024 @ 11:01 AM – 3:37 PM

CHAPTER 4: HOW TO HAVE A SUCCESSFUL MINISTRY AS A MAN OF GOD

63. Here are the Seven Steps to a successful Ministry!

64. **Successful Ministry Step 1:**

65. As a true Man of God, the instrument that you receive for a successful Ministry is the Gospel of Christ!

   i. **2 Corinthians 4:1 (KJV)** Therefore seeing we have this ministry, as we have received mercy, we faint not;

66. **Successful Ministry Step 2:**

67. You have to renounce all lying and all dishonesty. You will NOT handle the Word of God deceitfully! You will always walk in Truth and Righteosness!

   i. **2 Corinthians 4:2 (KJV)** But have renounced the hidden things of dishonesty, not walking in craftiness, nor handling the word of God deceitfully; but by manifestation of the truth commending ourselves to every man's conscience in the sight of God.

68. **Successful Ministry Step 3:**

69. You have to preach Christ always. Every sermon, every theme, every subject, every topic, and every doctrine that you teach in your entire Ministry has to glorify the LORD Jesus Christ, with the purpose of opening the blinded minds of all those who believe not the Gospel of Christ!

   i. **2 Corinthians 4:3 (KJV)** But if our gospel be hid, it is hid to them that are lost:

   ii. **2 Corinthians 4:4 (KJV)** In whom the god of this world hath blinded the minds of them which believe not, lest the light of the glorious gospel of Christ, who is the image of God, should shine unto them.

   iii. **2 Corinthians 4:5 (KJV)** For we preach not ourselves, but Christ Jesus the Lord; and ourselves your servants for Jesus' sake.

   iv. **2 Corinthians 4:6 (KJV)** For God, who commanded the light to shine out of darkness, hath shined in our hearts, to *give* the light of the knowledge of the glory of God in the face of Jesus Christ.

70. The revelation in **2 Corinthians 4:3-6 (KJV)** shows you that when the LORD Jesus Christ commanded you to heal the sick and open the eyes of the blind, the correct meaning is **2 Corinthians 4:3-6 (KJV)** whereby, you open the eyes of the blind whose eyes are in his head and NOT on his face, by means of teaching him the Gospel of Christ, which Gospel is the Light that leads him out of the darkness in which he dwells! Lack of knowledge, or ignorance, is blindness hence, as the knowledge of Christ is the Light that dispels the darkness and the blindness!

    i. **Isaiah 29:18 (KJV)** And in that day shall the deaf hear the words of the book, and the eyes of the blind shall see out of obscurity, and out of darkness.

    ii. **Matthew 4:16 (KJV)** The people which sat in darkness saw great light; and to them which sat in the region and shadow of death light is sprung up.

    iii. **Matthew 10:8 (KJV)** Heal the sick, cleanse the lepers, raise the dead, cast out devils: freely ye have received, freely give.

    iv. **Luke 7:22 (KJV)** Then Jesus answering said unto them, Go your way, and tell John what things ye have seen and heard; how that the blind see, the lame walk, the lepers are cleansed, the deaf hear, the dead are raised, to the poor the gospel is preached.

    v. **Luke 10:9 (KJV)** And heal the sick that are therein, and say unto them, The kingdom of God is come nigh unto you.

71. **Successful Ministry Step 4**:

72. The spiritual instrument of the Gospel of Christ and its power to heal the blind is a treasure that is hidden in the fragile human bodyframe of the Man of God that can be killed, and this combination of the excellent power of Christ housed in a weak human body is deliberate in order to produce utmost carefulness and circumspection on the part of the Man of God!

73. And the LORD God has made it so, so that such great power of Christ should NOT reside in invincible human beings who would then become aware of their power and invincibility and then begin to use it wickedly and destructively!

    i. **2 Corinthians 4:7 (KJV)** But we have this treasure in earthen vessels, that the excellency of the power may be of God, and not of us.

    ii. **Luke 9:51 (KJV)** And it came to pass, when the time was come that he should be received up, he stedfastly set his face to go to Jerusalem,

    iii. **Luke 9:52 (KJV)** And sent messengers before his face: and they went, and entered into a village of the Samaritans, to make ready for him.

    iv. **Luke 9:53 (KJV)** And they did not receive him, because his face was as though he would go to Jerusalem.

    v. **Luke 9:54 (KJV)** And when his disciples James and John saw *this*, they said, Lord, wilt thou that we command fire to come down from heaven, and consume them, even as Elias did?

    vi. **Luke 9:55 (KJV)** But he turned, and rebuked them, and said, Ye know not what manner of spirit ye are of.

    vii. **Luke 9:56 (KJV)** For the Son of man is not come to destroy men's lives, but to save *them*. And they went to another village.

74. **Successful Ministry Step 5**:

75. Being troubled, perplexed, persecuted, cast down, always bearing about in the body the dying of the Lord Jesus, always delivered unto death for Jesus' sake, daily reflecting the sufferings of Christ in our own flesh, often experiencing death that works in us, even as they are named in **2 Corinthians 4:8-12 (KJV)**, those are some of the elements of fragility that accompany the power of Christ in the true Man of God as a deliberate spiritual arrangement to buffet him and to knock him into place, so that he does NOT become oversized or rise up above Godly humility and service!

    i. **2 Corinthians 4:8 (KJV)** *We are* troubled on every side, yet not distressed; *we are* perplexed, but not in despair;

    ii. **2 Corinthians 4:9 (KJV)** Persecuted, but not forsaken; cast down, but not destroyed;

    iii. **2 Corinthians 4:10 (KJV)** Always bearing about in the body the dying of the Lord Jesus, that the life also of Jesus might be made manifest in our body.

    iv. **2 Corinthians 4:11 (KJV)** For we which live are alway delivered unto death for Jesus' sake, that the life also of Jesus might be made manifest in our mortal flesh.

    v. **2 Corinthians 4:12 (KJV)** So then death worketh in us, but life in you.

76. Here is just one example of Apostle Paul's fragility that accompany the power of Christ in the true Man of God as a deliberate spiritual arrangement to buffet him so that he does not fall into sin!

    i. **2 Corinthians 12:6 (KJV)** For though I would desire to glory, I shall not be a fool; for I will say the truth: but *now* I forbear, lest any man should think of me above that which he seeth me *to be*, or *that* he heareth of me.

    ii. **2 Corinthians 12:7 (KJV)** And lest I should be exalted above measure through the abundance of the revelations, there was given to me a thorn in the flesh, the messenger of Satan to buffet me, lest I should be exalted above measure.

    iii. **2 Corinthians 12:8 (KJV)** For this thing I besought the Lord thrice, that it might depart from me.

    iv. **2 Corinthians 12:9 (KJV)** And he said unto me, My grace is sufficient for thee: for my strength is made perfect in weakness. Most gladly therefore will I rather glory in my infirmities, that the power of Christ may rest upon me.

v. **2 Corinthians 12:10 (KJV)** Therefore I take pleasure in infirmities, in reproaches, in necessities, in persecutions, in distresses for Christ's sake: for when I am weak, then am I strong.

77. Successful Ministry Step 6:

78. The second reason for the elements of fragility that accompany the power of Christ in the true Man of God as a deliberate spiritual arrangement by God Almighty, is that these elements of fragility serve to orient the Man of God into the Faith of Christ, to anchor him deeper to trust God in all adversities, to cause him to focus on the unseen spiritual and faith and on the inner man whose replenishment is day by day, according as he the Man of God hmself walks in Truth and Righteousness!

i. **2 Corinthians 4:13 (KJV)** We having the same spirit of faith, according as it is written, I believed, and therefore have I spoken; we also believe, and therefore speak;

ii. **2 Corinthians 4:14 (KJV)** Knowing that he which raised up the Lord Jesus shall raise up us also by Jesus, and shall present *us* with you.

iii. **2 Corinthians 4:15 (KJV)** For all things *are* for your sakes, that the abundant grace might through the thanksgiving of many redound to the glory of God.

iv. **2 Corinthians 4:16 (KJV)** For which cause we faint not; but though our outward man perish, yet the inward *man* is renewed day by day.

v. **Lamentations 3:21 (KJV)** This I recall to my mind, therefore have I hope.

vi. **Lamentations 3:22 (KJV)** *It is of* the LORD'S mercies that we are not consumed, because his compassions fail not.

vii. **Lamentations 3:23 (KJV)** *They are* new every morning: great *is* thy faithfulness.

viii. **Matthew 6:11 (KJV)** Give us this day our daily bread.

ix. **Ephesians 4:23 (KJV)** And be renewed in the spirit of your mind;

x. **Ephesians 4:24 (KJV)** And that ye put on the new man, which after God is created in righteousness and true holiness.

79. Successful Ministry Step 7:

80. The true Man of God should count as nothing all the elements of fragility that accompany the power of Christ in Ministry, even as they are named in **2 Corinthians 4:8-12 (KJV)**: being troubled, perplexed, persecuted, cast down, always bearing about in the body the dying of the Lord Jesus, always delivered unto death for Jesus' sake, daily reflecting the sufferings of Christ in our own flesh, often experiencing death that works in us! The reason that the true Man of God should count all human suffering as nothing is that, compared to the glory that will be revealed in the true Man of God

who is able to do this thing, all the suffering on Earth are actually "light affliction, which is but for a moment"!

> i. **2 Corinthians 4:17 (KJV)** For our light affliction, which is but for a moment, worketh for us a far more exceeding *and* eternal weight of glory;
>
> ii. **Revelation 2:10 (KJV)** Fear none of those things which thou shalt suffer: behold, the devil shall cast *some* of you into prison, that ye may be tried; and ye shall have tribulation ten days: be thou faithful unto death, and I will give thee a crown of life.

81. In conclusion, the LORD God returns to re-emphasize the importance of focusing on the unseen spiritual and faith and on the inner man whose replenishment is day by day, according as he the Man of God hmself is walking in Truth and Righteousness, exorting the Man of God to learn that, for his Ministry to be successful, then, he must "NOT look at the things which are seen, but at the things which are not seen", meaning: cast out all physical forms of God-worship such as the use of oils, the use of water in Water Baptism, and the use of man-made oblations in Holy Commucion!

> i. **2 Corinthians 4:18 (KJV)** While we look not at the things which are seen, but at the things which are not seen: for the things which are seen *are* temporal; but the things which are not seen *are* eternal.

82. If you are a true Man of God, then, you do NOT walk by sight but by the unseen Faith of Christ, and to this declarion, I hear all the Men of God agreeing with me and sayng: Amen!

83. That is why all these same Men of God who are agreeing with me are fools to claim that you walk by the unseen Faith of Christ and yet, immediately after you have said that, you take filty physical Water Baptism excreta-infested rver water to baptize equally foolish people like you into Hell, and then, after that, you also pick up fiulthy man-made Holy Communion oblations of wafers, wine, and bread with your filthy hands and you begin to offer those same filthy things unto God Almighty as your worship!

84. Since when did Water Baptism excreta-infested rver water qualify as holy and acceptable in Heaven?

85. Since when did fiulthy man-made Holy Communion oblations of wafers, wine, and bread acquire a new definition as part of Faith?

> i. **2 Corinthians 4:1 (KJV)** Therefore seeing we have this ministry, as we have received mercy, we faint not;
>
> ii. **2 Corinthians 4:2 (KJV)** But have renounced the hidden things of dishonesty, not walking in craftiness, nor handling the word of God

deceitfully; but by manifestation of the truth commending ourselves to every man's conscience in the sight of God.

86. That is why the first step to having a successful Ministry referenced in **2 Corinthians 4:1-2 (KJV)** as a true Man of God is to operate and function, "not of the letter, but of the spirit", meaning that you must abandon the physical and focus on the spiritual, on Faith only, in all aspects of Ministry, and if you refuse to do so, then death in Hell is your reward, and this, for the very simple reason that, God is NOT physcal but a Spirit, and so, to present God with physical things as your way of worship is insulting, is disrespectful, and is a sin!

    i. **2 Corinthians 3:6 (KJV)** Who also hath made us able ministers of the new testament; not of the letter, but of the spirit: for the letter killeth, but the spirit giveth life.

    ii. **Romans 8:13 (KJV)** For if ye live after the flesh, ye shall die: but if ye through the Spirit do mortify the deeds of the body, ye shall live.

    iii. **John 4:23 (KJV)** But the hour cometh, and now is, when the true worshippers shall worship the Father in spirit and in truth: for the Father seeketh such to worship him.

    iv. **John 4:24 (KJV)** God *is* a Spirit: and they that worship him must worship *him* in spirit and in truth.

    v. **Micah 6:6 (KJV)** Wherewith shall I come before the LORD, *and* bow myself before the high God? shall I come before him with burnt offerings, with calves of a year old?

    vi. **Micah 6:7 (KJV)** Will the LORD be pleased with thousands of rams, *or* with ten thousands of rivers of oil? shall I give my firstborn *for* my transgression, the fruit of my body *for* the sin of my soul?

    vii. **Micah 6:8 (KJV)** He hath shewed thee, O man, what *is* good; and what doth the LORD require of thee, but to do justly, and to love mercy, and to walk humbly with thy God?

87. Surely, if you refuse to do so, then, not only is death in Hell is your reward, but even before that, you expose yourself as a blind, lost, and fake Man of God whis working to Satan!

    i. **2 Corinthians 4:3 (KJV)** But if our gospel be hid, it is hid to them that are lost:

    ii. **2 Corinthians 4:4 (KJV)** In whom the god of this world hath blinded the minds of them which believe not, lest the light of the glorious gospel of Christ, who is the image of God, should shine unto them.

Sunday 21st January 2024 @ 10:00 AM – 11:59 AM

CHAPTER 5: IMPORTANT TOPICS IN THE MINISTRY OF RECONCILIATION

88. The Ministry of Reconciliation is the main work that a true Man of God must do immediately after his calling, and in this chapter, we are going to learn the main topics that the Man of God is expected to preach and to teach in order to fulfill this Ministry of Reconciliation!

89. **Ministry of Reconciliation Topic #1:**
    i. **2 Corinthians 5:1 (KJV)** For we know that if our earthly house of *this* tabernacle were dissolved, we have a building of God, an house not made with hands, eternal in the heavens.
    ii. **2 Corinthians 5:2 (KJV)** For in this we groan, earnestly desiring to be clothed upon with our house which is from heaven:

90. You must begin to envision and walk in the concept of the hereafter, the life after your departure from the Earth, a realm of the spiritual and the non-physical hand of flesh!

91. **Ministry of Reconciliation Topic #2:**
    i. **2 Corinthians 5:3 (KJV)** If so be that being clothed we shall not be found naked.
    ii. **2 Corinthians 5:4 (KJV)** For we that are in *this* tabernacle do groan, being burdened: not for that we would be unclothed, but clothed upon, that mortality might be swallowed up of life.
    iii. **2 Corinthians 5:5 (KJV)** Now he that hath wrought us for the selfsame thing *is* God, who also hath given unto us the earnest of the Spirit.

92. While you work and execute your Ministry of Reconciliation in expectation of your life in Heaven, your assurance and guarantee that you will be successful come from your daily walk in Truth and Righteousness, led by the Holy Spirit of God!

93. You will know that you have the Holy Spirit when the thoughts of your head are always in the Gospel of Christ, because that is the only work that the Holy Spirit does!
    i. **John 14:26 (KJV)** But the Comforter, *which is* the Holy Ghost, whom the Father will send in my name, he shall teach you all things, and bring all things to your remembrance, whatsoever I have said unto you.
    ii. **John 15:26 (KJV)** But when the Comforter is come, whom I will send unto you from the Father, *even* the Spirit of truth, which proceedeth from the Father, he shall testify of me:
    iii. **John 16:13 (KJV)** Howbeit when he, the Spirit of truth, is come, he will guide you into all truth: for he shall not speak of himself; but

whatsoever he shall hear, *that* shall he speak: and he will shew you things to come.

    iv. **John 16:14 (KJV)** He shall glorify me: for he shall receive of mine, and shall shew *it* unto you.

    v. **Philippians 1:27 (KJV)** Only let your conversation be as it becometh the gospel of Christ: that whether I come and see you, or else be absent, I may hear of your affairs, that ye stand fast in one spirit, with one mind striving together for the faith of the gospel;

94. However, when your thoughts, your preaching, your actions, and your utterances are outside of the Gospel of Christ, then, know that you are of the Devil your father!

    i. **John 8:43 (KJV)** Why do ye not understand my speech? *even* because ye cannot hear my word.

    ii. **John 8:44 (KJV)** Ye are of *your* father the devil, and the lusts of your father ye will do. He was a murderer from the beginning, and abode not in the truth, because there is no truth in him. When he speaketh a lie, he speaketh of his own: for he is a liar, and the father of it.

    iii. **John 8:45 (KJV)** And because I tell *you* the truth, ye believe me not.

    iv. **Matthew 7:16 (KJV)** Ye shall know them by their fruits. Do men gather grapes of thorns, or figs of thistles?

    v. **Matthew 7:20 (KJV)** Wherefore by their fruits ye shall know them.

95. **Ministry of Reconciliation Topic #3:**

    i. **2 Corinthians 5:6 (KJV)** Therefore *we are* always confident, knowing that, whilst we are at home in the body, we are absent from the Lord:

    ii. **2 Corinthians 5:7 (KJV)** (For we walk by faith, not by sight:)

    iii. **2 Corinthians 5:8 (KJV)** We are confident, *I say*, and willing rather to be absent from the body, and to be present with the Lord.

    iv. **2 Corinthians 5:9 (KJV)** Wherefore we labour, that, whether present or absent, we may be accepted of him.

96. As a true Man of God who is executing your Ministry of Reconciliation, one of the topics that you should teach is: Where does the human spirit go after death?

97. And the answer is given you there in **2 Corinthians 5:6 (KJV)** saying:

    i. "Therefore *we are* always confident, knowing that, whilst we are at home in the body, we are absent from the Lord"!

98. So, it is an automatic transformation for the true child of God whereby:

    i. You exit this flesh body and you immediately enter your spiritual body from Heaven! OR

ii. In the case where you are a child of Satan, then, you exit this flesh body and you are immediately naked without any clothing and sent to the fire of Hell!

iii. **2 Corinthians 5:3 (KJV)** If so be that being clothed we shall not be found naked.

99. **Ministry of Reconciliation Topic #4**:

100. As a true Man of God who is executing your Ministry of Reconciliation, another topic that you should teach is mentioned in **2 Corinthians 5:7 (KJV)**!

i. **2 Corinthians 5:7 (KJV)** (For we walk by faith, not by sight:)

101. You must teach your followers and congregation that "we walk by faith and not by sight", meaning that all forms of physical items, such as your filthy Water Baptism river waters, your filthy Holy Communion wafers, wine, bread, your oils, your prophetic tokens, your lifeless concrete church buildings, they are all outlawed and contrary to true God-worship, even as the LORD Jesus Christ also taught!

i. **John 4:23 (KJV)** But the hour cometh, and now is, when the true worshippers shall worship the Father in spirit and in truth: for the Father seeketh such to worship him.

ii. **John 4:24 (KJV)** God *is* a Spirit: and they that worship him must worship *him* in spirit and in truth.

iii. **Ephesians 5:9 (KJV)** (For the fruit of the Spirit *is* in all goodness and righteousness and truth;)

iv. **Matthew 26:61 (KJV)** And said, This *fellow* said, I am able to destroy the temple of God, and to build it in three days.

v. **Mark 14:58 (KJV)** We heard him say, I will destroy this temple that is made with hands, and within three days I will build another made without hands.

vi. **John 2:19 (KJV)** Jesus answered and said unto them, Destroy this temple, and in three days I will raise it up.

vii. **Acts 7:48 (KJV)** Howbeit the most High dwelleth not in temples made with hands; as saith the prophet,

viii. **Acts 17:24 (KJV)** God that made the world and all things therein, seeing that he is Lord of heaven and earth, dwelleth not in temples made with hands;

ix. **Acts 17:25 (KJV)** Neither is worshipped with men's hands, as though he needed any thing, seeing he giveth to all life, and breath, and all things;

102. **Ministry of Reconciliation Topic #5**:

     i. **2 Corinthians 5:10 (KJV)** For we must all appear before the judgment seat of Christ; that every one may receive the things *done* in *his* body, according to that he hath done, whether *it be* good or bad.

     ii. **2 Corinthians 5:11 (KJV)** Knowing therefore the terror of the Lord, we persuade men; but we are made manifest unto God; and I trust also are made manifest in your consciences.

103.   As a true Man of God who is executing your Ministry of Reconciliation, another topic that you should teach is mentioned in **2 Corinthians 5:10-11 (KJV)** and it is the tipic of full accountability for every word and act that each of us has uttered and done in his or her lifetime on the earth!

     i. **Ecclesiastes 11:9 (KJV)** Rejoice, O young man, in thy youth; and let thy heart cheer thee in the days of thy youth, and walk in the ways of thine heart, and in the sight of thine eyes: but know thou, that for all these *things* God will bring thee into judgment.

     ii. **Romans 14:12 (KJV)** So then every one of us shall give account of himself to God.

     iii. **1 Peter 4:5 (KJV)** Who shall give account to him that is ready to judge the quick and the dead.

104.   **Ministry of Reconciliation Topic #6**:

     i. **2 Corinthians 5:12 (KJV)** For we commend not ourselves again unto you, but give you occasion to glory on our behalf, that ye may have somewhat to *answer* them which glory in appearance, and not in heart.

     ii. **2 Corinthians 5:13 (KJV)** For whether we be beside ourselves, *it is* to God: or whether we be sober, *it is* for your cause.

     iii. **2 Corinthians 5:14 (KJV)** For the love of Christ constraineth us; because we thus judge, that if one died for all, then were all dead:

     iv. **2 Corinthians 5:15 (KJV)** And *that* he died for all, that they which live should not henceforth live unto themselves, but unto him which died for them, and rose again.

     v. **2 Corinthians 5:16 (KJV)** Wherefore henceforth know we no man after the flesh: yea, though we have known Christ after the flesh, yet now henceforth know we *him* no more.

105.   As a true Man of God who is executing your Ministry of Reconciliation, another topic that you should teach is mentioned in **2 Corinthians 5:12-16 (KJV)** and it is the tipic of appropriating all the works and gifts of Christ through ONLY the knowledge and understanding of the Gospel of Christ!

  i. **2 Corinthians 5:5 (KJV)** Now he that hath wrought us for the selfsame thing *is* God, who also hath given unto us the earnest of the Spirit.

106. Meaning that, once you become truly born again and then you have "the earnest of the Spirit" from Heaven, then, you do not any longer need to repeat the works that the LORD Jesus Christ has already accomplished on your behalf freely, because Jesus Christ did every work once for all times!

  i. **Jeremiah 3:15 (KJV)** And I will give you pastors according to mine heart, which shall feed you with knowledge and understanding.

  ii. **Malachi 2:7 (KJV)** For the priest's lips should keep knowledge, and they should seek the law at his mouth: for he *is* the messenger of the LORD of hosts.

  iii. **John 5:24 (KJV)** Verily, verily, I say unto you, He that heareth my word, and believeth on him that sent me, hath everlasting life, and shall not come into condemnation; but is passed from death unto life.

  iv. **2 Corinthians 5:16 (KJV)** Wherefore henceforth know we no man after the flesh: yea, though we have known Christ after the flesh, yet now henceforth know we *him* no more.

  v. **Hebrews 10:10 (KJV)** By the which will we are sanctified through the offering of the body of Jesus Christ once *for all*.

  vi. **Romans 5:15 (KJV)** But not as the offence, so also *is* the free gift. For if through the offence of one many be dead, much more the grace of God, and the gift by grace, *which is* by one man, Jesus Christ, hath abounded unto many.

  vii. **Romans 5:17 (KJV)** For if by one man's offence death reigned by one; much more they which receive abundance of grace and of the gift of righteousness shall reign in life by one, Jesus Christ.)

107. Besides, if you are to compare what the LORD Jesus Christ accomplished to what you will be able to accomplish in one million years, yours will always be filthy, inadequate, and unacceptable in Heaven hence, the correct way of worship is always by knowledge and understanding, and NEVER BY PHYSICAL WORKS of Water Baptism or Holy Communion or Crucifixion or Circumcision!

108. As the LORD Jesus Christ Himself affirmed in **John 5:24 (KJV)**, all the fullness of the Christian's righteousness is embedded in just one thing: "He that heareth my word, and believeth on him that sent me"!

109. **Ministry of Reconciliation Topic #7:**

i. **2 Corinthians 5:17 (KJV)** Therefore if any man *be* in Christ, *he is* a new creature: old things are passed away; behold, all things are become new.

ii. **2 Corinthians 5:18 (KJV)** And all things *are* of God, who hath reconciled us to himself by Jesus Christ, and hath given to us the ministry of reconciliation;

iii. **2 Corinthians 5:19 (KJV)** To wit, that God was in Christ, reconciling the world unto himself, not imputing their trespasses unto them; and hath committed unto us the word of reconciliation.

iv. **2 Corinthians 5:20 (KJV)** Now then we are ambassadors for Christ, as though God did beseech *you* by us: we pray *you* in Christ's stead, be ye reconciled to God.

v. **2 Corinthians 5:21 (KJV)** For he hath made him *to be* sin for us, who knew no sin; that we might be made the righteousness of God in him.

110.   As a true Man of God who is executing your Ministry of Reconciliation, another topic that you should teach is mentioned in **2 Corinthians 5:17-21 (KJV)**, and it is the tipic of the newness of life for the newly born again!

111.   Now what the LORD God is showing you in **2 Corinthians 5:17-21 (KJV)** is that:

i. The moment that you, called Yaw Bonsu, becime truly saved with the seal of the Holy Spirit inside of you, that person called Yaw Bonsu died, and you are no loger that person because he is dead!

ii. You have a new living spirit from the Holy Ghost which was NOT inside that dead person!

iii. That dead spirit had a house which was your flesh and your body that everyone saw and and knew and called Yaw Bonsu!

iv. When the old dead spirit of yours was thrown out of its house, you received a new spirit from the Holy Ghost that took over the same house which was your flesh and your body that everyone saw and and knew and called Yaw Bonsu!

v. Because your old house and you new house are the same and look the same, people do not know that it is a new spirit that is now living inside of it and so, they still falsely think that you aare the same Yaw Bonsu that they knew many years before!

vi. The ONLY way that you can convince them that you are NOT the same Yaw Bonsu is when they now see you this time living in Truth and Righteousness daily, loving God, reading God's Word, searching

God's Word, obveying God, and living in the Light of the Knowledge of Christ the LORD!

Sunday 21st January 2024 @ 11:20 PM – Monday 22nd January 2024 @ 12:27 AM

CHAPTER 6: TEN JOB DESCRIPTIONS OF THE TRUE MINISTER OF GOD

112.   Is there a job description by which we can identify and know a true Man of God?

113.   **Job description #1**:

114.   The true Minister of God is first and foremost: a Worker in the enterprise of Salvation, to save souls into Heaven and unto eternal life!

     i. **2 Corinthians 6:1 (KJV)** We then, *as* workers together *with him*, beseech *you* also that ye receive not the grace of God in vain.

     ii. **2 Corinthians 6:2 (KJV)** (For he saith, I have heard thee in a time accepted, and in the day of salvation have I succoured thee: behold, now *is* the accepted time; behold, now *is* the day of salvation.)

115.   If the Man of God is a Worker, is his work then for free as some say that "freely ye have received, freely give"?

     i. **Matthew 10:8 (KJV)** Heal the sick, cleanse the lepers, raise the dead, cast out devils: freely ye have received, freely give.

116.   No, the work of the Man of God is NOT free, but, rather, it a doubly rewarded and a doubly remunerated work, both in this life, and then, in the life to come!

     i. **Matthew 19:27 (KJV)** Then answered Peter and said unto him, Behold, we have forsaken all, and followed thee; what shall we have therefore?

     ii. **Matthew 19:28 (KJV)** And Jesus said unto them, Verily I say unto you, That ye which have followed me, in the regeneration when the Son of man shall sit in the throne of his glory, ye also shall sit upon twelve thrones, judging the twelve tribes of Israel.

     iii. **Matthew 19:29 (KJV)** And every one that hath forsaken houses, or brethren, or sisters, or father, or mother, or wife, or children, or lands, for my name's sake, shall receive an hundredfold, and shall inherit everlasting life.

     iv. **Matthew 19:30 (KJV)** But many *that are* first shall be last; and the last *shall be* first.

     v. **1 Timothy 5:17 (KJV)** Let the elders that rule well be counted worthy of double honour, especially they who labour in the word and doctrine.

117.   **Job description #2**:

118.   The true Minister of God should NOT commit sin so that the Name of Christ is NOT shamed!

        i. **2 Corinthians 6:3 (KJV)** Giving no offence in any thing, that the ministry be not blamed:

119.   Job description #3:

120.   In times of afflictions, in necessities, and in distresses, still, the true Minister of God should NOT commit sin so that the Name of Christ is NOT shamed

        i. **2 Corinthians 6:4 (KJV)** But in all *things* approving ourselves as the ministers of God, in much patience, in afflictions, in necessities, in distresses,

121.   Job description #4:

122.   As part of the working conditions of the true Minister of God, he must also accept that, sometimes, he will be subjected to beatings, to imprisonments, to crowd agitations, to working with his own hands to feed himself and his family, often prayers and fastings!

        i. **2 Corinthians 6:5 (KJV)** In stripes, in imprisonments, in tumults, in labours, in watchings, in fastings;

123.   Job description #5:

124.   The true Minister of God shall also be known by the public as pure, blameless, knowledgeable in the Word of God, patient, kind, filled with the Holy Ghost, charitable in helping people, always speaking the truth, always demonstrating the power of God in his teaching of the Gospel of Christ to the saving of the soul, himself living daily in truth and righteousness, and he must be ready to receive condemnation, hatred, dishonour, evil report, and be condemned as a deceiver by all those who hate Truth and would prefer for him to stay silent in the face of evil deeds and corruption in the nation! His words and his deeds of Truth and Righteousness must reveal him as the living conscience of the nation!

        i. **2 Corinthians 6:6 (KJV)** By pureness, by knowledge, by longsuffering, by kindness, by the Holy Ghost, by love unfeigned,

        ii. **2 Corinthians 6:7 (KJV)** By the word of truth, by the power of God, by the armour of righteousness on the right hand and on the left,

        iii. **2 Corinthians 6:8 (KJV)** By honour and dishonour, by evil report and good report: as deceivers, and *yet* true;

125.   Job description #6:

126.   The true Minister of God shall also be sepaated from the people and he shall NOT be seen as a partaker of their carnal deeds that do NOT give glory to God Almighty. His works, utterances and his rebuke of sin and corruption in the nation should earn him much hatred and death from a good portion of the nation to the point of many wishing him dead, even as the LORD Jesus Christ also was treated!

i. **2 Corinthians 6:9 (KJV)** As unknown, and *yet* well known; as dying, and, behold, we live; as chastened, and not killed;

127.   Job description #7:

128.   The true Minister of God shall have have sorrow in Ministry but he should demonstrate joy at the sorrow! He shoudl welcome the sorrows as spiritually good for him instead of bemoaning himself! The true Minister of God shall be poor in the eyes of the world whereas his richness is counted in the excellency of the treasure of the knowledge of Christ in him!

i. **2 Corinthians 4:7 (KJV)** But we have this treasure in earthen vessels, that the excellency of the power may be of God, and not of us.

ii. **2 Corinthians 6:10 (KJV)** As sorrowful, yet alway rejoicing; as poor, yet making many rich; as having nothing, and *yet* possessing all things.

iii. **2 Corinthians 12:5 (KJV)** Of such an one will I glory: yet of myself I will not glory, but in mine infirmities.

iv. **2 Corinthians 12:9 (KJV)** And he said unto me, My grace is sufficient for thee: for my strength is made perfect in weakness. Most gladly therefore will I rather glory in my infirmities, that the power of Christ may rest upon me.

v. **2 Corinthians 12:10 (KJV)** Therefore I take pleasure in infirmities, in reproaches, in necessities, in persecutions, in distresses for Christ's sake: for when I am weak, then am I strong.

129.   Job description #8:

130.   The true Minister of God shall NOT partake in the beliefs and deeds of unbelievers and haters of God! It shall NOT be the lot of the true Man of God to promote the evil doctrines of unrighteousness and of darkness, but he shall focus ONLY in the Gospel of Christ, to meditate in it daily and to do it all the days of his life!

i. **2 Corinthians 6:14 (KJV)** Be ye not unequally yoked together with unbelievers: for what fellowship hath righteousness with unrighteousness? and what communion hath light with darkness?

ii. **2 Corinthians 6:15 (KJV)** And what concord hath Christ with Belial? or what part hath he that believeth with an infidel?

131.   Job description #9:

132.   The true Minister of God shall NOT partake in the pagan festivities of the people and then return to offer prayers in the church at the same time!

i. **2 Corinthians 6:16 (KJV)** And what agreement hath the temple of God with idols? for ye are the temple of the living God; as God hath said, I will dwell in them, and walk in *them*; and I will be their God, and they shall be my people.

133.   Job description #10:

134.   The life of a true Minister of God is a life of lifelong separation unto God untainted by none of the evil deeds that go on all around him!

    i. **2 Corinthians 6:17 (KJV)** Wherefore come out from among them, and be ye separate, saith the Lord, and touch not the unclean *thing*; and I will receive you,

    ii. **2 Corinthians 6:18 (KJV)** And will be a Father unto you, and ye shall be my sons and daughters, saith the Lord Almighty.

Monday 22nd January 2024 @ 10:40 AM – 11:51 AM

CHAPTER 7: WHAT IS THE DIFFERENCE BETWEEN SORROW UNTO DEATH, AND SORROW NOT UNTO DEATH?

135.   In other words, is it Godly to be sorrowful?

136.   When the sorrow is produced as a result of the rebuke from a true Minister of God because of some evil that was done, then that sorrow is a good thing!

137.   On the other hand, when the sorrow is produced because of some evil that was done while the person is NOT a child of God but is still a sinner, then, that sorrow is unto death!

138.   Just as thee is sin unto death and there is sin not unto death, so also, there is sorrow unto death, and there is sorrow not unto death!

  i.   **1 John 5:16 (KJV)** If any man see his brother sin a sin *which is* not unto death, he shall ask, and he shall give him life for them that sin not unto death. There is a sin unto death: I do not say that he shall pray for it.

  ii.   **1 John 5:17 (KJV)** All unrighteousness is sin: and there is a sin not unto death.

  iii. **1 John 5:18 (KJV)** We know that whosoever is born of God sinneth not; but he that is begotten of God keepeth himself, and that wicked one toucheth him not.

  iv.   **1 John 5:19 (KJV)** *And* we know that we are of God, and the whole world lieth in wickedness.

139.   There is a filthiness that the LORD God is teaching in **2 Corinthians 7:1-2 (KJV)**!

  i.   **2 Corinthians 7:1 (KJV)** Having therefore these promises, dearly beloved, let us cleanse ourselves from all filthiness of the flesh and spirit, perfecting holiness in the fear of God.

  ii.   **2 Corinthians 7:2 (KJV)** Receive us; we have wronged no man, we have corrupted no man, we have defrauded no man.

140.   This filthiness of the flesh and spirit in **2 Corinthians 7:1-2 (KJV)** is referring to the fellowship between righteousness and unrighteousness in **2 Corinthians 6:14-18 (KJV)** in

  i.   **2 Corinthians 6:14 (KJV)** Be ye not unequally yoked together with unbelievers: for what fellowship hath righteousness with unrighteousness? and what communion hath light with darkness?

  ii.   **2 Corinthians 6:15 (KJV)** And what concord hath Christ with Belial? or what part hath he that believeth with an infidel?

  iii. **2 Corinthians 6:16 (KJV)** And what agreement hath the temple of God with idols? for ye are the temple of the living God; as God hath said, I will dwell in them, and walk in *them*; and I will be their God, and they shall be my people.

    iv. **2 Corinthians 6:17 (KJV)** Wherefore come out from among them, and be ye separate, saith the Lord, and touch not the unclean *thing*; and I will receive you,

    v. **2 Corinthians 6:18 (KJV)** And will be a Father unto you, and ye shall be my sons and daughters, saith the Lord Almighty.

141.   Now, take note very carefully how the LORD God shows us how to receive cleansing from this filthiness of the flesh and spirit: You achieve it by "perfecting holiness in the fear of God"!

    i. **2 Corinthians 7:1 (KJV)** Having therefore these promises, dearly beloved, let us cleanse ourselves from all filthiness of the flesh and spirit, perfecting holiness in the fear of God.

142.   How can a man perfect holiness in the fear of God?

143.   That statement first means that God Almighty calls all Christians to be perfect, and so, it is false doctrine to say that "no one is perfect"!

    i. **Genesis 17:1 (KJV)** And when Abram was ninety years old and nine, the LORD appeared to Abram, and said unto him, I *am* the Almighty God; walk before me, and be thou perfect.

    ii. **2 Kings 20:3 (KJV)** I beseech thee, O LORD, remember now how I have walked before thee in truth and with a perfect heart, and have done *that which is* good in thy sight. And Hezekiah wept sore.

    iii. **1 Chronicles 28:9 (KJV)** And thou, Solomon my son, know thou the God of thy father, and serve him with a perfect heart and with a willing mind: for the LORD searcheth all hearts, and understandeth all the imaginations of the thoughts: if thou seek him, he will be found of thee; but if thou forsake him, he will cast thee off for ever.

    iv. **2 Chronicles 19:9 (KJV)** And he charged them, saying, Thus shall ye do in the fear of the LORD, faithfully, and with a perfect heart.

    v. **Psalm 101:2 (KJV)** I will behave myself wisely in a perfect way. O when wilt thou come unto me? I will walk within my house with a perfect heart.

    vi. **Isaiah 38:3 (KJV)** And said, Remember now, O LORD, I beseech thee, how I have walked before thee in truth and with a perfect heart, and have done *that which is* good in thy sight. And Hezekiah wept sore.

    vii. **Job 1:8 (KJV)** And the LORD said unto Satan, Hast thou considered my servant Job, that *there is* none like him in the earth, a perfect and an upright man, one that feareth God, and escheweth evil?

    viii. **Job 2:3 (KJV)** And the LORD said unto Satan, Hast thou considered my servant Job, that *there is* none like him in the earth, a perfect and an upright man, one that feareth God, and escheweth evil? and still he holdeth fast his integrity, although thou movedst me against him, to destroy him without cause.

    ix. **1 Corinthians 2:6 (KJV)** Howbeit we speak wisdom among them that are perfect: yet not the wisdom of this world, nor of the princes of this world, that come to nought:

    x. **1 John 4:17 (KJV)** Herein is our love made perfect, that we may have boldness in the day of judgment: because as he is, so are we in this world.

    xi. **Revelation 3:2 (KJV)** Be watchful, and strengthen the things which remain, that are ready to die: for I have not found thy works perfect before God.

144.   The second revelation is in the phrase: "in the fear of God". What shall a Christians do in order to demonstrate that he fears God? Here is the answer!

145.   You fear God by daily walking in Truth and Righteousness, obeying all the commandments of God, and hating covetuousness!

    i. **Exodus 18:21 (KJV)** Moreover thou shalt provide out of all the people able men, such as fear God, men of truth, hating covetousness; and place *such* over them, *to be* rulers of thousands, *and* rulers of hundreds, rulers of fifties, and rulers of tens:

    ii. **Ecclesiastes 12:13 (KJV)** Let us hear the conclusion of the whole matter: Fear God, and keep his commandments: for this *is* the whole *duty* of man.

146.   Therefore, when the LORD God says "perfecting holiness in the fear of God", it means that "you become holy through your daily walking in Truth and Righteousness, obeying all the commandments of God, and hating covetuousness"!

    i. **2 Corinthians 7:1 (KJV)** Having therefore these promises, dearly beloved, let us cleanse ourselves from all filthiness of the flesh and spirit, perfecting holiness in the fear of God.

147.   Then, we have the third and fnal revelation in **2 Corinthians 7:1 (KJV)**, which says: "let us cleanse ourselves"!

148.   How can a Christian cleanse himself/herself?

149.   Again, the answer is inside the Word of God, meaning that you must use the Word of God, or, the water in the Word of God "to cleanse ourselves from all filthiness of the flesh and spirit"!

150.   In practical terms, as you are:

i. "Daily walking in Truth and Righteousness, obeying all the commandments of God, and hating covetuousness"!

ii. As you are doing that, you are automatically being cleansed by the Holy Spirit with the pure water in the Word of God!

iii. **John 17:17 (KJV)** Sanctify them through thy truth: thy word is truth.

iv. **Ephesians 5:26 (KJV)** That he might sanctify and cleanse it with the washing of water by the word,

v. **John 4:10 (KJV)** Jesus answered and said unto her, If thou knewest the gift of God, and who it is that saith to thee, Give me to drink; thou wouldest have asked of him, and he would have given thee living water.

vi. **John 7:38 (KJV)** He that believeth on me, as the scripture hath said, out of his belly shall flow rivers of living water.

151. From what I have taught you so far, this is the quality of the Man of God that you should be following!

i. "Daily walking in Truth and Righteousness, obeying all the commandments of God, and hating covetuousness"!

152. A Man of God who is NOT teaching you how to daily walk in Truth and Righteousness, how to daily obey all the commandments of God, and how to daily hate covetuousness, that same Man of God has wronged you, has corrupted you, and has defrauded you!

153. A Man of God who is NOT doing that in his Ministry is the same who has wronged you, who has corrupted you, and who has defrauded you! Flee from such a Man of Satan!

i. **2 Corinthians 7:2 (KJV)** Receive us; we have wronged no man, we have corrupted no man, we have defrauded no man.

154. Take note though, that in a true Ministry of Christ where the true Man of God is teaching you how to daily walk in Truth and Righteousness, how to daily obey all the commandments of God, and how to daily hate covetuousness, Satan will surely raise much persecution, pain, and sorrow against both the Man of God and the congregation!

i. **2 Corinthians 7:5 (KJV)** For, when we were come into Macedonia, our flesh had no rest, but we were troubled on every side; without *were* fightings, within *were* fears.

ii. **2 Corinthians 7:6 (KJV)** Nevertheless God, that comforteth those that are cast down, comforted us by the coming of Titus;

iii. **2 Corinthians 7:7 (KJV)** And not by his coming only, but by the consolation wherewith he was comforted in you, when he told us your earnest desire, your mourning, your fervent mind toward me; so that I rejoiced the more.

iv. **2 Corinthians 7:8 (KJV)** For though I made you sorry with a letter, I do not repent, though I did repent: for I perceive that the same epistle hath made you sorry, though *it were* but for a season.

v. **2 Corinthians 7:9 (KJV)** Now I rejoice, not that ye were made sorry, but that ye sorrowed to repentance: for ye were made sorry after a godly manner, that ye might receive damage by us in nothing.

vi. **2 Corinthians 7:10 (KJV)** For godly sorrow worketh repentance to salvation not to be repented of: but the sorrow of the world worketh death.

vii. **2 Corinthians 7:11 (KJV)** For behold this selfsame thing, that ye sorrowed after a godly sort, what carefulness it wrought in you, yea, *what* clearing of yourselves, yea, *what* indignation, yea, *what* fear, yea, *what* vehement desire, yea, *what* zeal, yea, *what* revenge! In all *things* ye have approved yourselves to be clear in this matter.

viii. **2 Corinthians 7:12 (KJV)** Wherefore, though I wrote unto you, *I did it* not for his cause that had done the wrong, nor for his cause that suffered wrong, but that our care for you in the sight of God might appear unto you.

ix. **2 Corinthians 7:13 (KJV)** Therefore we were comforted in your comfort: yea, and exceedingly the more joyed we for the joy of Titus, because his spirit was refreshed by you all.

x. **2 Corinthians 7:14 (KJV)** For if I have boasted any thing to him of you, I am not ashamed; but as we spake all things to you in truth, even so our boasting, which *I made* before Titus, is found a truth.

xi. **2 Corinthians 7:15 (KJV)** And his inward affection is more abundant toward you, whilst he remembereth the obedience of you all, how with fear and trembling ye received him.

xii. **2 Corinthians 7:16 (KJV)** I rejoice therefore that I have confidence in you in all *things.*

155. Now, when the persecution, pain, and sorrow come because of sin among the congregation, then, the Man of God has to condemn it and punish the sinner!

i. **1 Corinthians 5:1 (KJV)** It is reported commonly *that there is* fornication among you, and such fornication as is not so much as named among the Gentiles, that one should have his father's wife.

     ii. **1 Corinthians 5:2 (KJV)** And ye are puffed up, and have not rather mourned, that he that hath done this deed might be taken away from among you.

     iii. **1 Corinthians 5:13 (KJV)** But them that are without God judgeth. Therefore put away from among yourselves that wicked person.

156.   When the sinner repents and turns away from the sin after bearing his rebuke, after his punishment and sorrow, then, that sorrow unto repentance was Godly and NOT the sorrow unto death!

157.   However, if the sinner bears his sorrow from sin and continues to remain in the sin, then, that is when the sorrow is unto death, because he will die in his sins!

     i. **Ezekiel 3:16 (KJV)** And it came to pass at the end of seven days, that the word of the LORD came unto me, saying,

     ii. **Ezekiel 3:17 (KJV)** Son of man, I have made thee a watchman unto the house of Israel: therefore hear the word at my mouth, and give them warning from me.

     iii. **Ezekiel 3:18 (KJV)** When I say unto the wicked, Thou shalt surely die; and thou givest him not warning, nor speakest to warn the wicked from his wicked way, to save his life; the same wicked *man* shall die in his iniquity; but his blood will I require at thine hand.

     iv. **Ezekiel 3:19 (KJV)** Yet if thou warn the wicked, and he turn not from his wickedness, nor from his wicked way, he shall die in his iniquity; but thou hast delivered thy soul.

     v. **Ezekiel 3:20 (KJV)** Again, When a righteous *man* doth turn from his righteousness, and commit iniquity, and I lay a stumblingblock before him, he shall die: because thou hast not given him warning, he shall die in his sin, and his righteousness which he hath done shall not be remembered; but his blood will I require at thine hand.

     vi. **Ezekiel 3:21 (KJV)** Nevertheless if thou warn the righteous *man*, that the righteous sin not, and he doth not sin, he shall surely live, because he is warned; also thou hast delivered thy soul.

     vii. **Ezekiel 18:21 (KJV)** But if the wicked will turn from all his sins that he hath committed, and keep all my statutes, and do that which is lawful and right, he shall surely live, he shall not die.

     viii. **Ezekiel 18:22 (KJV)** All his transgressions that he hath committed, they shall not be mentioned unto him: in his righteousness that he hath done he shall live.

      ix. **Ezekiel 18:23 (KJV)** Have I any pleasure at all that the wicked should die? saith the Lord GOD: *and* not that he should return from his ways, and live?

      x. **Ezekiel 18:24 (KJV)** But when the righteous turneth away from his righteousness, and committeth iniquity, *and* doeth according to all the abominations that the wicked *man* doeth, shall he live? All his righteousness that he hath done shall not be mentioned: in his trespass that he hath trespassed, and in his sin that he hath sinned, in them shall he die.

158.   Finally, when a sinner turns away from sin in sorrow and in repentance unto Christ, there is great rejoicing in the true Man of God and in Heaven!

      i. **2 Corinthians 7:4 (KJV)** Great *is* my boldness of speech toward you, great *is* my glorying of you: I am filled with comfort, I am exceeding joyful in all our tribulation.

Monday 22nd January 2024 @ 6:21 AM – 11:57 PM

CHAPTER 8: THE DOCTRINE OF RECIPROCAL EQUIVALENCE IN CHRISTIAN GIVING

159.   Christian Giving is a Christian Arrangement for Gospel Financing that is based on freewill liberal voluntary small contributions of money or goods from many Christians in order to attain a greater sum for a previously declared purpose of solving a problem, usually, to alleviate the suffering and poverty of poor saints!

    i.   **2 Corinthians 8:1 (KJV)** Moreover, brethren, we do you to wit of the grace of God bestowed on the churches of Macedonia;

160.   Christian Giving is never for the benefit of the rich!

    i.   **Luke 6:24 (KJV)** But woe unto you that are rich! for ye have received your consolation.

161.   In the Doctrine of Reciprocal Equivalence of Christian Giving, all Christians, both poor and rich, are permitted to give according as the LORD God has blessed them and according as they are able to give!

    i.   **2 Corinthians 8:2 (KJV)** How that in a great trial of affliction the abundance of their joy and their deep poverty abounded unto the riches of their liberality.

    ii.   **2 Corinthians 8:3 (KJV)** For to *their* power, I bear record, yea, and beyond *their* power *they were* willing of themselves;

162.   It is very important to note very carefully, that, inlcuding this very example of Christian Giving, all the instances of Christian Giving in the entire Holy Bible are for the benefit of the poor, the needy, the widow, the stranger, the fatherless, and the destitute, never for the rich!

    i.   **2 Corinthians 8:4 (KJV)** Praying us with much intreaty that we would receive the gift, and *take upon us* the fellowship of the ministering to the saints.

163.   Truly, truly, it is a curse to give gifts to the rich?

    i.   **Proverbs 22:16 (KJV)** He that oppresseth the poor to increase his *riches, and* he that giveth to the rich, *shall* surely *come* to want.

    ii.   **Luke 6:24 (KJV)** But woe unto you that are rich! for ye have received your consolation.

164.   The blessing in Christian Giving is assured when the giver is a Christian and not a sinner!

    i.   **2 Corinthians 8:5 (KJV)** And *this they did*, not as we hoped, but first gave their own selves to the Lord, and unto us by the will of God.!

165.   Truly, in order to attract the spiritual blessing in the giving, the Christian Giver must qualify to give before he or she is permitted to give, because, according to

Leviticus 22:25 (KJV), it is an abomination to receive money or offering for the work of the LORD God from filthy hands! Here are the four qualifications according to **2 Corinthians 8:7 (KJV)**:

     i.   **ONE** – The Christian Giver must first have had a prior confession of faith/believing in the Testimony of Christ.

     ii.   **TWO** – His/her speech must be sound in the knowledge of the Word of God.

     iii.   **THREE** – He or she must have demonstrated diligence in obeying the Word of God, and

     iv.   **FOUR** – He or she must have demonstrated charity/love toward the Brethren and Sisters in the fellowship!

     v.   **2 Corinthians 8:7 (KJV)** Therefore, as ye abound in every *thing, in* faith, and utterance, and knowledge, and *in* all diligence, and *in* your love to us, *see* that ye abound in this grace also.

     vi.   **Proverbs 30:12 (KJV)** *There is* a generation *that are* pure in their own eyes, and *yet* is not washed from their filthiness.

     vii.   **Leviticus 22:25 (KJV)** Neither from a stranger's hand shall ye offer the bread of your God of any of these; because their corruption *is* in them, *and* blemishes *be* in them: they shall not be accepted for you.

166.   The richness of the Qualified Christian Giver is measured NOT in worldly material things, but in the excellent knowledge of Christ that he possesses!

     i.   **2 Corinthians 8:8 (KJV)** I speak not by commandment, but by occasion of the forwardness of others, and to prove the sincerity of your love.

     ii.   **2 Corinthians 8:9 (KJV)** For ye know the grace of our Lord Jesus Christ, that, though he was rich, yet for your sakes he became poor, that ye through his poverty might be rich.

167.   Brother, ye that are quick to pervert the Gospel of Christ, this Word of God here in **2 Corinthians 8:9 (KJV)**, is NOT talking about money at all! God Almighty is NOT teaching you that the LORD Jesus Christ became materially and moneywise poor so that you can become a millionnaire!

168.   The emptying of the rich Glory of the LORD Jesus Christ in Heaven before HE came down to you in your filthy self on Earth to save us is what God means by: "our Lord Jesus Christ, that, though he was rich, yet for your sakes he became poor, that ye through his poverty might be rich"! Hence, your richness is in your partaking of the Glory of Christ in Heaven, and NOT in your filthy and greedy amassing of millions of filthy money!

    i. **John 17:4 (KJV)** I have glorified thee on the earth: I have finished the work which thou gavest me to do.

    ii. **John 17:5 (KJV)** And now, O Father, glorify thou me with thine own self with the glory which I had with thee before the world was.

169.   The ability of a poor Christian to give toward the good cause of alleviating the suffering of another poor Christian comes from his or her rich and abundant reservoir of the Word of God in him/her, of his/her charity, and of the love of Christ in him/her!

170.   Without first that rich spiritual abundance in the knowledge of Christ and obedience thereto, the giving will not come, and if it does come, it will NOT come from a clean heart/mind, and it is therefore profane and corrupted in the sight of God Almighty!

171.   Christian Giving must never be taken from borrowed money such as bank credit cards, neither should it be given from money that you do NOT own! It is a curse before God Almighty that you should give for a Christian cause from money that you have borrowed or from money that you do NOT own!

    i. **2 Corinthians 8:11 (KJV)** Now therefore perform the doing *of it*; that as *there was* a readiness to will, so *there may be* a performance also out of that which ye have.

    ii. **2 Corinthians 8:12 (KJV)** For if there be first a willing mind, *it is* accepted according to that a man hath, *and* not according to that he hath not.

172.   Very importantly, the Christian Giving must never be coerced, induced, forced, threatened, wrested out from fear, but only based on freewill liberal voluntary willing small contributions!

173.   Another very important condition for Reciprocal Christian Giving to be acceptable in Heaven is its reciprocity or equality!

    i. **2 Corinthians 8:13 (KJV)** For *I mean* not that other men be eased, and ye burdened:

    ii. **2 Corinthians 8:14 (KJV)** But by an equality, *that* now at this time your abundance *may be a supply* for their want, that their abundance also may be *a supply* for your want: that there may be equality:

    iii. **2 Corinthians 8:15 (KJV)** As it is written, He that *had gathered* much had nothing over; and he that *had gathered* little had no lack.

174.   Christian Giving is never accomplished, Christian Giving is a perversion, Christian Giving is evil, Christian Giving is a robbery, when one party is burdened because of the giving, when one party is deprived because of the giving, or when one party receives nothing in return or in exchange for the giving! When you give without

gaining back or receiving back, then, it is a loss and a robbery caused by he who received your giving!

    i. **Exodus 20:17 (KJV)** Thou shalt not covet thy neighbour's house, thou shalt not covet thy neighbour's wife, nor his manservant, nor his maidservant, nor his ox, nor his ass, nor any thing that *is* thy neighbour's.

    ii. **Romans 13:9 (KJV)** For this, Thou shalt not commit adultery, Thou shalt not kill, Thou shalt not steal, Thou shalt not bear false witness, Thou shalt not covet; and if *there be* any other commandment, it is briefly comprehended in this saying, namely, Thou shalt love thy neighbour as thyself.

175.   In the case of a Man of God and true Christians, the principle of equality in that the LORD God has revealed in **2 Corinthians 8:13-15 (KJV)** is revealed in these words:

    i. "Your abundance *may be a supply* for their want, that their abundance also may be *a supply* for your want: that there may be equality"!

176.   In other words, if one Christian or the Man of God is deep in the knowledge of God whereas the other Christian has this world's material goods or money, then the Doctrine of Reciprocal Equivalence in Christian Giving works whereby, the one gives some knowledge of Christ unto good discipleship or unto edification whereas the other gives material things or money, thus, you accomplish the exchange and the equality, and this is aceptable in Heaven!

    i. **Romans 15:27 (KJV)** It hath pleased them verily; and their debtors they are. For if the Gentiles have been made partakers of their spiritual things, their duty is also to minister unto them in carnal things.

177.   Now, when this equivalence in Christian Reciprocal Giving is NOT respected by any one of the two parties, then, a curse follows the offender to destroy him/her!

    i. **Exodus 21:19 (KJV)** If he rise again, and walk abroad upon his staff, then shall he that smote *him* be quit: only he shall pay *for* the loss of his time, and shall cause *him* to be thoroughly healed.

    ii. **Jeremiah 22:13 (KJV)** Woe unto him that buildeth his house by unrighteousness, and his chambers by wrong; *that* useth his neighbour's service without wages, and giveth him not for his work;

    iii. **Matthew 10:12 (KJV)** And when ye come into an house, salute it.

    iv. **Matthew 10:13 (KJV)** And if the house be worthy, let your peace come upon it: but if it be not worthy, let your peace return to you.

     v. **Matthew 10:14 (KJV)** And whosoever shall not receive you, nor hear your words, when ye depart out of that house or city, shake off the dust of your feet.

     vi. **Matthew 10:15 (KJV)** Verily I say unto you, It shall be more tolerable for the land of Sodom and Gomorrha in the day of judgment, than for that city.

178.   One last very important part of the Ministry of Reciprocal Equivalence in Christian Giving is Accountability! You must give account of every penny that comes into your hand if you do not want to be called a thief and a robber of curches!

     i. **Matthew 12:36 (KJV)** But I say unto you, That every idle word that men shall speak, they shall give account thereof in the day of judgment.

     ii. **Luke 16:1 (KJV)** And he said also unto his disciples, There was a certain rich man, which had a steward; and the same was accused unto him that he had wasted his goods.

     iii. **Luke 16:2 (KJV)** And he called him, and said unto him, How is it that I hear this of thee? give an account of thy stewardship; for thou mayest be no longer steward.

     iv. **Ephesians 6:21 (KJV)** But that ye also may know my affairs, *and* how I do, Tychicus, a beloved brother and faithful minister in the Lord, shall make known to you all things:

     v. **2 Corinthians 8:18 (KJV)** And we have sent with him the brother, whose praise *is* in the gospel throughout all the churches;

     vi. **2 Corinthians 8:19 (KJV)** And not *that* only, but who was also chosen of the churches to travel with us with this grace, which is administered by us to the glory of the same Lord, and *declaration of* your ready mind:

     vii. **2 Corinthians 8:20 (KJV)** Avoiding this, that no man should blame us in this abundance which is administered by us:

179.   The requirement for the true Man of God to be truthful, plain, and transparent in all things money in the church is not just for himself and by himself in prayer and in his closet, but equally very importantly, in the sight of all men!

180.   The more many Brethren know of the finances of the church, the better and the more trustworthy and the more transparent, but the more church money is shrouded in secrecy and expenses are not discussed and disclosed, the many more evil opportunities the Pastor has to steal church money and to rob the congregation, and he will eventually go to Hell for all his thefts!

     i. **2 Corinthians 8:21 (KJV)** Providing for honest things, not only in the sight of the Lord, but also in the sight of men.

ii. **2 Corinthians 8:22 (KJV)** And we have sent with them our brother, whom we have oftentimes proved diligent in many things, but now much more diligent, upon the great confidence which *I have* in you.

iii. **2 Corinthians 8:23 (KJV)** Whether *any do inquire* of Titus, *he is* my partner and fellowhelper concerning you: or our brethren *be inquired of, they are* the messengers of the churches, *and* the glory of Christ.

iv. **2 Corinthians 8:24 (KJV)** Wherefore shew ye to them, and before the churches, the proof of your love, and of our boasting on your behalf.

Tuesday 23rd January 2024 @ 10:59 AM – 1:12 PM

CHAPTER 9: THE ONE PERSON GIVING SPIRITUAL KNOWLEDGE/TEACHING WHEREAS THE OTHER PERSON IS GIVING MATERIAL GOOD OR MONEY

181.   In **2 Corinthians 9 (KJV)**, we have a contiinuation of the teaching on the Ministry of Reciprocal Equivalence in Christian Giving, which is also clled the Ministry of Helps!

182.   Remember, as we said in the previous chapter, that the purpose for this money collection in the church remains a freewill liberal voluntary small contributions of money or goods from many Christians in order to attain a greater sum for a previously declared purpose of solving a problem, usually, to alleviate the suffering and poverty of poor saints!

183.   Now, here is the additional information that we learn:

    i. **2 Corinthians 9:6 (KJV)** But this *I say*, He which soweth sparingly shall reap also sparingly; and he which soweth bountifully shall reap also bountifully.

    ii. **2 Corinthians 9:7 (KJV)** Every man according as he purposeth in his heart, *so let him give*; not grudgingly, or of necessity: for God loveth a cheerful giver.

    iii. **2 Corinthians 9:8 (KJV)** And God *is* able to make all grace abound toward you; that ye, always having all sufficiency in all *things*, may abound to every good work:

184.   You remember that one of the main requirements for the Ministry of Reciprocal Equivalence in Christian Giving is an exchange of each other's possession that solves each other's need! In other words, the one person is giving spiritual knowledge whereas the other person is giving material good or money:

    i. "Your abundance *may be a supply* for their want, that their abundance also may be *a supply* for your want: that there may be equality"!

185.   It also so happens that sometimes, it is not only the giving of spiritual knowledge but the need for prayer for the other person who is doing the material Christian Giving, and such is the case that we see here in **2 Corinthians 9:8-11 (KJV)** where Apostle Paul is offering up prayer for the money that was collected to reduce the suffering of the poor saints in Jerusalem!

    i. **2 Corinthians 9:8 (KJV)** And God *is* able to make all grace abound toward you; that ye, always having all sufficiency in all *things*, may abound to every good work:

    ii. **2 Corinthians 9:9 (KJV)** (As it is written, He hath dispersed abroad; he hath given to the poor: his righteousness remaineth for ever.

   iii. **2 Corinthians 9:10 (KJV)** Now he that ministereth seed to the sower both minister bread for *your* food, and multiply your seed sown, and increase the fruits of your righteousness;)

   iv. **2 Corinthians 9:11 (KJV)** Being enriched in every thing to all bountifulness, which causeth through us thanksgiving to God.

186.   Again, someone gives material thing or money, and the other person gives spiritual knowledge/teaching, or prayer!

   i. **2 Corinthians 9:12 (KJV)** For the administration of this service not only supplieth the want of the saints, but is abundant also by many thanksgivings unto God;

   ii. **2 Corinthians 9:13 (KJV)** Whiles by the experiment of this ministration they glorify God for your professed subjection unto the gospel of Christ, and for *your* liberal distribution unto them, and unto all *men*;

   iii. **2 Corinthians 9:14 (KJV)** And by their prayer for you, which long after you for the exceeding grace of God in you.

   iv. **2 Corinthians 9:15 (KJV)** Thanks *be* unto God for his unspeakable gift.

Tuesday 23rd January 2024 @ 7:40 PM – 8:50 PM

CHAPTER 10: OFFER UNTO GOD WORDS, LIVING WORDS

187.   As the LORD Jesus Christ showed us that the flesh profiteth nothing, and again as the LORD showed us that the flesh is weak but the spirit is willing, and again as the LORD showed us that HE was cricified in the flesh but quickened in the Spirit, so also we have this treasure in an earthern temporary vessel of flesh that is also weak and base but carrying the excellency of the eternal knowledge of Christ!

    i. **2 Corinthians 10:1 (KJV)** Now I Paul myself beseech you by the meekness and gentleness of Christ, who in presence *am* base among you, but being absent am bold toward you:

    ii. **2 Corinthians 10:2 (KJV)** But I beseech *you*, that I may not be bold when I am present with that confidence, wherewith I think to be bold against some, which think of us as if we walked according to the flesh.

188.   It is for this very reason of the weakness, unrpifitableness, and baseness of the flesh that everything that we do with the flesh, such as Holy Communion offerings and Water Baptism sacrifices, are already filthy and condemned and unacceptable in Heaven!

    i. **Matthew 26:41 (KJV)** Watch and pray, that ye enter not into temptation: the spirit indeed *is* willing, but the flesh *is* weak.

    ii. **Mark 14:38 (KJV)** Watch ye and pray, lest ye enter into temptation. The spirit truly *is* ready, but the flesh *is* weak.

    iii. **John 6:63 (KJV)** It is the spirit that quickeneth; the flesh profiteth nothing: the words that I speak unto you, *they* are spirit, and *they* are life.

    iv. **Romans 7:18 (KJV)** For I know that in me (that is, in my flesh,) dwelleth no good thing: for to will is present with me; but *how* to perform that which is good I find not.

189.   Moreover, and most imprtantly, the LORD God Almighty DOES NOT accept dead lifeless things, such as the fruits of the ground, as sacrifice, and if God did NOT accept them from Cain, then, how deep is your stupidity to think that the same God will accept from your filthy hands what God has already rejected?

    i. **Genesis 4:3 (KJV)** And in process of time it came to pass, that Cain brought of the fruit of the ground an offering unto the LORD.

    ii. **Genesis 4:4 (KJV)** And Abel, he also brought of the firstlings of his flock and of the fat thereof. And the LORD had respect unto Abel and to his offering:

iii. **Genesis 4:5 (KJV)** But unto Cain and to his offering he had not respect. And Cain was very wroth, and his countenance fell.

iv. **Genesis 4:6 (KJV)** And the LORD said unto Cain, Why art thou wroth? and why is thy countenance fallen?

v. **Genesis 4:7 (KJV)** If thou doest well, shalt thou not be accepted? and if thou doest not well, sin lieth at the door. And unto thee *shall be* his desire, and thou shalt rule over him.

vi. **Micah 6:6 (KJV)** Wherewith shall I come before the LORD, *and* bow myself before the high God? shall I come before him with burnt offerings, with calves of a year old?

vii. **Micah 6:7 (KJV)** Will the LORD be pleased with thousands of rams, *or* with ten thousands of rivers of oil? shall I give my firstborn *for* my transgression, the fruit of my body *for* the sin of my soul?

viii. **Micah 6:8 (KJV)** He hath shewed thee, O man, what *is* good; and what doth the LORD require of thee, but to do justly, and to love mercy, and to walk humbly with thy God?

190.	The above reasons are also why the Old Testament was condemned unto removal and abogation by reason of its weakness and unprofitableness seeing that it leadeth to the works of the Law and of the flesh, which works cannot save anyone, but the New Testament was deemed excellent and better Covenant because it tendeth and leadeth to the spirit and NOT to the flesh/letter!

i. **Galatians 2:16 (KJV)** Knowing that a man is not justified by the works of the law, but by the faith of Jesus Christ, even we have believed in Jesus Christ, that we might be justified by the faith of Christ, and not by the works of the law: for by the works of the law shall no flesh be justified.

ii. **Hebrews 7:18 (KJV)** For there is verily a disannulling of the commandment going before for the weakness and unprofitableness thereof.

iii. **Hebrews 7:19 (KJV)** For the law made nothing perfect, but the bringing in of a better hope *did*; by the which we draw nigh unto God.

iv. **Hebrews 7:20 (KJV)** And inasmuch as not without an oath *he was made priest*:

v. **Hebrews 8:6 (KJV)** But now hath he obtained a more excellent ministry, by how much also he is the mediator of a better covenant, which was established upon better promises.

      vi. **Hebrews 12:24 (KJV)** And to Jesus the mediator of the new covenant, and to the blood of sprinkling, that speaketh better things than *that of* Abel.

191.   By reason of the perpetual condition of the flesh as weak, unrpifitable, and base, everything that we do with the flesh, such as Holy Communion offerings and Water Baptism sacrifices, are already filthy and condemned and unacceptable in Heaven!

      i. **Haggai 2:10 (KJV)** In the four and twentieth *day* of the ninth *month*, in the second year of Darius, came the word of the LORD by Haggai the prophet, saying,

      ii. **Haggai 2:11 (KJV)** Thus saith the LORD of hosts; Ask now the priests *concerning* the law, saying,

      iii. **Haggai 2:12 (KJV)** If one bear holy flesh in the skirt of his garment, and with his skirt do touch bread, or pottage, or wine, or oil, or any meat, shall it be holy? And the priests answered and said, No.

      iv. **Haggai 2:13 (KJV)** Then said Haggai, If *one that is* unclean by a dead body touch any of these, shall it be unclean? And the priests answered and said, It shall be unclean.

      v. **Haggai 2:14 (KJV)** Then answered Haggai, and said, So *is* this people, and so *is* this nation before me, saith the LORD; and so *is* every work of their hands; and that which they offer there *is* unclean.

      vi. **Romans 7:18 (KJV)** For I know that in me (that is, in my flesh,) dwelleth no good thing: for to will is present with me; but *how* to perform that which is good I find not.

192.   There is no Man of God living who has yet attained unto the spiritual level of Apostle Paul! Therefore, if Apostle Paul can say in **Romans 7:18 (KJV)** that I know that in me (that is, in my flesh,) dwelleth no good thing, then, you the Holy Communion and Water Baptism Pastors of today, there is far more filth in your flesh than there was in Apostle Paul who went to Paradise in Heaven and returned, whereas you did not!

      i. **2 Corinthians 12:1 (KJV)** It is not expedient for me doubtless to glory. I will come to visions and revelations of the Lord.

      ii. **2 Corinthians 12:2 (KJV)** I knew a man in Christ above fourteen years ago, (whether in the body, I cannot tell; or whether out of the body, I cannot tell: God knoweth;) such an one caught up to the third heaven.

      iii. **2 Corinthians 12:3 (KJV)** And I knew such a man, (whether in the body, or out of the body, I cannot tell: God knoweth;)

    iv. **2 Corinthians 12:4 (KJV)** How that he was caught up into paradise, and heard unspeakable words, which it is not lawful for a man to utter.

    v. **2 Corinthians 12:5 (KJV)** Of such an one will I glory: yet of myself I will not glory, but in mine infirmities.

    vi. **2 Corinthians 12:6 (KJV)** For though I would desire to glory, I shall not be a fool; for I will say the truth: but *now* I forbear, lest any man should think of me above that which he seeth me *to be*, or *that* he heareth of me.

    vii. **2 Corinthians 12:7 (KJV)** And lest I should be exalted above measure through the abundance of the revelations, there was given to me a thorn in the flesh, the messenger of Satan to buffet me, lest I should be exalted above measure.

    viii. **2 Corinthians 12:8 (KJV)** For this thing I besought the Lord thrice, that it might depart from me.

    ix. **2 Corinthians 12:9 (KJV)** And he said unto me, My grace is sufficient for thee: for my strength is made perfect in weakness. Most gladly therefore will I rather glory in my infirmities, that the power of Christ may rest upon me.

    x. **2 Corinthians 12:10 (KJV)** Therefore I take pleasure in infirmities, in reproaches, in necessities, in persecutions, in distresses for Christ's sake: for when I am weak, then am I strong.

193. And so, if by way of comparison, you are worse and filthier than Apostle Paul, and Apostle Paul did NOT water baptize people, then, where is your scriptural justification to do Water Baptism and Holy Communion?

    i. **1 Corinthians 1:17 (KJV)** For Christ sent me not to baptize, but to preach the gospel: not with wisdom of words, lest the cross of Christ should be made of none effect.

    ii. **1 Corinthians 6:20 (KJV)** For ye are bought with a price: therefore glorify God in your body, and in your spirit, which are God's.

    iii. **1 Corinthians 11:20 (KJV)** When ye come together therefore into one place, *this* is not to eat the Lord's supper.

    iv. **1 Corinthians 15:50 (KJV)** Now this I say, brethren, that flesh and blood cannot inherit the kingdom of God; neither doth corruption inherit incorruption.

194. The sum of what I have said so far is this:

    i. You have flesh and you have a spirit. **1 Corinthians 6:20 (KJV)**

    ii. Your flesh is weak, unrpifitable, and base. **John 6:63 (KJV), Romans 7:18 (KJV)**

iii. Everything that your flesh offers to God Almighty is filthy and unacceptable in Heaven! **Micah 6:6-8 (KJV), Haggai 2:10-14 (KJV)**

iv. Therefore, the flesh is forever disqualified from offering anytging unto God Almighty!

v. What you now have left is only your spirit!

vi. The spirit eats and produces only one thing: words!

vii. Therefore, offer unto God words, living words, living words that come from a living human spirit, living words that are produced from the spirit in which dwells the Holy Spirit, living words that are produced from the spirit that is washed with the water of the Word, living words that are produced from the spirit that is a well of rivers of living waters, living words that are produced from the spirit that has been and is being renewed everyday in the Gospel of Christ, living words that God Almighty Himself has given you!

viii. **Micah 6:8 (KJV)** He hath shewed thee, O man, what *is* good; and what doth the LORD require of thee, but to do justly, and to love mercy, and to walk humbly with thy God?

ix. **Hosea 14:2 (KJV)** Take with you words, and turn to the LORD: say unto him, Take away all iniquity, and receive *us* graciously: so will we render the calves of our lips.

x. **John 3:34 (KJV)** For he whom God hath sent speaketh the words of God: for God giveth not the Spirit by measure *unto him.*

xi. **1 Corinthians 6:17 (KJV)** But he that is joined unto the Lord is one spirit.

xii. **John 14:17 (KJV)** *Even* the Spirit of truth; whom the world cannot receive, because it seeth him not, neither knoweth him: but ye know him; for he dwelleth with you, and shall be in you.

xiii. **Romans 8:11 (KJV)** But if the Spirit of him that raised up Jesus from the dead dwell in you, he that raised up Christ from the dead shall also quicken your mortal bodies by his Spirit that dwelleth in you.

xiv. **Ephesians 5:26 (KJV)** That he might sanctify and cleanse it with the washing of water by the word,

xv. **John 4:10 (KJV)** Jesus answered and said unto her, If thou knewest the gift of God, and who it is that saith to thee, Give me to drink; thou wouldest have asked of him, and he would have given thee living water.

xvi. **John 4:14 (KJV)** But whosoever drinketh of the water that I shall give him shall never thirst; but the water that I shall give him shall be in him a well of water springing up into everlasting life.

xvii. **John 7:38 (KJV)** He that believeth on me, as the scripture hath said, out of his belly shall flow rivers of living water.

xviii. **John 15:3 (KJV)** Now ye are clean through the word which I have spoken unto you.

xix. **Ephesians 4:23 (KJV)** And be renewed in the spirit of your mind;

xx. **John 17:8 (KJV)** For I have given unto them the words which thou gavest me; and they have received *them*, and have known surely that I came out from thee, and they have believed that thou didst send me.

195. All the above are the reasons why "we do not war after the flesh"! All the above are the reasons why "the weapons of our warfare *are* not carnal"!

i. **2 Corinthians 10:3 (KJV)** For though we walk in the flesh, we do not war after the flesh:

ii. **2 Corinthians 10:4 (KJV)** (For the weapons of our warfare *are* not carnal, but mighty through God to the pulling down of strong holds;)

196. Now, pause a while and ask yourself:

197. The filthy Water Baptism river and pool waters, and the Holy Comunion wafers, wine, and bread that we offer in all the churches, are they "in the flesh"? YES!

i. Then, they are disqualified because they stand against and are contrary to **2 Corinthians 10:3-4 (KJV)**!

198. The filthy Water Baptism river and pool waters, and the Holy Comunion wafers, wine, and bread that we offer in all the churches, are they "after the flesh"? YES!

i. Then, they are disqualified because they stand against and are contrary to **2 Corinthians 10:3-4 (KJV)**!

199. The filthy Water Baptism river and pool waters, and the Holy Comunion wafers, wine, and bread that we offer in all the churches, are they part of the Christian life of war? NO!

i. Then, they are disqualified because they stand against and are contrary to **2 Corinthians 10:3-4 (KJV)**!

200. The filthy Water Baptism river and pool waters, and the Holy Comunion wafers, wine, and bread that we offer in all the churches, are they "weapons of our warfare"? NO!

i. Then, they are disqualified because they stand against and are contrary to **2 Corinthians 10:3-4 (KJV)**!

201. The filthy Water Baptism river and pool waters, and the Holy Comunion wafers, wine, and bread that we offer in all the churches, are they mighty warfare items in God? NO!

       i. Then, they are disqualified because they stand against and are contrary to **2 Corinthians 10:3-4 (KJV)**!

202. The filthy Water Baptism river and pool waters, and the Holy Comunion wafers, wine, and bread that we offer in all the churches, are you able to use them to pull down of strong holds? NO!

       i. Then, they are disqualified because they stand against and are contrary to **2 Corinthians 10:3-4 (KJV)**!

203. Will demons of the strong holds recognize, fear, respond to, and obey your filthy Water Baptism river and pool waters, and your Holy Comunion wafers, wine, and bread that we offer in all the churches? NO!

       i. Then, they are disqualified because they stand against and are contrary to **2 Corinthians 10:3-4 (KJV)**!

204. Let us conside some more evidences:

       i. **2 Corinthians 10:5 (KJV)** Casting down imaginations, and every high thing that exalteth itself against the knowledge of God, and bringing into captivity every thought to the obedience of Christ;

       ii. **2 Corinthians 10:6 (KJV)** And having in a readiness to revenge all disobedience, when your obedience is fulfilled.

205. Furthermore, are you able to use your filthy Water Baptism river and pool waters, and your Holy Comunion wafers, wine, and bread to "cast down imaginations, and every high thing that exalteth itself against the knowledge of God"? NO!

       i. Then, they are disqualified because they stand against and are contrary to **2 Corinthians 10:5-6 (KJV)**!

206. Then, are you able to use your filthy Water Baptism river and pool waters, and your Holy Comunion wafers, wine, and bread to "bring into captivity every thought to the obedience of Christ"? NO!

       i. Then, they are disqualified because they stand against and are contrary to **2 Corinthians 10:5-6 (KJV)**!

207. Brother Pastor and Bishop, do you now see how nakedly shameful you look because you do NOT know the Holy Scriptures and yet you claim to have been called into the Ministry?

208. Did you ever read anywhere in the entire Holy Bible Bible from Genesis to Revelation, that the LORD God Almighty sends fools and ignorant bastards like you into the Ministry?

       i. **Exodus 28:3 (KJV)** And thou shalt speak unto all *that are* wise hearted, whom I have filled with the spirit of wisdom, that they may make Aaron's garments to consecrate him, that he may minister unto me in the priest's office.

      ii. **Exodus 31:3 (KJV)** And I have filled him with the spirit of God, in wisdom, and in understanding, and in knowledge, and in all manner of workmanship,

      iii. **Exodus 35:31 (KJV)** And he hath filled him with the spirit of God, in wisdom, in understanding, and in knowledge, and in all manner of workmanship;

      iv. **Luke 2:40 (KJV)** And the child grew, and waxed strong in spirit, filled with wisdom: and the grace of God was upon him.

209.   Do you now see that it was NOT the LORD Jesus Christ who called you into the Ministry and that you called yourself?

210.   Do you now see that if you were not a liar and you truly had the Holy Spirit, then HE would have taught you all these mysteries in the Gospel of Christ?

211.   Brother, Sister, do you now see and admit that it is ONLY words, living words, the words of God, that are able to do all the above things that your filthy Water Baptism river and pool waters, and your Holy Comunion wafers, wine, and bread are NOT able to do?

212.   So, therefore, USE ONLY WORDS, THE WORD OF GOD, TO ACCOMPLISH ALL WORSHIP AND ALL SACRIFICES, INCLUDING WATER BAPTISM AND HOLY COMMUNION!

213.   As a true man of God, should you operate by what you see and feel? NO!

      i. **2 Corinthians 10:7 (KJV)** Do ye look on things after the outward appearance? If any man trust to himself that he is Christ's, let him of himself think this again, that, as he *is* Christ's, even so *are* we Christ's.

      ii. **2 Corinthians 4:18 (KJV)** While we look not at the things which are seen, but at the things which are not seen: for the things which are seen *are* temporal; but the things which are not seen *are* eternal.

214.   If, therefore, the LORD God commanded you to NOT operate in Ministry by what you see and feel because all those things are temporal, carnal, worldly, defiled, corrupt, and NOT of God, but instead God commanded you to operate by "the things which are not seen" because they share the same eternal attributes with God Almighty, and now, you on your part, you have defied God Almighty and you are operating and serving God in Ministry with "the things which are seen" such as your filthy Water Baptism river and pool waters, and your Holy Comunion wafers, wine, and bread, then, is it not plainly obvious that it was NOT the LORD Jesus Christ who called you into the Ministry?

215.   Is it not plainly obvious that it was NOT the LORD Holy Spirit who called you into the Ministry?

216.   Is it not plainly obvious that it was Satan who called you into the Ministry and that is why you are defying God Almighty and obeying Satan?

217.   If the LORD God Almighty gave you four commands in **2 Corinthians 10:5-8 (KJV)**, and you failed all of them, you are not obeying any of them, then, how is it that you do not have shame to continue to call yourself a Pastor or a bishop? Can a Man oif God defy God and still be a Man of God?

    i. **Amos 3:3 (KJV)** Can two walk together, except they be agreed?

    ii. **2 Corinthians 6:15 (KJV)** And what concord hath Christ with Belial? or what part hath he that believeth with an infidel?

    iii. **2 Corinthians 6:16 (KJV)** And what agreement hath the temple of God with idols? for ye are the temple of the living God; as God hath said, I will dwell in them, and walk in *them*; and I will be their God, and they shall be my people.

218.   Now, when that which is perfect is already come, it is only the preaching and teaching of the Word of God that is now needful and NOT the offering of useless physical oblations in useless church sacrifices that have zero ability to save anyone!

    i. **2 Corinthians 10:16 (KJV)** To preach the gospel in the *regions* beyond you, *and* not to boast in another man's line of things made ready to our hand.

    ii. **2 Corinthians 10:17 (KJV)** But he that glorieth, let him glory in the Lord.

    iii. **2 Corinthians 10:18 (KJV)** For not he that commendeth himself is approved, but whom the Lord commendeth.

    iv. **1 Corinthians 13:10 (KJV)** But when that which is perfect is come, then that which is in part shall be done away.

    v. **Luke 10:41 (KJV)** And Jesus answered and said unto her, Martha, Martha, thou art careful and troubled about many things:

    vi. **Luke 10:42 (KJV)** But one thing is needful: and Mary hath chosen that good part, which shall not be taken away from her.

    vii. **Revelation 1:11 (KJV)** Saying, I am Alpha and Omega, the first and the last: and, What thou seest, write in a book, and send *it* unto the seven churches which are in Asia; unto Ephesus, and unto Smyrna, and unto Pergamos, and unto Thyatira, and unto Sardis, and unto Philadelphia, and unto Laodicea.

219.   The LORD God Almighty, the LORD Jesus Christ, never commended anyone for excellent in sacrificing sheep and goats, neither did the LORD Jesus Christ commend anyone for excellence in sacrificing Holy Communion wafers, wine, and bread, but the LORD Jesus Christ surely commended HIS Disciples for excellence in

Teaching the Word of God unto Salvation! So, then, choose which function you want to receive commendation in: whether in the carnal filthy Holy Communion physical things, and Water Baptism, or, in the teaching of the Word of God ONLY!

 i. **2 Corinthians 10:18 (KJV)** For not he that commendeth himself is approved, but whom the Lord commendeth.

 ii. **Acts 18:9 (KJV)** Then spake the Lord to Paul in the night by a vision, Be not afraid, but speak, and hold not thy peace:

 iii. **Acts 18:10 (KJV)** For I am with thee, and no man shall set on thee to hurt thee: for I have much people in this city.

 iv. **Acts 18:11 (KJV)** And he continued *there* a year and six months, teaching the word of God among them.

 v. **Acts 23:11 (KJV)** And the night following the Lord stood by him, and said, Be of good cheer, Paul: for as thou hast testified of me in Jerusalem, so must thou bear witness also at Rome.

 vi. **Amos 5:21 (KJV)** I hate, I despise your feast days, and I will not smell in your solemn assemblies.

 vii. **Amos 5:22 (KJV)** Though ye offer me burnt offerings and your meat offerings, I will not accept *them*: neither will I regard the peace offerings of your fat beasts.

 viii. **Amos 5:23 (KJV)** Take thou away from me the noise of thy songs; for I will not hear the melody of thy viols.

 ix. **Amos 5:24 (KJV)** But let judgment run down as waters, and righteousness as a mighty stream.

 x. **Amos 5:25 (KJV)** Have ye offered unto me sacrifices and offerings in the wilderness forty years, O house of Israel?

 xi. **Amos 5:26 (KJV)** But ye have borne the tabernacle of your Moloch and Chiun your images, the star of your god, which ye made to yourselves.

 xii. **Amos 5:27 (KJV)** Therefore will I cause you to go into captivity beyond Damascus, saith the LORD, whose name *is* The God of hosts.

 xiii. **Acts 7:42 (KJV)** Then God turned, and gave them up to worship the host of heaven; as it is written in the book of the prophets, O ye house of Israel, have ye offered to me slain beasts and sacrifices *by the space of forty years in the wilderness?*

Wednesday 24th January 2024 @ 11:01 AM – 3:27 PM

CHAPTER 11: CHRISTIANITY IS SPIRITUAL MARRIAGE

220.   Why did the LORD Jesus Christ not marry?

221.   Because HE was already married!

      i. **2 Corinthians 11:1 (KJV)** Would to God ye could bear with me a little in *my* folly: and indeed bear with me.

      ii. **2 Corinthians 11:2 (KJV)** For I am jealous over you with godly jealousy: for I have espoused you to one husband, that I may present *you as* a chaste virgin to Christ.

222.   Christianity is spiritual marriage between Christ and HIS Bride called The Church, and the means of producing children into this marriage is by using the Word of God as **1 Corinthians 4:15 (KJV)** says, NOT human biologocal male sperm!

      i. **1 Corinthians 4:15 (KJV)** For though ye have ten thousand instructors in Christ, yet *have ye* not many fathers: for in Christ Jesus I have begotten you through the gospel.

      ii. **Romans 7:4 (KJV)** Wherefore, my brethren, ye also are become dead to the law by the body of Christ; that ye should be married to another, *even* to him who is raised from the dead, that we should bring forth fruit unto God.

      iii. **Revelation 21:9 (KJV)** And there came unto me one of the seven angels which had the seven vials full of the seven last plagues, and talked with me, saying, Come hither, I will shew thee the bride, the Lamb's wife.

223.   The superior spiritual Heavenly Seed/Sperm is the Word of God, whereas the inferior physical earthly seed is the male sperm!

      i. **Matthew 13:19 (KJV)** When any one heareth the word of the kingdom, and understandeth *it* not, then cometh the wicked *one*, and catcheth away that which was sown in his heart. This is he which received seed by the way side.

      ii. **Matthew 13:20 (KJV)** But he that received the seed into stony places, the same is he that heareth the word, and anon with joy receiveth it;

      iii. **Matthew 13:22 (KJV)** He also that received seed among the thorns is he that heareth the word; and the care of this world, and the deceitfulness of riches, choke the word, and he becometh unfruitful.

      iv. **Matthew 13:23 (KJV)** But he that received seed into the good ground is he that heareth the word, and understandeth *it*; which also beareth fruit, and bringeth forth, some an hundredfold, some sixty, some thirty.

    v. **Luke 8:11 (KJV)** Now the parable is this: The seed is the word of God.

224.   The superior spiritual Heavenly vagina and reproductive organ is the human mind, whereas the inferior physical earthly vagina and reproductive organ is the female vagina and her internal biological reproductive system!

225.   Hence, virginity in the spiritual realm is located in the mind and NOT in the biological genitalia! Furthermore, virginity is destroyed and lost NOT by reason of human biological intercourse, but by means of preaching and teaching wrong false evil doctrines of devils, and here is the evidence in **2 Corinthians 11:1-4 (KJV)**!

    i. **2 Corinthians 11:1 (KJV)** Would to God ye could bear with me a little in *my* folly: and indeed bear with me.

    ii. **2 Corinthians 11:2 (KJV)** For I am jealous over you with godly jealousy: for I have espoused you to one husband, that I may present *you as* a chaste virgin to Christ.

    iii. **2 Corinthians 11:3 (KJV)** But I fear, lest by any means, as the serpent beguiled Eve through his subtilty, so your minds should be corrupted from the simplicity that is in Christ.

    iv. **2 Corinthians 11:4 (KJV)** For if he that cometh preacheth another Jesus, whom we have not preached, or *if* ye receive another spirit, which ye have not received, or another gospel, which ye have not accepted, ye might well bear with *him*.

226.   Spirits use words and the mind to reproduce, NOT flesh! Therefore, when the words that come forth are evil, then, the children or the human beings or the products of the words or he or she that received the evil words, becomes automatically children of the spirit or children of the person who first issued those evil words!

    i. **Romans 6:16 (KJV)** Know ye not, that to whom ye yield yourselves servants to obey, his servants ye are to whom ye obey; whether of sin unto death, or of obedience unto righteousness?

227.   Likewise, when the words that come forth are good words, then whosoever receives those same good words, becomes the child of he/spirit who first issued those good words!

    i. **John 6:63 (KJV)** It is the spirit that quickeneth; the flesh profiteth nothing: the words that I speak unto you, *they* are spirit, and *they* are life.

    ii. **John 21:5 (KJV)** Then Jesus saith unto them, Children, have ye any meat? They answered him, No.

    iii. **1 John 2:1 (KJV)** My little children, these things write I unto you, that ye sin not. And if any man sin, we have an advocate with the Father, Jesus Christ the righteous:

    iv. **1 John 2:13 (KJV)** I write unto you, fathers, because ye have known him *that is* from the beginning. I write unto you, young men, because ye have overcome the wicked one. I write unto you, little children, because ye have known the Father.

    v. **1 John 2:18 (KJV)** Little children, it is the last time: and as ye have heard that antichrist shall come, even now are there many antichrists; whereby we know that it is the last time.

    vi. **1 John 2:28 (KJV)** And now, little children, abide in him; that, when he shall appear, we may have confidence, and not be ashamed before him at his coming.

    vii. **1 John 4:4 (KJV)** Ye are of God, little children, and have overcome them: because greater is he that is in you, than he that is in the world.

228.   Here is the evidence of the link between the spiritual mind (I knew thee) and the physical female womb (I formed thee in the belly)!

    i. **Jeremiah 1:5 (KJV)** Before I formed thee in the belly I knew thee; and before thou camest forth out of the womb I sanctified thee, *and* I ordained thee a prophet unto the nations.

229.   There is the Serpent Seed Doctrine that Mr. William Marrion Branham (April 6, 1909 – December 24, 1965) rebranded into Christianity following the racist white supremacy doctrine of Wesley A. Swift! Serpent Seed is the name of a teaching that is based on the Serpent (Satan or the Devil) having had sexual intercourse with Eve!

    i. **Revelation 12:9 (KJV)** And the great dragon was cast out, that old serpent, called the Devil, and Satan, which deceiveth the whole world: he was cast out into the earth, and his angels were cast out with him.

230.   Yet, here is the Truth of God Almighty showing exactly what happened between Satan and Eve! It was NOT any sexual intercouse seeing that spirits have no flash and bones, and seeing that it is impossible for fleshless spirits to mate with flesh humans!

    i. **Matthew 22:29 (KJV)** Jesus answered and said unto them, Ye do err, not knowing the scriptures, nor the power of God.

    ii. **Matthew 22:30 (KJV)** For in the resurrection they neither marry, nor are given in marriage, but are as the angels of God in heaven.

    iii. **Luke 24:36 (KJV)** And as they thus spake, Jesus himself stood in the midst of them, and saith unto them, Peace *be* unto you.

iv. **Luke 24:37 (KJV)** But they were terrified and affrighted, and supposed that they had seen a spirit.

v. **Luke 24:38 (KJV)** And he said unto them, Why are ye troubled? and why do thoughts arise in your hearts?

vi. **Luke 24:39 (KJV)** Behold my hands and my feet, that it is I myself: handle me, and see; for a spirit hath not flesh and bones, as ye see me have.

vii. **Luke 24:40 (KJV)** And when he had thus spoken, he shewed them *his* hands and *his* feet.

231.   In **2 Corinthians 11:3 (KJV)**, the LORD God Almighty reveals to us exactly what happened between Satan and Eve!

i. **2 Corinthians 11:3 (KJV)** But I fear, lest by any means, as the serpent beguiled Eve through his subtilty, so your minds should be corrupted from the simplicity that is in Christ.

232.   Now, from the revelation in **2 Corinthians 11:3 (KJV)**, and all the above verses that I have just shown you, especially, the truth that spirits have no flesh and bones, and that spirits cannot intermarry with humans, therefore, the only option that is left between Satan and Eve is the spiritual procreation method of words + mind, and that is excatly what Satan did with Eve, even as the LORD Holy Spirit also reveals in **2 Corinthians 11:3 (KJV)**!

233.   Satan gave Eve evil corrupted words as **2 Corinthians 11:3 (KJV)** says, Eve accepted and received the evil words in her mind, and in that same moment, Eve became a child of Satan by reason of the spiritual law of **Romans 6:16 (KJV)**, and since Eve was the first woman, therefore, all her offspring also became corrupted and owned by Satan since they issued from the already corrupted Tree/Eve!

234.   In the spieitual realm, a virgin is NOT of the flesh, but is one whose mind has not been corrupted by evil doctrines from the time that he or she became born again!

i. **2 Corinthians 11:2 (KJV)** For I am jealous over you with godly jealousy: for I have espoused you to one husband, that I may present *you as* a chaste virgin to Christ.

ii. **Isaiah 1:1 (KJV)** The vision of Isaiah the son of Amoz, which he saw concerning Judah and Jerusalem in the days of Uzziah, Jotham, Ahaz, *and* Hezekiah, kings of Judah.

iii. **Isaiah 1:2 (KJV)** Hear, O heavens, and give ear, O earth: for the LORD hath spoken, I have nourished and brought up children, and they have rebelled against me.

iv. **Hosea 1:2 (KJV)** The beginning of the word of the LORD by Hosea. And the LORD said to Hosea, Go, take unto thee a wife of whoredoms and children of whoredoms: for the land hath committed great whoredom, *departing* from the LORD.

235. In the spiritual realm, here are the three different ways for producing children:
    i. ONE – Through preaching/teaching.
    ii. TWO – Through receiving words/concept/ideas/thoughts (remember that words are spirits as I showed you). **John 6:63 (KJV)**
    iii. THREE – through another gospel!
    iv. **2 Corinthians 11:4 (KJV)** For if he that cometh preacheth another Jesus, whom we have not preached, or *if* ye receive another spirit, which ye have not received, or another gospel, which ye have not accepted, ye might well bear with *him*.

236. Christianity is the acquisition of the knowledge of Christ and obedience to that knowledge!
    i. **2 Corinthians 11:6 (KJV)** But though *I be* rude in speech, yet not in knowledge; but we have been throughly made manifest among you in all things.
    ii. **Matthew 10:8 (KJV)** Heal the sick, cleanse the lepers, raise the dead, cast out devils: freely ye have received, freely give.

237. To all those who have this ready-made statement in their mouth: "freely ye have received, freely give", without finding out whether they have understood it and are using it correctly or not, here is **2 Corinthians 11:7 (KJV)** showing you that you have been wrong all along!
    i. **2 Corinthians 11:7 (KJV)** Have I committed an offence in abasing myself that ye might be exalted, because I have preached to you the gospel of God freely?
    ii. **2 Corinthians 11:8 (KJV)** I robbed other churches, taking wages *of them*, to do you service.
    iii. **2 Corinthians 12:13 (KJV)** For what is it wherein ye were inferior to other churches, except *it be* that I myself was not burdensome to you? forgive me this wrong.
    iv. **1 Corinthians 9:13 (KJV)** Do ye not know that they which minister about holy things live *of the things* of the temple? and they which wait at the altar are partakers with the altar?
    v. **1 Corinthians 9:14 (KJV)** Even so hath the Lord ordained that they which preach the gospel should live of the gospel.

238. As you can see in **2 Corinthians 11:7-8 (KJV)**, when you are a Man of God and you preach or teach the Word of God freely, then:
    i. ONE – You are committing an offence!

    ii.   **TWO** – You are abasing yourself!

    iii.   **THREE** – You are robbing that place where you receive the wages that should rather have come from the group or congregation that received the preaching/teaching from you!

    iv.   **FOUR** – It is ordained of God Amighty for the Man of God to receive wages for his work!

    v.   **FIVE** – The church, the group, and the congregation that refuses to administer the material and financial burden of the true Man of God is in an inferior spiritual position compared to the congregation that obeys this Spiritual Law of Christian Reciprocal Giving!

    vi.   **SIX** – The Pastor or the Man of God who declines the congregational administration of their duty of the Spiritual Law of Christian Reciprocal Giving is himself doing wrong!

239.   It is correct Christian doctrine that the true Man of God must be given wages for his work!

    i.   **2 Corinthians 11:9 (KJV)** And when I was present with you, and wanted, I was chargeable to no man: for that which was lacking to me the brethren which came from Macedonia supplied: and in all *things* I have kept myself from being burdensome unto you, and *so* will I keep *myself.*

240.   Take note very crefully, that in these Last Days, Satan does NOT come with plain evil words and thoughts, but he comes with words and thoughts that look very much like the words and thoughts of the LORD God Almighty!

    i.   **2 Corinthians 11:13 (KJV)** For such *are* false apostles, deceitful workers, transforming themselves into the apostles of Christ.

    ii.   **2 Corinthians 11:14 (KJV)** And no marvel; for Satan himself is transformed into an angel of light.

    iii.   **2 Corinthians 11:15 (KJV)** Therefore *it is* no great thing if his ministers also be transformed as the ministers of righteousness; whose end shall be according to their works.

    iv.   **Jeremiah 23:30 (KJV)** Therefore, behold, I *am* against the prophets, saith the LORD, that steal my words every one from his neighbour.

241.   Here is Satan coming to quote Holy Scriptures to the LORD Jesus Christ in order to deveive HIM, but he failed!

    i.   **Matthew 4:5 (KJV)** Then the devil taketh him up into the holy city, and setteth him on a pinnacle of the temple,

    ii.   **Matthew 4:6 (KJV)** And saith unto him, If thou be the Son of God, cast thyself down: for it is written, He shall give his angels charge concerning thee: and in *their* hands they shall bear thee up, lest at any time thou dash thy foot against a stone.

iii. **Matthew 4:7 (KJV)** Jesus said unto him, It is written again, Thou shalt not tempt the Lord thy God.

242.   Here is how to trace Jewishness! A Jew in the flesh must come from the lineage of Abraham, Isaac, and Jacob! Without that lineage, then, he/she is NOT a Jew!

i. **2 Corinthians 11:22 (KJV)** Are they Hebrews? so *am* I. Are they Israelites? so *am* I. Are they the seed of Abraham? so *am* I.

243.   The credentials of every true Man of God must include personal suffering, without which personal suffering, he is NOT yet a Man of God!

i. **2 Corinthians 11:23 (KJV)** Are they ministers of Christ? (I speak as a fool) I *am* more; in labours more abundant, in stripes above measure, in prisons more frequent, in deaths oft.

ii. **2 Corinthians 11:24 (KJV)** Of the Jews five times received I forty *stripes* save one.

iii. **2 Corinthians 11:25 (KJV)** Thrice was I beaten with rods, once was I stoned, thrice I suffered shipwreck, a night and a day I have been in the deep;

iv. **2 Corinthians 11:26 (KJV)** *In* journeyings often, *in* perils of waters, *in* perils of robbers, *in* perils by *mine own* countrymen, *in* perils by the heathen, *in* perils in the city, *in* perils in the wilderness, *in* perils in the sea, *in* perils among false brethren;

v. **2 Corinthians 11:27 (KJV)** In weariness and painfulness, in watchings often, in hunger and thirst, in fastings often, in cold and nakedness.

vi. **2 Corinthians 11:28 (KJV)** Beside those things that are without, that which cometh upon me daily, the care of all the churches.

vii. **2 Corinthians 11:29 (KJV)** Who is weak, and I am not weak? who is offended, and I burn not?

Thursday 25th January 2024 @ 11:25 AM – 2:11 PM

CHAPTER 12: IN HEAVEN, THEY SPEAK HUMAN LANGUAGES, NOT UNKNOWN TONGUES

244.   The LORD God reveals to us that there are three Heavens in the spiritual realm!

     i. **2 Corinthians 12:1 (KJV)** It is not expedient for me doubtless to glory. I will come to visions and revelations of the Lord.

     ii. **2 Corinthians 12:2 (KJV)** I knew a man in Christ above fourteen years ago, (whether in the body, I cannot tell; or whether out of the body, I cannot tell: God knoweth;) such an one caught up to the third heaven.

245.   Apostle Paul, in his Ministry, wen to The Third Heaven:

     i. **2 Corinthians 12:3 (KJV)** And I knew such a man, (whether in the body, or out of the body, I cannot tell: God knoweth;)

246.   Now, there are some who say that there is a Heavenly language that Satan does not understand, and so, when they speak in their incomprehensible gibberish, then, it is that Heavenly language! Yet, the LORD God calls all of them liars in **2 Corinthians 12:4 (KJV)**!

     i. **2 Corinthians 12:4 (KJV)** How that he was caught up into paradise, and heard unspeakable words, which it is not lawful for a man to utter.

247.   Surely, we have the evidence in **2 Corinthians 12:4 (KJV)**, that in Heaven, even in The Third Heaven, the language that is spoken over there is comprehensible, is understandable, to the Children of God!

248.   Furtheremore, if there should be any secret language in Heaven that these evil demonic tongue-speaking Christians are speaking, then, who would be in a better position to hear it, to understand it, and to speak it?

     i.   **Revelation 12:7 (KJV)** And there was war in heaven: Michael and his angels fought against the dragon; and the dragon fought and his angels,

     ii. **Revelation 12:8 (KJV)** And prevailed not; neither was their place found any more in heaven.

     iii. **Revelation 12:9 (KJV)** And the great dragon was cast out, that old serpent, called the Devil, and Satan, which deceiveth the whole world: he was cast out into the earth, and his angels were cast out with him.

     iv. **Revelation 12:10 (KJV)** And I heard a loud voice saying in heaven, Now is come salvation, and strength, and the kingdom of our God, and the power of his Christ: for the accuser of our brethren is cast down, which accused them before our God day and night.

v. **Revelation 12:11 (KJV)** And they overcame him by the blood of the Lamb, and by the word of their testimony; and they loved not their lives unto the death.

vi. **Revelation 12:12 (KJV)** Therefore rejoice, *ye* heavens, and ye that dwell in them. Woe to the inhabiters of the earth and of the sea! for the devil is come down unto you, having great wrath, because he knoweth that he hath but a short time.

vii. **Revelation 12:13 (KJV)** And when the dragon saw that he was cast unto the earth, he persecuted the woman which brought forth the man *child*.

viii. **Revelation 12:14 (KJV)** And to the woman were given two wings of a great eagle, that she might fly into the wilderness, into her place, where she is nourished for a time, and times, and half a time, from the face of the serpent.

249.   The answer is, Satan, because he lived in Heaven before he was cast out, whereas you never lived there!

250.   The second reason why all you gibberish evil demonic tongue-speakers are evil beasts is that, here are two spirits: the LORD Jesus Christ and Satan!

i. They both lived in Heaven, and they have both come down to the Earth!

ii. Therefore, naturally, they will communicate in the same language that they both spoke to each other in Heaven!

iii. And what is that language? IT IS A HUMAN LANGUAGE!

iv. **Matthew 4:1 (KJV)** Then was Jesus led up of the Spirit into the wilderness to be tempted of the devil.

v. **Matthew 4:2 (KJV)** And when he had fasted forty days and forty nights, he was afterward an hungred.

vi. **Matthew 4:3 (KJV)** And when the tempter came to him, he said, If thou be the Son of God, command that these stones be made bread.

vii. **Matthew 4:4 (KJV)** But he answered and said, It is written, Man shall not live by bread alone, but by every word that proceedeth out of the mouth of God.

viii. **Matthew 4:5 (KJV)** Then the devil taketh him up into the holy city, and setteth him on a pinnacle of the temple,

ix. **Matthew 4:6 (KJV)** And saith unto him, If thou be the Son of God, cast thyself down: for it is written, He shall give his angels charge concerning thee: and in *their* hands they shall bear thee up, lest at any time thou dash thy foot against a stone.

x. **Matthew 4:7 (KJV)** Jesus said unto him, It is written again, Thou shalt not tempt the Lord thy God.

xi. **Matthew 4:8 (KJV)** Again, the devil taketh him up into an exceeding high mountain, and sheweth him all the kingdoms of the world, and the glory of them;

xii. **Matthew 4:9 (KJV)** And saith unto him, All these things will I give thee, if thou wilt fall down and worship me.

xiii. **Matthew 4:10 (KJV)** Then saith Jesus unto him, Get thee hence, Satan: for it is written, Thou shalt worship the Lord thy God, and him only shalt thou serve.

xiv. **Matthew 4:11 (KJV)** Then the devil leaveth him, and, behold, angels came and ministered unto him.

251. Here is the third evidence against all you gibberish evil demonic tongue-speaking evil beasts! Here is the LORD God Almighty speaking with the LORD Yeshua Christ in Heaven, and there are no humans there in their midst, and what language are they using? IT IS A HUMAN LANGUAGE!

i. **Psalm 110:1 (KJV)** A Psalm of David. The LORD said unto my Lord, Sit thou at my right hand, until I make thine enemies thy footstool.

ii. **Hebrews 1:13 (KJV)** But to which of the angels said he at any time, Sit on my right hand, until I make thine enemies thy footstool?

252. So, all you gibberish evil demonic tongue-speaking evil beasts, do you now see how very stupidly ignorant you are?

i. **Matthew 22:29 (KJV)** Jesus answered and said unto them, Ye do err, not knowing the scriptures, nor the power of God.

253. Here is one example wherein affliction of the true Man of God can be spiritually good, beneficial, and a bridge to higher spiritual levels!

i. **2 Corinthians 12:7 (KJV)** And lest I should be exalted above measure through the abundance of the revelations, there was given to me a thorn in the flesh, the messenger of Satan to buffet me, lest I should be exalted above measure.

ii. **2 Corinthians 12:8 (KJV)** For this thing I besought the Lord thrice, that it might depart from me.

iii. **2 Corinthians 12:9 (KJV)** And he said unto me, My grace is sufficient for thee: for my strength is made perfect in weakness. Most gladly therefore will I rather glory in my infirmities, that the power of Christ may rest upon me.

iv. **2 Corinthians 12:10 (KJV)** Therefore I take pleasure in infirmities, in reproaches, in necessities, in persecutions, in distresses for Christ's sake: for when I am weak, then am I strong.

254.　　　In the Christian Ministry, as revealed in **2 Corinthians 12:14-15 (KJV)**, a father is one who feeds the congregation with understanding in the Word of God!

i. **2 Corinthians 12:14 (KJV)** Behold, the third time I am ready to come to you; and I will not be burdensome to you: for I seek not yours, but you: for the children ought not to lay up for the parents, but the parents for the children.

ii. **2 Corinthians 12:15 (KJV)** And I will very gladly spend and be spent for you; though the more abundantly I love you, the less I be loved.

iii. **Jeremiah 3:15 (KJV)** And I will give you pastors according to mine heart, which shall feed you with knowledge and understanding.

iv. **Lamentations 2:12 (KJV)** They say to their mothers, Where *is* corn and wine? when they swooned as the wounded in the streets of the city, when their soul was poured out into their mothers' bosom.

v. **Malachi 2:7 (KJV)** For the priest's lips should keep knowledge, and they should seek the law at his mouth: for he *is* the messenger of the LORD of hosts.

vi. **John 21:15 (KJV)** So when they had dined, Jesus saith to Simon Peter, Simon, *son* of Jonas, lovest thou me more than these? He saith unto him, Yea, Lord; thou knowest that I love thee. He saith unto him, Feed my lambs.

vii. **John 21:16 (KJV)** He saith to him again the second time, Simon, *son* of Jonas, lovest thou me? He saith unto him, Yea, Lord; thou knowest that I love thee. He saith unto him, Feed my sheep.

viii. **John 21:17 (KJV)** He saith unto him the third time, Simon, *son* of Jonas, lovest thou me? Peter was grieved because he said unto him the third time, Lovest thou me? And he said unto him, Lord, thou knowest all things; thou knowest that I love thee. Jesus saith unto him, Feed my sheep.

ix. **Luke 11:11 (KJV)** If a son shall ask bread of any of you that is a father, will he give him a stone? or if *he ask* a fish, will he for a fish give him a serpent?

x. **Luke 11:12 (KJV)** Or if he shall ask an egg, will he offer him a scorpion?

xi. **Luke 11:13 (KJV)** If ye then, being evil, know how to give good gifts unto your children: how much more shall *your* heavenly Father give the Holy Spirit to them that ask him?

255.　　　A successful Ministry of a true Man of God is the one where the Man of God is able to say on the witness of the congregation that "I have NOT made any gain out of you"! A Man of God who hesitates to say that, or who cannot make that declaration, is already guilty of theft of church money!

i. **2 Corinthians 12:17 (KJV)** Did I make a gain of you by any of them whom I sent unto you?

ii. **2 Corinthians 12:18 (KJV)** I desired Titus, and with *him* I sent a brother. Did Titus make a gain of you? walked we not in the same spirit? *walked we* not in the same steps?

iii. **2 Corinthians 12:19 (KJV)** Again, think ye that we excuse ourselves unto you? we speak before God in Christ: but *we do* all things, dearly beloved, for your edifying.

256.　　　Sin is an uncleanness! Sin is a filthiness! And the true Man of God is he who bewails and bemoans the evil in the congregation and rebukes the sin sharply without mercy!

i. **2 Corinthians 12:20 (KJV)** For I fear, lest, when I come, I shall not find you such as I would, and *that* I shall be found unto you such as ye would not: lest *there be* debates, envyings, wraths, strifes, backbitings, whisperings, swellings, tumults:

ii. **2 Corinthians 12:21 (KJV)** *And* lest, when I come again, my God will humble me among you, and *that* I shall bewail many which have sinned already, and have not repented of the uncleanness and fornication and lasciviousness which they have committed.

Thursday 25th January 2024 @ 9:14 PM – 11:07 PM

CHAPTER 13: HOW TO COUNSEL CONCERNING SIN IN THE CONGREGATION

257.   The Man of God must first hear the matter and then search and establish whether, truly, the person being accused or suspected has truly committed the sin so named, and he should establish the truth at the mouth of two or three witnesses!!

      i.   **2 Corinthians 13:1 (KJV)** This *is* the third *time* I am coming to you. In the mouth of two or three witnesses shall every word be established.

258.   The Man of God shall NOT condone sin in the congregation!

      i.   **2 Corinthians 13:2 (KJV)** I told you before, and foretell you, as if I were present, the second time; and being absent now I write to them which heretofore have sinned, and to all other, that, if I come again, I will not spare:.

259.   The Man of God shall rely ONLY on the Gospel of Christ to guide him in deliberate the sin!

      i.   **2 Corinthians 13:3 (KJV)** Since ye seek a proof of Christ speaking in me, which to you-ward is not weak, but is mighty in you.

      ii. **2 Corinthians 13:4 (KJV)** For though he was crucified through weakness, yet he liveth by the power of God. For we also are weak in him, but we shall live with him by the power of God toward you.

260.   The parties themselves shall examine themselves in the Woird of God whether their action is approved in the Word of God, or not!

      i.   **2 Corinthians 13:5 (KJV)** Examine yourselves, whether ye be in the faith; prove your own selves. Know ye not your own selves, how that Jesus Christ is in you, except ye be reprobates?

      ii. **2 Corinthians 13:6 (KJV)** But I trust that ye shall know that we are not reprobates.

261.   The matter shall be decided on the side of Truth and never by favouritism or by respecting persons, for that is evil!

      i.   **2 Corinthians 13:7 (KJV)** Now I pray to God that ye do no evil; not that we should appear approved, but that ye should do that which is honest, though we be as reprobates.

      ii. **2 Corinthians 13:8 (KJV)** For we can do nothing against the truth, but for the truth.

      iii. **Deuteronomy 1:17 (KJV)** Ye shall not respect persons in judgment; *but* ye shall hear the small as well as the great; ye shall not be afraid of the face of man; for the judgment *is* God's: and the cause that is too hard for you, bring *it* unto me, and I will hear it.

iv. **Deuteronomy 16:19 (KJV)** Thou shalt not wrest judgment; thou shalt not respect persons, neither take a gift: for a gift doth blind the eyes of the wise, and pervert the words of the righteous.

v. **Proverbs 28:21 (KJV)** To have respect of persons *is* not good: for for a piece of bread *that* man will transgress.

vi. **Acts 10:34 (KJV)** Then Peter opened *his* mouth, and said, Of a truth I perceive that God is no respecter of persons:

vii. **James 2:1 (KJV)** My brethren, have not the faith of our Lord Jesus Christ, *the Lord* of glory, with respect of persons.

262. While counseling in a matter of sin in the congregation, the Man of God shall be perfect in doctrine and in the application of the doctrine of Christ!

i. **2 Corinthians 13:9 (KJV)** For we are glad, when we are weak, and ye are strong: and this also we wish, *even* your perfection.

ii. **2 Corinthians 13:10 (KJV)** Therefore I write these things being absent, lest being present I should use sharpness, according to the power which the Lord hath given me to edification, and not to destruction.

iii. **2 Corinthians 13:11 (KJV)** Finally, brethren, farewell. Be perfect, be of good comfort, be of one mind, live in peace; and the God of love and peace shall be with you.

iv. **Matthew 18:15 (KJV)** Moreover if thy brother shall trespass against thee, go and tell him his fault between thee and him alone: if he shall hear thee, thou hast gained thy brother.

v. **Matthew 18:16 (KJV)** But if he will not hear *thee, then* take with thee one or two more, that in the mouth of two or three witnesses every word may be established.

vi. **Matthew 18:17 (KJV)** And if he shall neglect to hear them, tell *it* unto the church: but if he neglect to hear the church, let him be unto thee as an heathen man and a publican.

263. While counseling in a matter of sin in the congregation, the Man of God shall always aim for the edification and unity of the congregation in one accord with the Trinity of the Godhead!

i. **2 Corinthians 13:12 (KJV)** Greet one another with an holy kiss.

ii. **2 Corinthians 13:13 (KJV)** All the saints salute you.

iii. **2 Corinthians 13:14 (KJV)** The grace of the Lord Jesus Christ, and the love of God, and the communion of the Holy Ghost, *be* with you all. Amen. The second *epistle* to the Corinthians was written from Philippi, *a city* of Macedonia, by Titus and Lucas.

264.   Here is the Trinity of the Godhead:
  i.   The Lord Jesus Christ.
  ii.   The Lord God Almighty.
  iii.   The Lord Holy Ghost.

Saturday 27th January 2024 @ 1:11 AM – 2:08 AM

CHAPTER 4
GENERAL CONCLUSION

AKOMA
"The heart"

Asante philosophical symbol of Patience, Love, Goodwill, Tolerance, Faithfulness, Fondness, Endurance, Consistency

We have come to the end of this Book – *Complete Bible Curriculum: How to Examine Pastors, Vol. 4 – Fundamental Concepts for Successful Christian Life: Covering 1 & 2 Corinthians* – in which we have taught all and everything that the LORD God Almighty has embedded and revealed to me concerning Pastoral Examination and how to verify the doctrines of Pastors in the Books of *1 & 2 Corinthians*, in order to know whether they were called of God or whether they work for Satan!

This is a most valuable study and reference material for the Spiritual Bible Training of Ministers so that the Man of God should be well equipped and adequately furnished to respond to all spiritual questions regarding the doctrines in the Books of *1 & 2 Corinthians*!

> **Jeremiah 3:15 (KJV)** And I will give you pastors according to mine heart, which shall feed you with knowledge and understanding.

> **Malachi 2:7 (KJV)** For the priest's lips should keep knowledge, and they should seek the law at his mouth: for he *is* the messenger of the LORD of hosts.

2 Timothy 3:16 (KJV) All Scripture *is* given by inspiration of God, and *is* profitable for doctrine, for reproof, for correction, for instruction in righteousness:

2 Timothy 3:17 (KJV) That the man of God may be perfect, throughly furnished unto all good works.

We used the Scriptures from Genesis to Revelation as our main and only research material according to the methodology of Bible research and doctrine that God Almighty revealed in the Holy Scriptures:

Isaiah 8:20 (KJV) To the law and to the testimony: if they speak not according to this word, *it is* because *there is* no light in them.

Jeremiah 23:28 (KJV) The prophet that hath a dream, let him tell a dream; and he that hath my word, let him speak my word faithfully. What *is* the chaff to the wheat? saith the LORD.

Galatians 1:8 (KJV) But though we, or an angel from heaven, preach any other gospel unto you than that which we have preached unto you, let him be accursed.

Galatians 1:9 (KJV) As we said before, so say I now again, If any *man* preach any other gospel unto you than that ye have received, let him be accursed.

Throughout our research, we have solidified our belief that while all other things shall pass away, only the Word of God will remain. That observation further reveals that, given the capital importance of the Word of God and its power of Salvation to them that believe, in other words, its ability to become your Ticket to Heaven, God Almighty also did not leave carnal humans to decide how to teach it, nor even to determine the foolishness or otherwise of the Scriptures, seeing that God Almighty uses the foolish things of the world to confound the wise:

1 Corinthians 1:26 (KJV) For ye see your calling, brethren, how that not many wise men after the flesh, not many mighty, not many noble, *are called*:

1 Corinthians 1:27 (KJV) But God hath chosen the foolish things of the world to confound the wise; and God hath chosen the weak things of the world to confound the things which are mighty;

1 Corinthians 1:28 (KJV) And base things of the world, and things which are despised, hath God chosen, *yea*, and things which are not, to bring to nought things that are:

1 Corinthians 1:29 (KJV) That no flesh should glory in his presence.

The following groups of people will find excellent use for this Christian Theological Research Textbook:

1. Already established Ministers who are still teaching the Word of God.
2. Newly ordained Ministers in churches who are seeking Pastoral Training on how to approach and understanding spiritual proverbs and parables as a foundation to understanding the entire Holy Bible.
3. Theological Scholars who are researching theological questions in the Holy Scriptures.
4. Bible Students at the following levels of academic and spiritual pursuit:
5. **SUMMARY OF DEGREE PROGRAMS IN THE BIBLE UNIVERSITY**:
    The Bible University offers the following Degree Programs:
    i. Occupational Certificate: **Religious Associate Professional (Christian Religious Practitioner): South African Qualifications Authority (SAQA)ID 101997.**
    ii. Certificate in Theology (C. Th.) (for just one topic or two) – 1 month
    iii. Diploma in Theology (Dip. Th.) is a self-paced one-year diploma program of purely Bible Study, Bible Translation, and Bible Interpretation
    iv. Bachelor of Theology (B.Th.) – 2-year degree program to complete 22 self-selected Books of the Holy Bible
    v. Master of Theology (M.Th.) – 2-year degree program to complete 44 self-selected Books of the Holy Bible
    i. Doctor of Theology (Th.D.) – 4-year degree program to complete all 66 Books of the Holy Bible
    ii. Diploma in Chaplaincy Training Program for Pastors
    iii. Diploma in Church Financial Management Training Program for Pastors
    iv. Diploma in General Counseling Training Program for Pastors
    v. Diploma in Marriage Counseling Training Program for Pastors
    vi. Diploma in Sermon Preparation for Ministers of the Gospel

vii. Preparation of Bible Topics for Christian Conference and award of Conference Certificates to Participants

The Scriptures the Word of God are in two parts, and possessing one part but lacking the other invalidates what you have! The two parts are:

i. The written Scriptures, and
ii. The Holy Spirit

When those two do not combine, you do not have the Word of God! Just as you do not have a ship and you will die if you purchase one from the market and you lack the professionally approved Pilot to captain the ship and navigate the treacherous waters for you, so also, you do not have Scriptures the Word of God, and you will die, if you purchase one Holy Bible from the open market but you lack the Driver called Holy Spirit to help you navigate the treacherous spiritual realm within it! Here is the evidence:

Luke 24:48 (KJV) And ye are witnesses of these things.

Luke 24:49 (KJV) And, behold, I send the promise of my Father upon you: but tarry ye in the city of Jerusalem, until ye be endued with power from on high.

John 14:15 (KJV) If ye love me, keep my commandments.

John 14:16 (KJV) And I will pray the Father, and he shall give you another Comforter, that he may abide with you for ever;

John 14:17 (KJV) *Even* the Spirit of truth; whom the world cannot receive, because it seeth him not, neither knoweth him: but ye know him; for he dwelleth with you, and shall be in you.

John 16:12 (KJV) I have yet many things to say unto you, but ye cannot bear them now.

John 16:13 (KJV) Howbeit when he, the Spirit of truth, is come, he will guide you into all truth: for he shall not speak of himself; but whatsoever he shall hear, *that* shall he speak: and he will shew you things to come.

John 16:14 (KJV) He shall glorify me: for he shall receive of mine, and shall shew *it* unto you.

Romans 8:9 (KJV) But ye are not in the flesh, but in the Spirit, if so be that the Spirit of God dwell in you. Now if any man have not the Spirit of Christ, he is none of his.

Romans 8:14 (KJV) For as many as are led by the Spirit of God, they are the sons of God.

THE DOCTRINE OF THE BIBLE UNIVERSITY

In this section, I identify thirteen foundational pillars of The Bible University Doctrine! This is our doctrine and this is where we stand in the Holy Scriptures. Let us consider the following verses to confirm our doctrine:

1. In The Bible University, we teach ONLY the Holy Bible the Word of God, from Genesis to Revelation, without any denominational influence!

    i. **Matthew 28:18 (KJV)** And Jesus came and spake unto them, saying, All power is given unto me in heaven and in earth.

    ii. **Matthew 28:19 (KJV)** Go ye therefore, and teach all nations, baptizing them in the name of the Father, and of the Son, and of the Holy Ghost:

    iii. **Matthew 28:20 (KJV)** Teaching them to observe all things whatsoever I have commanded you: and, lo, I am with you alway, *even* unto the end of the world. Amen.

2. In The Bible University, we question everything by the Scriptures, we question every church practise, we question every church doctrine, we judge everything, and we judge every Man of God… by the Scriptures!

    i. **John 7:24 (KJV)** Judge not according to the appearance, but judge righteous judgment.

    ii. **Acts 17:11 (KJV)** These were more noble than those in Thessalonica, in that they received the word with all readiness of mind, and searched the scriptures daily, whether those things were so.

    iii. **1 Corinthians 14:29 (KJV)** Let the prophets speak two or three, and let the other judge.

    iv. **1 Thessalonians 5:21 (KJV)** Prove all things; hold fast that which is good.

    v. **1 John 4:1 (KJV)** Beloved, believe not every spirit, but try the spirits whether they are of God: because many false prophets are gone out into the world.

3. In The Bible University, our foundational doctrine is that there is ONLY ONE WAY to teach, to translate, and to interpret the Word of God, which is: YOU MUST TEACH THE WORD OF GOD TO AGREE WITH THE WORD OF GOD!

     i.   **Proverbs 21:30 (KJV)** *There is* no wisdom nor understanding nor counsel against the LORD.

     ii.   **Isaiah 8:20 (KJV)** To the law and to the testimony: if they speak not according to this word, *it is* because *there is* no light in them.

     iii.   **Jeremiah 23:28 (KJV)** The prophet that hath a dream, let him tell a dream; and he that hath my word, let him speak my word faithfully. What *is* the chaff to the wheat? saith the LORD.

     iv.   **John 10:35 (KJV)** If he called them gods, unto whom the word of God came, and the scripture cannot be broken;

     v.   **Galatians 1:8 (KJV)** But though we, or an angel from heaven, preach any other gospel unto you than that which we have preached unto you, let him be accursed.

     vi.   **Galatians 1:9 (KJV)** As we said before, so say I now again, If any *man* preach any other gospel unto you than that ye have received, let him be accursed.

4. In The Bible University, our foundational doctrine is that: TO QUALIFY AS A MAN OF GOD, YOU MUST THINK, SPEAK, AND OBEY THE WORD OF GOD COMPLETELY TO REFLECT THAT HOLY SPIRIT LIVES IN YOU!

     i.   **Joshua 1:8 (KJV)** This book of the law shall not depart out of thy mouth; but thou shalt meditate therein day and night, that thou mayest observe to do according to all that is written therein: for then thou shalt make thy way prosperous, and then thou shalt have good success.

     ii.   **John 6:63 (KJV)** It is the spirit that quickeneth; the flesh profiteth nothing: the words that I speak unto you, *they* are spirit, and *they* are life.

     iii.   **John 14:17 (KJV)** *Even* the Spirit of truth; whom the world cannot receive, because it seeth him not, neither knoweth him: but ye know him; for he dwelleth with you, and shall be in you.

     iv.   **John 15:7 (KJV)** If ye abide in me, and my words abide in you, ye shall ask what ye will, and it shall be done unto you.

     v.   **Colossians 1:9 (KJV)** For this cause we also, since the day we heard *it*, do not cease to pray for you, and to desire that ye might be filled with the knowledge of his will in all wisdom and spiritual understanding;

5. In The Bible University, by means of the Word of God, we identify, analyze, dissect, point out, prove, show, expose, and overthrow evil church doctrines and practices that have no basis in the Holy Bible, that violate the Holy Scriptures, and that are contrary

to the Gospel of Jesus Christ! We rebuke sharply, sparing no man or woman, to the intent "that they may be sound in the faith"!

    i. **2 Corinthians 13:10 (KJV)** Therefore I write these things being absent, lest being present I should use sharpness, according to the power which the Lord hath given me to edification, and not to destruction.

    ii. **1 Timothy 5:20 (KJV)** Them that sin rebuke before all, that others also may fear.

    iii. **Titus 1:13 (KJV)** This witness is true. Wherefore rebuke them sharply, that they may be sound in the faith;

6. In The Bible University, we judge the spiritual controversies of Jesus Christ and Apostle Paul with the Word of God Almighty!

    i. **Deuteronomy 17:8 (KJV)** If there arise a matter too hard for thee in judgment, between blood and blood, between plea and plea, and between stroke and stroke, *being* matters of controversy within thy gates: then shalt thou arise, and get thee up into the place which the LORD thy God shall choose;

    ii. **Deuteronomy 19:17 (KJV)** Then both the men, between whom the controversy *is*, shall stand before the LORD, before the priests and the judges, which shall be in those days;

    iii. **Deuteronomy 21:5 (KJV)** And the priests the sons of Levi shall come near; for them the LORD thy God hath chosen to minister unto him, and to bless in the name of the LORD; and by their word shall every controversy and every stroke be *tried*:

    iv. **Deuteronomy 25:1 (KJV)** If there be a controversy between men, and they come unto judgment, that *the judges* may judge them; then they shall justify the righteous, and condemn the wicked.

    v. **Jeremiah 25:31 (KJV)** A noise shall come *even* to the ends of the earth; for the LORD hath a controversy with the nations, he will plead with all flesh; he will give them *that are* wicked to the sword, saith the LORD.

    vi. **Ezekiel 44:24 (KJV)** And in controversy they shall stand in judgment; *and* they shall judge it according to my judgments: and they shall keep my laws and my statutes in all mine assemblies; and they shall hallow my sabbaths.

    vii. **1 Timothy 3:16 (KJV)** And without controversy great is the mystery of godliness: God was manifest in the flesh, justified in the Spirit, seen of angels, preached unto the Gentiles, believed on in the world, received up into glory.

viii. **2 Chronicles 19:8 (KJV)** Moreover in Jerusalem did Jehoshaphat set of the Levites, and *of* the priests, and of the chief of the fathers of Israel, for the judgment of the LORD, and for controversies, when they returned to Jerusalem.

7. In The Bible University, we maintain The Offence of the Cross!

i. **John 6:61 (KJV)** When Jesus knew in himself that his disciples murmured at it, he said unto them, Doth this offend you?

ii. **Galatians 5:11 (KJV)** And I, brethren, if I yet preach circumcision, why do I yet suffer persecution? then is the offence of the cross ceased.

iii. **James 3:2 (KJV)** For in many things we offend all. If any man offend not in word, the same *is* a perfect man, *and* able also to bridle the whole body.

8. In The Bible University, we do not shy away from Bible errors and contradictions, because we have Bible theories to explain the errors, omissions, corruptions, contradictions, inconsistences and foolishness in the Holy Bible as God-ordained spiritual seals and sieves for good purpose, and for the weeding out and cleansing of the corrupt!

i. **Isaiah 30:28 (KJV)** And his breath, as an overflowing stream, shall reach to the midst of the neck, to sift the nations with the sieve of vanity: and *there shall be* a bridle in the jaws of the people, causing *them* to err.

ii. **Amos 9:9 (KJV)** For, lo, I will command, and I will sift the house of Israel among all nations, like as *corn* is sifted in a sieve, yet shall not the least grain fall upon the earth.

iii. **2 Corinthians 2:17 (KJV)** For we are not as many, which corrupt the word of God: but as of sincerity, but as of God, in the sight of God speak we in Christ.

9. In The Bible University, we are only virtual and worldwide!

i. **Matthew 28:18 (KJV)** And Jesus came and spake unto them, saying, All power is given unto me in heaven and in earth.

ii. **Matthew 28:19 (KJV)** Go ye therefore, and teach all nations, baptizing them in the name of the Father, and of the Son, and of the Holy Ghost:

iii. **Matthew 28:20 (KJV)** Teaching them to observe all things whatsoever I have commanded you: and, lo, I am with you alway, *even* unto the end of the world. Amen.

10. In The Bible University, our aim is Salvation by The Bible only!

  i. **1 Timothy 4:13 (KJV)** Till I come, give attendance to reading, to exhortation, to doctrine.

  ii. **1 Timothy 4:16 (KJV)** Take heed unto thyself, and unto the doctrine; continue in them: for in doing this thou shalt both save thyself, and them that hear thee.

  iii. **James 1:21 (KJV)** Wherefore lay apart all filthiness and superfluity of naughtiness, and receive with meekness the engrafted word, which is able to save your souls.

11. In The Bible University, we teach that Christianity is a School whose only pursuit is to seek the knowledge of God Almighty and Jesus Christ, from Genesis to Revelation!

  i. **Hosea 6:6 (KJV)** For I desired mercy, and not sacrifice; and the knowledge of God more than burnt offerings.

  ii. **Psalm 2:10 (KJV)** Be wise now therefore, O ye kings: be instructed, ye judges of the earth.

  iii. **Proverbs 9:10 (KJV)** The fear of the LORD *is* the beginning of wisdom: and the knowledge of the holy *is* understanding.

  iv. **Proverbs 15:28 (KJV)** The heart of the righteous studieth to answer: but the mouth of the wicked poureth out evil things.

  v. **Jeremiah 3:15 (KJV)** And I will give you pastors according to mine heart, which shall feed you with knowledge and understanding.

  vi. **Jeremiah 6:8 (KJV)** Be thou instructed, O Jerusalem, lest my soul depart from thee; lest I make thee desolate, a land not inhabited.

  vii. **Matthew 13:52 (KJV)** Then said he unto them, Therefore every scribe *which is* instructed unto the kingdom of heaven is like unto a man *that is* an householder, which bringeth forth out of his treasure *things* new and old.

  viii. **Matthew 28:18 (KJV)** And Jesus came and spake unto them, saying, All power is given unto me in heaven and in earth.

  ix. **Matthew 28:19 (KJV)** Go ye therefore, and teach all nations, baptizing them in the name of the Father, and of the Son, and of the Holy Ghost:

  x. **Matthew 28:20 (KJV)** Teaching them to observe all things whatsoever I have commanded you: and, lo, I am with you alway, *even* unto the end of the world. Amen.

  xi. **1 Timothy 4:13 (KJV)** Till I come, give attendance to reading, to exhortation, to doctrine.

  xii. **2 Timothy 2:15 (KJV)** Study to shew thyself approved unto God, a workman that needeth not to be ashamed, rightly dividing the word of truth.

12. In The Bible University, we teach that the best way to know God is to obey the commandments of Jesus Christ!

    i. **Exodus 19:5 (KJV)** Now therefore, if ye will obey my voice indeed, and keep my covenant, then ye shall be a peculiar treasure unto me above all people: for all the earth *is* mine:

    ii. **Jeremiah 7:23 (KJV)** But this thing commanded I them, saying, Obey my voice, and I will be your God, and ye shall be my people: and walk ye in all the ways that I have commanded you, that it may be well unto you.

    iii. **Jeremiah 9:23 (KJV)** Thus saith the LORD, Let not the wise *man* glory in his wisdom, neither let the mighty *man* glory in his might, let not the rich *man* glory in his riches:

    iv. **Jeremiah 9:24 (KJV)** But let him that glorieth glory in this, that he understandeth and knoweth me, that I *am* the LORD which exercise lovingkindness, judgment, and righteousness, in the earth: for in these *things* I delight, saith the LORD.

    v. **Jeremiah 22:15 (KJV)** Shalt thou reign, because thou closest *thyself* in cedar? did not thy father eat and drink, and do judgment and justice, *and* then *it was* well with him?

    vi. **Jeremiah 22:16 (KJV)** He judged the cause of the poor and needy; then *it was* well *with him: was* not this to know me? saith the LORD.

    vii. **John 14:23 (KJV)** Jesus answered and said unto him, If a man love me, he will keep my words: and my Father will love him, and we will come unto him, and make our abode with him.

    viii. **John 14:24 (KJV)** He that loveth me not keepeth not my sayings: and the word which ye hear is not mine, but the Father's which sent me.

13. In The Bible University, we teach that the best way to obey the commandments of Jesus Christ is to correctly understand them!

    i. **Nehemiah 8:3 (KJV)** And he read therein before the street that *was* before the water gate from the morning until midday, before the men and the women, and those that could understand; and the ears of all the people *were attentive* unto the book of the law.

    ii. **Nehemiah 8:7 (KJV)** Also Jeshua, and Bani, and Sherebiah, Jamin, Akkub, Shabbethai, Hodijah, Maaseiah, Kelita, Azariah, Jozabad, Hanan, Pelaiah, and the Levites, caused the people to understand the law: and the people *stood* in their place.

   iii. **Nehemiah 8:8 (KJV)** So they read in the book in the law of God distinctly, and gave the sense, and caused *them* to understand the reading.

   iv. **Nehemiah 8:13 (KJV)** And on the second day were gathered together the chief of the fathers of all the people, the priests, and the Levites, unto Ezra the scribe, even to understand the words of the law.

   v. **Psalm 14:2 (KJV)** The LORD looked down from heaven upon the children of men, to see if there were any that did understand, *and* seek God.

   vi. **Psalm 53:2 (KJV)** God looked down from heaven upon the children of men, to see if there were *any* that did understand, that did seek God.

   vii. **Isaiah 28:9 (KJV)** Whom shall he teach knowledge? and whom shall he make to understand doctrine? *them that are* weaned from the milk, *and* drawn from the breasts.

   viii. **Daniel 8:16 (KJV)** And I heard a man's voice between *the banks of* Ulai, which called, and said, Gabriel, make this *man* to understand the vision.

   ix. **Matthew 15:10 (KJV)** And he called the multitude, and said unto them, Hear, and understand:

   x. **Mark 13:14 (KJV)** But when ye shall see the abomination of desolation, spoken of by Daniel the prophet, standing where it ought not, (let him that readeth understand,) then let them that be in Judaea flee to the mountains:

   xi. **Luke 24:45 (KJV)** Then opened he their understanding, that they might understand the scriptures,

The best way to correctly understand the Word of God and the commandments of Jesus Christ is why The Bible University textbooks were written for you: ***Complete Bible Curriculum***! There are two channels of training as follows. Everything is virtual:

1. Pastoral Training for Ministry
2. Personal Training for Spiritual Growth

Group 1 Members will register at

WWW.THEBIBLEUNIVERSITY.ORG for Pastoral training and a Degree Certificate at completion.

Group 2 Members will register at

WWW.THEBIBLEUNIVERSITYCHURCH.ORG for proper Christian education and spiritual growth.

The LORD Jesus Christ be with your spirit. The LORD Jesus Christ give you understanding.

Rev. Prof. PETER PRYCE,
DSEF, BA, MA, B.Soc.Sc Pol Sci, IBA, PhD
A Scribe of the Law of the God of Heaven
Prophet of the Word of God
Professor of French, Silver Spring, MD, USA
Scholar of the Institute of Theologians, USA
WWW.THEBIBLEUNIVERSITY.ORG
Accreditation Number: 07-QCTO/SDP120723172836
SAQA QUAL ID: Identification # 101997
WWW.BOOKSTORESITE.ORG
WWW.THEBIBLEUNIVERSITYCHURCH.ORG

Tuesday 15th March 2022 @ 3:37 PM – 5:07 PM
While hearing and meditating on the Word of God

RESEARCH METHODOLOGY

We used the Christian Holy Scriptures the Bible as the main and only source of research data, beginning from ***Genesis to Revelation***. In this discovery research specifically focused on the Holy Bible, covering ***1 & 2 Corinthians,*** we began from the broad to the specific. We searched the Scriptures from Genesis to Revelation in order to find out everything that God Almighty has embedded in the Holy Scriptures, for the purpose of strengthening the Body of Christ by these teachings so that Ministers and Christians alike would be fully equipped for Ministry Service.

The type of Bible Interpretation exemplified in this book is ***intralingual translation*** and we used the English Bible, the King James Version, throughout. It is well understood that in translation, you render ***meaning of thought*** by means of entities called *words* or *identifiers* or *signs* or *symbols* that constitute into a main idea text or speech. Therefore, *words*, *identifiers*, *signs*, and *symbols* are ***linguistic vehicles*** that carry meanings.

Just as meaning does not derive independent of the pre-text, the text, the context, the post-text, as well as the unseen spirit behind the text, so also Bible Translation, whether interlingual or intralingual, must respect the correct Biblical Hermeneutics of the ***perfect harmony of the Scriptures.***

The ***Perfect Harmony Theory for Bible Translation and Interpreting (Pryce, 2011)*** simply means that Bible teaching or interpreting must not in any way contradict any part of the Bible from Genesis to Revelation, and, therefore, the meaning of the text must come from the text itself, not from outside the text!

The exposition of the ***Perfect Harmony Theory for Bible Translation and Interpreting (Pryce, 2011)*** prescribes that there is ONLY ONE methodology to teach, to translate, to explain, to interpret, to write, and to expound the Holy Scriptures the Word of God, which methodology is this: YOU MUST TEACH THE WORD OF GOD TO AGREE WITH THE WORD OF GOD, and here are the evidences!

> i. **Proverbs 21:30 (KJV)** *There is* no wisdom nor understanding nor counsel against the LORD.

ii. **Isaiah 8:20 (KJV)** To the law and to the testimony: if they speak not according to this word, *it is* because *there is* no light in them.

iii. **Jeremiah 23:28 (KJV)** The prophet that hath a dream, let him tell a dream; and he that hath my word, let him speak my word faithfully. What *is* the chaff to the wheat? saith the LORD.

iv. **John 10:35 (KJV)** If he called them gods, unto whom the word of God came, and the Scripture cannot be broken;

v. **Galatians 1:8 (KJV)** But though we, or an angel from heaven, preach any other gospel unto you than that which we have preached unto you, let him be accursed.

vi. **Galatians 1:9 (KJV)** As we said before, so say I now again, If any *man* preach any other gospel unto you than that ye have received, let him be accursed.

To master the Hermeneutics of the ***Perfect Harmony Theory for Bible Translation and Interpreting (Pryce, 2011)*** is to successfully blend the communicative objective of translation and interpreting with thorough Bible scholarship enriched by research and the study of the Word of God from Genesis to Revelation, without losing the scientific edge of Bible Interpretation where ***scientific*** means that the interpretation that is finally presented is independently verifiable and replicable through research in much the same intellectual way as you can subject a text to translation analysis using proper ***translation assessment strategies***.

The hallmark of this method is a total agreement between what is presented as the meaning of the verse and what the rest of the Bible, from Genesis to Revelation, says. There must be no variation or contradiction between what is presented as meaning of the verses and what the Bible says in order to fulfil the commandment of God that we must be of one mind and in one accord with the Scriptures:

> **2 Corinthians 13:11 (KJV)** Finally, brethren, farewell. Be perfect, be of good comfort, be of one mind, live in peace; and the God of love and peace shall be with you.

> **Philippians 1:27 (KJV)** Only let your conversation be as it becometh the gospel of Christ: that whether I come and see you, or else be absent, I may hear of your affairs, that ye stand fast in one spirit, with one mind striving together for the faith of the gospel;

> **Philippians 2:2 (KJV)** Fulfil ye my joy, that ye be likeminded, having the same love, *being* of one accord, of one mind.

1 Peter 3:8 (KJV) Finally, *be ye* all of one mind, having compassion one of another, love as brethren, *be* pitiful, *be* courteous:

In other words, one interpretation at one part of the Bible should not contradict another interpretation at another part of the Bible thus, creating perfect harmony. Due to the verse comparison and verification that is required, the ***Perfect Harmony Theory (Pryce, 2011)*** is also a tool to test ***faithfulness*** in Bible Translation and Interpreting.

RESEARCH APPROACH

This has been a qualitative research in as much as it aligns with a Biblical Exegesis and constructivist paradigm of re-interpreting Scripture in a way that impacts spiritual and redemptive thought to the saving of the soul:

> **Exodus 20:20 (KJV)** And Moses said unto the people, Fear not: for God is come to prove you, and that his fear may be before your faces, that ye sin not.

> **1 John 2:1 (KJV)** My little children, these things write I unto you, that ye sin not. And if any man sin, we have an advocate with the Father, Jesus Christ the righteous:

We approached this research with methodical data collection from Genesis to Revelation. In fact, we did a verse-by-verse reading and analysis of each verse. We followed the Bible reference selections with an in-depth critical analysis of Scripture and hypotheses, using both inductive and deductive reasoning as part of the methodical approach:

> **1 Samuel 12:7 (KJV)** Now therefore stand still, that I may reason with you before the LORD of all the righteous acts of the LORD, which he did to you and to your fathers.

> **Job 13:3 (KJV)** Surely I would speak to the Almighty, and I desire to reason with God.

> **Job 37:19 (KJV)** Teach us what we shall say unto him; *for* we cannot order *our speech* by reason of darkness.

> **Isaiah 1:18 (KJV)** Come now, and let us reason together, saith the LORD: though your sins be as scarlet, they shall be as white as snow; though they be red like crimson, they shall be as wool.

> **Isaiah 41:21 (KJV)** Produce your cause, saith the LORD; bring forth your strong *reasons*, saith the King of Jacob.

> **Ecclesiastes 8:5 (KJV)** Whoso keepeth the commandment shall feel no evil thing: and a wise man's heart discerneth both time and judgment.

> **Hebrews 5:14 (KJV)** But strong meat belongeth to them that are of full age, *even* those who by reason of use have their senses exercised to discern both good and evil.

> **1 Peter 3:15 (KJV)** But sanctify the Lord God in your hearts: and *be* ready always to *give* an answer to every man that asketh you a reason of the hope that is in you with meekness and fear:

The research in this textbook also draws from two research methods: (1) Constructive Research methods, using the **Perfect Harmony Theory for Translation and Interpreting (Pryce, 2011),** by which we have thus far developed solutions and answers to some **2492** Scripture questions on multiple platforms, producing some 64 Christian Theological Research Textbooks of Holy Scriptures and Bible Commentaries in the process. Just a few of the full list of all my 127 books are listed at the end of this book.

The second research method used in this book is the Empirical Research by which we tested the feasibility and applicability of the **Perfect Harmony Theory for Translation and Interpreting (Pryce, 2011)** to discover scriptural solutions to relevant spiritual questions. The multiple testing platforms were:

- Face-to-face Bible Lecture Series
- Campus Students' Bible Lecture Series
- Writing Christian Theological Research Textbooks and Bible Commentary
- Bible Lecture Series in churches
- Radio Bible Lecture Series on Channel-R Radio on 92.7 FM in Accra, Ghana
- Radio Bible Lecture Series on Radio Spring 102.7 FM in Accra, Ghana
- Radio Bible Lecture Series on Radio Peace 88.9 FM in Winneba
- TV Bible Lecture Series on 1st Digital TV in Accra, Ghana
- Bible and Qur'an Lecture Series on Qibla FM Radio in New York, USA
- Bible Lecture Series on ELWA and ELBC FM Radio stations in Liberia
- Bible Lecture Series via WhatsApp
- Pastors' Bible Lecture Series
- YouTube Bible Lecture Series – type Rev. Prof. Peter Pryce and scroll down for all his 100 works
- Radio Bible Lecture Series on 90.3 FM WDIH Radio in Salisbury, Maryland, USA

- **Bible Lecture Series of the Christian Sunday Live Zoom Podcast, USA – Sunday, October 23, 2022**

Quite specifically, there is ONLY ONE spiritual law that governs how to translate, interpret, explain, teach, and understand the Word of God! That law is stated twice: one in the Old Testament and the other in the New Testament, as follows: "turn not from it *to* the right hand or *to* the left"! That was the spiritual approach that we adopted throughout our Bible research:

Proverbs 21:30 (KJV) *There is* no wisdom nor understanding nor counsel against the LORD.

Isaiah 8:20 (KJV) To the law and to the testimony: if they speak not according to this word, *it is* because *there is* no light in them.

Deuteronomy 28:14 (KJV) And thou shalt not go aside from any of the words which I command thee this day, *to* the right hand, or *to* the left, to go after other gods to serve them.

Joshua 1:7 (KJV) Only be thou strong and very courageous, that thou mayest observe to do according to all the law, which Moses my servant commanded thee: turn not from it *to* the right hand or *to* the left, that thou mayest prosper whithersoever thou goest.

Galatians 1:8 (KJV) But though we, or an Angel from heaven, preach any other gospel unto you than that which we have preached unto you, let him be accursed.

Galatians 1:9 (KJV) As we said before, so say I now again, If any *man* preach any other gospel unto you than that ye have received, let him be accursed.

In other words, the only approach to Bible Teaching that is acceptable in Heaven is the one that will "turn not from it *to* the right hand or *to* the left"!

EXPRESSION OF PERSONAL OPINION

We hope that Ministers and Christians will verify the contents of this textbook by the Holy Scriptures, and yield to the teachings contained herein in as much as they conform 100% to the Holy Bible. Then, their spiritual life would greatly advance to the acknowledgment of the Truth of the Gospel of Jesus Christ and, most importantly, to the obedience of the Word of God unto Salvation.

It is our hope that you will trust the Word of God the Scriptures as the final authority in all matters spiritual while using this textbook as supplementary reading material in your Spiritual School of Heaven on Earth. In whatever way this book is useful to you, believe only the Word of God, believe the LORD Jesus Christ as the final authority in all matters spiritual:

> **Ephesians 6:19 (KJV)** And for me, that utterance may be given unto me, that I may open my mouth boldly, to make known the mystery of the gospel,

> **Ephesians 6:20 (KJV)** For which I am an ambassador in bonds: that therein I may speak boldly, as I ought to speak.

> **Ephesians 6:21 (KJV)** But that ye also may know my affairs, *and* how I do, Tychicus, a beloved brother and faithful minister in the Lord, shall make known to you all things:

The following groups of people will find an excellent use for the **Complete Bible Curriculum** series:

1. Already established Ministers who are still teaching the Word of God.
2. Newly ordained Ministers in churches who are seeking Pastoral Training in sermon preparation.
3. Theological Scholars who are researching theological questions in the Holy Scriptures.
4. **The Bible University** students who are in the following levels of academic and spiritual education:
6. **SUMMARY OF DEGREE PROGRAMS IN THE BIBLE UNIVERSITY**: The Bible University offers the following Degree Programs:

vi. Occupational Certificate: **Religious Associate Professional (Christian Religious Practitioner): South African Qualifications Authority (SAQA)ID 101997**.

vii. Certificate in Theology (C. Th.) (for just one topic or two) – 1 month

viii. Diploma in Theology (Dip. Th.) is a self-paced one-year diploma program of purely Bible Study, Bible Translation, and Bible Interpretation

ix. Bachelor of Theology (B. Th.) – 2-year degree program to complete 22 self-selected Books of the Holy Bible

x. Master of Theology (M. Th.) – 2-year degree program to complete 44 self-selected Books of the Holy Bible

xii. Doctor of Theology (Th. D.) – 4-year degree program to complete all 66 Books of the Holy Bible

xiii. Diploma in Chaplaincy Training Program for Pastors

xiv. Diploma in Church Financial Management Training Program for Pastors

xv. Diploma in General Counseling Training Program for Pastors

xvi. Diploma in Marriage Counseling Training Program for Pastors

xvii. Diploma in Sermon Preparation for Ministers of the Gospel

xviii. Preparation of Bible Topics for Christian Conference and award of Conference Certificates to Participants

Jeremiah 23:15 (KJV) Therefore thus saith the LORD of hosts concerning the prophets; Behold, I will feed them with wormwood, and make them drink the water of gall: for from the prophets of Jerusalem is profaneness gone forth into all the land.

2 Corinthians 2:17 (KJV) For we are not as many, which corrupt the word of God: but as of sincerity, but as of God, in the sight of God speak we in Christ.

1 Timothy 4:13 (KJV) Till I come, give attendance to reading, to exhortation, to doctrine.

1 Timothy 6:5 (KJV) Perverse disputings of men of corrupt minds, and destitute of the truth, supposing that gain is godliness: from such withdraw thyself.

2 Timothy 2:15 (KJV) Study to shew thyself approved unto God, a workman that needeth not to be ashamed, rightly dividing the word of truth.

I pray that by the power of the knowledge and wisdom of the Holy Spirit, I shall continue to be able to make known the mystery of the Gospel of Jesus Christ according to the will of the LORD God Almighty:

> **Romans 16:25 (KJV)** Now to him that is of power to stablish you according to my gospel, and the preaching of Jesus Christ, according to the revelation of the mystery, which was kept secret since the world began,

> **Ephesians 6:18 (KJV)** Praying always with all prayer and supplication in the Spirit, and watching thereunto with all perseverance and supplication for all saints;

> **Ephesians 6:19 (KJV)** And for me, that utterance may be given unto me, that I may open my mouth boldly, to make known the mystery of the gospel,

> **Ephesians 6:20 (KJV)** For which I am an ambassador in bonds: that therein I may speak boldly, as I ought to speak.

Please, do not just quietly steal the ideas and teachings in this intellectual project/work and use them without any form of reward to me, so that you do not reveal yourself as a thief bound for Hell rather than as a true Minister of Jesus Christ. Instead of stealing my work, contact me, work with me, collaborate with me, and partner with me, so that I can also receive the due reward for my many hours, days, months, and years of labour in the Wisdom of God Almighty, for the edification of the Body of Christ:

> **Jeremiah 22:13 (KJV)** Woe unto him that buildeth his house by unrighteousness, and his chambers by wrong; *that* useth his neighbour's service without wages, and giveth him not for his work;

> **1 Thessalonians 4:6 (KJV)** That no *man* go beyond and defraud his brother in *any* matter: because that the Lord *is* the avenger of all such, as we also have forewarned you and testified.

> **1 Thessalonians 4:7 (KJV)** For God hath not called us unto uncleanness, but unto holiness.

FUTURE EXPECTATIONS

For the future, as we are able to secure funding for research, interior formatting, graphic designing, printing, and publishing, we pray to be able to continue writing Scriptures, and to keep writing on relevant topics that the Holy Spirit would teach us so that we can produce Christian Theological Research Textbooks to the world, especially to edify the Body of Christ in knowledge and in Truth.

These are intellectual, academic, and spiritual resources to all people around the world, who desire study materials for Spiritual Pastoral Training, for the edification of the Christian, and for the edification of the Church.

> **2 Timothy 2:15 (KJV)** Study to shew thyself approved unto God, a workman that needeth not to be ashamed, rightly dividing the word of truth.

As we conducted the research to produce this textbook, take note very carefully that we used only the Word of God the Scriptures and allowed the Holy Bible to speak for itself, not turning to the right or to the left to use any other book according to the requirement for research in Bible Translation and Interpretation that is laid down in **Deuteronomy 28:14 (KJV)** and in the following Scriptures:

> **Deuteronomy 17:18 (KJV)** And it shall be, when he sitteth upon the throne of his kingdom, that he shall write him a copy of this law in a book out of *that which is* before the priests the Levites:

> **Deuteronomy 17:19 (KJV)** And it shall be with him, and he shall read therein all the days of his life: that he may learn to fear the LORD his God, to keep all the words of this law and these statutes, to do them:

> **Deuteronomy 28:14 (KJV)** And thou shalt not go aside from any of the words which I command thee this day, *to* the right hand, or *to* the left, to go after other gods to serve them.

> **Joshua 1:8 (KJV)** This book of the law shall not depart out of thy mouth; but thou shalt meditate therein day and night, that thou mayest observe to do

according to all that is written therein: for then thou shalt make thy way prosperous, and then thou shalt have good success.

Luke 10:26 (KJV) He said unto him, What is written in the law? how readest thou?

John 5:39 (KJV) Search the Scriptures; for in them ye think ye have eternal life: and they are they which testify of me.

2 Peter 1:19 (KJV) We have also a more sure word of prophecy; whereunto ye do well that ye take heed, as unto a light that shineth in a dark place, until the day dawn, and the day star arise in your hearts:

2 Peter 1:20 (KJV) Knowing this first, that no prophecy of the Scripture is of any private interpretation.

The LORD God Almighty let His face shine upon you. The LORD Jesus Christ give you understanding. The Holy Spirit be with your spirit…Amen.

THE END!
Saturday 27ᵗʰ January 2024 @ 12:17 PM
While hearing and meditating on the Word of God.

+ + + + + + +
Rev. Prof. PETER PRYCE,
DSEF, BA, MA, B.Soc.Sc Pol Sci, IBA, PhD
A Scribe of the Law of the God of Heaven
Prophet of the Word of God
Professor of French, Silver Spring, MD, USA
Scholar of the Institute of Theologians, USA
WWW.THEBIBLEUNIVERSITY.ORG
Accreditation Number: 07-QCTO/SDP120723172836
SAQA QUAL ID: Identification # 101997
WWW.BOOKSTORESITE.ORG
WWW.THEBIBLEUNIVERSITYCHURCH.ORG

Contact Info:
Phone: +1-301-793-7190
E-mail: Dr.Pryce@gmail.com

PRINCIPAL REFERENCE

The Holy Scriptures - King James Version

OTHER PRINCIPAL REFERENCES

Abdullah, Yusuf Ali. "The Meanings of the Holy Qur'an."
http://www.islam101.com/quran/YusufAli/index.htm:
9 October 2013.

http://www.islam101.com/quran/yusufAli/
14th September 2016.

https://www.google.com/?gfe_rd=cr&ei=g9EPVrb6Euyr8wf0m44CA#safe=active&q=abdullah+yusuf+ali
(Friday 16th September, 2016).

For a detailed study of the Holy Qur'an: English Translation and Commentary by Abdullah Yusuf Ali, both his original and modified versions, see these three works:
https://www.al-islam.org/tahrif/yusufali/
(Friday 16th September, 2016).

Original
The Glorious Kur'an - Translation and Commentary
 (Dar al-Fikr, Beirut) (n.d.)

Amana
The Meaning of The Holy Qur'an
New Edition with Revised Translation, Commentary and Newly Compiled Comprehensive Index. Amana Publications, First edition, 1408 AH/1989 AC by Amana Corporation

IFTA
The Holy Qur'an - English Translation of the Meanings and Commentary Revised and Edited by The Presidency of Islamic Researches, IFTA, Call and Guidance, King Fahd Holy Qur'an Printing Complex

Abdullah, Yusuf Ali. *The Meaning of the Holy Qur'an: [English] Translation and Commentary*. 10th Edition. Maryland: Amana Corporation, 1935, 1989, 1993.

Ally, Dr. Shabir. "What Are Some Examples of Parables in the Quran?"

http://www.onislam.net/english/ask-about-islam/faith-and-worship/quran-andScriptures/462015-what-are-some-examples-of-parables-in-thequran.html?Scriptures:
30th October 2014.

Khali, Ibrahim. "The Sons of God in Bible and Quran."
http://www.streetdirectory.com/travel_guide/105306/religion/the_sons_of_god_in_bibl_and_quran.html:
1 August 2014.

King Fahd Holy Qur'an. The Holy Qur'an: English Translation of the Meanings and Commentary, King Fahd Holy Qur'an Printing Complex, P O Box 3561, Al-Madinah, Al-Munawarah:
http://qurancomplex.gov.sa/Quran/Targama/Targama.asp?TabID=4&SubItemID=1&l=eng&t=eng&SecOrder=4&SubSecOrder=1)

King Fahd Complex for the Printing of the Holy Qur'an,
http://qurancomplex.gov.sa/Quran/Targama/Targama.asp?TabID=4&SubItemID=1&l=eng&t=eng&SecOrder=4&SubSecOrder=1

Memsuah, Mansoor "The Son of God in the Bible and the Qur'an."
http://www.answeringislam.org/Authors/Memsuah/son_of_god_bq.htm:
1 August 2014.

"Father and Son Definitions".
http://www.answering-christianity.com,
http://www.answeringchristianity.com/definition_son_of_god.htm:
1 August 2014.

GENERAL BIBLIOGRAPHY

Allen, Jeff. "The Bible as Resource for Translation Software". http://www.multilingual.com/articleDetaillosthisislam.php?id=614: December 21, 2012.

Bearth T. « Exégèse et herméneutique biblique du point de vue d'un linguiste ». *Cahiers de traduction biblique 15*, 1991.

Beekman, John and **Callow, John**. *Translating "the Word of God"*. Grand Rapids Michigan: Zondervan Publishing House, 1997, pp. 23, 24, 33-39.

Berman, A. "Translation and the Trials of the Foreign", in Lawrence Venuti (ed.), *The Translation Studies Reader*. London: Routledge, 2000, p. 297.

Bernard, H. Russell. *Research Methods in Anthropology: Qualitative and Quantitative Approaches, 6th Edition*. Lanham: Rowman and Littlefield, 2002, pp. 437-490.

Blum-Kulka, Shoshana. "Shifts of Cohesion and Coherence in Translation", in J. House and S. Blum-Kulka (eds), *Interlingual and Intercultural Communication*. Tübingen: Gunter Narr, 1986, pp. 17-35.

Bodine J. E. « Discourse Analysis of Biblical Literature: What it is and what it offers ». *Discourse Analysis of Biblical Literature*. Atlanta: Scholars Press, 1995, pp. 1-20.

Catford, John C. *A Linguistic Theory of Translation*. Oxford: Oxford University Press. 1965.

Chesterman, Andrew. *Memes of Translation*. Amsterdam: Benjamins, 1997.

Delisle, Jean et al. *Terminologie de la traduction*. Amsterdam: Benjamins. 1999.

Dye, Thurlow Wayne. *Bible Translation Strategy, an Analysis of Its Spiritual Impact*. Rev. ed. Dallas, TX: Wycliffe Bible Translators, 1985.

Escande J. « Pour une réflexion sémiotique sur la traduction des textes bibliques », *ETR 53,3*, 1978.

Even-Zohar, Itamar. "The Position of Translated Literature within the Literary Polysystem", in *Poetics Today 11/1*, 1990 pp. 45-51.

Even-Zohar, Itamar. "Polysystem Theory" in *Poetics Today 11*: 1 Spring, 1990, pp. 9-26.

Fairclough, Norman. *Analysing Discourse, Textual Analysis for Social Research*, London, Routledge. 2001, pp. 19-39.

Garnet, Paul. « The Concept of a Sacred Language: Help or Hindrance in New Testament Translation? » *TTR, 3, 2, 2e semestre*, 1990, pp. 71-79.

Gentzler, Edwin. "Translation without Borders". http://translation.fusp.it/. October 4, 2014.

Gentzler, Edwin. *Contemporary Translation Theories*. Clevedon: Cromwell Press Ltd. 2001.

Greimas A. J. « La traduction et La Bible ». *Sémiotique et Bible 32*, 1983.

Greenstein E. L. *Essays on biblical method and translation*. Atlanta: Scholars Press, 1989.

Gutt, Ernst-August. Translation and Relevance, Oxford: Basil Blackwell, 1991.

Gutt, Ernst-August. "Translation as Interlingual Interpretive Use." in *The Translation Studies Reader*. Lawrence Venuti (ed.), London: Routledge, 1991, 2000, 2001 pp. 376-96.

Hatim, Basil, and **Ian Mason**. The Translator as Communicator, London & New York: Routledge, vii, 1997, pp. 14, 193.

Hervey, Sándor and **Higgins, Ian**. *Thinking Translation: A Course in Translation Method: French to English*. London: Routledge, 1992.

Irving, Thomas Ballantine, Ahmad, Khurshid, and **Ahsan, Mohammad Manazir**. The Qur'an. Basic Teachings. Leicester, UK. The Islamic Foundation, 1992, pp. 109-112.

Jakobson, Roman. "On Linguistic Aspects of Translation." in R. Jakobson (ed.), *Selected Writings, II*, The Hague: Mouton, 1971 [1959], pp. 260-266.

Jakobson, Roman O. "On Linguistic Aspects of Translation" in L. Venuti (ed), *The Translation Studies Reader*. London, New York and Canada: Routledge, 2004, pp. 113-118.

Lategan, B.C. "Target Audience and Bible Translation", *JNSL 19*, 1993.

Lefevere, André. (ed.) Translation, History and Culture, London: Pinter Publishing Ltd. 1990.

Lockyer, Sharon. In Lisa M. Given (ed.), *The Sage Encyclopaedia of Qualitative Research Methods Vols. 1 & 2*, Thousand Oaks, California, SAGE Publications, Inc., 2008. pp. 706-711.

Margot, Jean-Claude. « Langues sacrées et méthode de traduction ». *TTR, 3, 2, 2e semestre*, 1990, pp. 15-31.

Mossop, Brian. *"Translating as Reporting: A Theoretical Characterization of the Translator"*. Paper read at EST Congress "Translating / Interpreting as Intercultural Communication", Prague 28-30 September, 1995.

Mossop, Brian. "Objective Translational Error and the Cultural Norm of Translation" in R. Larose (ed.), *L'Erreur en Traduction, TTR 2/2*, 1989, pp. 55-70.

Mullins P. « Sacred Text in Electronic Age », *BTB 20/3002E*, 1990.

Newmark, Peter. *Approaches to Translation.* New York and London: Prentice Hall, 1988a.

Nida, Eugene A. *Toward a Science of Translating*, Leiden: E. J. Brill, 1964.

Nida, Eugene A, and William D. Reyburn. *Meaning across Cultures.* Maryknoll, New York: Orbis Press, 1981.

O'Donnell M. B. « Translation and the Exegetical Process, Using Mark 5:1-10, "The Binding of the Strong Man" as a Test Case ». *Translating the Bible*, Sheffield: Academic Press, 1999.

Patte D. « Speech Act Theory and Biblical Exegesis. » *Semeia 41*, 1988, pp. 85-102.

Popovic, Anton. "Aspects of metatext". *Canadian Review of Comparative Literature* 3, 1976, pp. 225-235.

Pryce, Peter. *Measuring Attitudes in Translation: A Study of Nokia Business Reports*, Helsinki: Helsinki University Printing House, 2006, p. 150.

Reiss, Katharina and **Vermeer, Hans J**. *Grundlegung einer allgemeinen Translationstheorie.* Tübingen: Niemeyer, 1984.

Rivers, W. M. and **Temperley, M. S**. A Practical Guide to the Teaching of English as a Second or Foreign Language, Oxford: Oxford University Press, 1978, p. 329.

Robyns, Clem. *Translation and Discursive Identity*, in Robyns, C. (ed.), 1994, pp. 57-81.

Seleskovitch, Danica. « Take care of the sense and the sounds will take care of themselves or Why interpreting is not tantamount to Translating Languages. » *The Incorporated Linguist, 16*, 1977, pp. 27-33.

Seleskovitch, Danica. & Lederer, Marianne. *Traduire pour interpréter*. Publication de la Sorbonne: Didier Erudition, Coll. « Traductologie 1 », 1993.

Seleskovitch, Danica, et Marianne Lederer. *Interpréter pour traduire, Quatrième édition*. Paris: Didier Erudition, 2001.

Simon, Sherry. « La traduction biblique : Modèle des Modèles? ». *TTR, 3, 2, 2e semestre*, 1990, pp. 111-120.

Simms, Karl, (ed.) *Translating Sensitive Texts: Linguistic Aspects*. Amsterdam: Rodopi, 1997.

Toury, Gideon. *Descriptive Translation Studies and Beyond*. Amsterdam: Benjamins, 1995.

Turner, Charles. V. *Biblical Bible Translating*. Lafayette: Sovereign Grace Publishers Inc., Lighting Source Inc., 2001.

Vatican Insider Newspaper, La Stampa, of Tuesday 8th March 2011. http://vaticaninsider.lastampa.it/en/documents/detail/articolo/bibbia-bible-biblia-6531/ Friday April 12, 2013.

Venuti, Lawrence. *The Translation Studies Reader London: Routledge*. 2000.

Vinay, Jean-Paul, and **Jean Darbelnet**. *Comparative Stylistics of French and English: a Methodology for Translation*. Juan C. Sager and M.-J. Hamel, (ed. and translators), Amsterdam: John Benjamin, 1995 [1958].

Wilhelm, J. E. « Herméneutique et traduction: La question de l'appropriation ou le rapport du propre à l'étranger ». *Meta, 49, 4*, 2004, pp. 768-776.

BIBLIOGRAPHY FOR BIBLE TRANSLATION METHODS

Barnwell, Katharine G. L. *Bible Translation an Introductory Course in Translation Principles*. 3d ed. Dallas, TX: Institute of Linguistics, 1992.

Barnwell, Katharine G. L., and Summer Institute of Linguistics. *Introduction to Semantics and Translation with Special Reference to Bible Translation*. 2d ed. Introduction to Practical Linguistics. High Wycombe: Summer Institute of Linguistics, 1980.

Bible. *The Psalms in English*. Penguin Classics. London New York: Penguin Books, 1996.

Bible., and **Norman Messenger**. *The Creation Story*. New York: DK Pub., 2001.

Budick, Sanford, and **Wolfgang. Iser**. *The Translatability of Cultures Figurations of the Space Between*. Stanford, Calif.: Stanford University Press, 1996.

Cavanaugh, Jack. *Beyond the Sacred Page a Novel : The Tyndale Translation*. Grand Rapids, Mich.: Zondervan, 2003.

Clendenen, E. Ray. *Inclusive Language in Bible Translation a Reply to Mark Strauss*, 1998.

De Groot, Martien. *Assessment of Bible Translation and Literacy Needs of the Samburu Language Group*. Nairobi: Bible Translation and Literacy (EA), 1987.

Dye, Thurlow Wayne. *Bible Translation Strategy an Analysis of Its Spiritual Impact*. Rev. (ed.) Dallas, TX: Wycliffe Bible Translators, 1985.

Fritz, Paul J. *Sermons for the Nigerian Pastor*. Jos, Nigeria: Nigeria Bible Translation Trust, 1989.

General Conference of Seventh-Day Adventists. *Problems in Bible Translation*. Washington: Review and Herald, 1954.

Griffiths, Richard. *The Bible in the Renaissance Essays on Biblical Commentary and Translation in the Fifteenth and the Sixteenth Centuries*. St. Andrews Studies in Reformation History. Aldershot, Hants, UK Burlington, USA: Ashgate, 2001.

Hammer, Reuven. *The Classic Midrash Tannaitic Commentaries on the Bible*. Classics of Western Spirituality. New York: Paulist Press, 1995.

Hampton, Roberta S. *A Guide to Reading is Easy, Understand with Your Eyes!* Tamale, Ghana: Ghana Institute of Linguistics, Literacy and Bible Translation, 1994.

Lewins, Frank. (1992). *Social Science Methodology: A Brief but Critical Introduction*, South Melbourne, Australia: Macmillan Education Australia, Pty Ltd. P. 11.

Louw, J. P. *Lexicography and Translation with Special Reference to Bible Translation*. Cape Town: Bible Society of South Africa, 1985.

McGrath, Alister E. *In the Beginning the Story of the King James Bible and How It Changed a Nation, a Language and a Culture*. London: Hodder & Stoughton, 2002.

Pryce, Peter. "Méthode de traduction intralinguale de thèmes bibliques." Paper presented at the 8th Inter-University Conference on the Co-Existence of Languages in West Africa, Department of French Education, University of Education, Winneba, Ghana, Monday, 13th June 2011 – Saturday 18th June, 2011.

Strauss, Mark L. *Distorting Scripture? The Challenge of Bible Translation & Gender Accuracy*. Downers Grove, Ill: Inter Varsity Press, 1998.

Turner, Charles V. *Biblical Bible Translating the Biblical Basis for Bible Translating: With an Introduction to Semantics and Applications Made to Bible Translation Principles*. Bowie, Tex. (Box 1450, Bowie 76230): Baptist Bible Translators, Institute of Missiology International, 1988.

OTHER BOOKS BY THE SAME AUTHOR

These Christian Research Theological Textbooks are recommended as **Supplementary Course Literature** for training in The Bible University (WWW.THEBIBLEUNIVERSITY.ORG), and for a better understanding of the Holy Scriptures. They are methodically reasoned and are perfectly harmonized expositions of the Scriptures – written by Rev. Prof. Peter Pryce for the *Bible Lecture Series*.

1. Studies and Teachings on The Prophetic
2. Translation of Dreams
3. The Law of Writing Scriptures
4. Key to the Bible - Complete Bible Curriculum Vol. 1
5. Key to the Bible - Complete Bible Curriculum Vol. 2
6. Studies and Teachings on Abraham
7. Studies and Teachings on Water Baptism – From Genesis to Revelation
8. BOOK # 5 – Studies and Teachings on The Gentile
9. Studies and Teachings on Fasting
10. BOOK # 9 – Studies and Teachings on The Child of God
11. Studies and Teachings on Sin
12. BOOK # 15 – Studies and Teachings on Perfect
13. Studies and Teachings on The Spiritual
14. Studies and Teachings on Freely ye have received, Freely Give
15. Studies and Teachings on Prayer
16. Studies and Teachings on The Dog
17. Studies and Teachings on The Church
18. Studies and Teachings on Kingdom of Heaven, Kingdom of God
19. Studies and Teachings on Miracle
20. Studies and Teachings on Healing
21. Studies and Teachings on The Holy Communion
22. Studies and Teachings on The Poor
23. Studies and Teachings on The Servant of God
24. Studies and Teachings on Understanding Parables
25. Studies and Teachings on Death
26. Studies and Teachings on Faith
27. Studies and Teachings on Angels

28. Studies and Teachings on Christian Conflict Resolution
29. Studies and Teachings on Bible Translation and Interpreting
30. Studies and Teachings on Suffering
31. Studies and Teachings on Sabbath
32. Studies and Teachings on Definition of Jews
33. Studies and Teachings on Birthday
34. Studies and Teachings on The Multi-Dimensional Personalities of Jesus Christ
35. Studies and Teachings on Reincarnation
36. Studies and Teachings on The Scribe
37. Studies and Teachings on Tongues
38. Studies and Teachings on The Bereaved
39. Studies and Teachings on The Place of Worship
40. Studies and Teachings on Customs, Culture, and Traditions
41. Studies and Teachings on Discernment
42. Studies and Teachings on Deliverance
43. Topics in Translation Review – Testing the Perfect Harmony Theory of Translation and Interpreting
44. Qibla Files
45. Bible Translation of the Qur'an
46. Spirituals of Money
47. Hope for Christian-Muslim Fellowship
48. Perfect Harmony Theory for Translators and Interpreters – Méthode de traduction intralinguale de thèmes bibliques.

SCHOLAR OF THE INSTITUTE OF THEOLOGIANS

hereby elect

Dr. Peter Pryce, *S.Inst.T.*

Scholar of the Institute Of Theologians

Together with all the rights, privileges, and honor appertaining thereunto in consideration of satisfactory completion of the prescribed requirements.

In testimony wherefore, the seal of the Institute and Signatures as authorized by the Board of Trustees are hereunto affixed in the State of North Carolina. Given at Dallas, North Carolina, in the year of our Lord, Two Thousand Eighteen, The Month of December.

Dr. Moses Nueman Sr., Th.D., D.Miss., President

Dr. Robert Eng III Ph.D. Th.D., Vice President

INDEX

I

J

L

M

N

P

Put that sinner out of the church forthwith and immediately so that he/she does not corrupt the rest of the congregation! Treat his/her lifestyle as poison that can kill the entire congregation!...................**141**

Q

R

S

T

U

V

W

Y

Milton Keynes UK
Ingram Content Group UK Ltd.
UKHW050437290524
443153UK00006B/11